I've been so busy lately for the first time in a while. I haven't been able go out and play for days. When I can't go out and play, I have nothing to write here. So when I'm busy, I wish this segment didn't exist. I've already spent four hours thinking of what to write. Good, it's filled now!

-Tite Kubo

BLEACH is author Tite Kubo's second title. Kubo made his debut with *ZOMBIEPOWDER.*, a four-volume series for *WEEKLY SHONEN JUMP*. To date, *BLEACH* has been translated into numerous languages and has also inspired an animated TV series that began airing in the U.S. in 2006. Beginning its serialization in 2001, *BLEACH* is still a mainstay in the pages of *WEEKLY SHONEN JUMP*. In 2005, *BLEACH* was awarded the prestigious Shogakukan Manga Award in the *shonen* (boys) category.

BLEACH
Vol. 51: LOVE ME BITTERLY LOTH ME SWEETLY
SHONEN JUMP Manga Edition

STORY AND ART BY
TITE KUBO

Translation/Joe Yamazaki
Touch-up Art & Lettering/James Dashiell
Design/Yukiko Whitley, Kam Li
Editor/Alexis Kirsch

BLEACH © 2001 by Tite Kubo. All rights reserved. First published
in Japan in 2001 by SHUEISHA Inc., Tokyo. English translation rights
arranged by SHUEISHA Inc.

The rights of the author(s) of the work(s) in this publication to be so
identified have been asserted in accordance with Copyright, Designs and
Patents Act 1988. A CIP catalogue record for this book is available from
the British Library.

The stories, characters and incidents mentioned in this publication are
entirely fictional.

No portion of this book may be reproduced or transmitted in any form
or by any means without written permission from the copyright holders.

Printed in the U.S.A.

Published by VIZ Media, LLC
P.O. Box 77010
San Francisco, CA 94107

10 9 8 7 6 5 4 3 2 1
First printing, November 2012

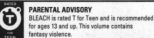

PARENTAL ADVISORY
BLEACH is rated T for Teen and is recommended
for ages 13 and up. This volume contains
fantasy violence.
ratings.viz.com

www.viz.com

THE WORLD'S
MOST POPULAR MANGA
SHONEN JUMP
www.shonenjump.com

Don't put your finger

In my heart

BLEACH51 Love me Bitterly Loth me Sweetly

STARS AND

Orihime Inoue

Chad Yasutora

Ichigo Kurosaki

Ichigo Kurosaki meets Soul Reaper Rukia Kuchiki and ends up helping her eradicate Hollows. After developing his powers as a Soul Reaper, Ichigo enters battle against Aizen and his dark ambitions! Ichigo finally defeats Aizen in exchange for his powers as a Soul Reaper.

With the battle over, Ichigo regains his normal daily life. But his tranquil life ends when Ishida is attacked by an unknown assailant. Ichigo then meets Ginjo, whose objective is to help Ichigo regain his Soul Reaper powers. Ichigo then begins his training to gain a new power known as Fullbring. At the same time, Orihime comes in contact with a mysterious figure named Tsukishima. Ichigo grows impatient when he learns he is the target!!

BLEACH ALL

月島秀九郎

Shukuro Tsukishima

銀城空吾

Kugo Ginjo

Riruka Dokugamine

毒ヶ峰リルカ

STORIES

BLEACH 51

Love me Bitterly Loth me Sweetly

Contents

HEY, WHERE YOU GOING? YOU HAVE TO UNDO YOUR DOLLHOUSE WHEN HE FINISHES.

STAY HERE AND WATCH.

HEY!

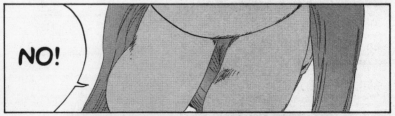

NO!

442. Battlefield Shallows, Otherfield Abyss

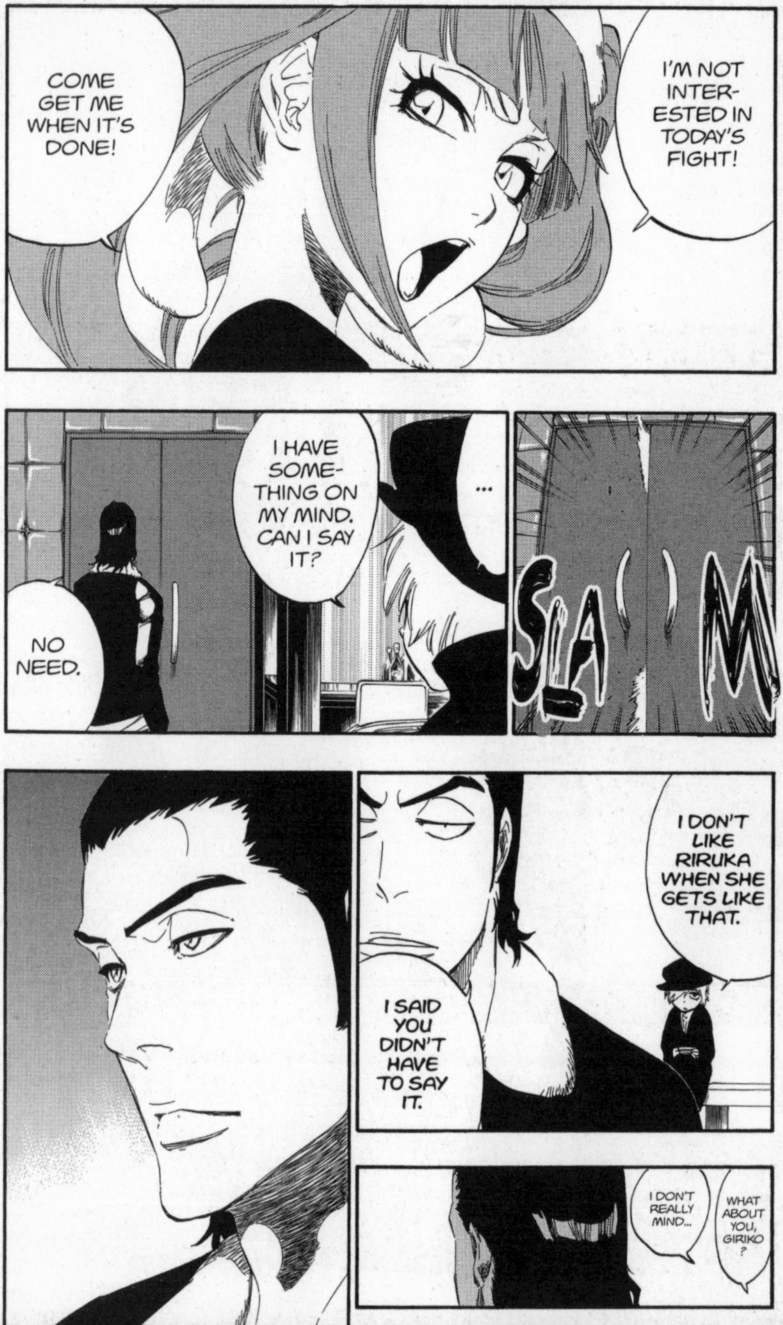
I'M NOT INTER-ESTED IN TODAY'S FIGHT!
COME GET ME WHEN IT'S DONE!
SLAM
...
I HAVE SOME-THING ON MY MIND. CAN I SAY IT?
NO NEED.
I DON'T LIKE RIRUKA WHEN SHE GETS LIKE THAT.
I SAID YOU DIDN'T HAVE TO SAY IT.
WHAT ABOUT YOU, GIRIKO?
I DON'T REALLY MIND...

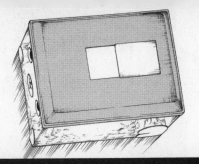

BLEACH

442.

**Battlefield Shallows,
Otherfield Abyss**

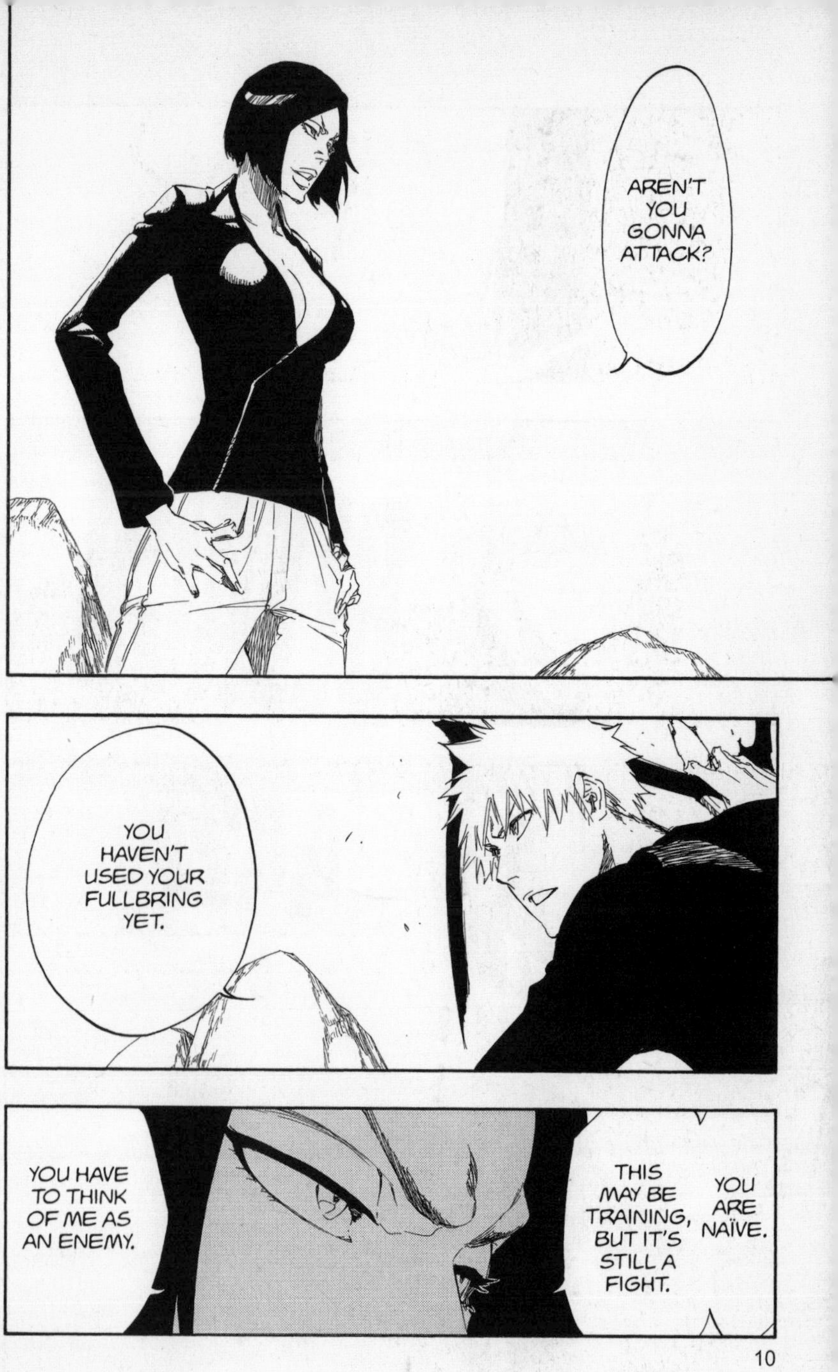
AREN'T YOU GONNA ATTACK?
YOU HAVEN'T USED YOUR FULLBRING YET.
YOU ARE NAÏVE.
THIS MAY BE TRAINING, BUT IT'S STILL A FIGHT.
YOU HAVE TO THINK OF ME AS AN ENEMY.

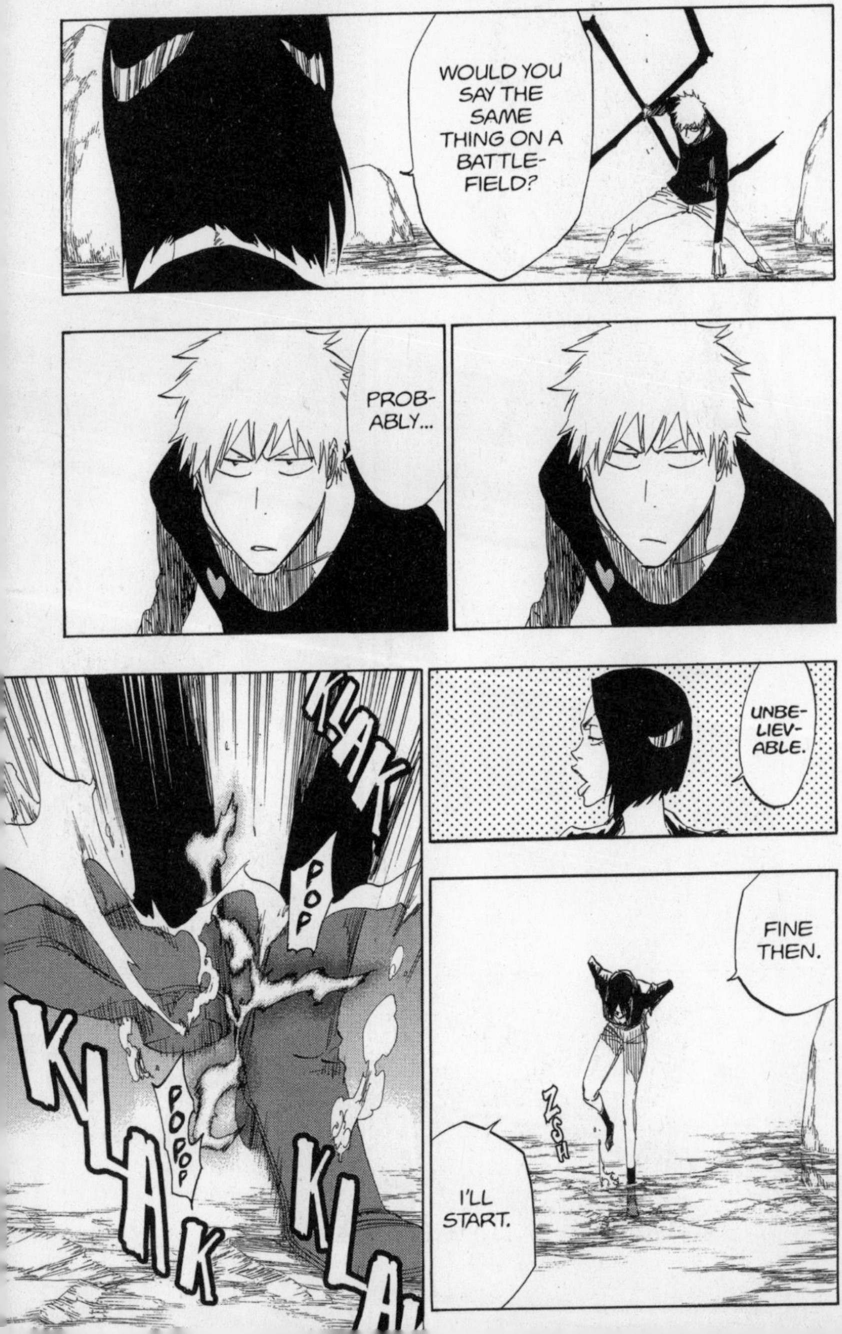
WOULD YOU SAY THE SAME THING ON A BATTLE-FIELD?
PROB-ABLY...
UNBE-LIEV-ABLE.
FINE THEN.
ZSH
I'LL START.
KLAK
POP POP
KLAK
POPOPOP
KLAK

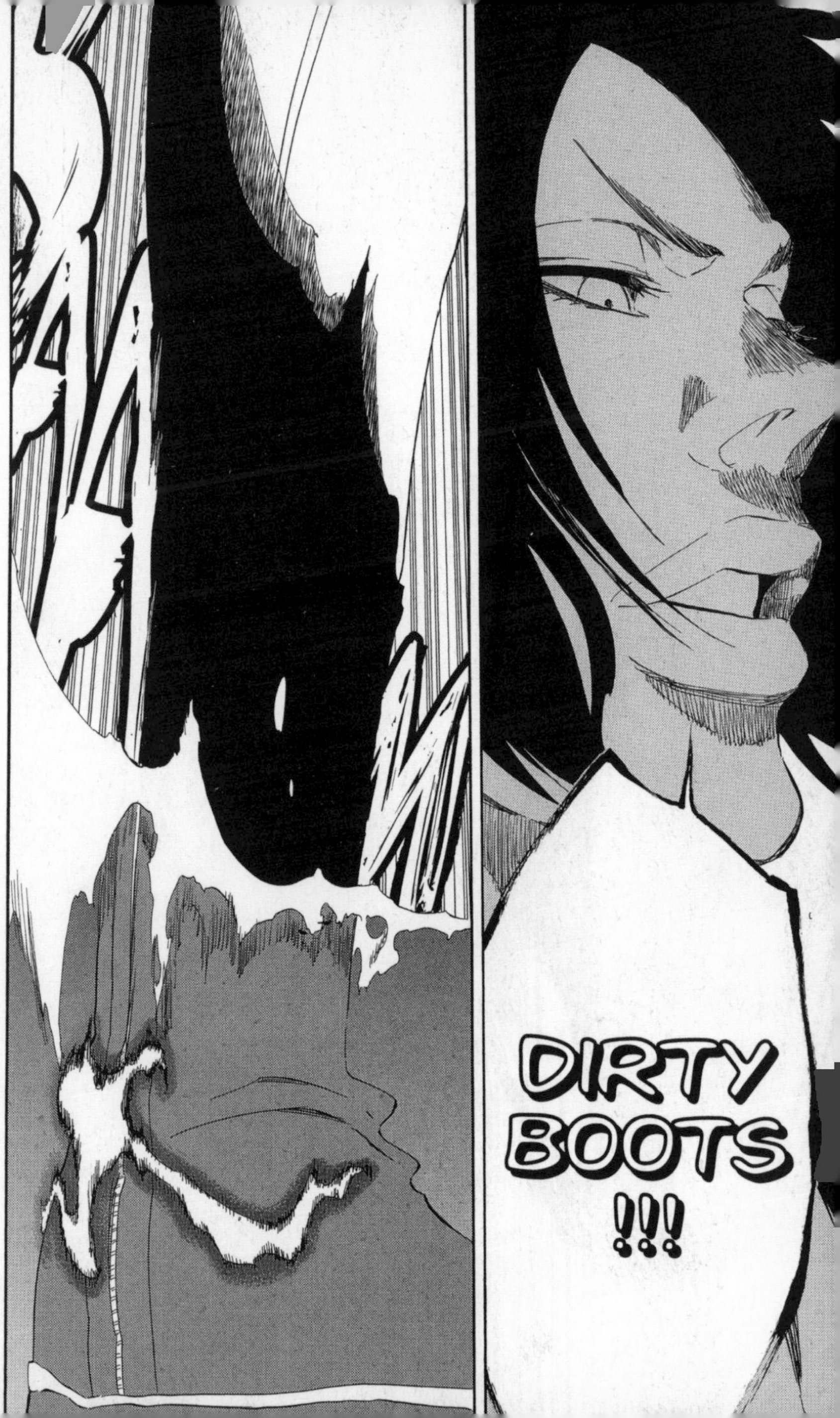
DIRTY BOOTS !!!

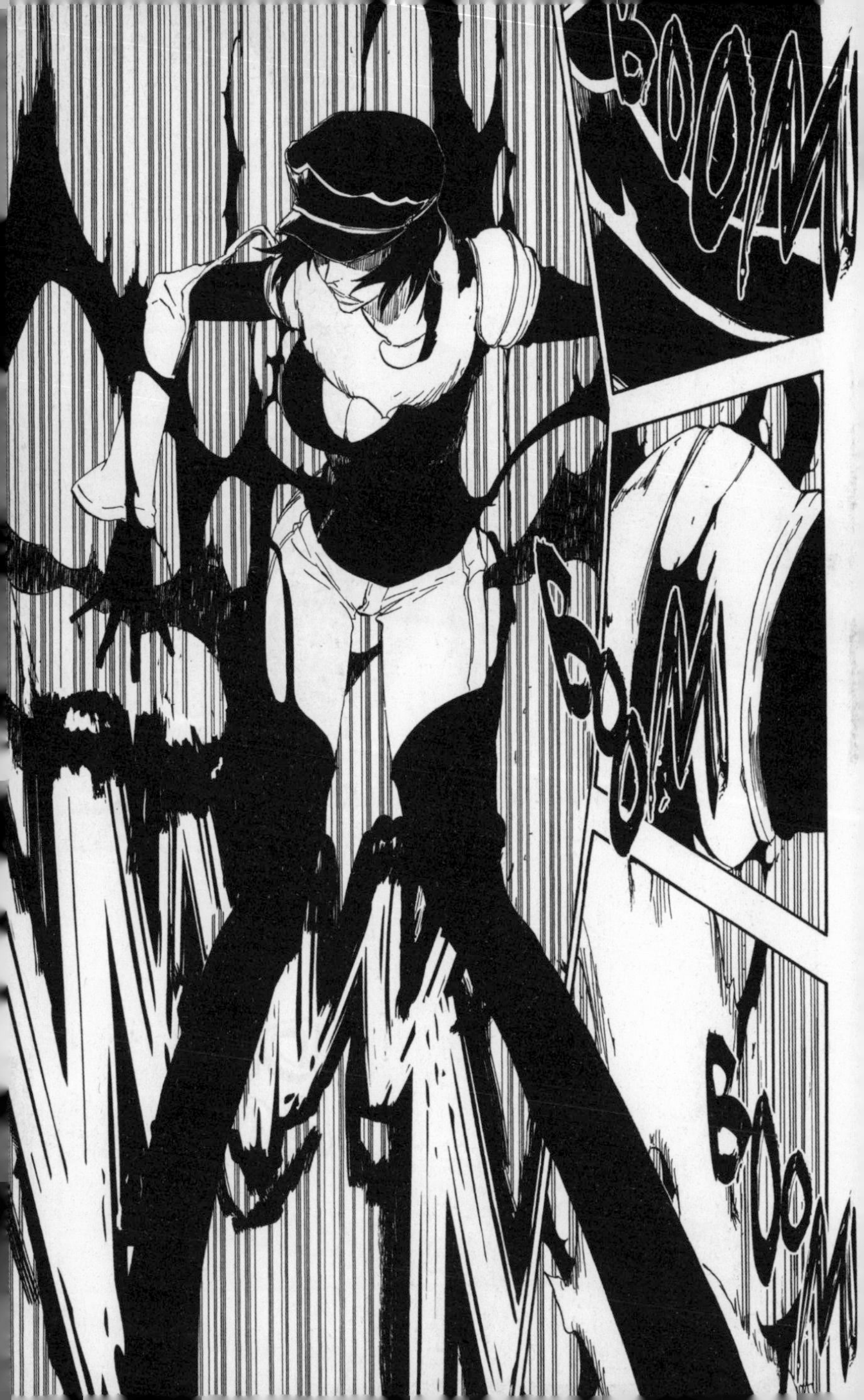
BOOM
BOOM
BOOM

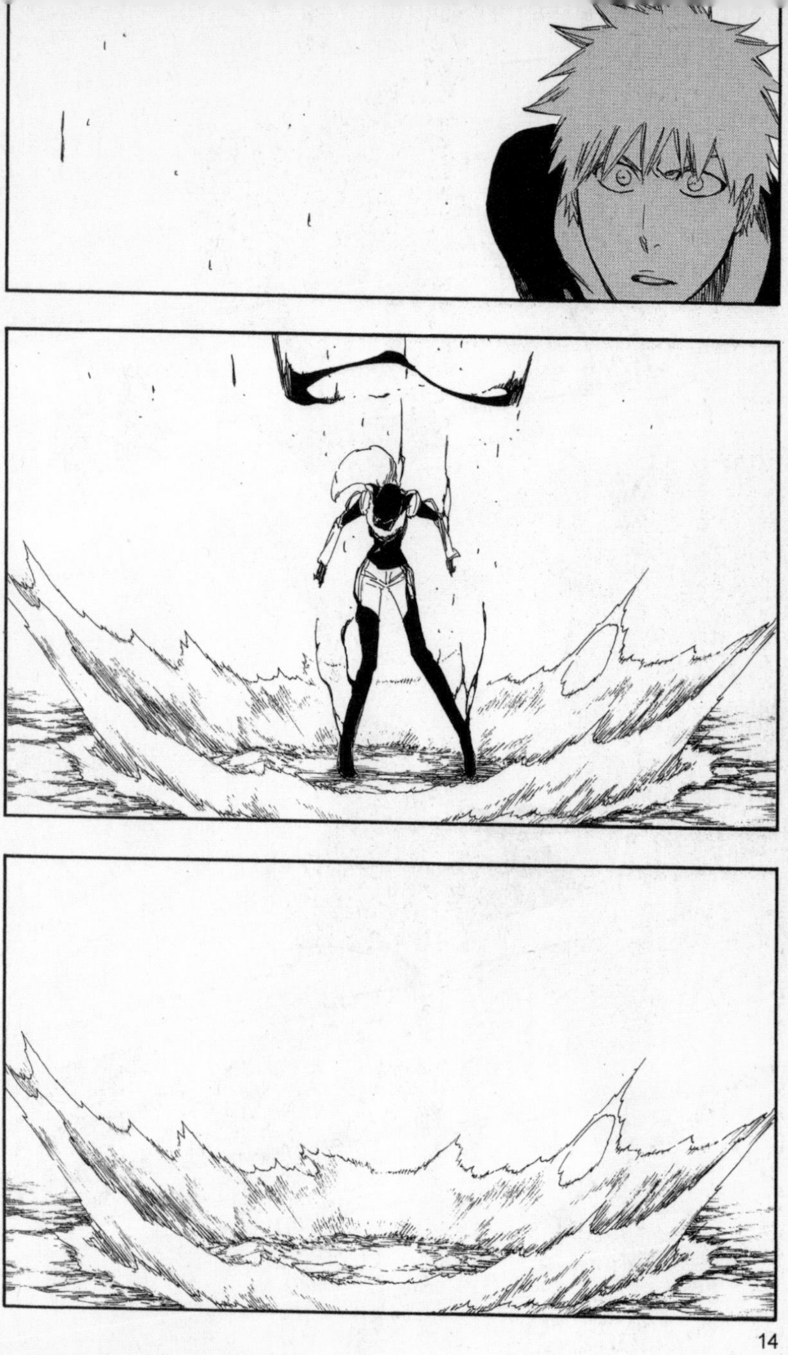

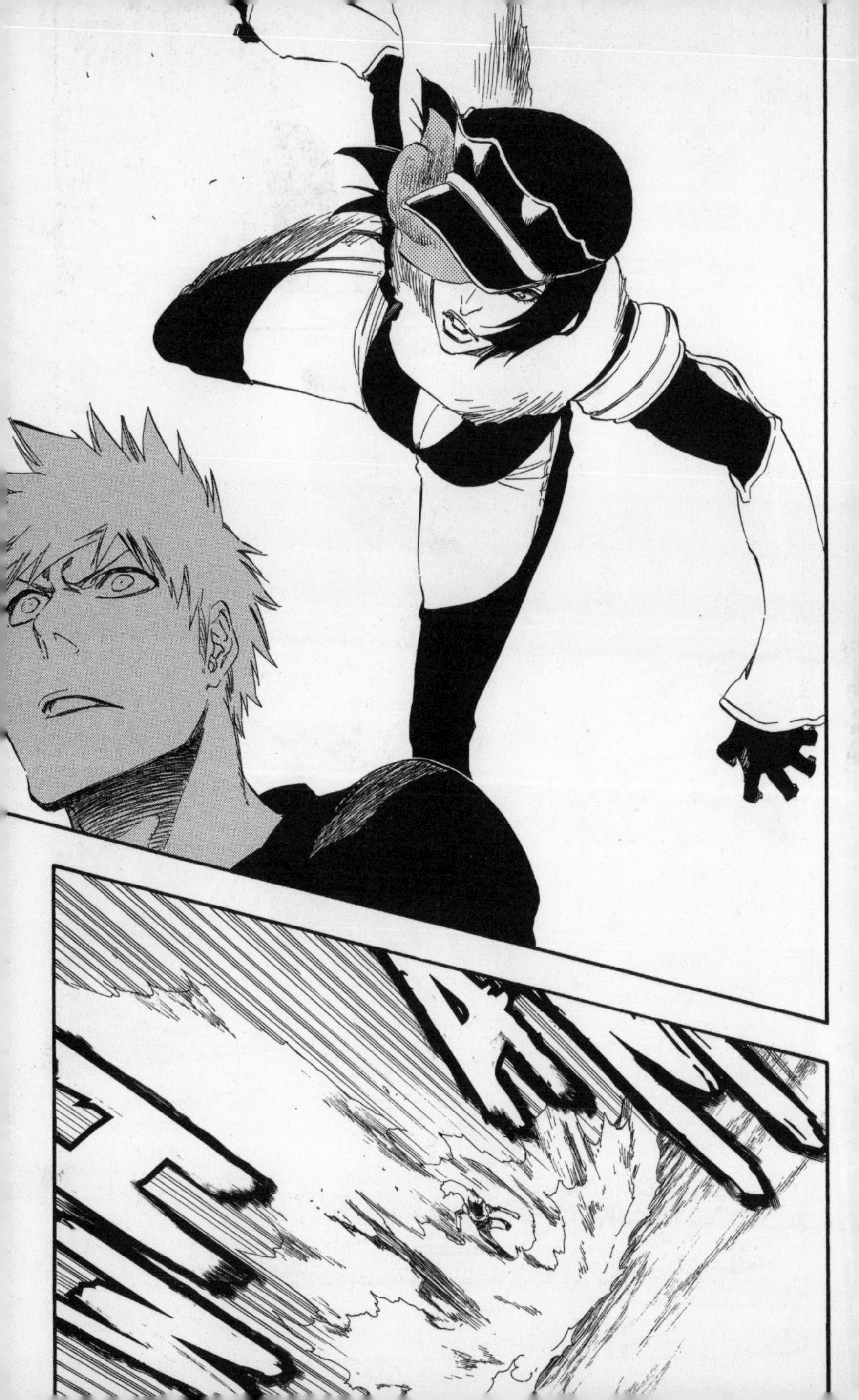

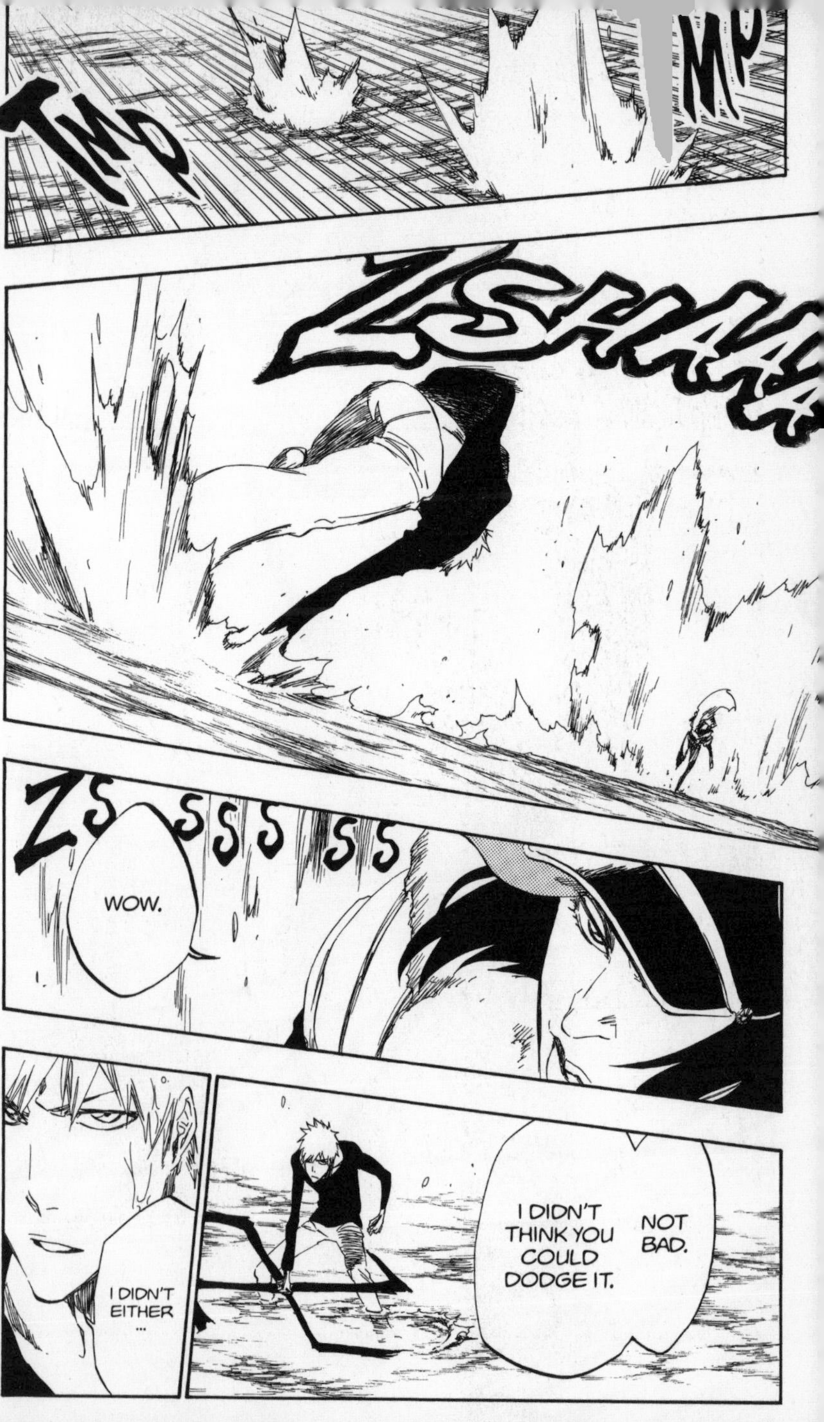
MP
TMP
ZSHAA
ZSSSSSS
WOW.
NOT BAD.
I DIDN'T THINK YOU COULD DODGE IT.
I DIDN'T EITHER ...

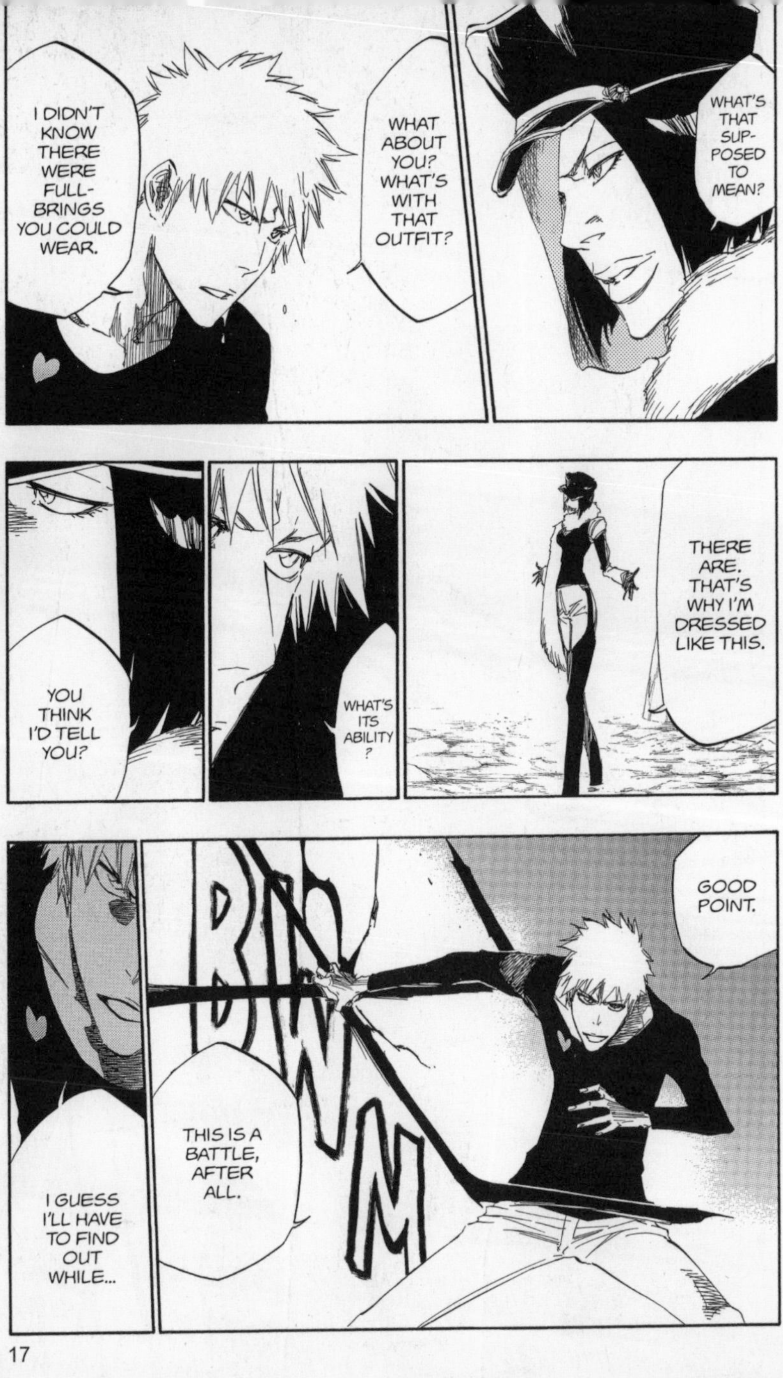
WHAT'S THAT SUP-POSED TO MEAN?
WHAT ABOUT YOU? WHAT'S WITH THAT OUTFIT?
I DIDN'T KNOW THERE WERE FULL-BRINGS YOU COULD WEAR.
THERE ARE. THAT'S WHY I'M DRESSED LIKE THIS.
WHAT'S ITS ABILITY?
YOU THINK I'D TELL YOU?
GOOD POINT.
THIS IS A BATTLE, AFTER ALL.
I GUESS I'LL HAVE TO FIND OUT WHILE...

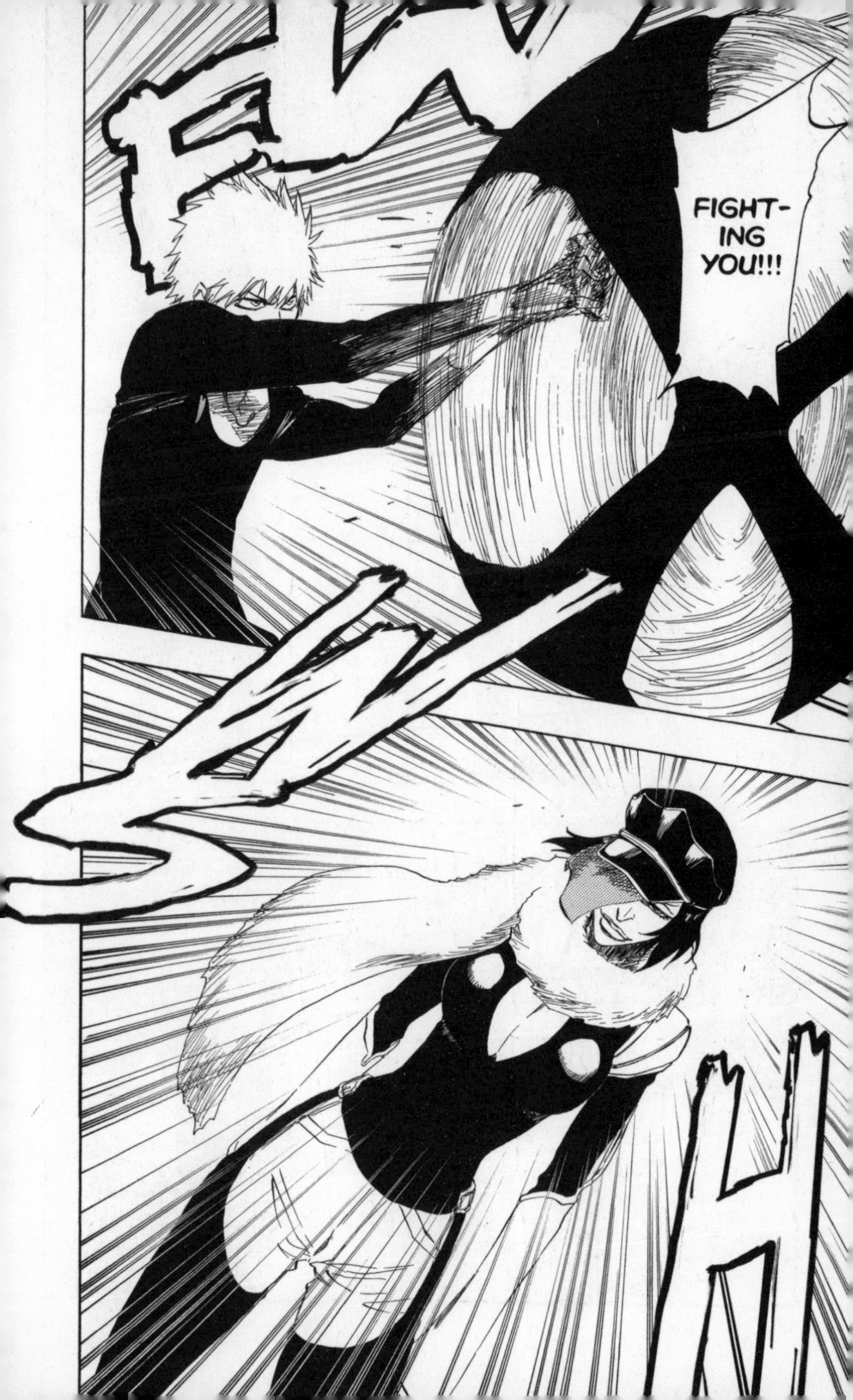
FIGHT-ING YOU!!!

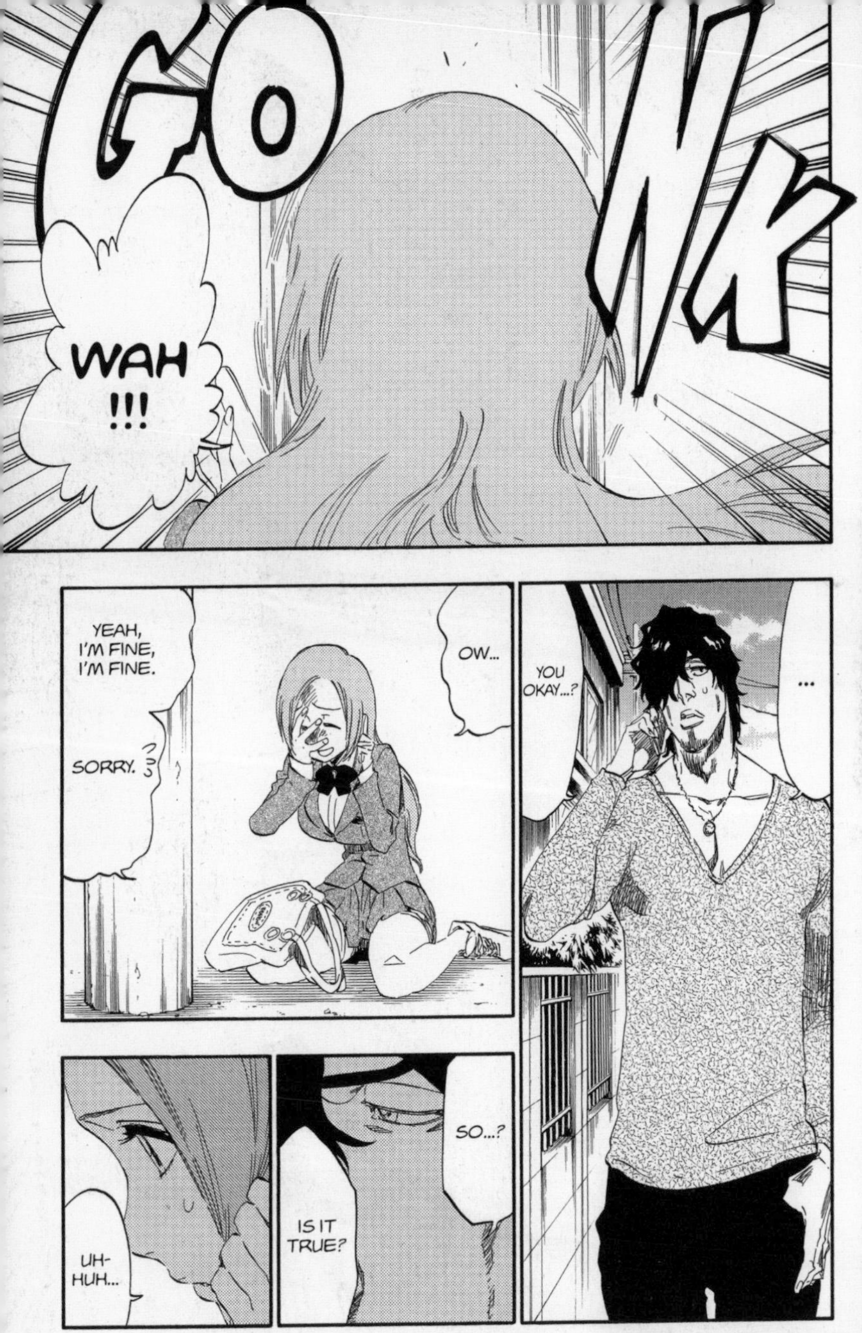
GONK
WAH !!!
...
YOU OKAY...?
OW...
YEAH, I'M FINE, I'M FINE.
SORRY.
SO...?
IS IT TRUE?
UH-HUH...

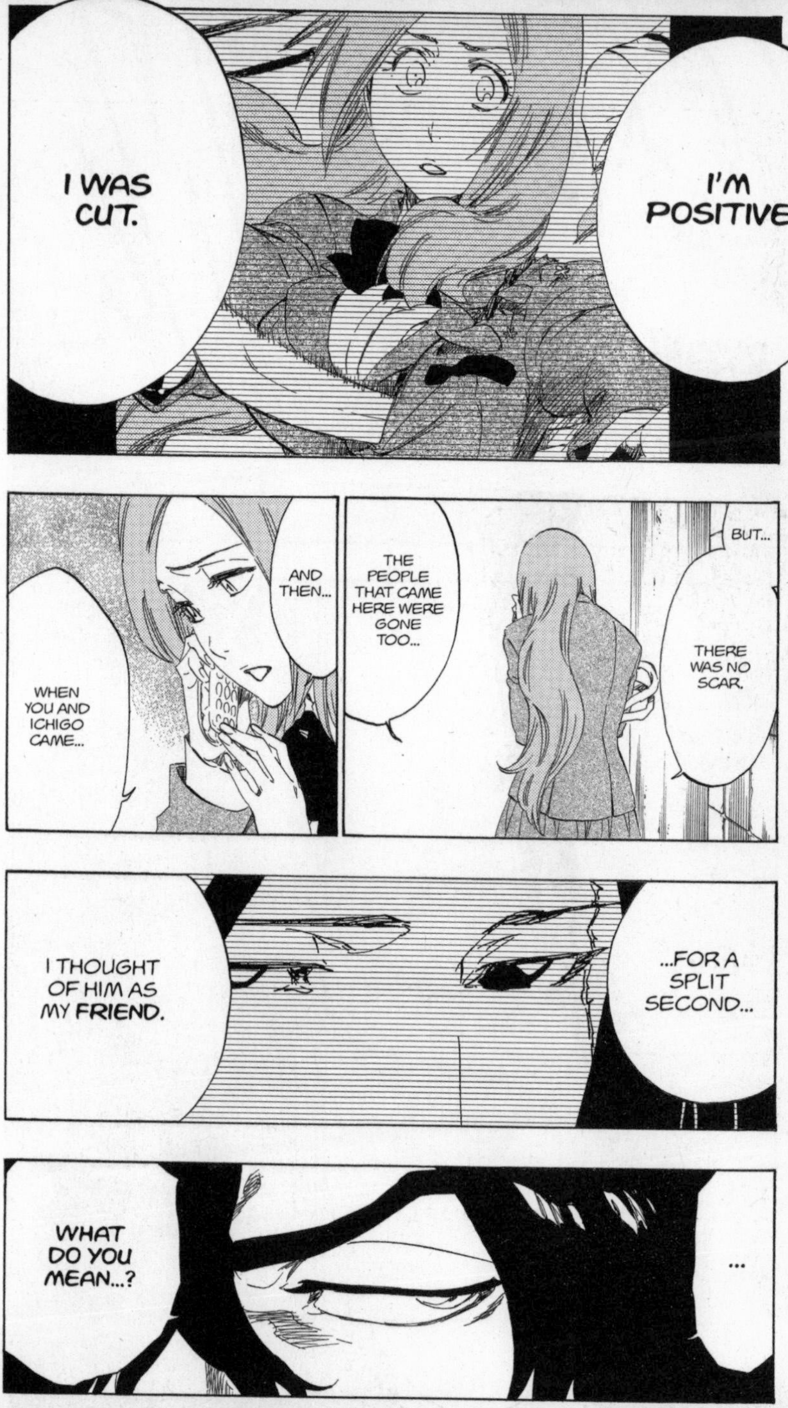
I'M POSITIVE...
I WAS CUT.
BUT...
THERE WAS NO SCAR.
THE PEOPLE THAT CAME HERE WERE GONE TOO...
AND THEN...
WHEN YOU AND ICHIGO CAME...
...FOR A SPLIT SECOND...
I THOUGHT OF HIM AS MY FRIEND.
...
WHAT DO YOU MEAN...?

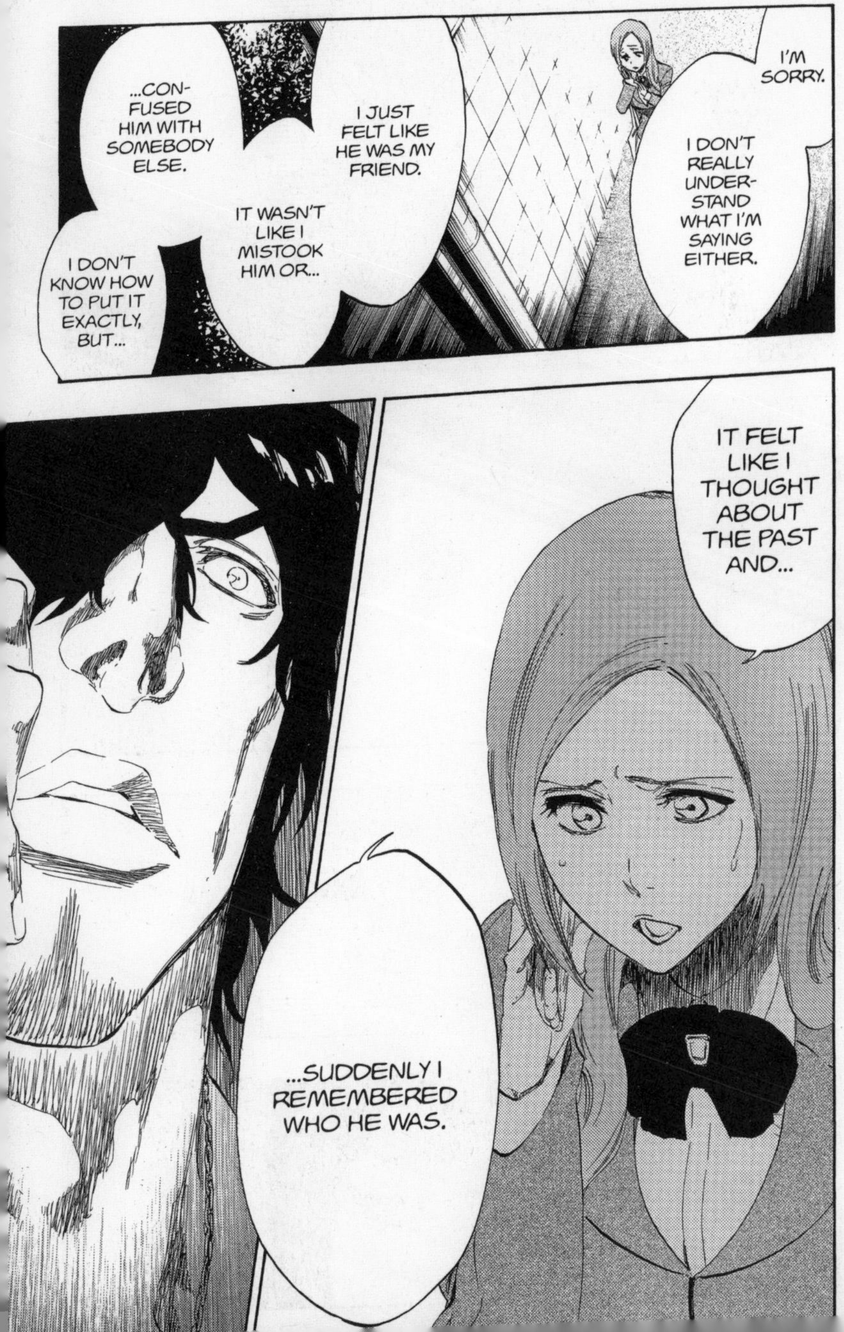
I'M SORRY.
I DON'T REALLY UNDER-STAND WHAT I'M SAYING EITHER.
I JUST FELT LIKE HE WAS MY FRIEND.
IT WASN'T LIKE I MISTOOK HIM OR...
...CON-FUSED HIM WITH SOMEBODY ELSE.
I DON'T KNOW HOW TO PUT IT EXACTLY, BUT...
IT FELT LIKE I THOUGHT ABOUT THE PAST AND...
...SUDDENLY I REMEMBERED WHO HE WAS.

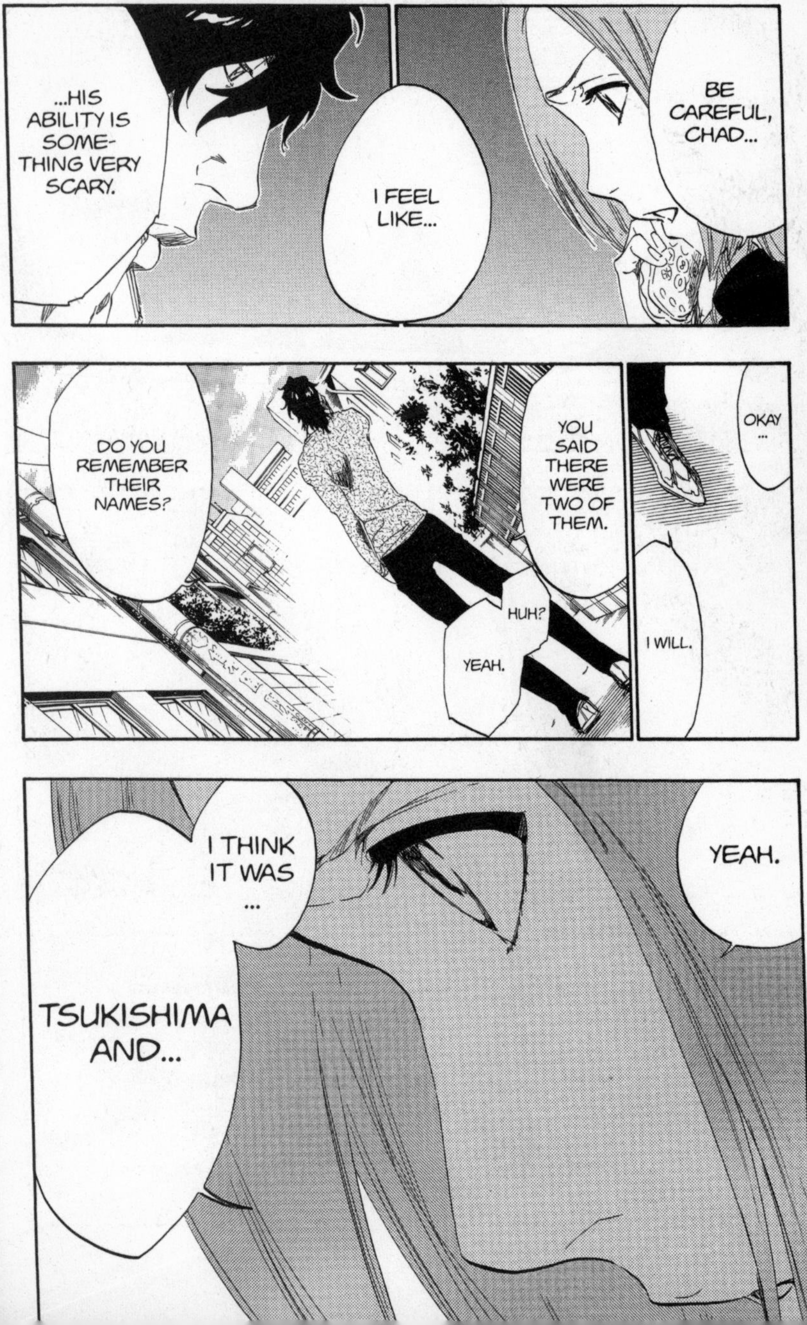
BE CAREFUL, CHAD...
I FEEL LIKE...
...HIS ABILITY IS SOME-THING VERY SCARY.
OKAY ...
I WILL.
YOU SAID THERE WERE TWO OF THEM.
HUH?
YEAH.
DO YOU REMEMBER THEIR NAMES?
YEAH.
I THINK IT WAS ...
TSUKISHIMA AND...

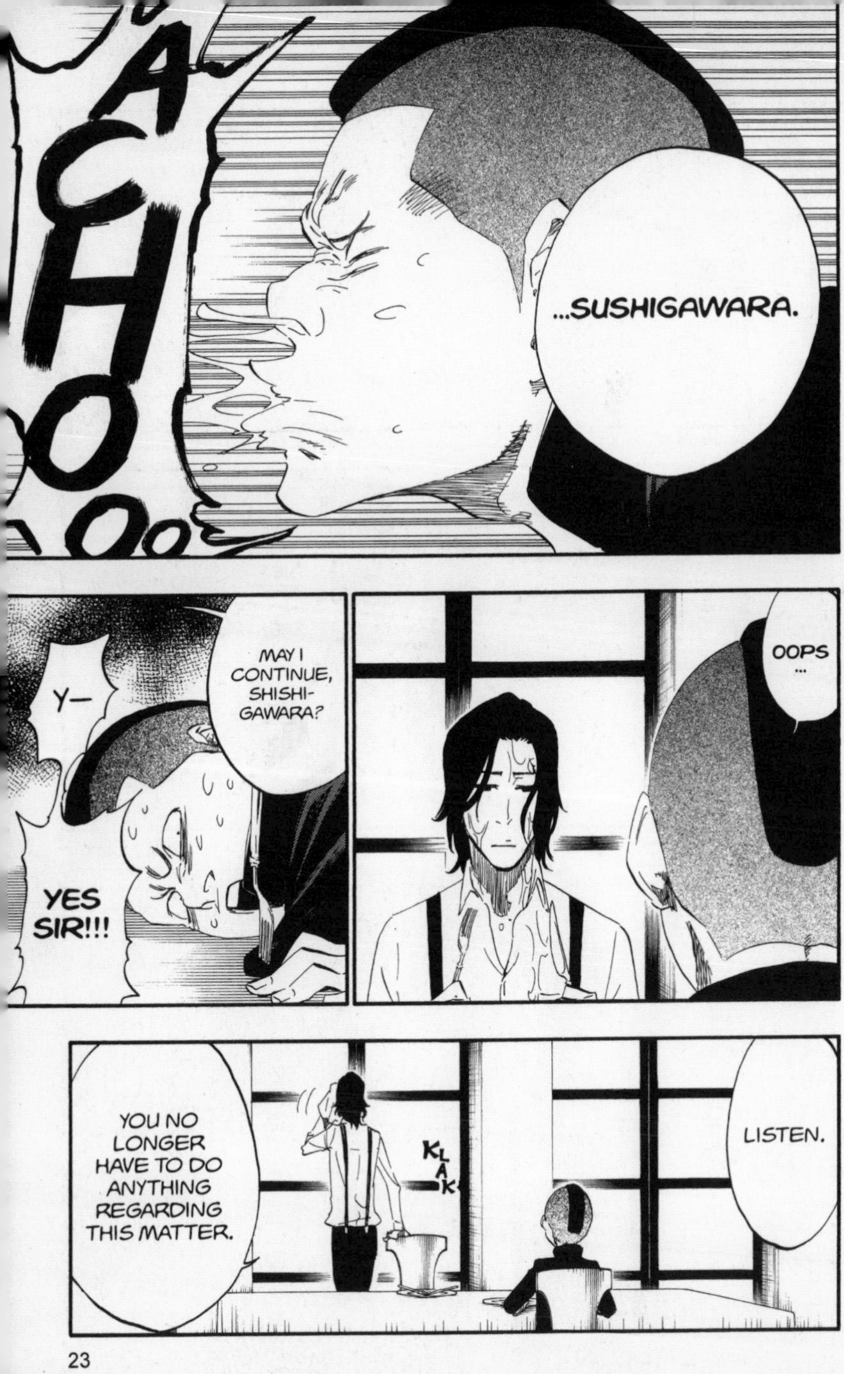
ACHOOO
...SUSHIGAWARA.
OOPS ...
MAY I CONTINUE, SHISHI-GAWARA?
Y—
YES SIR!!!
LISTEN.
KLAK
YOU NO LONGER HAVE TO DO ANYTHING REGARDING THIS MATTER.

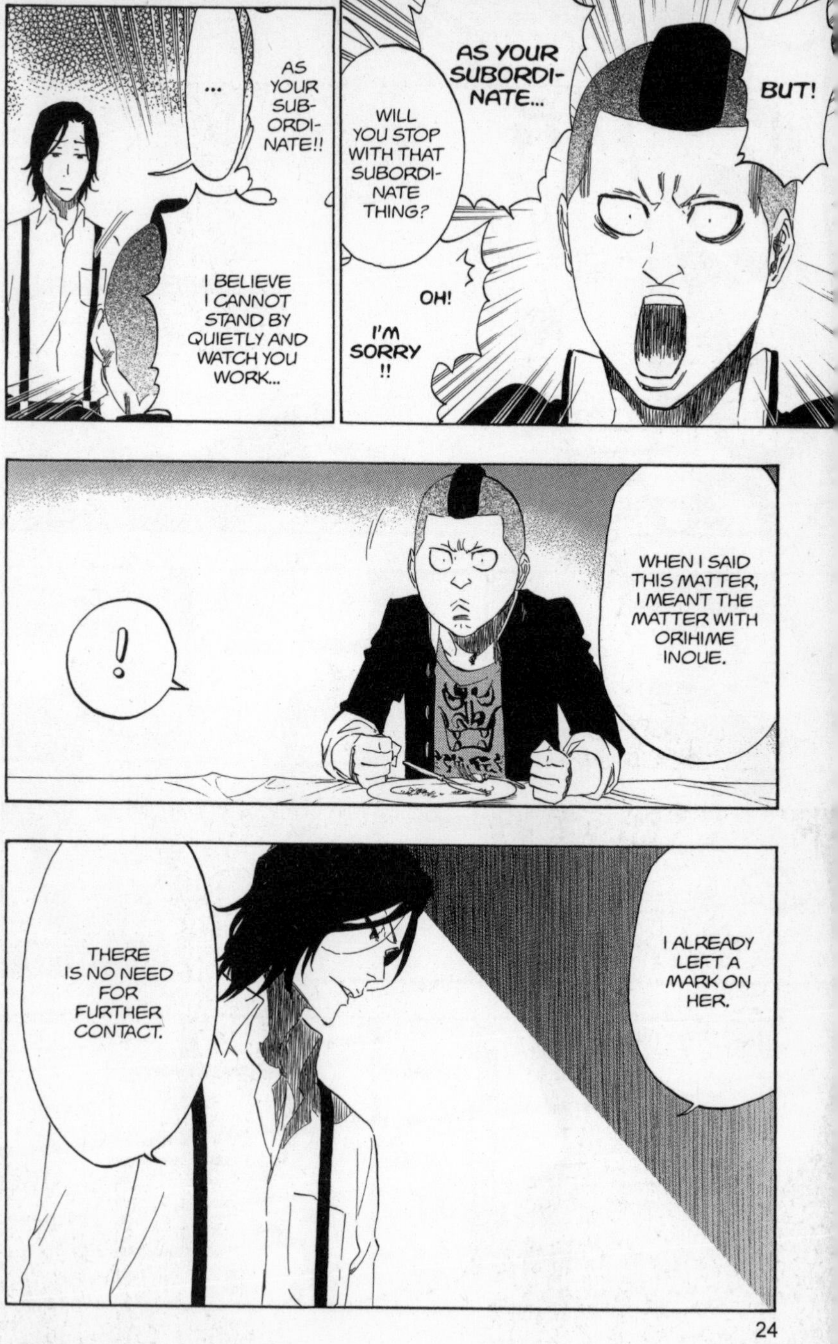
BUT!
AS YOUR SUBORDI-NATE...
WILL YOU STOP WITH THAT SUBORDI-NATE THING?
OH!
I'M SORRY!!
AS YOUR SUB-ORDI-NATE!!
...
I BELIEVE I CANNOT STAND BY QUIETLY AND WATCH YOU WORK...
WHEN I SAID THIS MATTER, I MEANT THE MATTER WITH ORIHIME INOUE.
!
I ALREADY LEFT A MARK ON HER.
THERE IS NO NEED FOR FURTHER CONTACT.

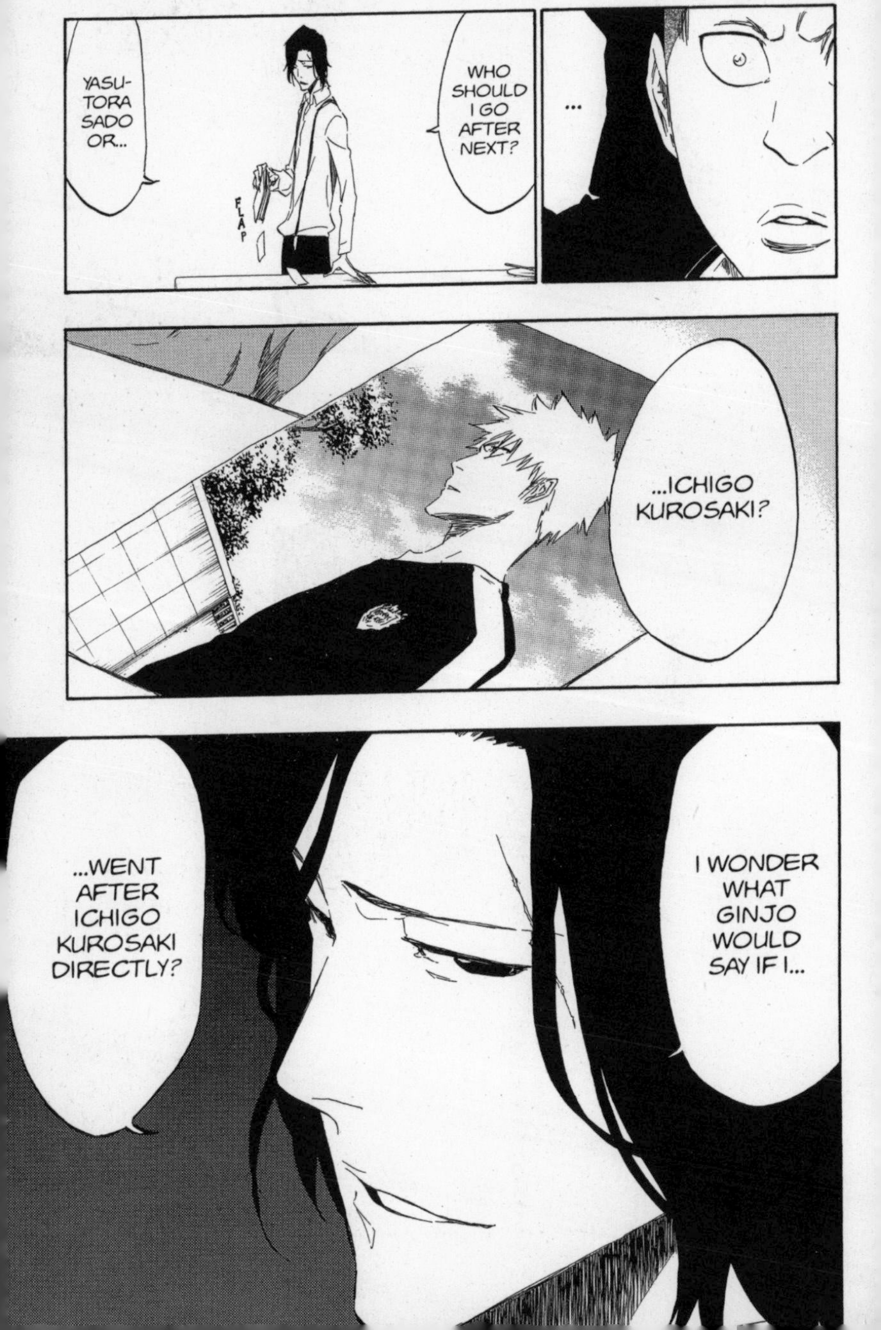
...
WHO SHOULD I GO AFTER NEXT?
YASU-TORA SADO OR...
FLAP
...ICHIGO KUROSAKI?
I WONDER WHAT GINJO WOULD SAY IF I...
...WENT AFTER ICHIGO KUROSAKI DIRECTLY?

SHISHIGAWARA'S
T-SHIRT

LEGENDARY
STRENGTH

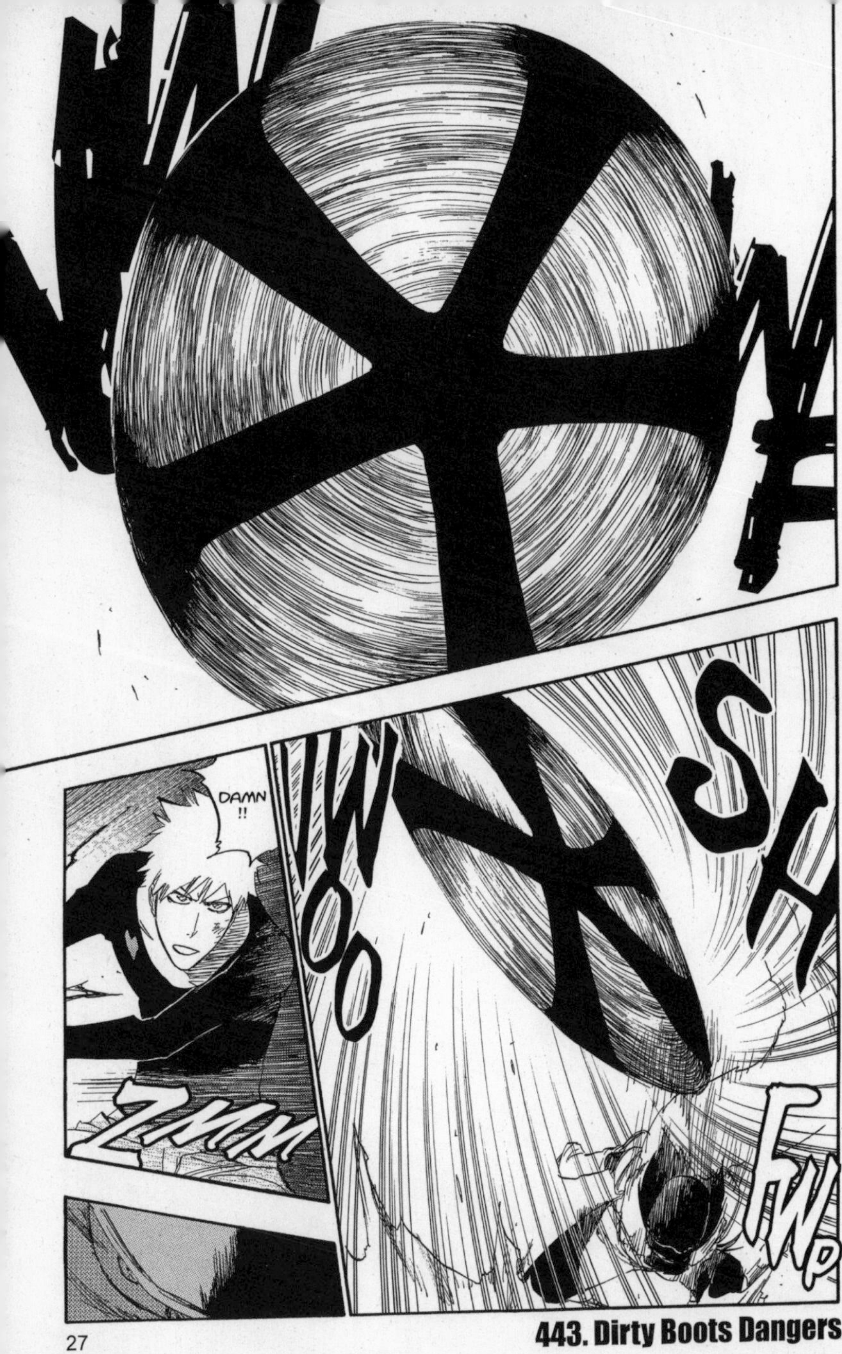
DAMN
!!

443. Dirty Boots Dangers

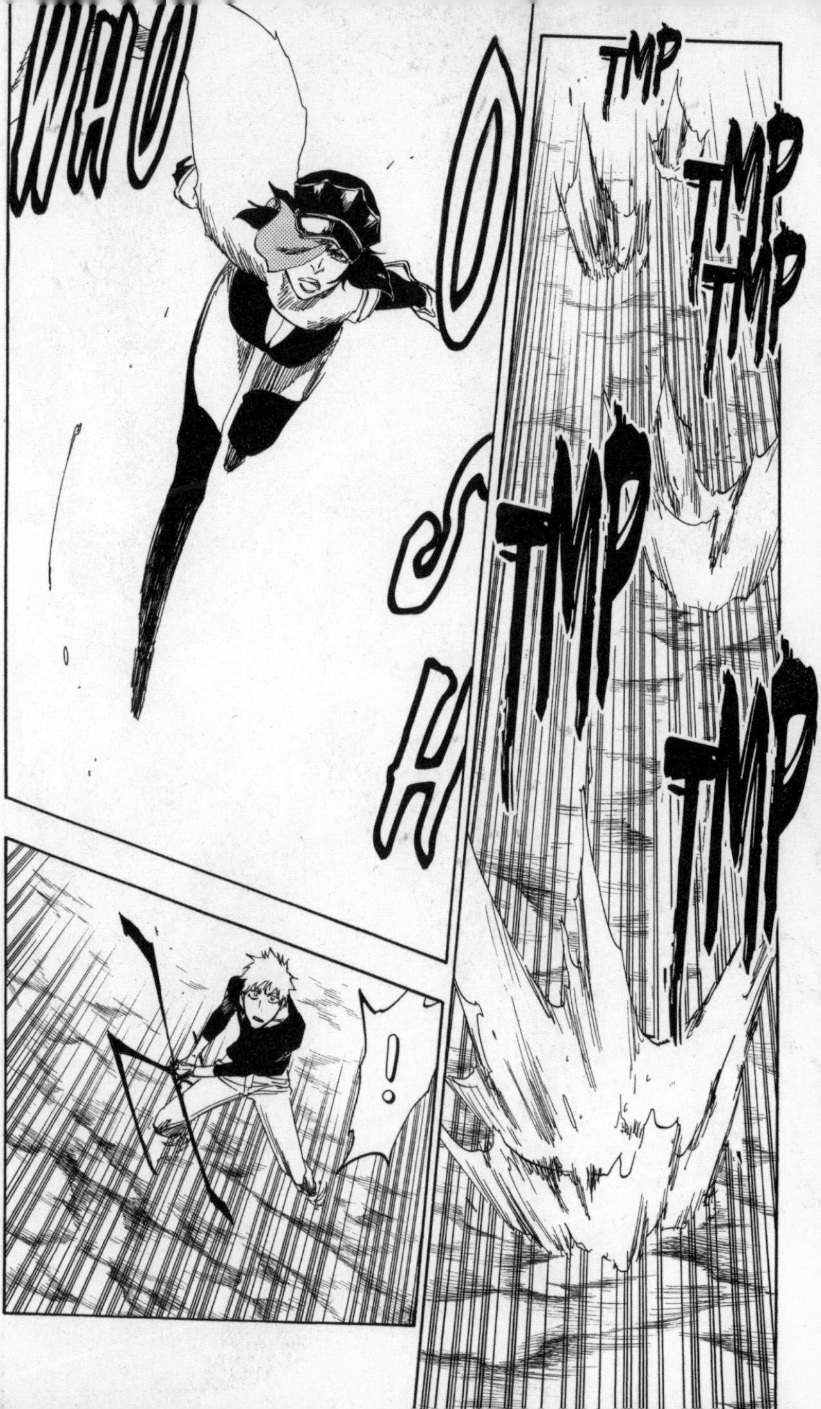
TMP
TMP
TMP
TMP
TMP
!

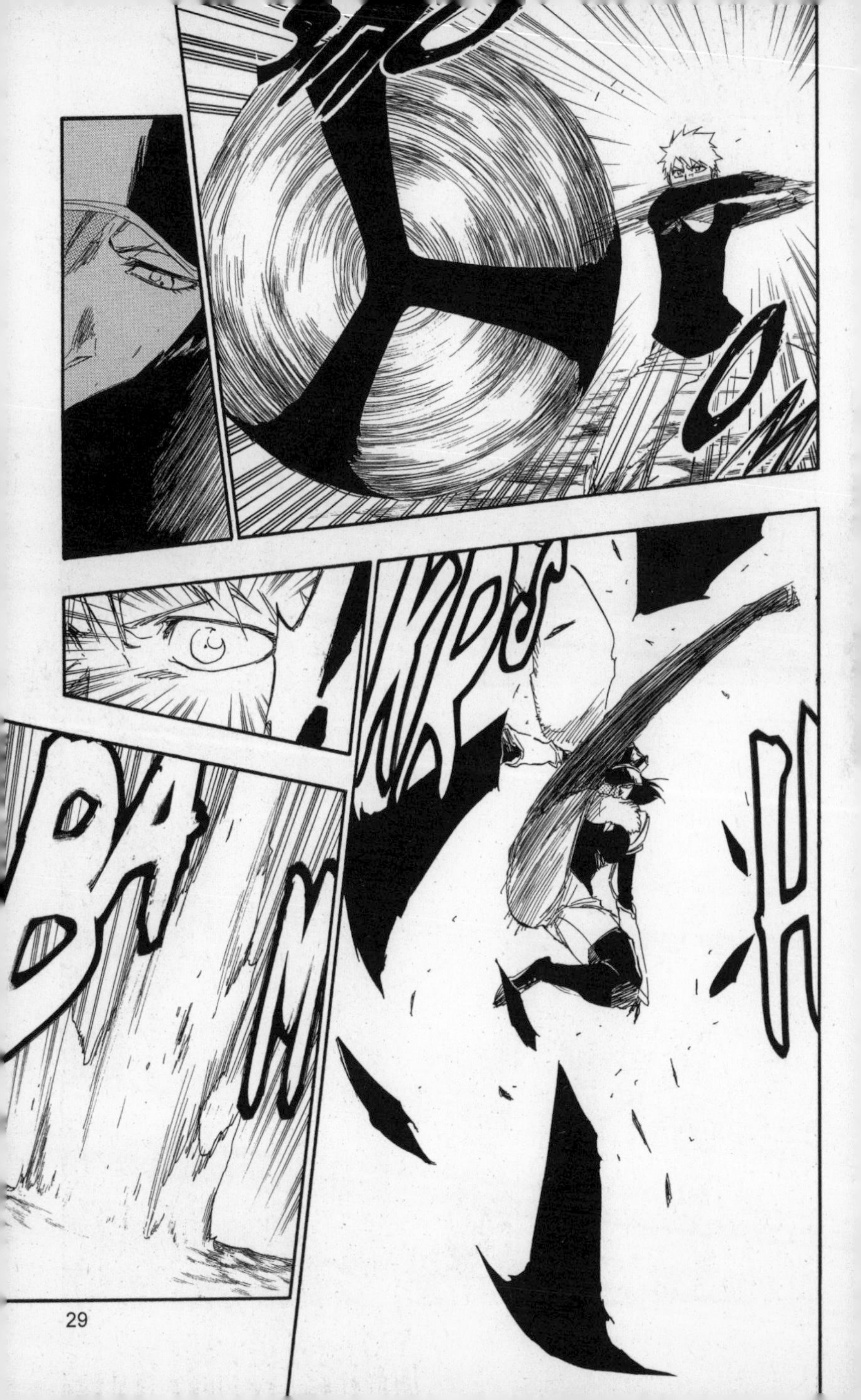
WHOOSH
BAM

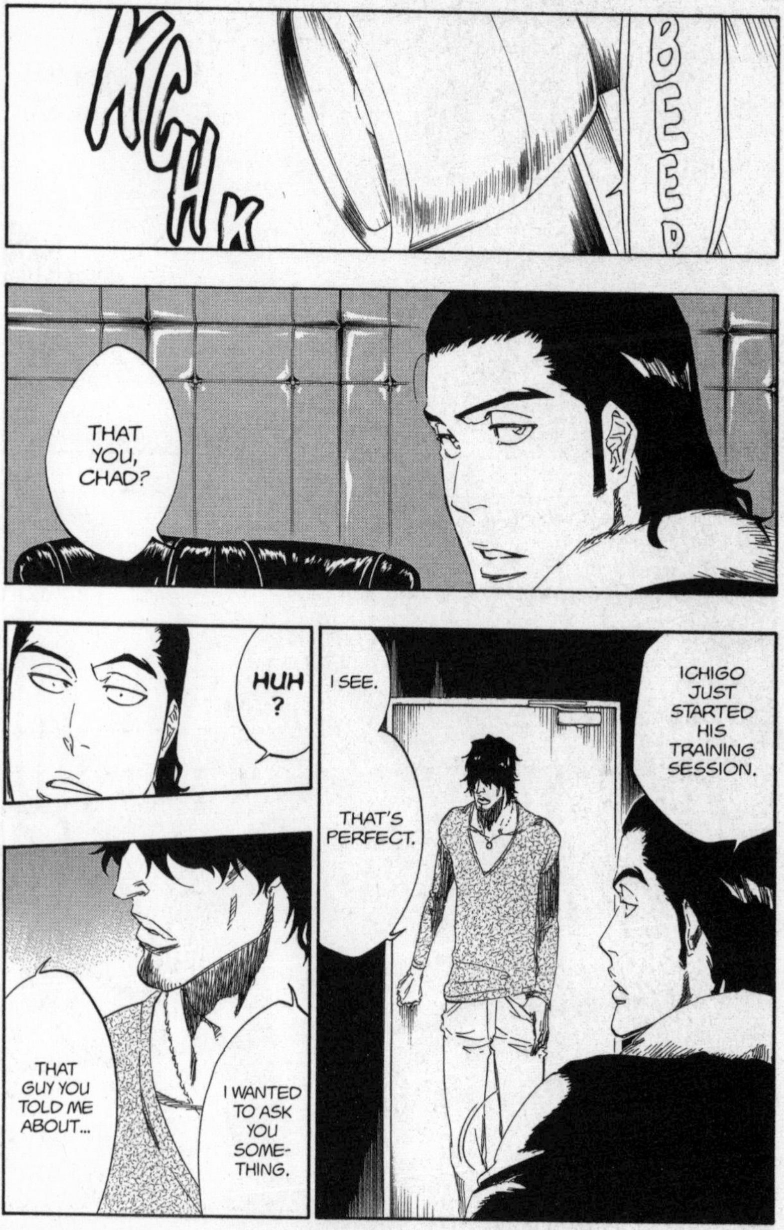
BEEP
KCHK
THAT YOU, CHAD?
ICHIGO JUST STARTED HIS TRAINING SESSION.
I SEE.
THAT'S PERFECT.
HUH?
I WANTED TO ASK YOU SOMETHING.
THAT GUY YOU TOLD ME ABOUT...

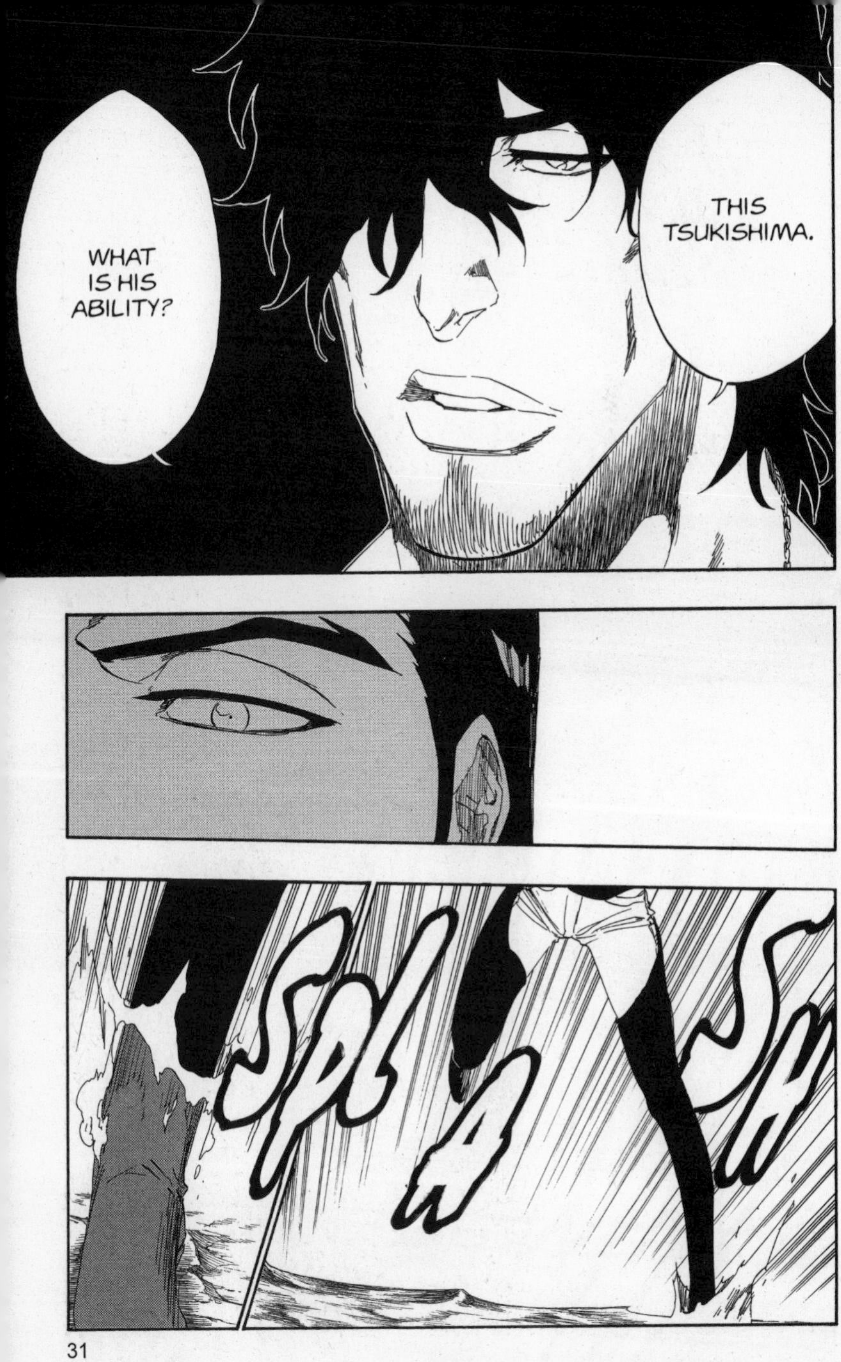
THIS TSUKISHIMA.
WHAT IS HIS ABILITY?

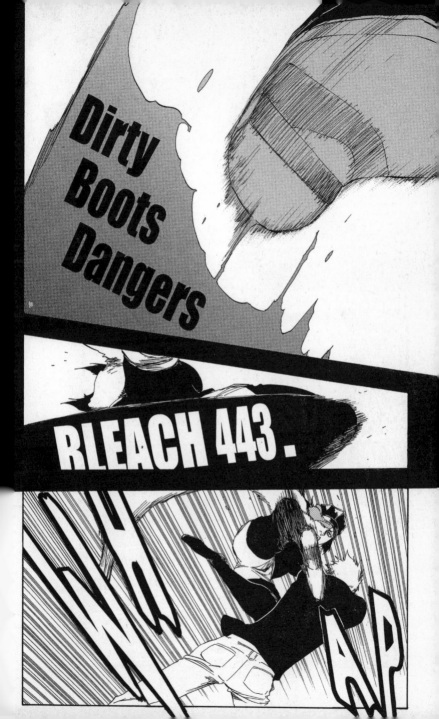

Dirty
Boots
Dangers

BLEACH 443.

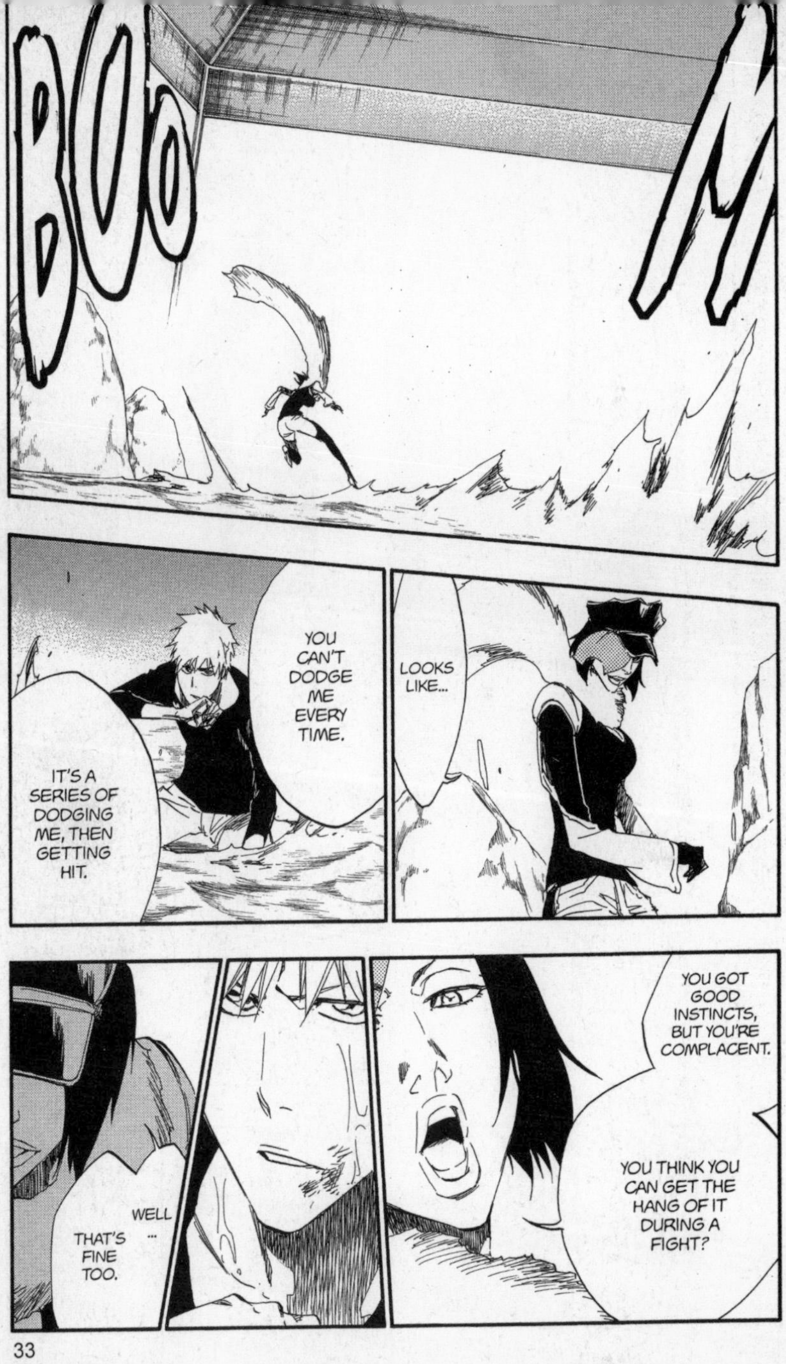
BOOOM
LOOKS LIKE...
YOU CAN'T DODGE ME EVERY TIME.
IT'S A SERIES OF DODGING ME, THEN GETTING HIT.
YOU GOT GOOD INSTINCTS, BUT YOU'RE COMPLACENT.
YOU THINK YOU CAN GET THE HANG OF IT DURING A FIGHT?
WELL...
THAT'S FINE TOO.

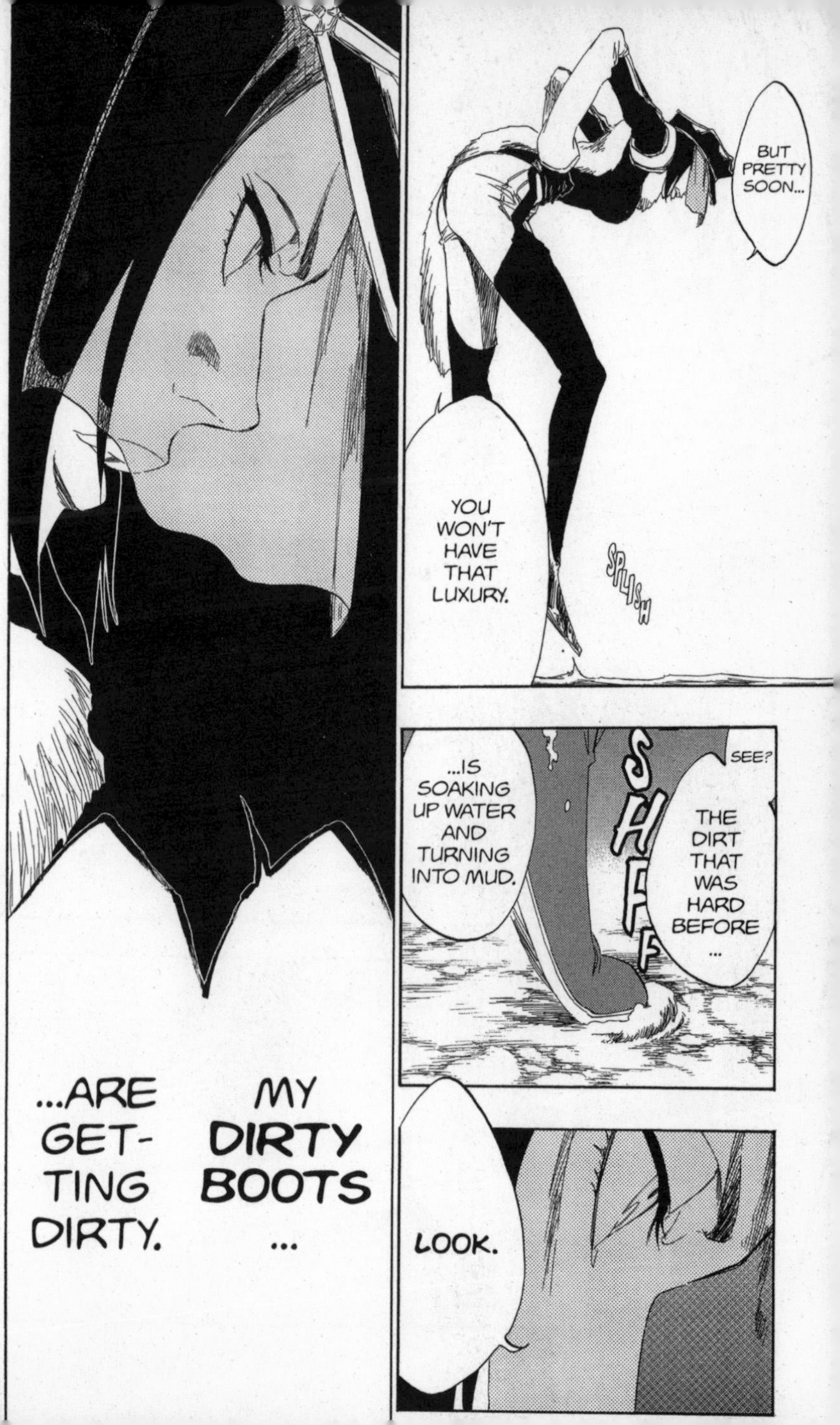
BUT PRETTY SOON...
YOU WON'T HAVE THAT LUXURY.
SPLISH
SEE?
THE DIRT THAT WAS HARD BEFORE...
SHFF
...IS SOAKING UP WATER AND TURNING INTO MUD.
LOOK.
MY DIRTY BOOTS...
...ARE GET-TING DIRTY.

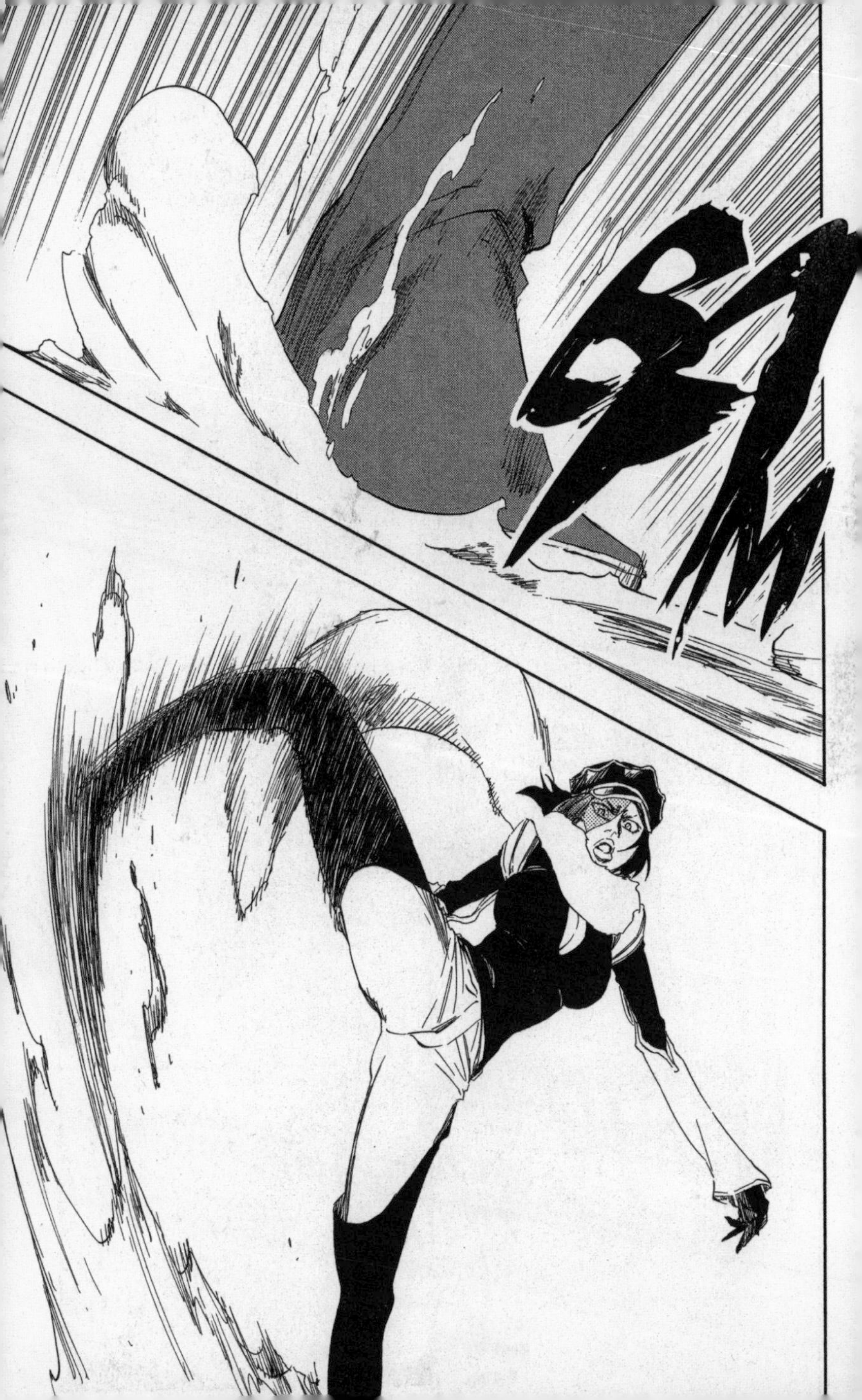
BAMM

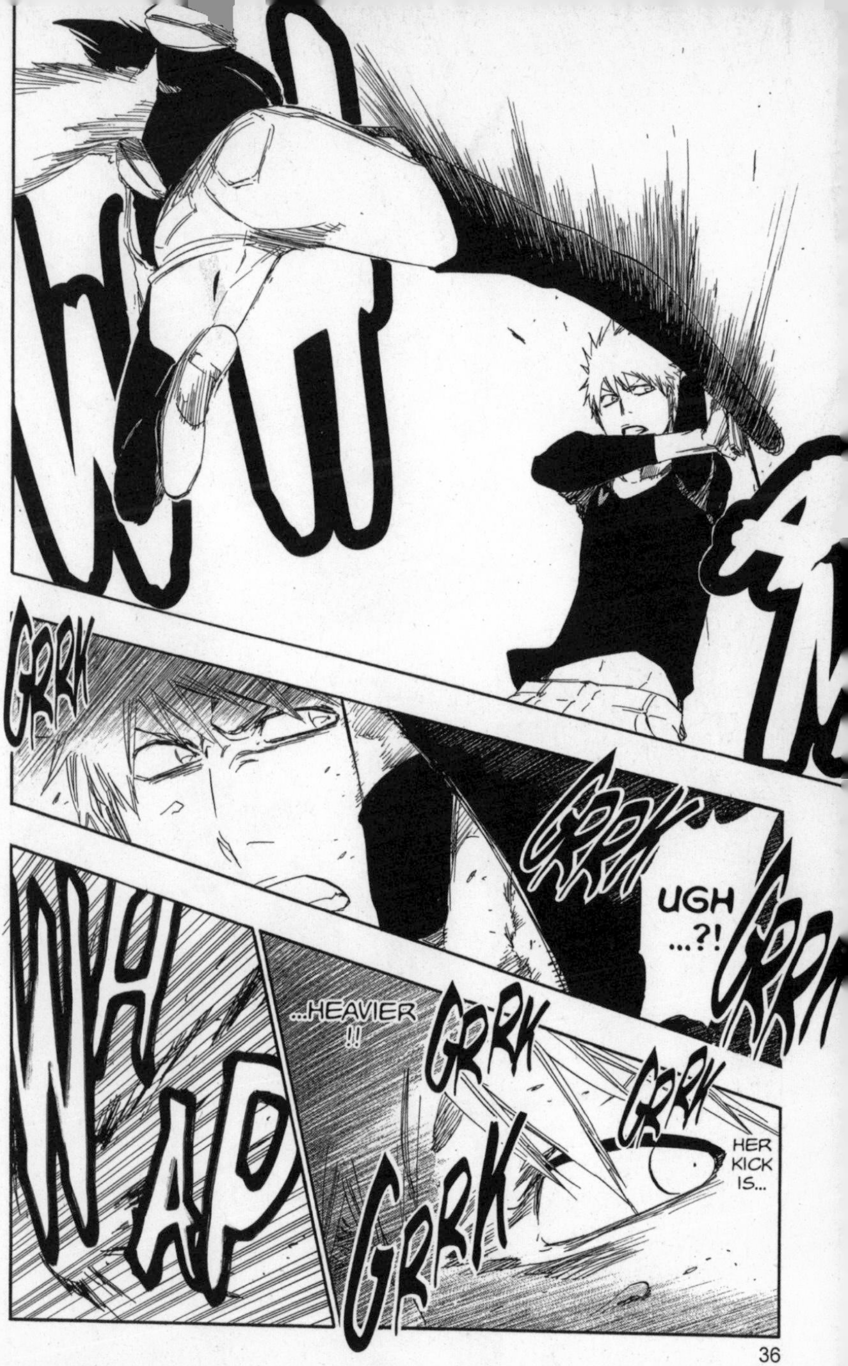
GRRK
UGH ...?!
GRRK
GRRK
HER KICK IS...
GRRK
GRRK
GRRK
...HEAVIER !!
WHAP

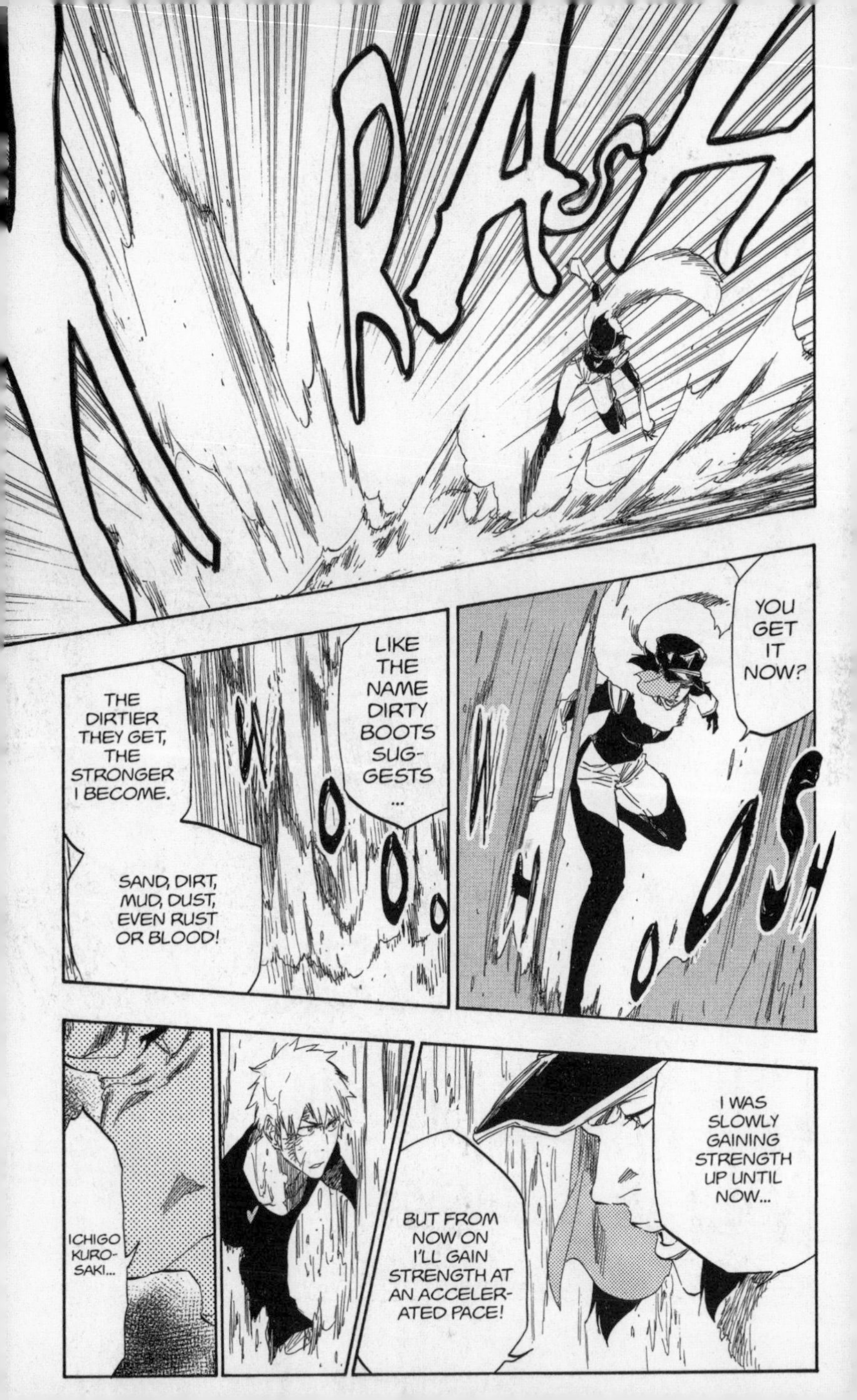
YOU GET IT NOW?
LIKE THE NAME DIRTY BOOTS SUGGESTS...
THE DIRTIER THEY GET, THE STRONGER I BECOME.
SAND, DIRT, MUD, DUST, EVEN RUST OR BLOOD!
I WAS SLOWLY GAINING STRENGTH UP UNTIL NOW...
BUT FROM NOW ON I'LL GAIN STRENGTH AT AN ACCELERATED PACE!
ICHIGO KUROSAKI...

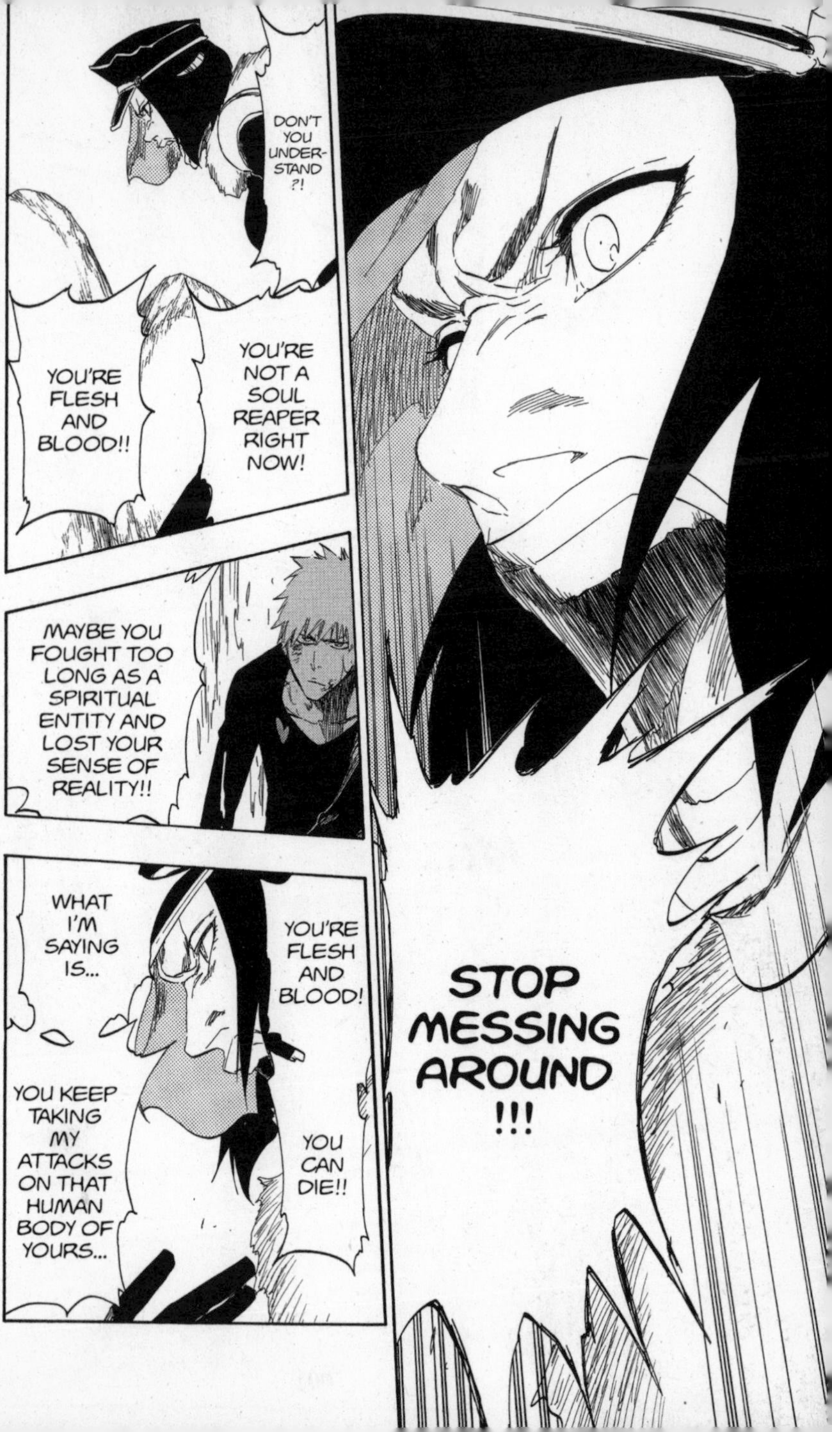
STOP MESSING AROUND !!!
DON'T YOU UNDER-STAND ?!
YOU'RE NOT A SOUL REAPER RIGHT NOW!
YOU'RE FLESH AND BLOOD!!
MAYBE YOU FOUGHT TOO LONG AS A SPIRITUAL ENTITY AND LOST YOUR SENSE OF REALITY!!
WHAT I'M SAYING IS...
YOU'RE FLESH AND BLOOD!
YOU KEEP TAKING MY ATTACKS ON THAT HUMAN BODY OF YOURS...
YOU CAN DIE!!

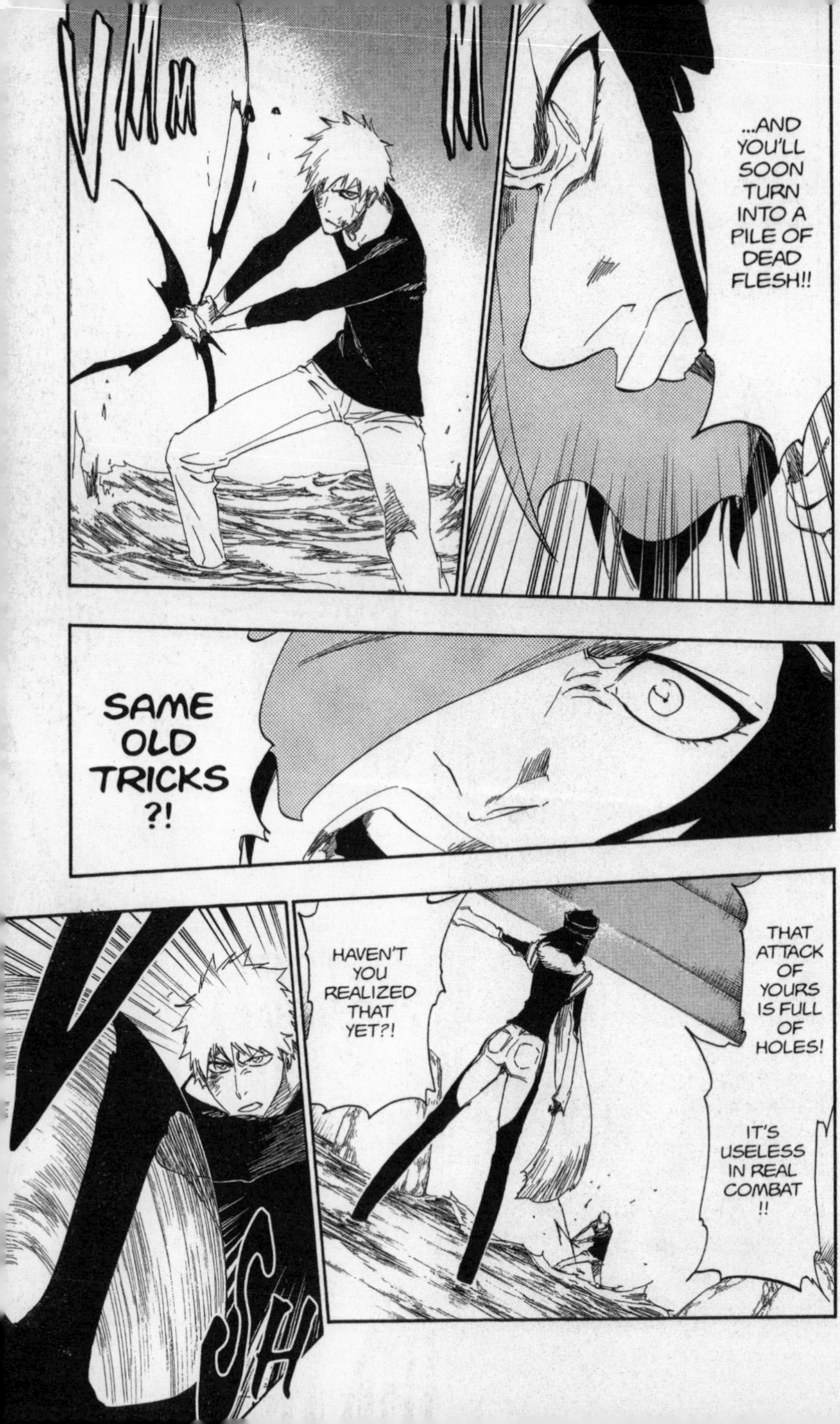
...AND YOU'LL SOON TURN INTO A PILE OF DEAD FLESH!!
SAME OLD TRICKS ?!
THAT ATTACK OF YOURS IS FULL OF HOLES!
IT'S USELESS IN REAL COMBAT !!
HAVEN'T YOU REALIZED THAT YET?!

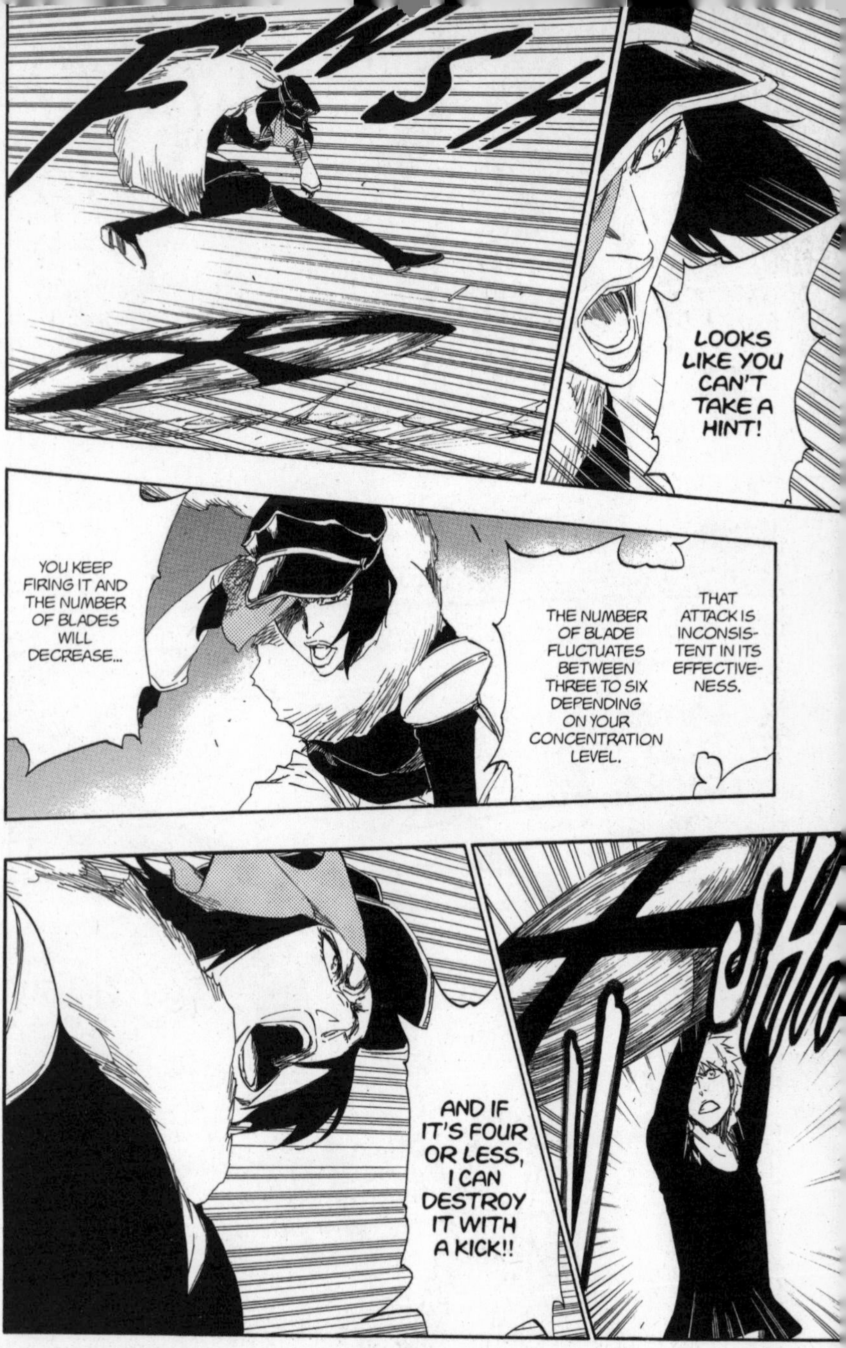
LOOKS LIKE YOU CAN'T TAKE A HINT!
FWSH
THAT ATTACK IS INCONSISTENT IN ITS EFFECTIVENESS.
THE NUMBER OF BLADE FLUCTUATES BETWEEN THREE TO SIX DEPENDING ON YOUR CONCENTRATION LEVEL.
YOU KEEP FIRING IT AND THE NUMBER OF BLADES WILL DECREASE...
AND IF IT'S FOUR OR LESS, I CAN DESTROY IT WITH A KICK!!

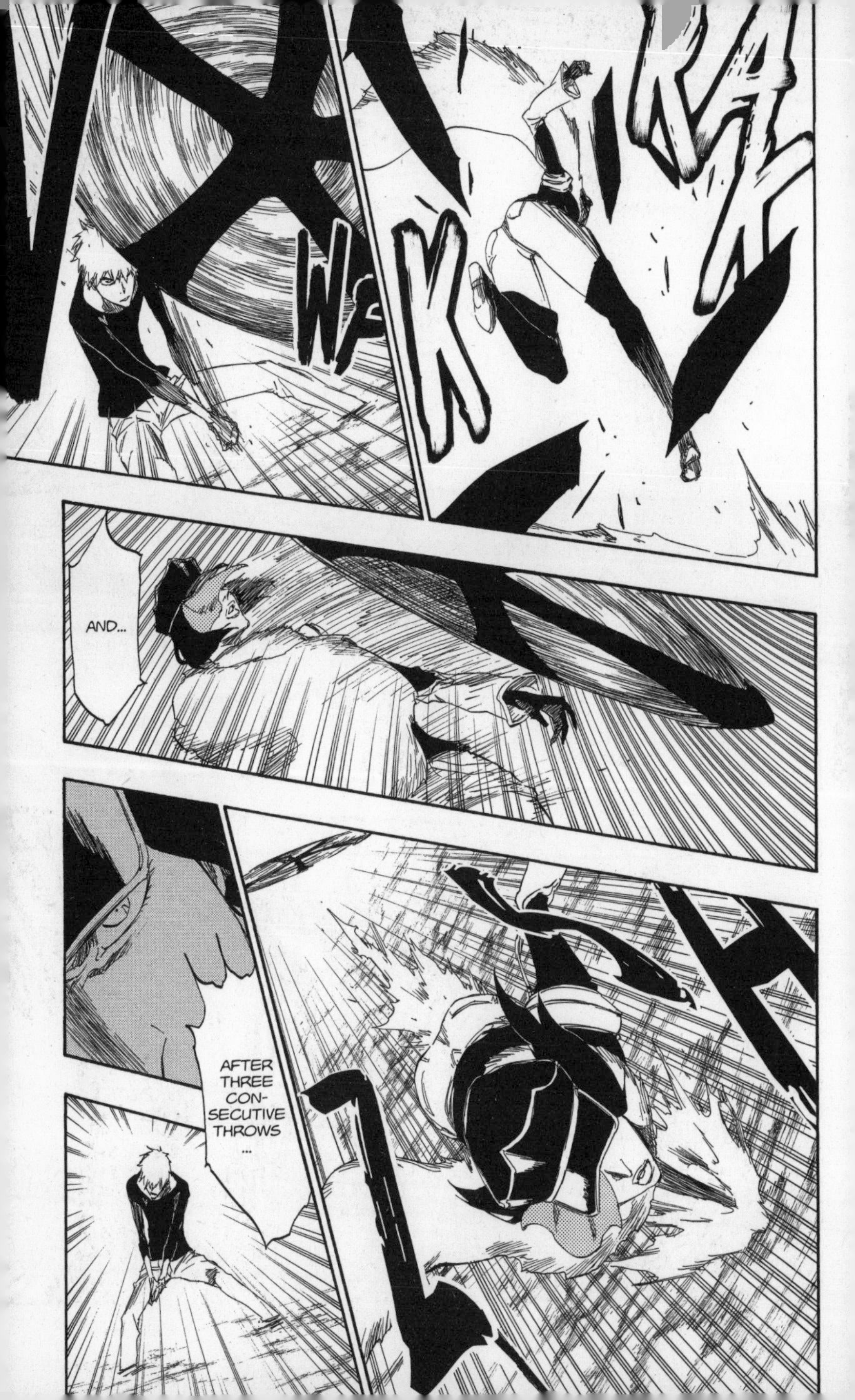
AND...
AFTER THREE CON-SECUTIVE THROWS ...

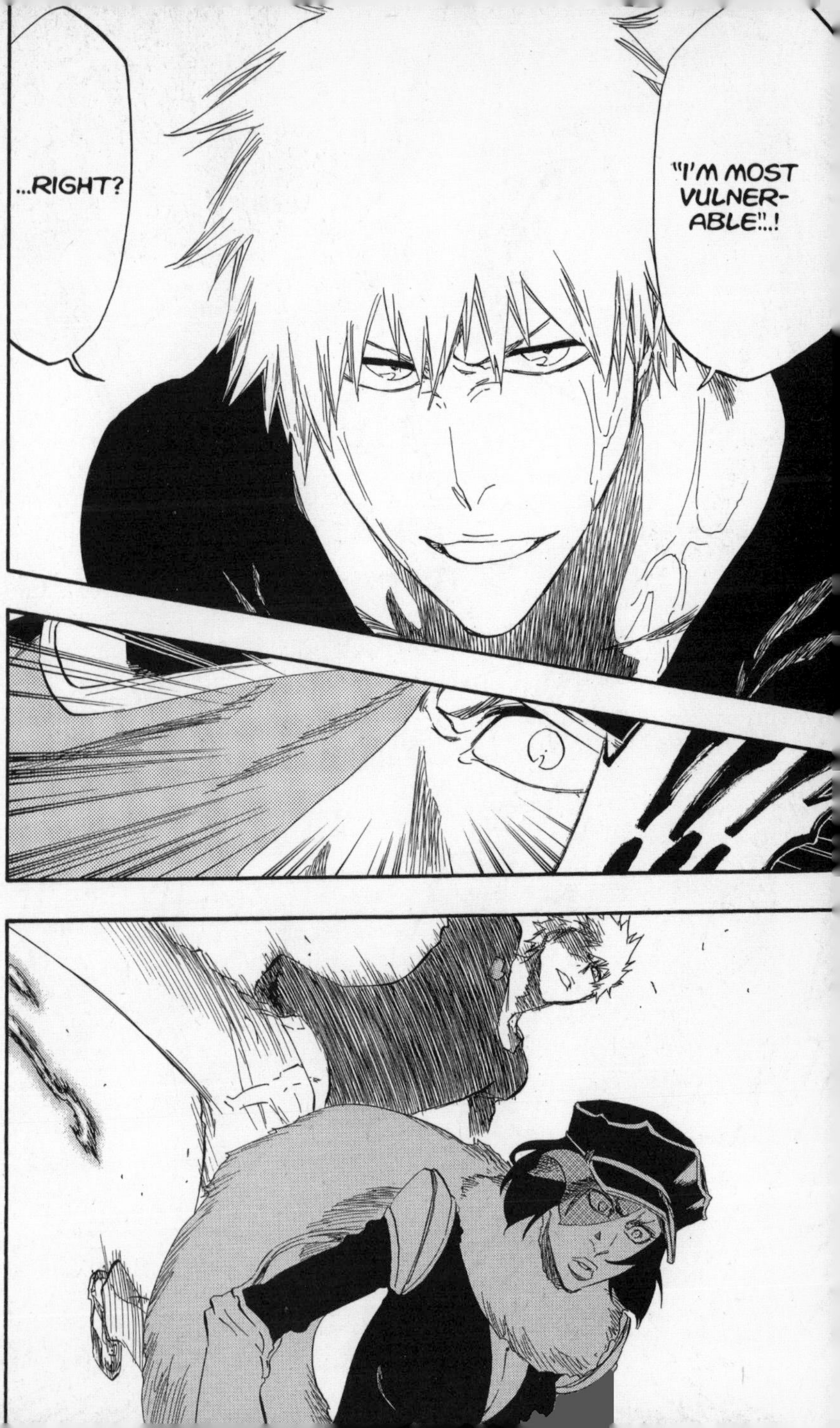
"I'M MOST VULNER-ABLE"...!
...RIGHT?

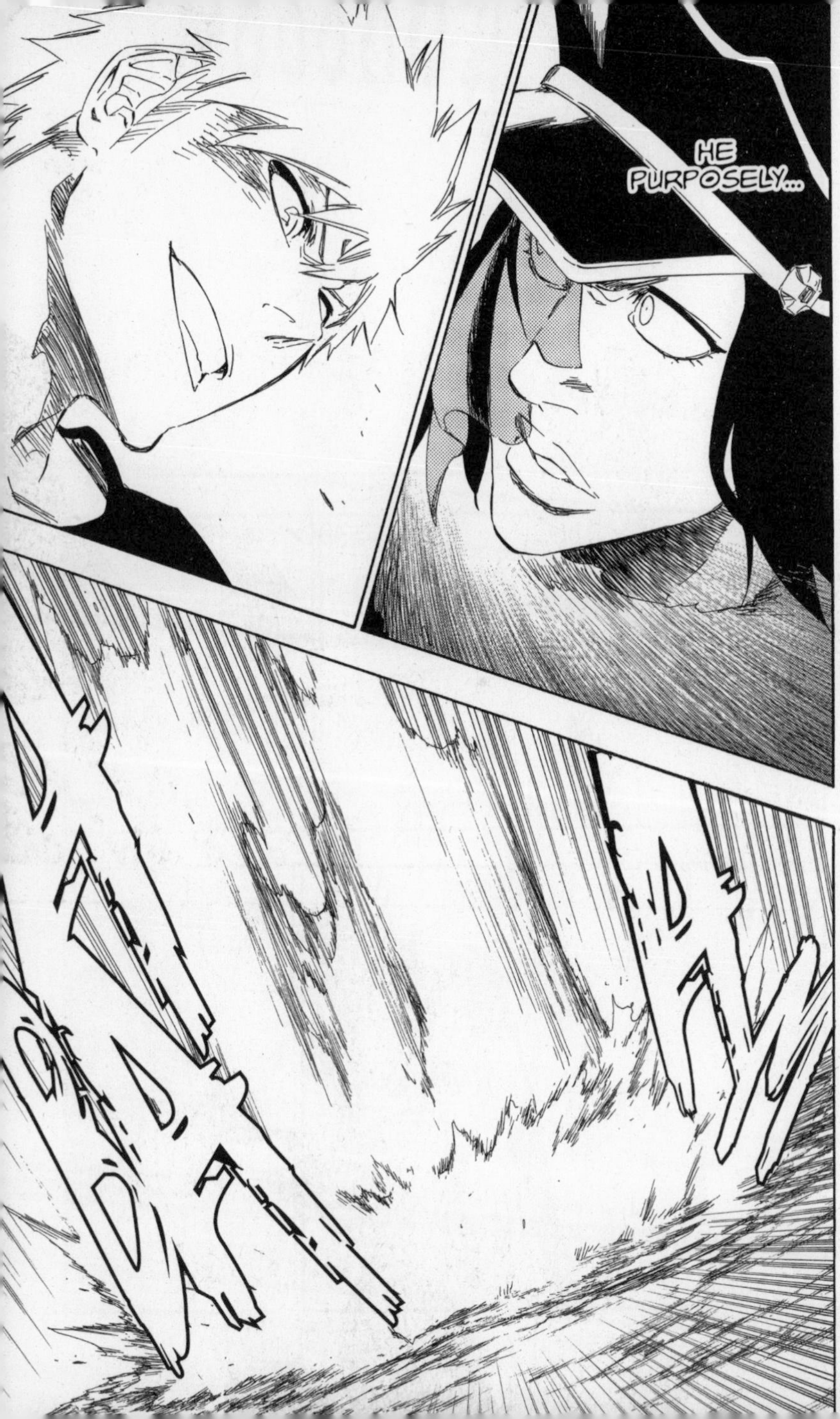
HE PURPOSELY...

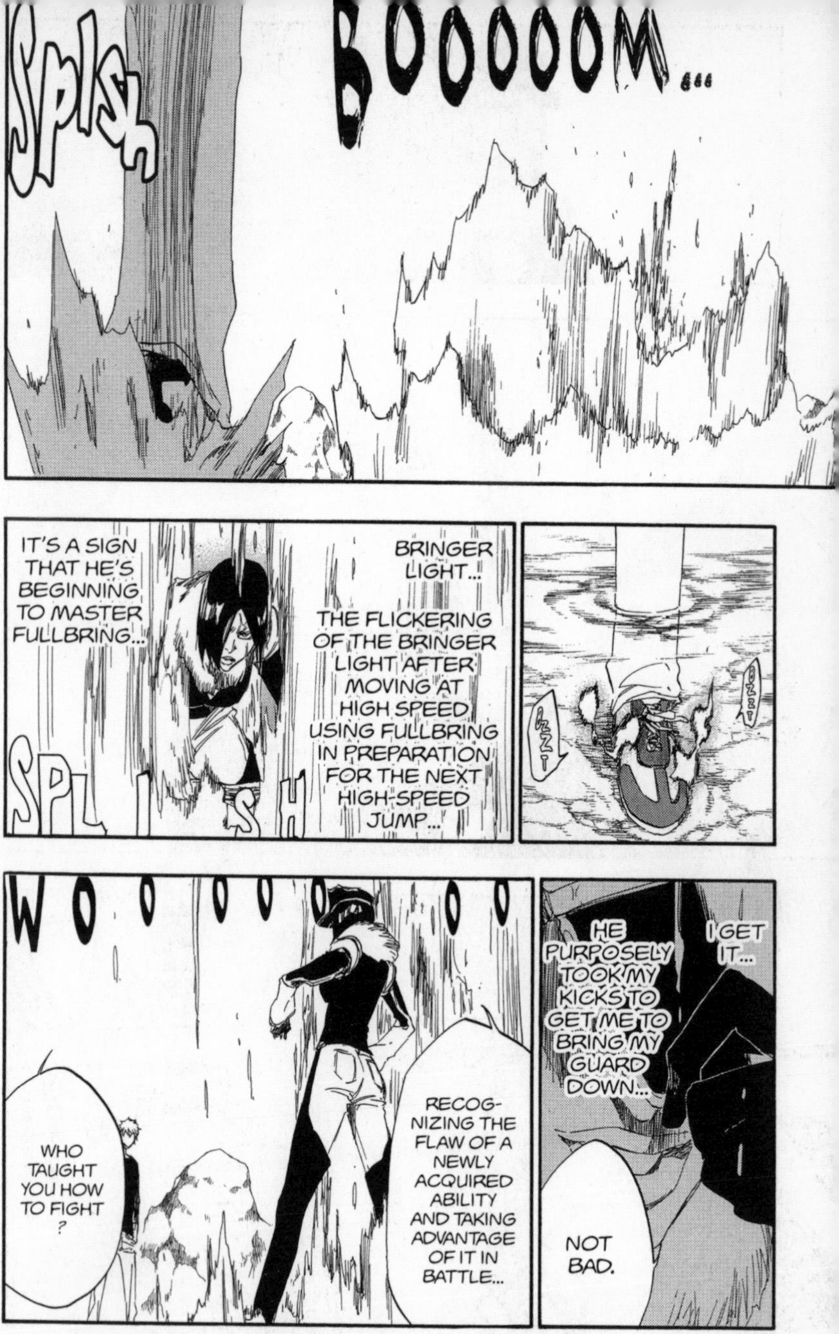
BOOOOM...
Splsh
BZZT
BZZT
BRINGER LIGHT...
THE FLICKERING OF THE BRINGER LIGHT AFTER MOVING AT HIGH SPEED USING FULLBRING IN PREPARATION FOR THE NEXT HIGH-SPEED JUMP...
IT'S A SIGN THAT HE'S BEGINNING TO MASTER FULLBRING...
SPLISH
I GET IT...
HE PURPOSELY TOOK MY KICKS TO GET ME TO BRING MY GUARD DOWN...
NOT BAD.
WOOOOOO
RECOGNIZING THE FLAW OF A NEWLY ACQUIRED ABILITY AND TAKING ADVANTAGE OF IT IN BATTLE...
WHO TAUGHT YOU HOW TO FIGHT?

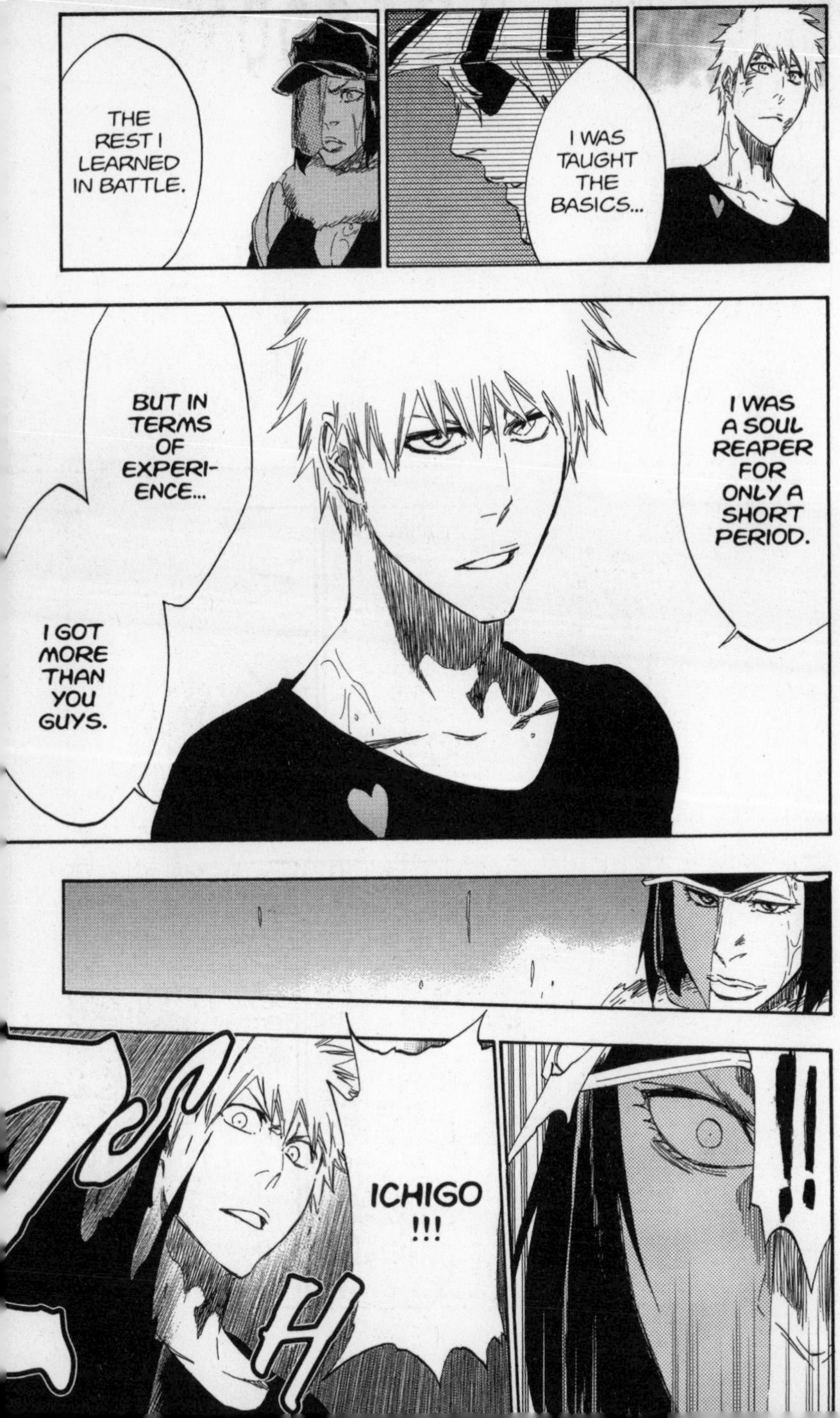
I WAS TAUGHT THE BASICS...
THE REST I LEARNED IN BATTLE.
I WAS A SOUL REAPER FOR ONLY A SHORT PERIOD.
BUT IN TERMS OF EXPERIENCE...
I GOT MORE THAN YOU GUYS.
!!
ICHIGO !!!

RIRUKA
REALLY
DIDN'T
RETURN...

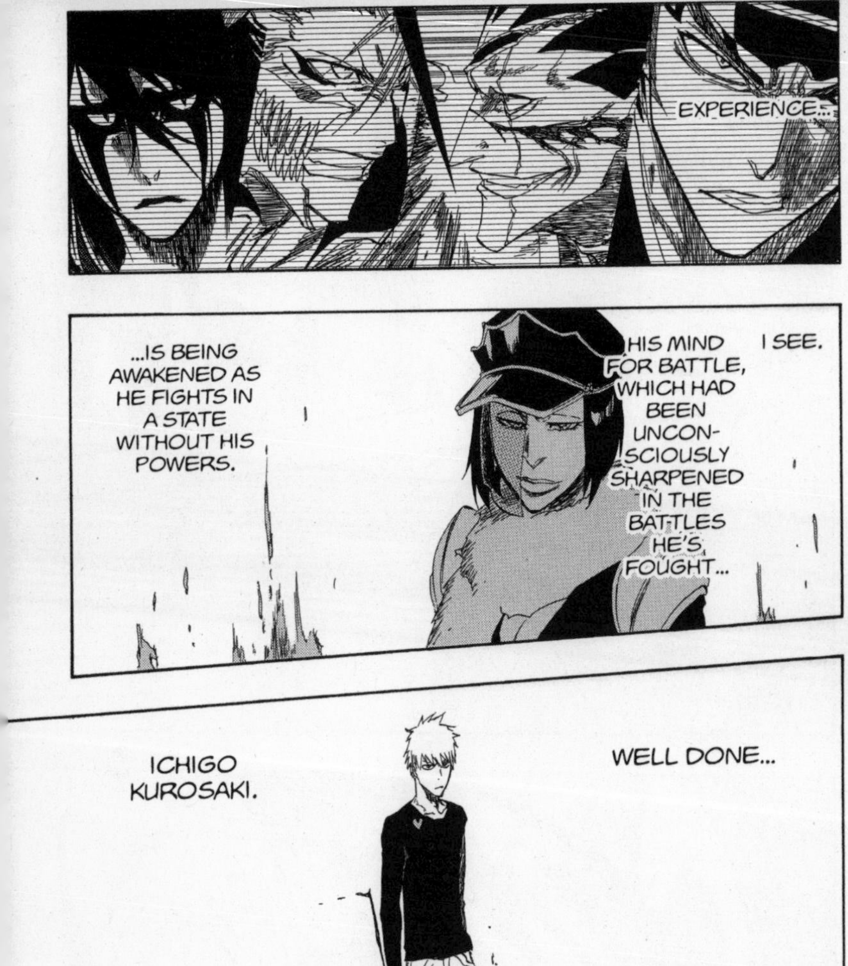
EXPERIENCE...
I SEE.
HIS MIND FOR BATTLE, WHICH HAD BEEN UNCONSCIOUSLY SHARPENED IN THE BATTLES HE'S FOUGHT...
...IS BEING AWAKENED AS HE FIGHTS IN A STATE WITHOUT HIS POWERS.
WELL DONE...
ICHIGO KUROSAKI.

444. THE RISING

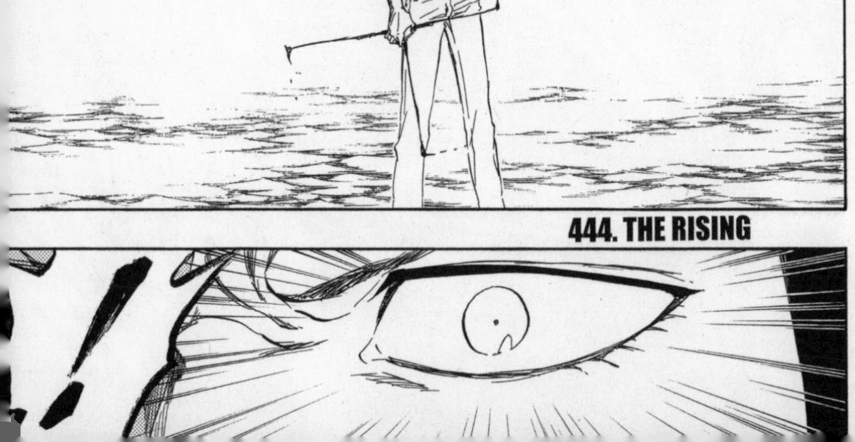

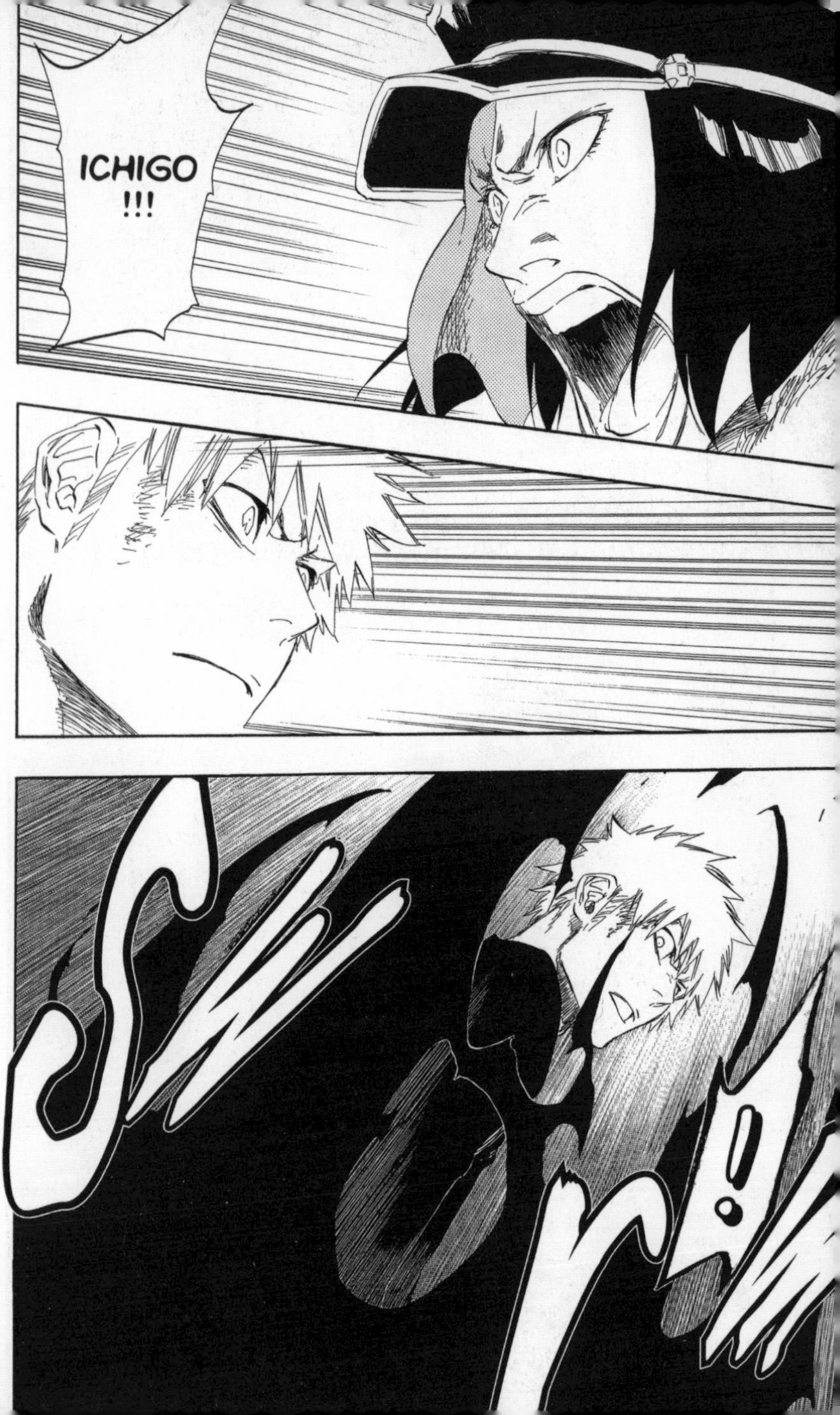
ICHIGO
!!!
!!

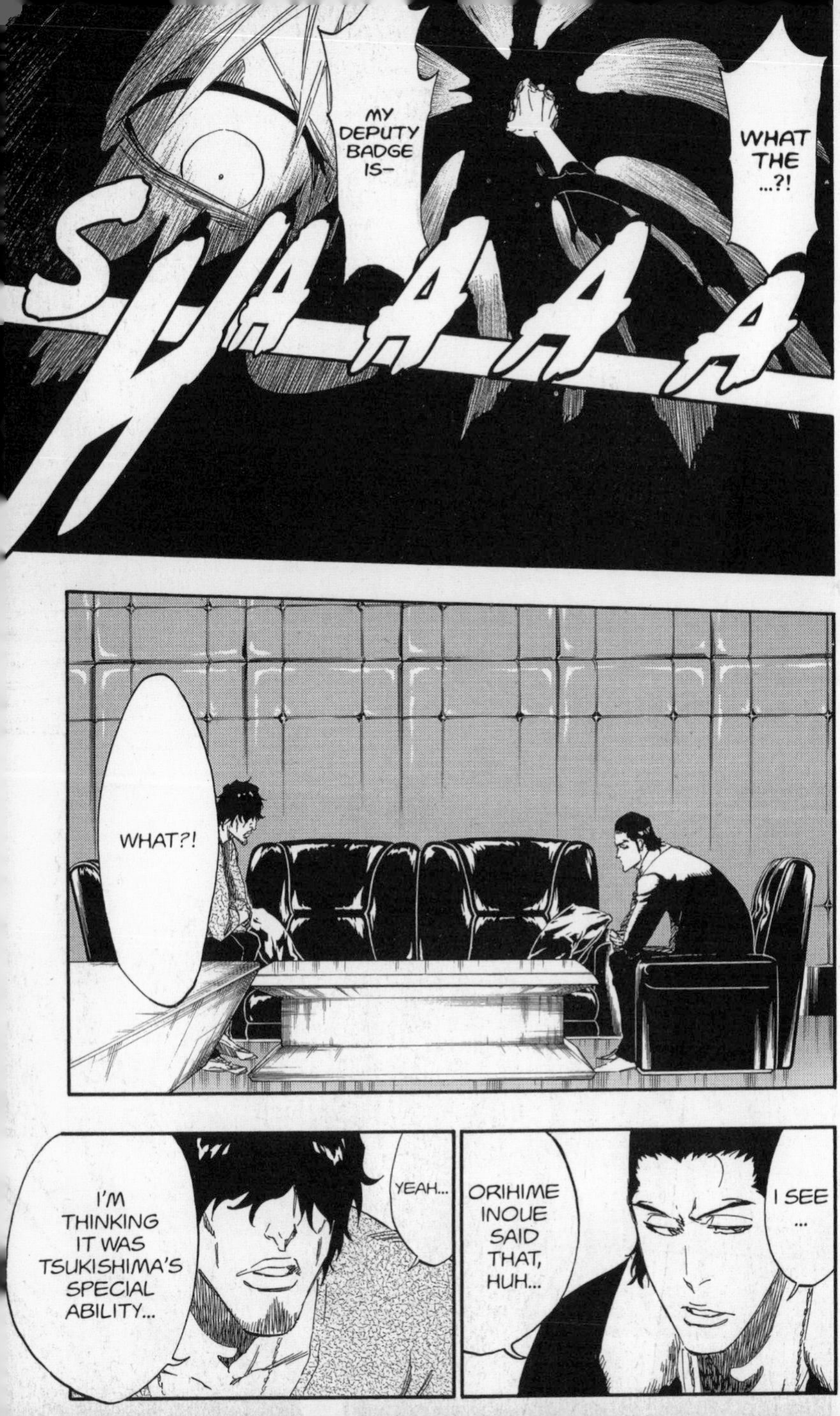
WHAT THE ...?!
MY DEPUTY BADGE IS–
SHAAAA
WHAT?!
I SEE ...
ORIHIME INOUE SAID THAT, HUH...
YEAH...
I'M THINKING IT WAS TSUKISHIMA'S SPECIAL ABILITY...

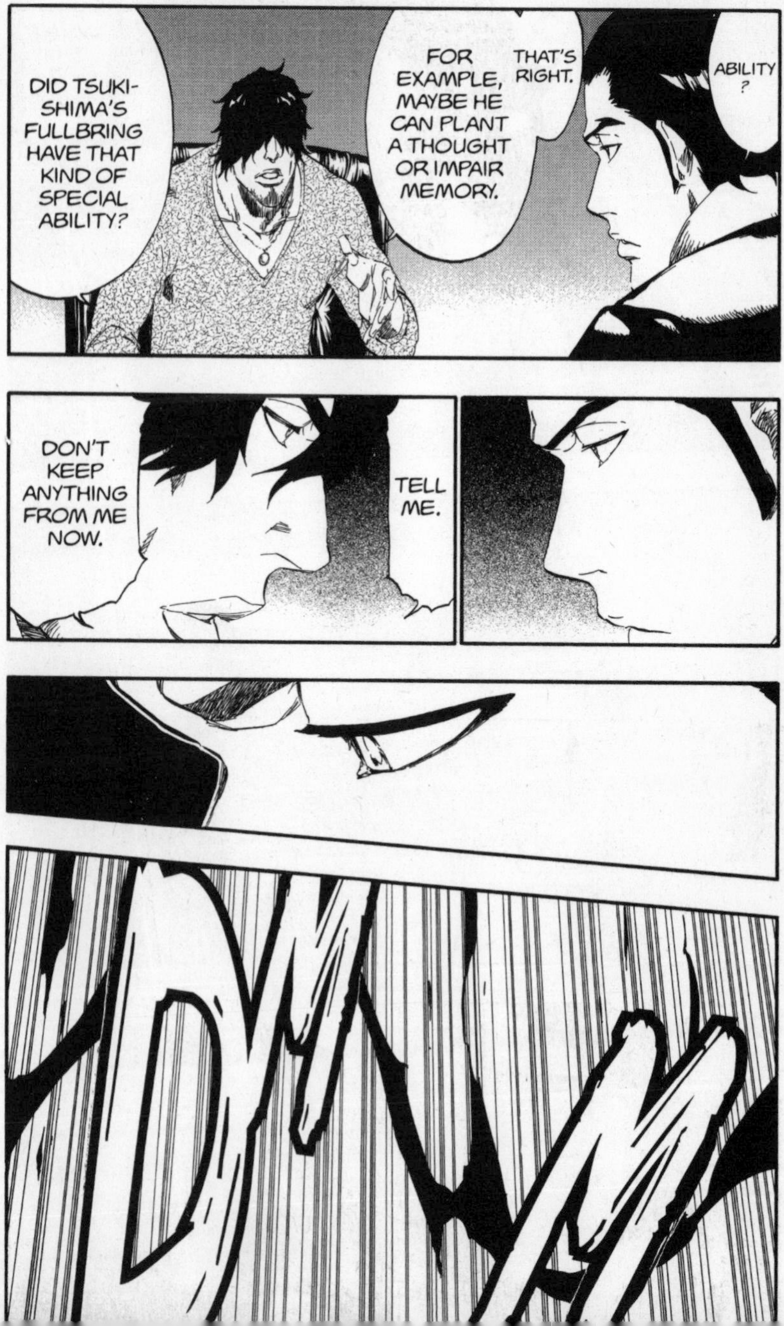
ABILITY?
THAT'S RIGHT.
FOR EXAMPLE, MAYBE HE CAN PLANT A THOUGHT OR IMPAIR MEMORY.
DID TSUKI-SHIMA'S FULLBRING HAVE THAT KIND OF SPECIAL ABILITY?
TELL ME.
DON'T KEEP ANYTHING FROM ME NOW.

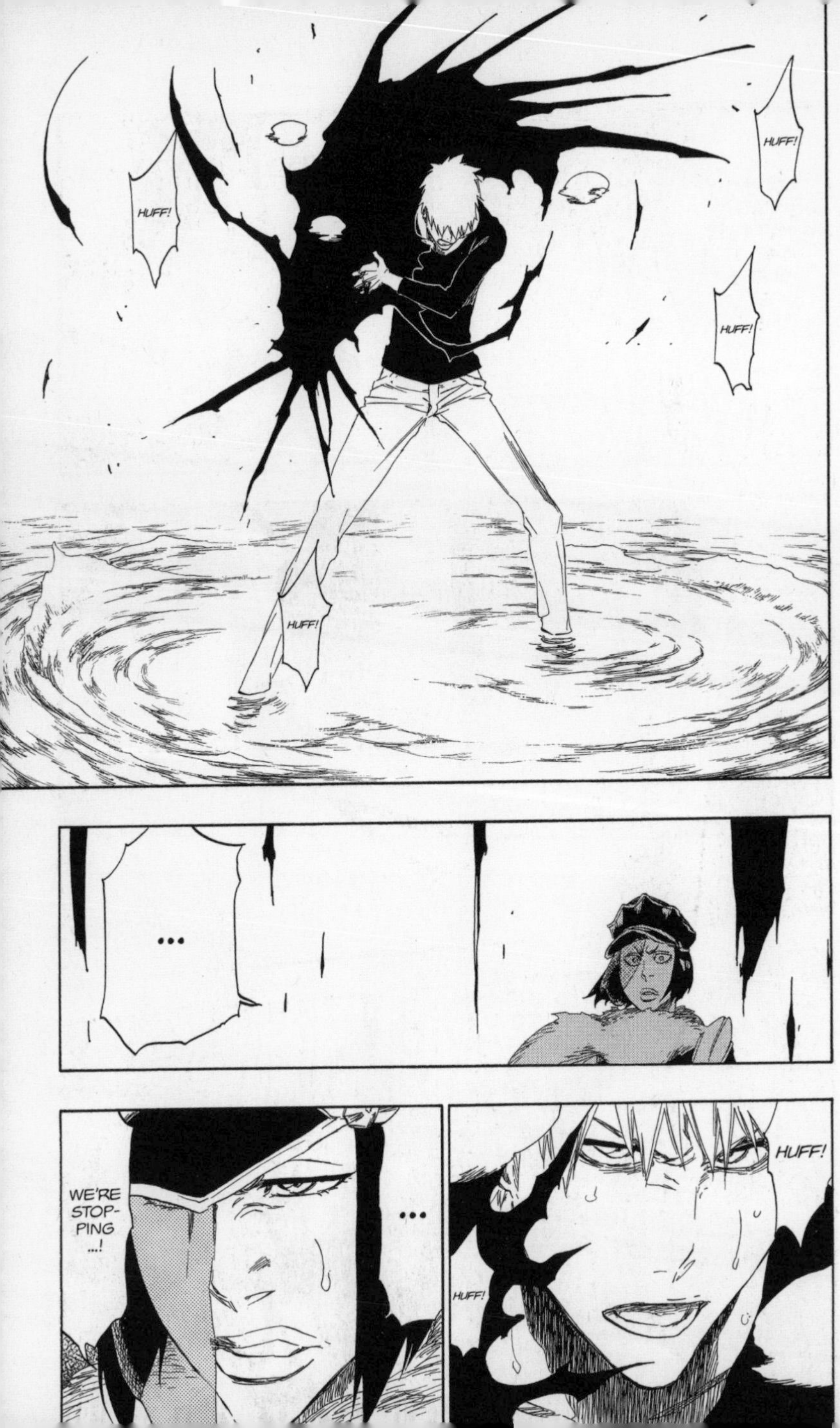
HUFF!
HUFF!
HUFF!
HUFF!
...
HUFF!
HUFF!
...
WE'RE STOP-PING ...!

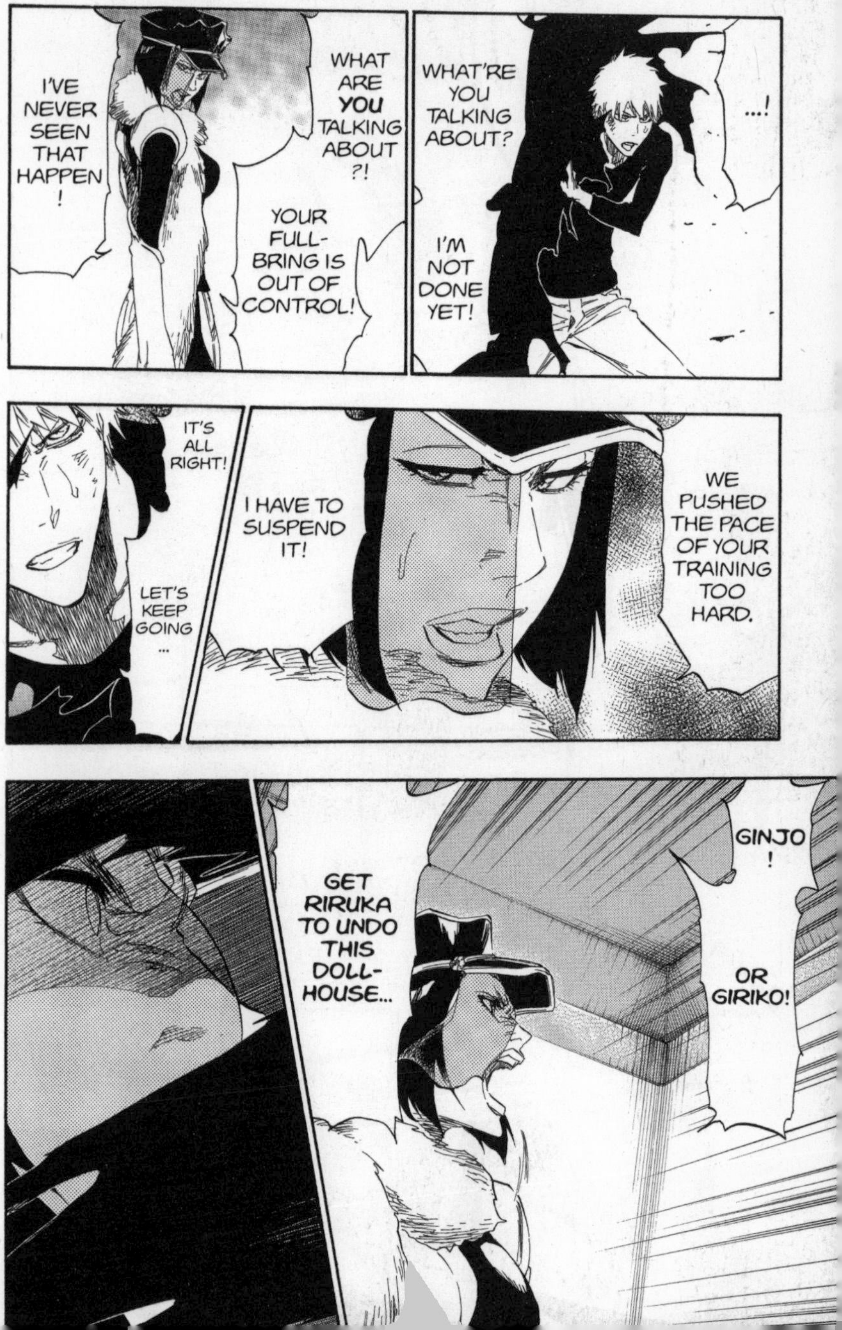
...!
WHAT'RE YOU TALKING ABOUT?
I'M NOT DONE YET!
WHAT ARE **YOU** TALKING ABOUT?!
YOUR FULLBRING IS OUT OF CONTROL!
I'VE NEVER SEEN THAT HAPPEN!
WE PUSHED THE PACE OF YOUR TRAINING TOO HARD.
I HAVE TO SUSPEND IT!
IT'S ALL RIGHT!
LET'S KEEP GOING...
GINJO!
OR GIRIKO!
GET RIRUKA TO UNDO THIS DOLLHOUSE...

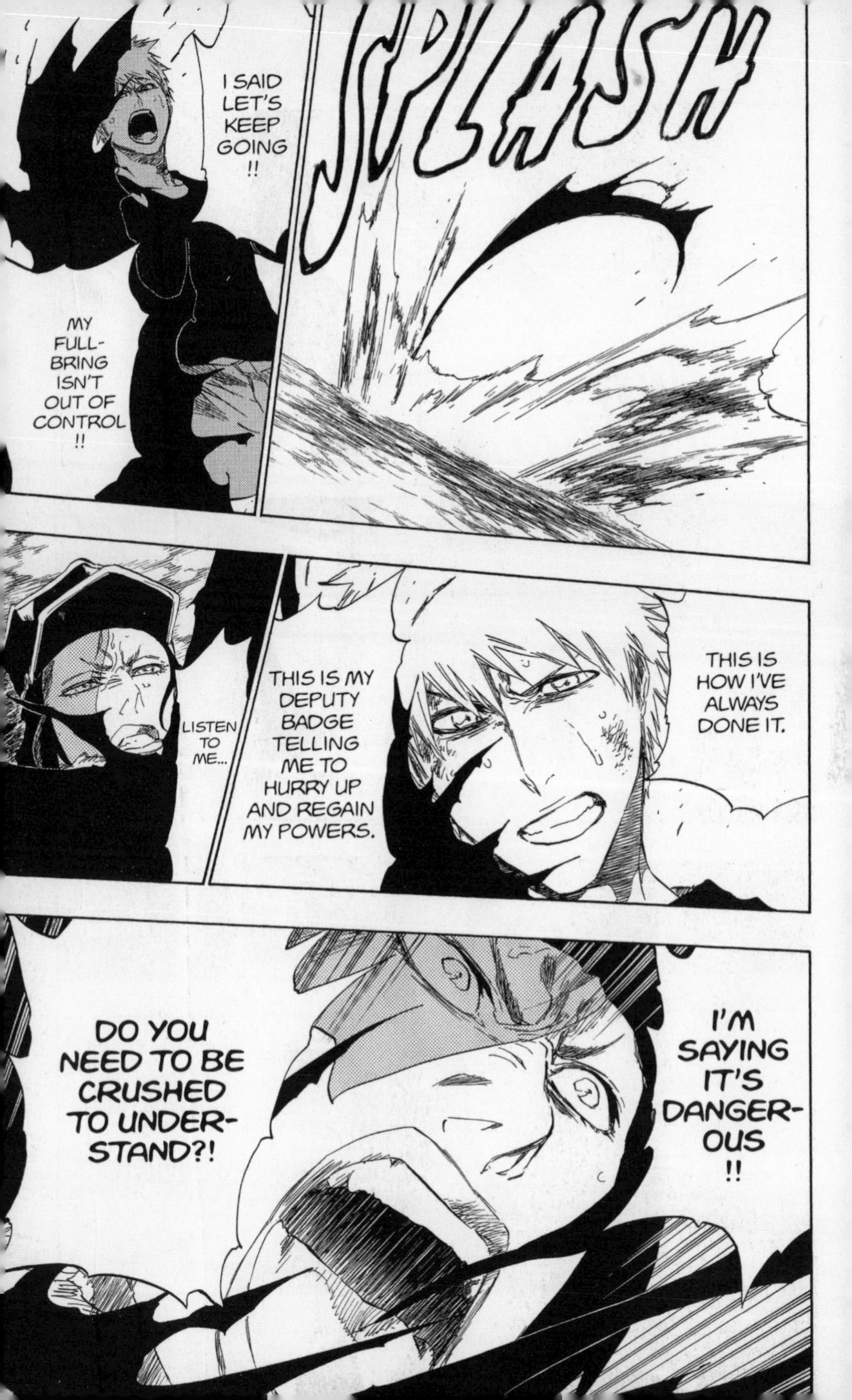
SPLASH
I SAID LET'S KEEP GOING!!
MY FULL-BRING ISN'T OUT OF CONTROL!!
THIS IS HOW I'VE ALWAYS DONE IT.
THIS IS MY DEPUTY BADGE TELLING ME TO HURRY UP AND REGAIN MY POWERS.
LISTEN TO ME...
I'M SAYING IT'S DANGER-OUS!!
DO YOU NEED TO BE CRUSHED TO UNDER-STAND?!

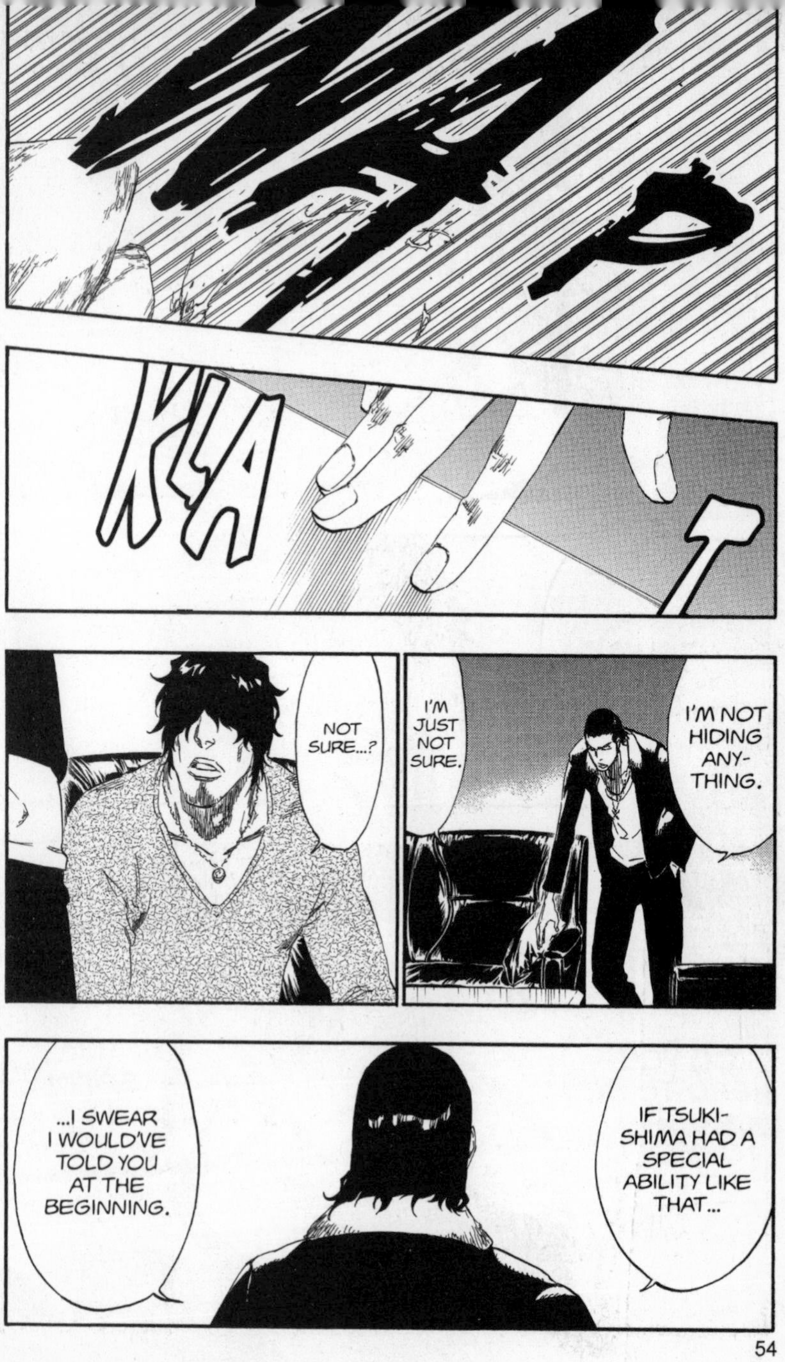
WHAP
KLAT
I'M NOT HIDING ANY-THING.
I'M JUST NOT SURE.
NOT SURE...?
IF TSUKI-SHIMA HAD A SPECIAL ABILITY LIKE THAT...
...I SWEAR I WOULD'VE TOLD YOU AT THE BEGINNING.

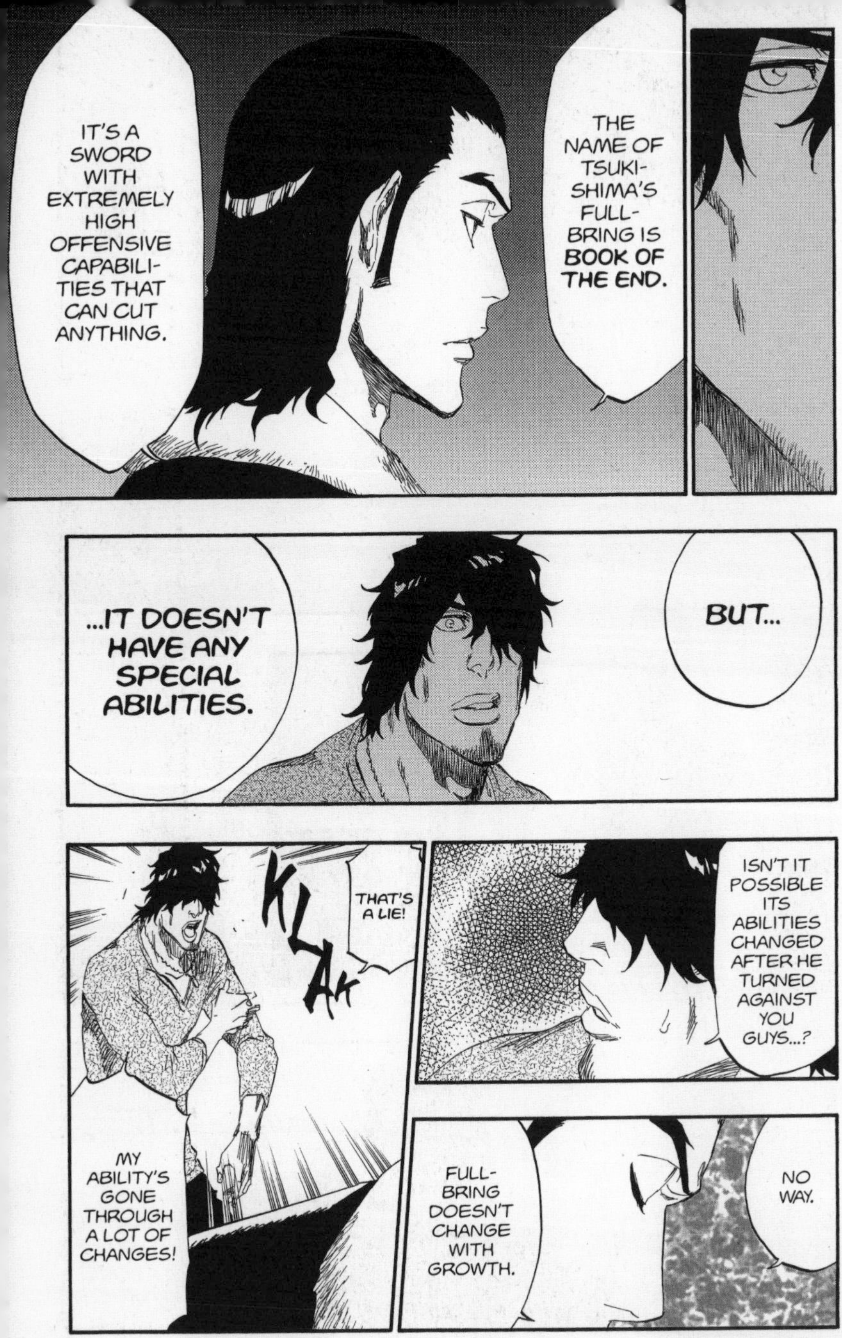
THE NAME OF TSUKI-SHIMA'S FULL-BRING IS BOOK OF THE END.
IT'S A SWORD WITH EXTREMELY HIGH OFFENSIVE CAPABILI-TIES THAT CAN CUT ANYTHING.
BUT...
...IT DOESN'T HAVE ANY SPECIAL ABILITIES.
ISN'T IT POSSIBLE ITS ABILITIES CHANGED AFTER HE TURNED AGAINST YOU GUYS...?
NO WAY.
FULL-BRING DOESN'T CHANGE WITH GROWTH.
THAT'S A LIE!
KLAK
MY ABILITY'S GONE THROUGH A LOT OF CHANGES!

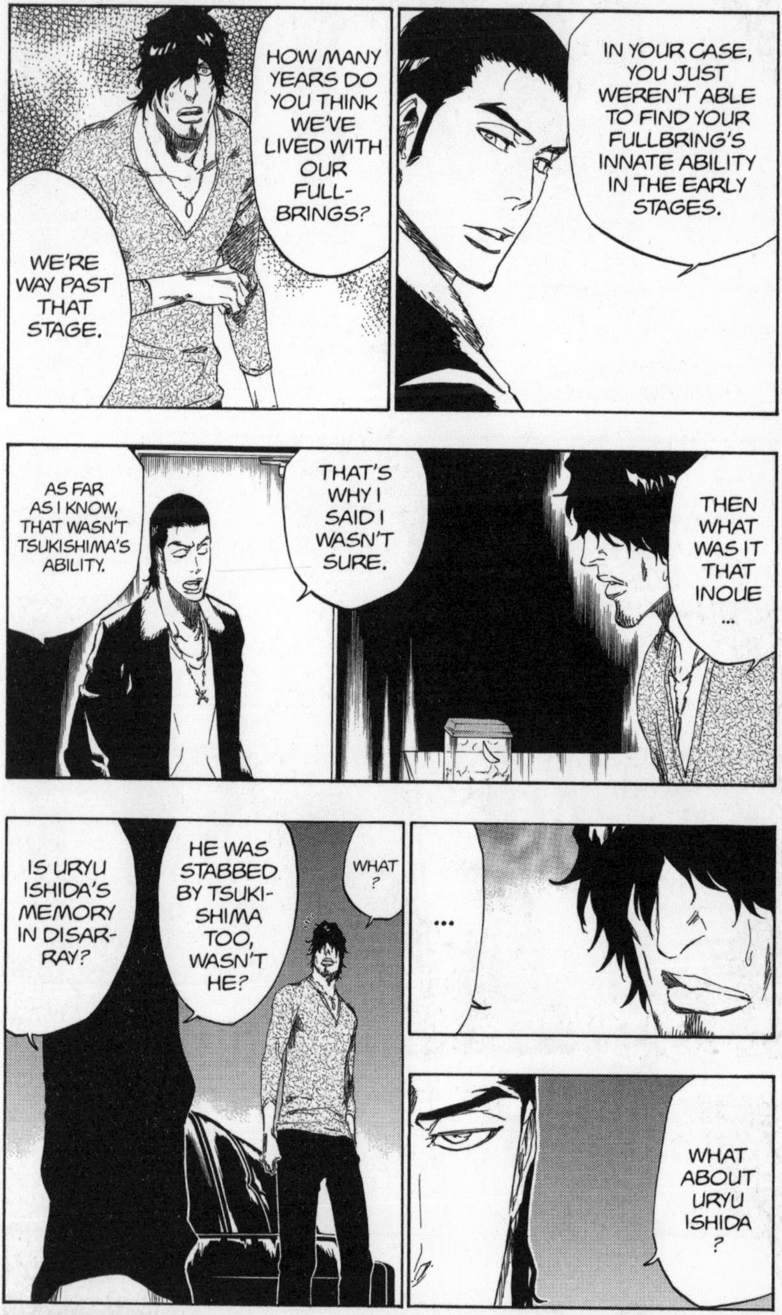
IN YOUR CASE, YOU JUST WEREN'T ABLE TO FIND YOUR FULLBRING'S INNATE ABILITY IN THE EARLY STAGES.
HOW MANY YEARS DO YOU THINK WE'VE LIVED WITH OUR FULL-BRINGS?
WE'RE WAY PAST THAT STAGE.
THEN WHAT WAS IT THAT INOUE ...
THAT'S WHY I SAID I WASN'T SURE.
AS FAR AS I KNOW, THAT WASN'T TSUKISHIMA'S ABILITY.
...
WHAT ABOUT URYU ISHIDA ?
WHAT ?
HE WAS STABBED BY TSUKI-SHIMA TOO, WASN'T HE?
IS URYU ISHIDA'S MEMORY IN DISAR-RAY?

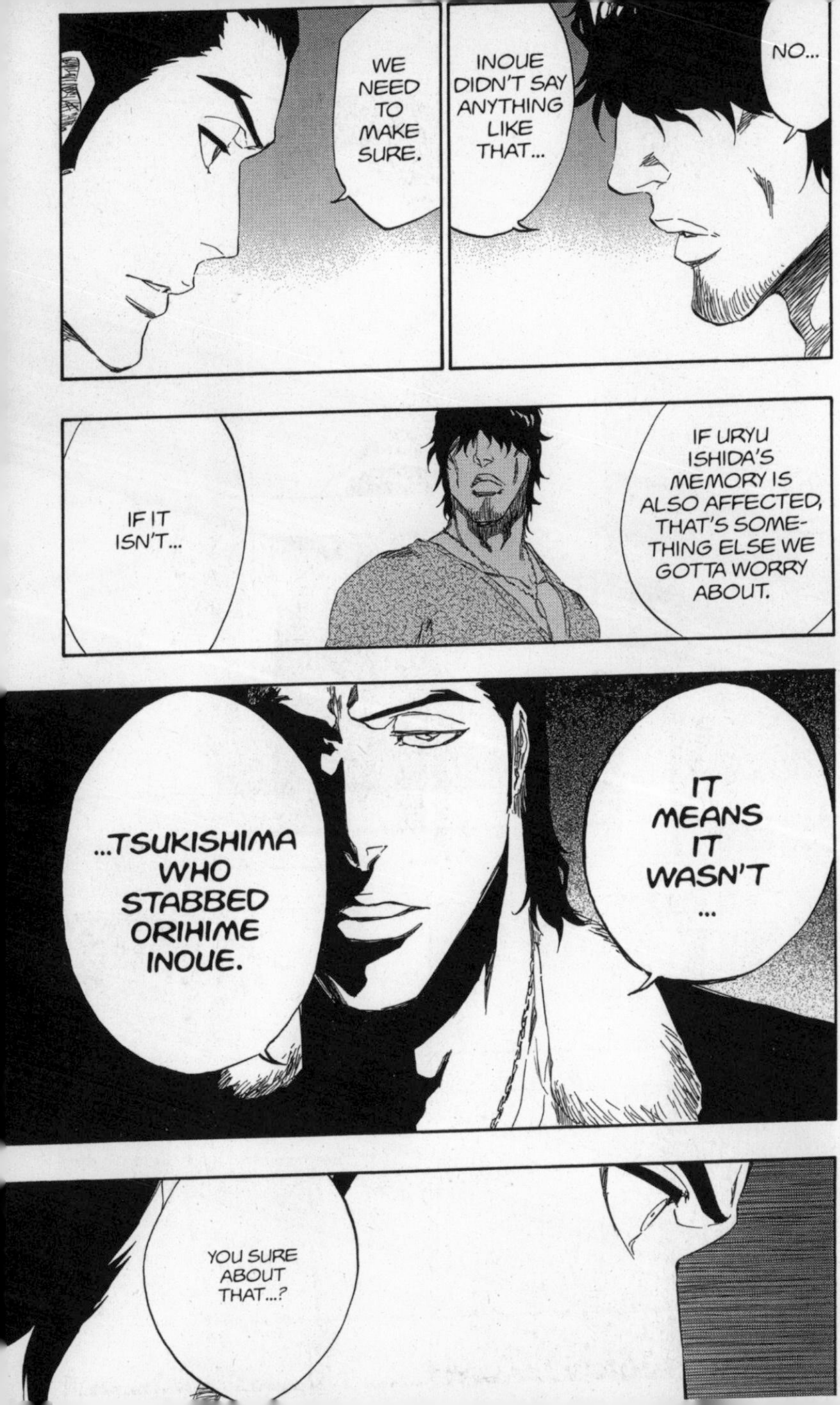
NO...
INOUE DIDN'T SAY ANYTHING LIKE THAT...
WE NEED TO MAKE SURE.
IF URYU ISHIDA'S MEMORY IS ALSO AFFECTED, THAT'S SOME-THING ELSE WE GOTTA WORRY ABOUT.
IF IT ISN'T...
IT MEANS IT WASN'T ...
...TSUKISHIMA WHO STABBED ORIHIME INOUE.
YOU SURE ABOUT THAT...?

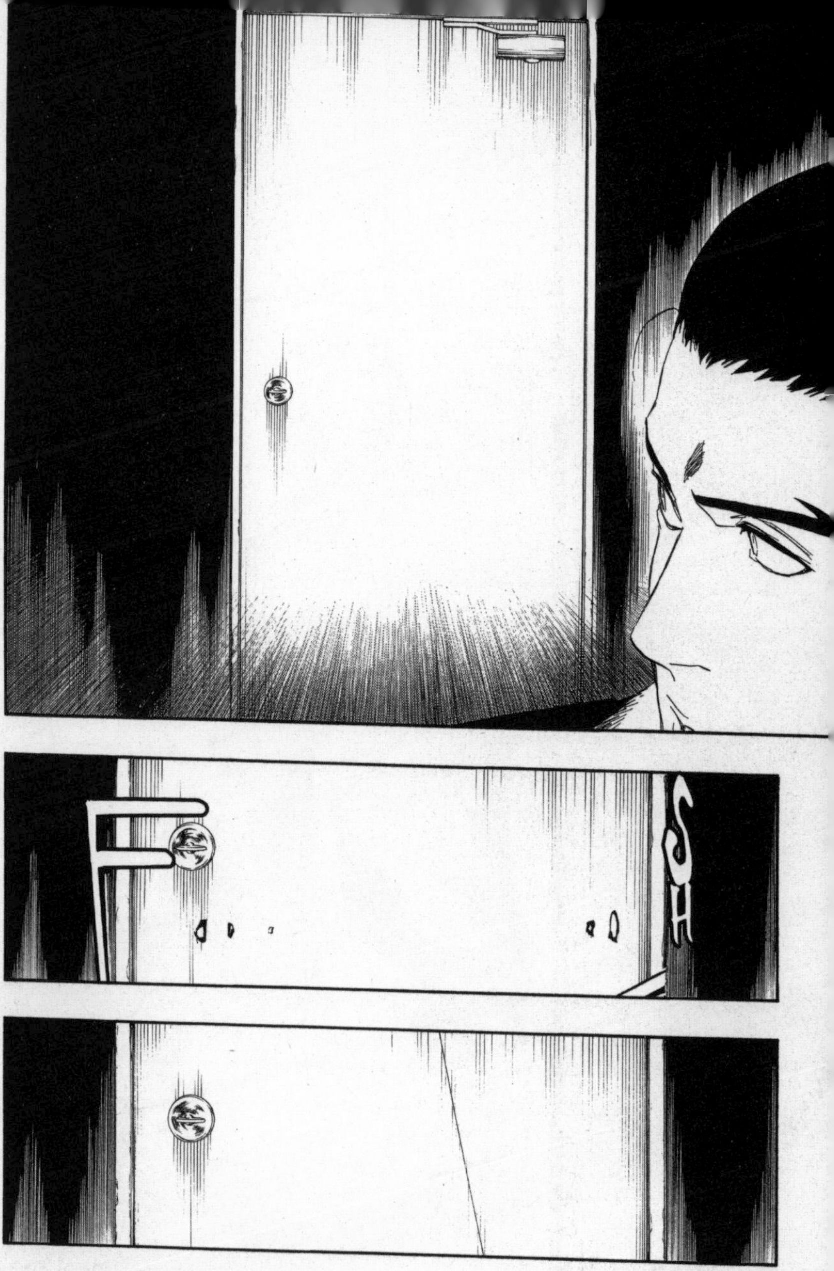

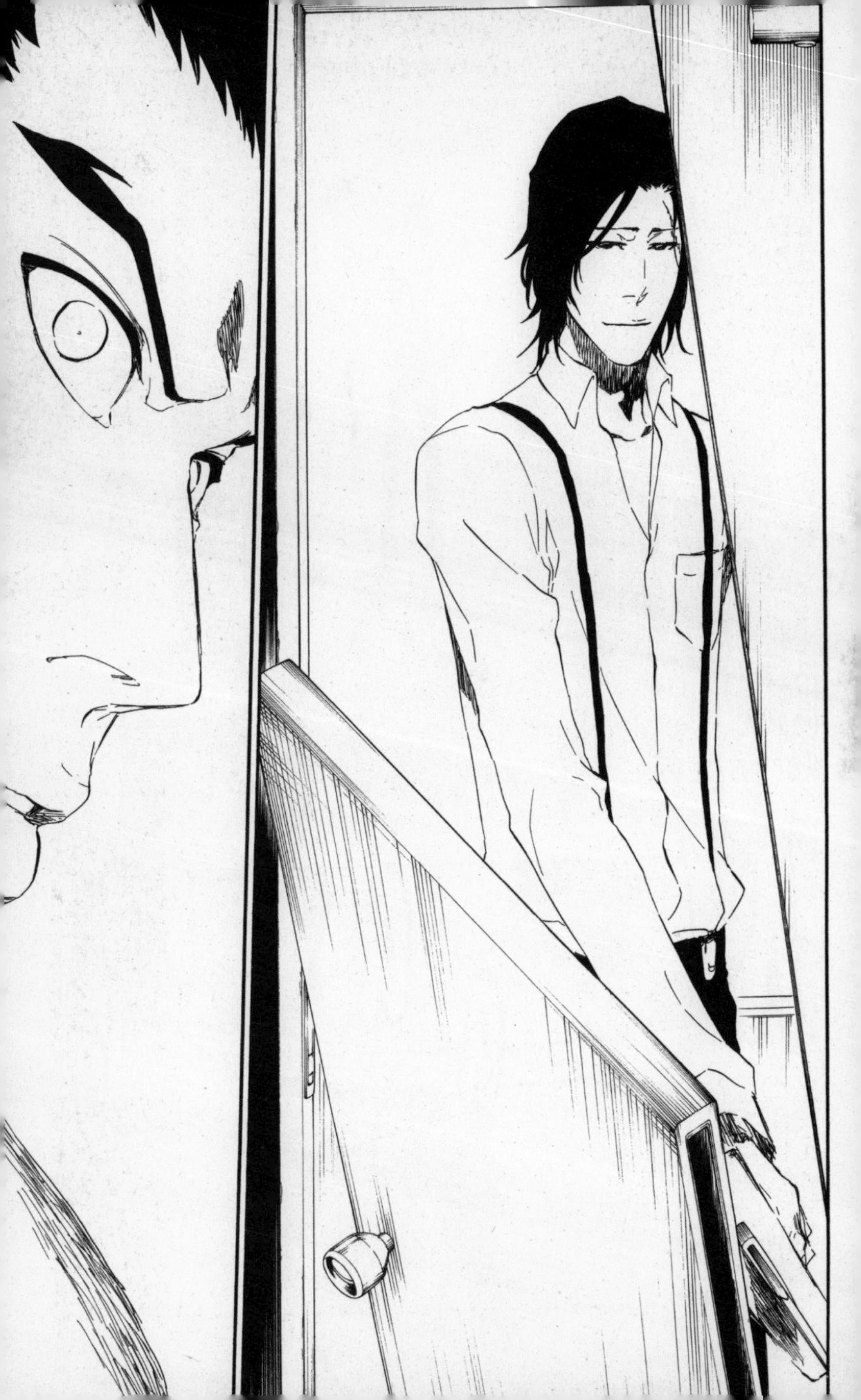

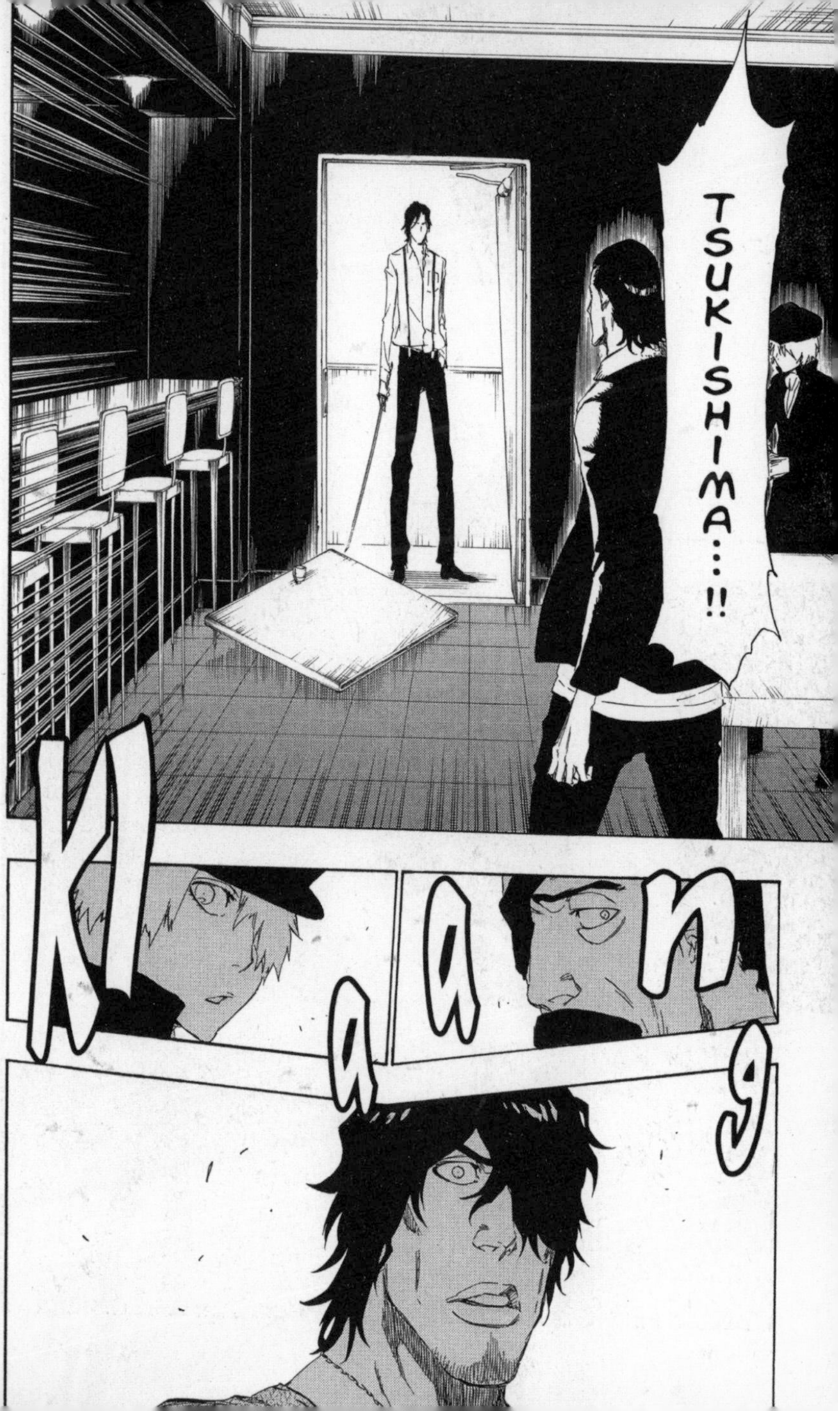
TSUKISHIMA...!!
Klaang

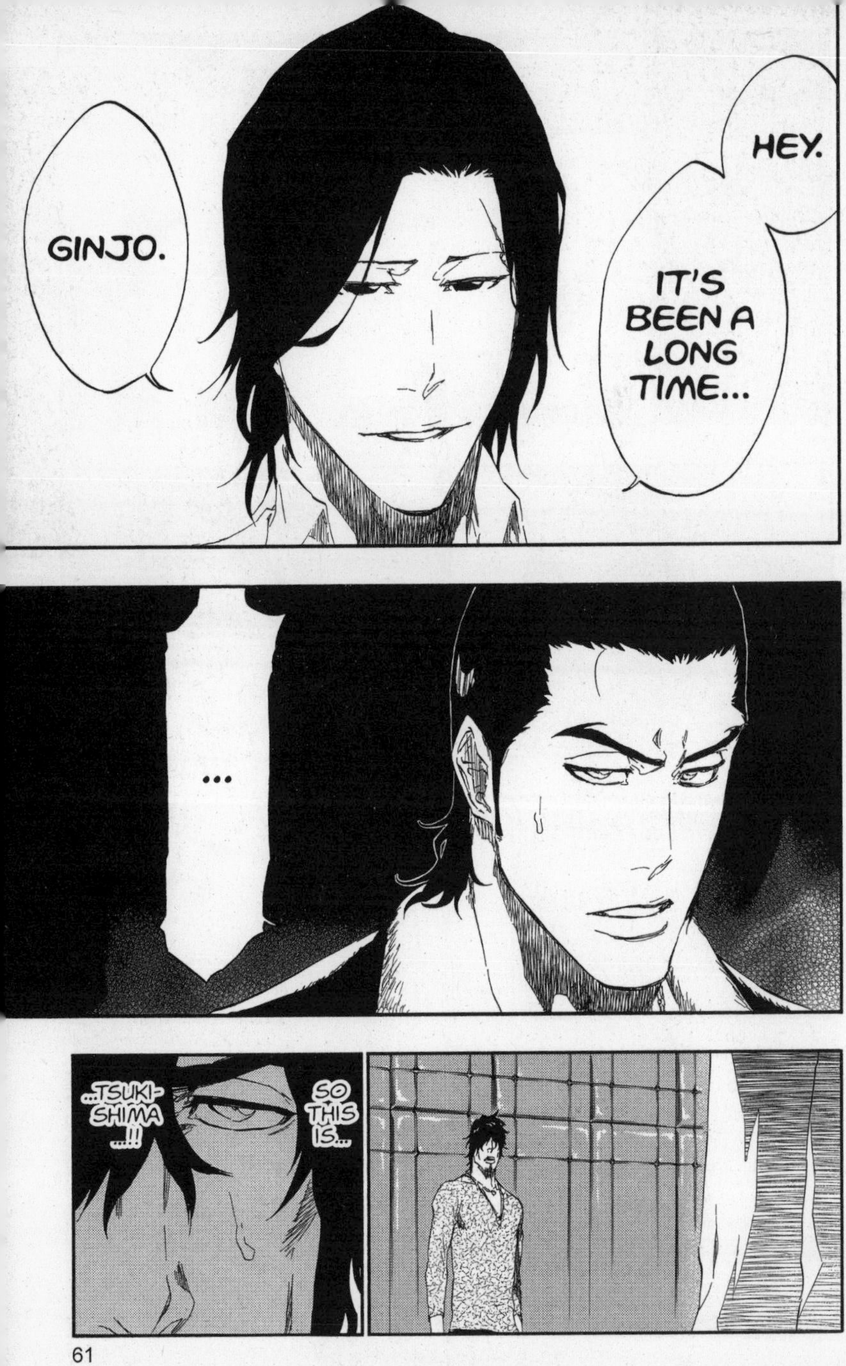
HEY.
IT'S BEEN A LONG TIME...
GINJO.
...
SO THIS IS...
...TSUKISHIMA ...!!

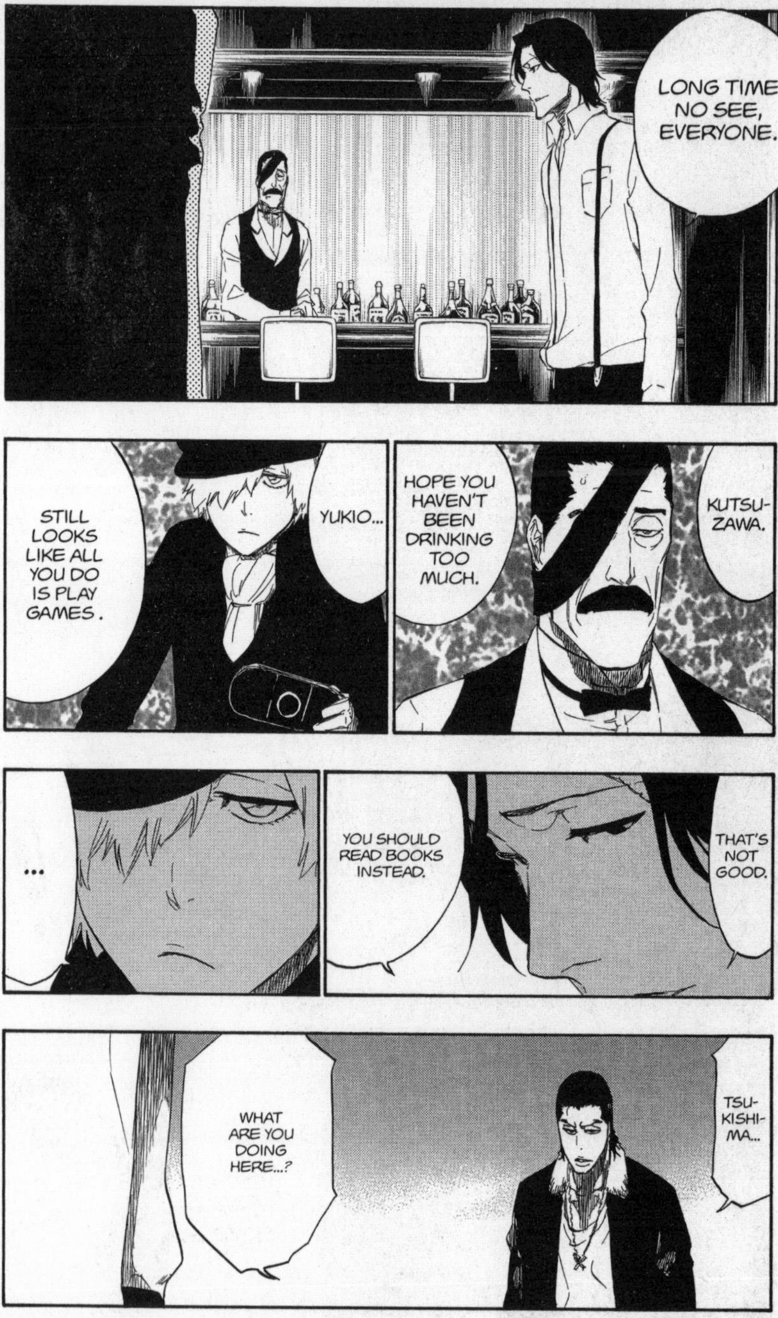
LONG TIME NO SEE, EVERYONE.
KUTSU-ZAWA.
HOPE YOU HAVEN'T BEEN DRINKING TOO MUCH.
YUKIO...
STILL LOOKS LIKE ALL YOU DO IS PLAY GAMES.
THAT'S NOT GOOD.
YOU SHOULD READ BOOKS INSTEAD.
...
TSU-KISHI-MA...
WHAT ARE YOU DOING HERE...?

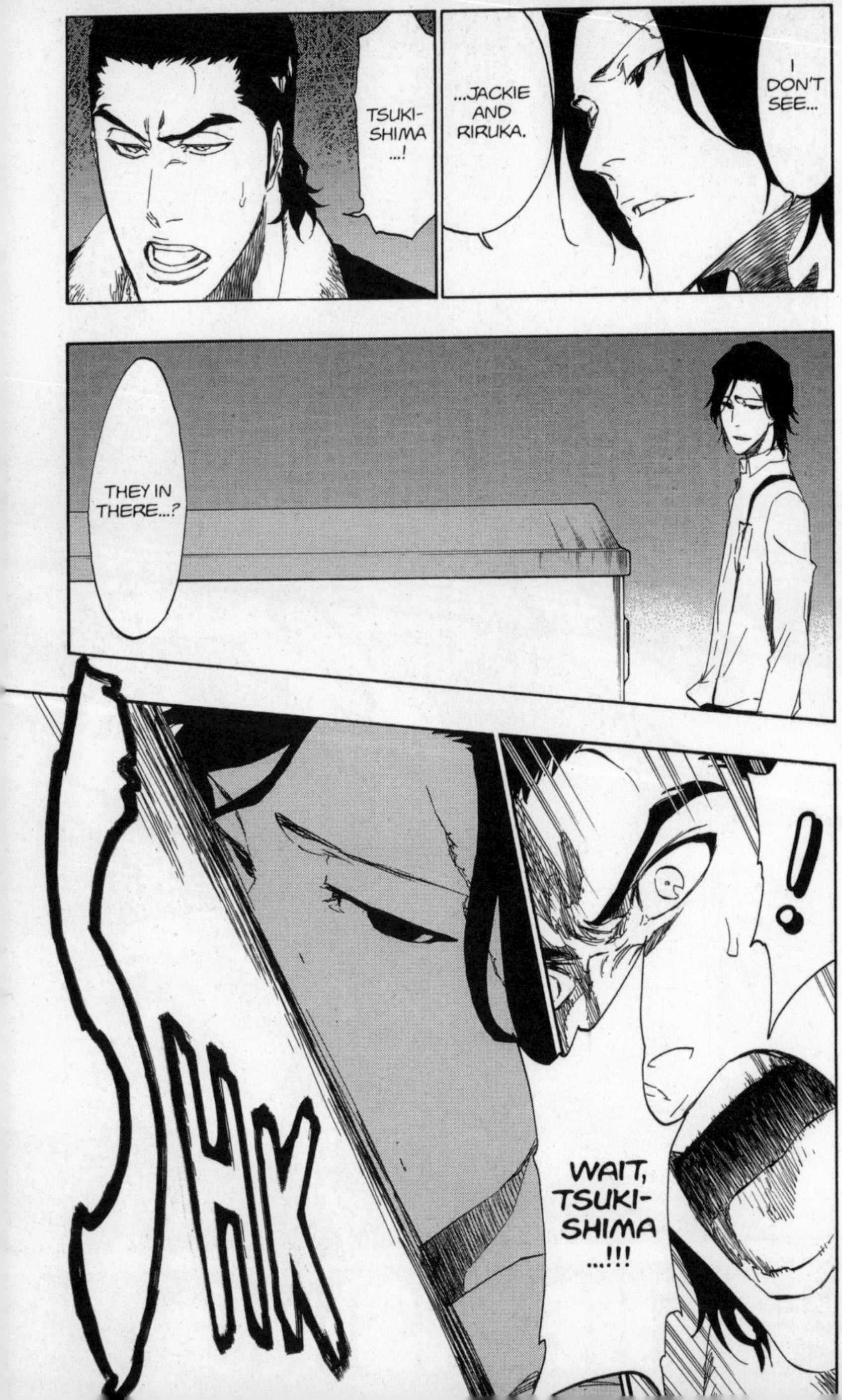
I DON'T SEE...
...JACKIE AND RIRUKA.
TSUKI-SHIMA ...!
THEY IN THERE...?
!
WAIT, TSUKI-SHIMA ...!!!
SHK

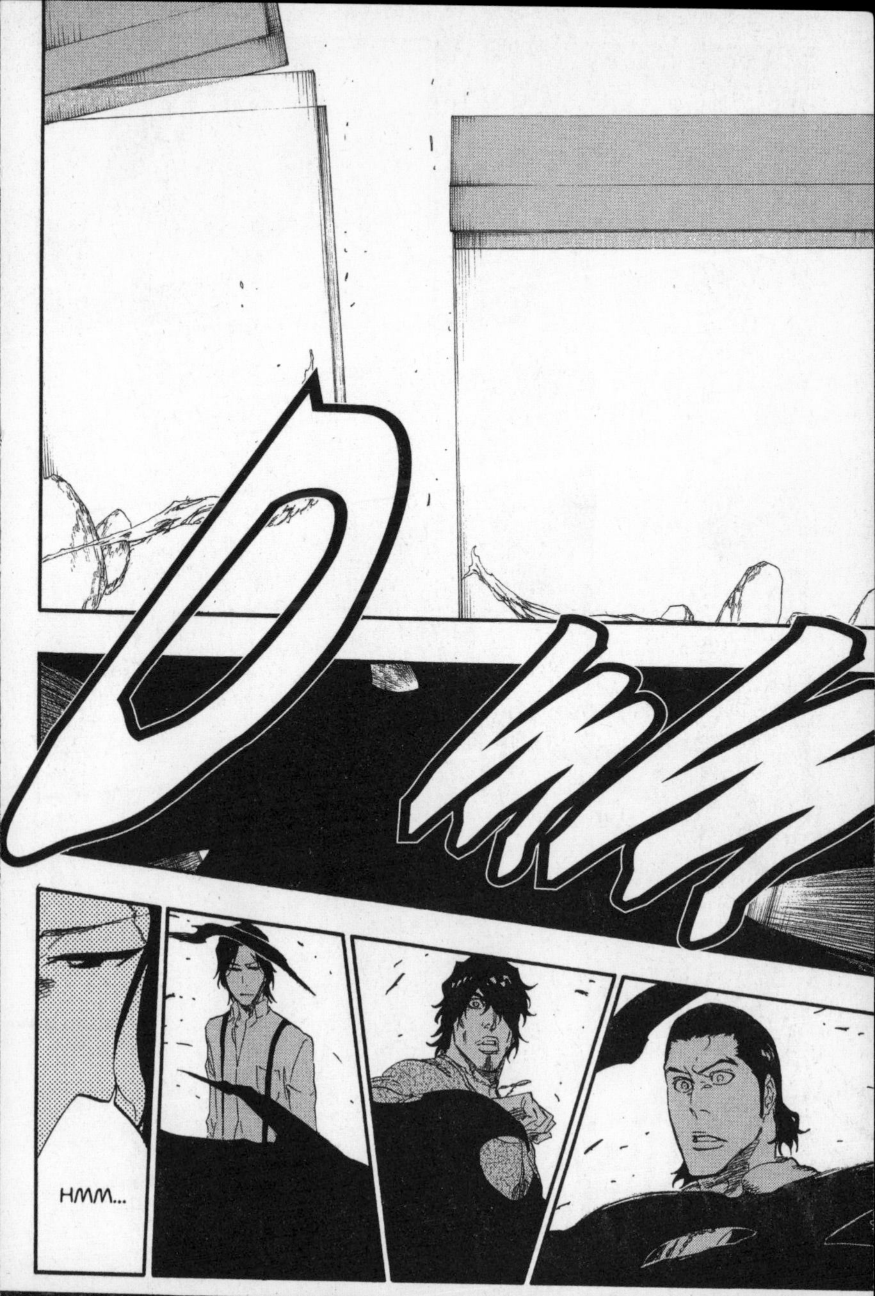
HMM...

THE RISING

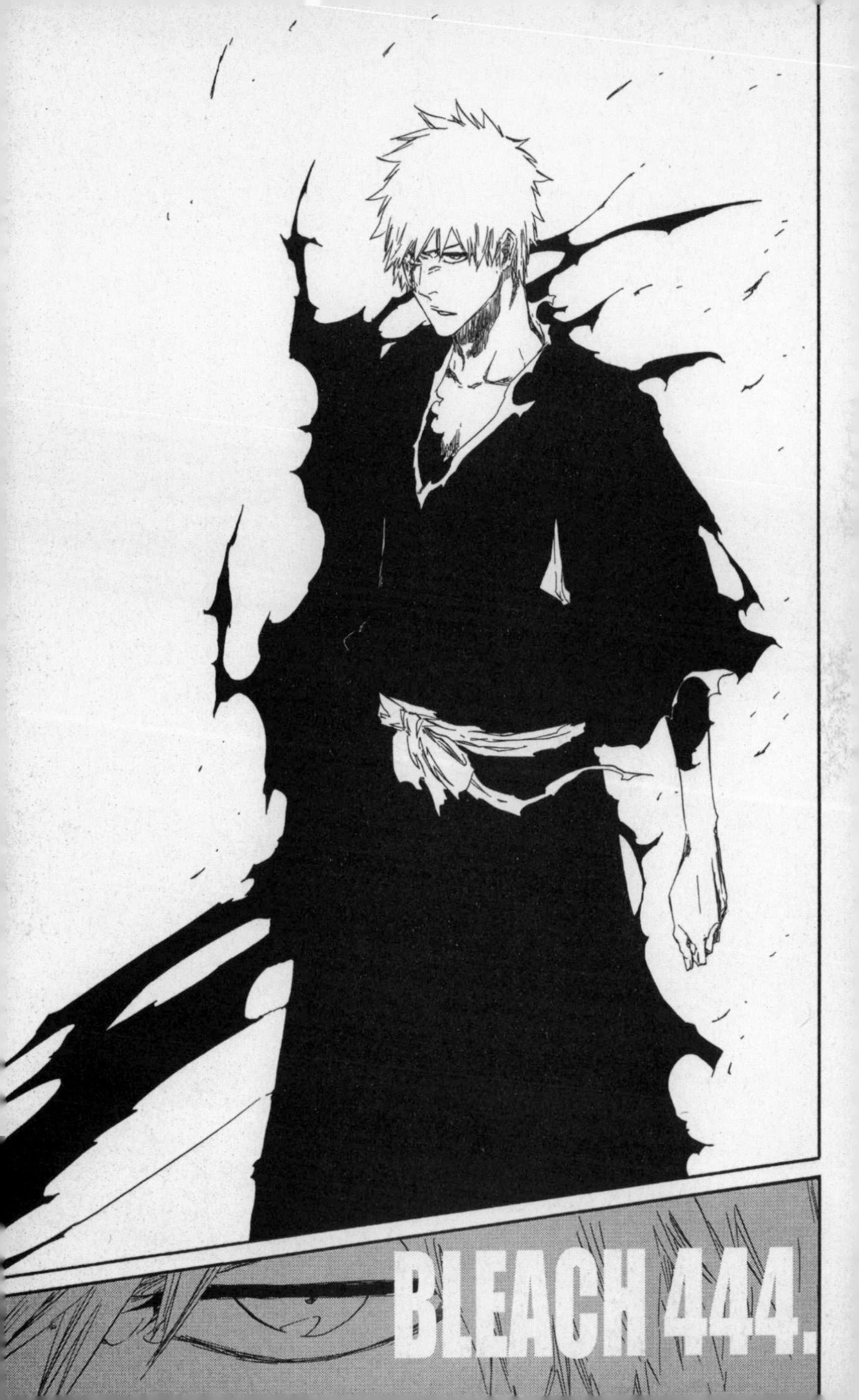
BLEACH 444.

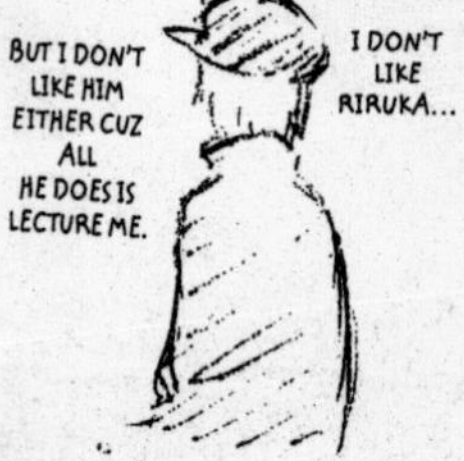
I DON'T LIKE RIRUKA...
BUT I DON'T LIKE HIM EITHER CUZ ALL HE DOES IS LECTURE ME.

445. THE DARK BEAT

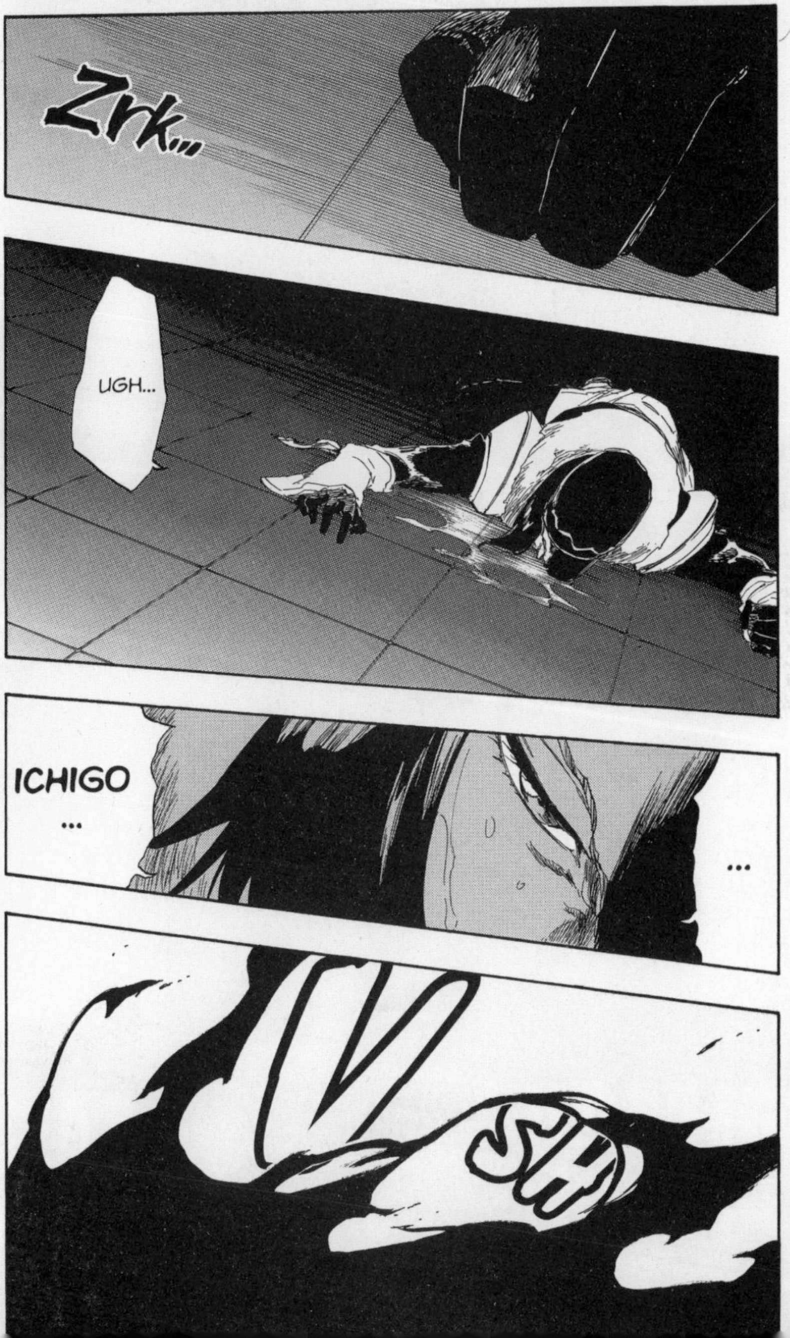
Zrk...
UGH...
...
ICHIGO
...
SH

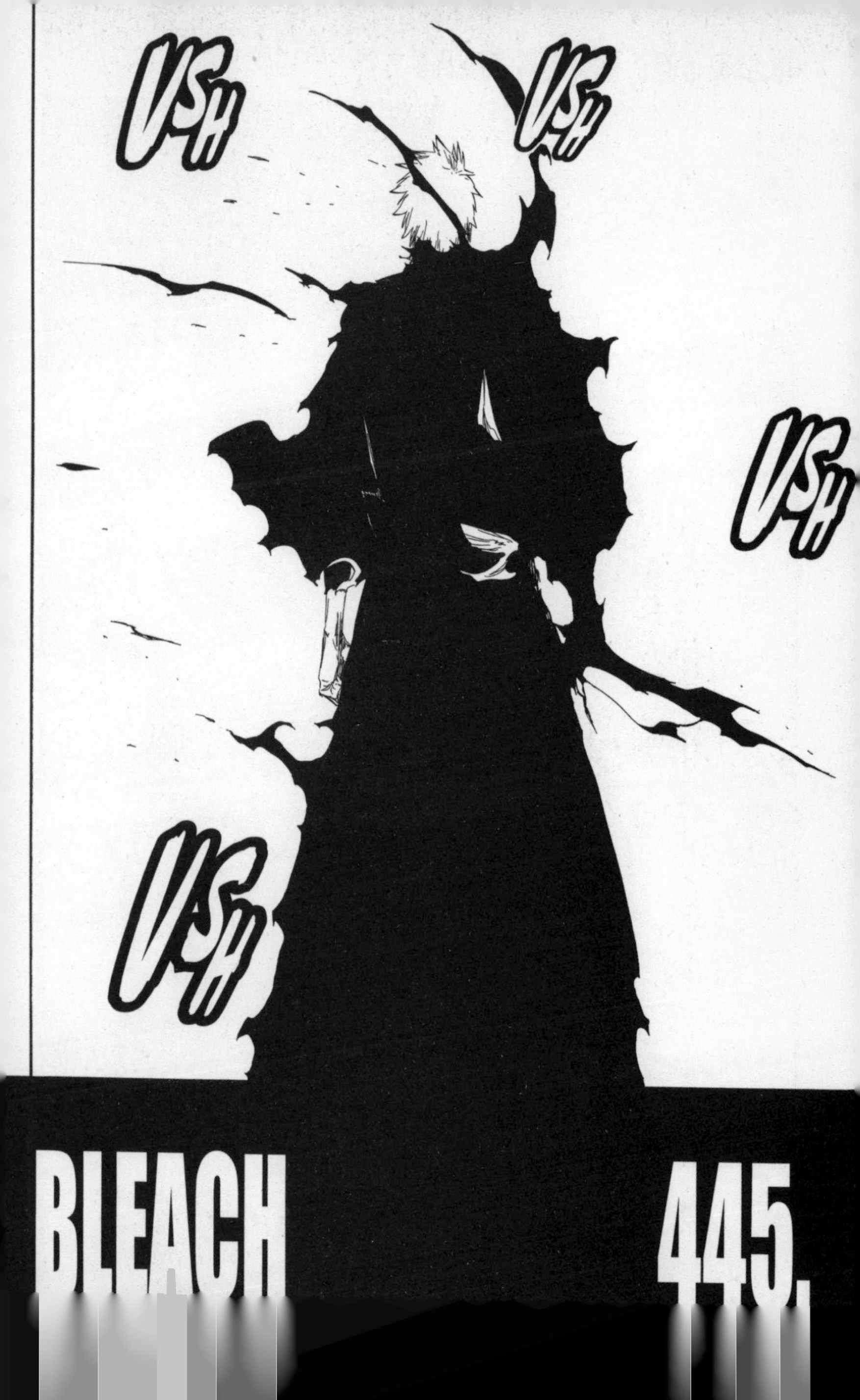
VSH
VSH
VSH
VSH
BLEACH
445.

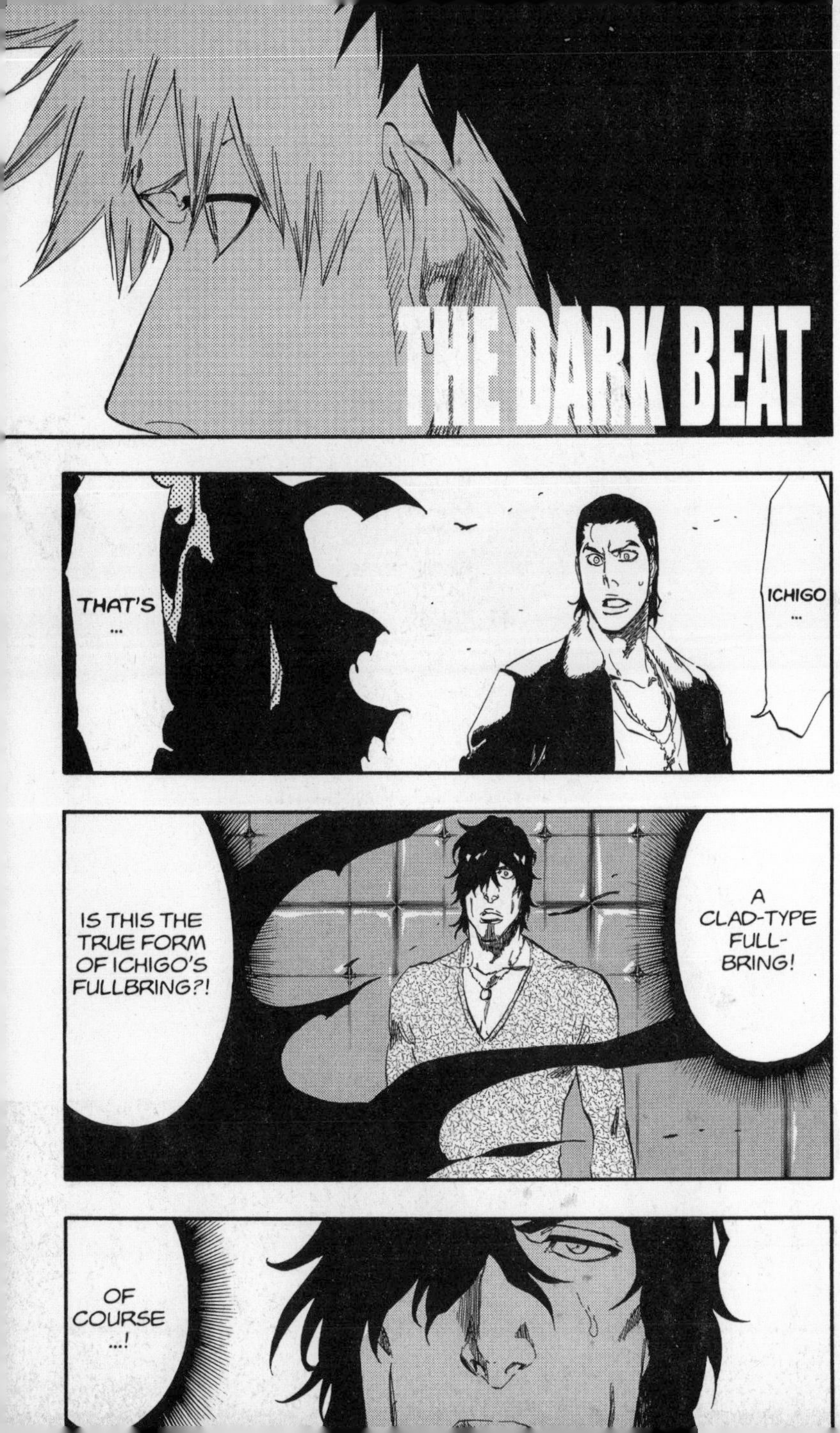
THE DARK BEAT
ICHIGO ...
THAT'S ...
A CLAD-TYPE FULL-BRING!
IS THIS THE TRUE FORM OF ICHIGO'S FULLBRING?!
OF COURSE ...!

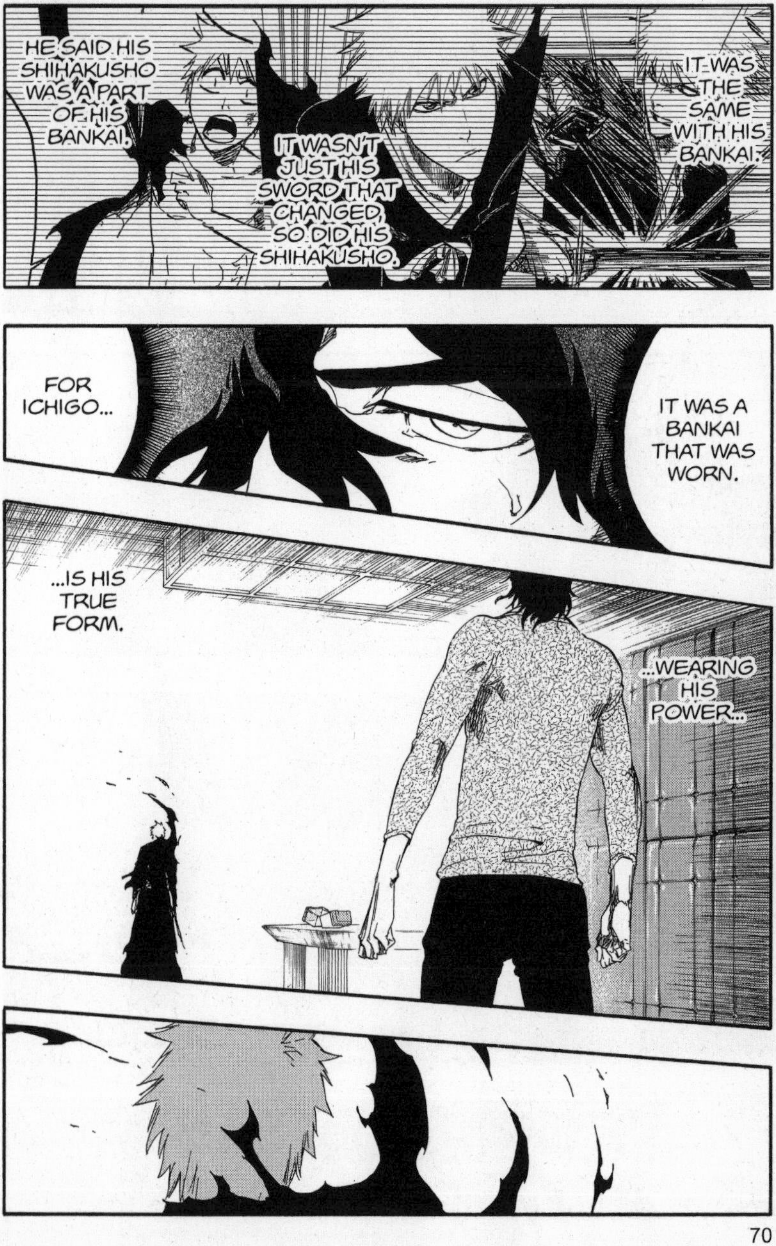
IT WAS THE SAME WITH HIS BANKAI.
IT WASN'T JUST HIS SWORD THAT CHANGED, SO DID HIS SHIHAKUSHO.
HE SAID HIS SHIHAKUSHO WAS A PART OF HIS BANKAI.
IT WAS A BANKAI THAT WAS WORN.
FOR ICHIGO...
...WEARING HIS POWER...
...IS HIS TRUE FORM.

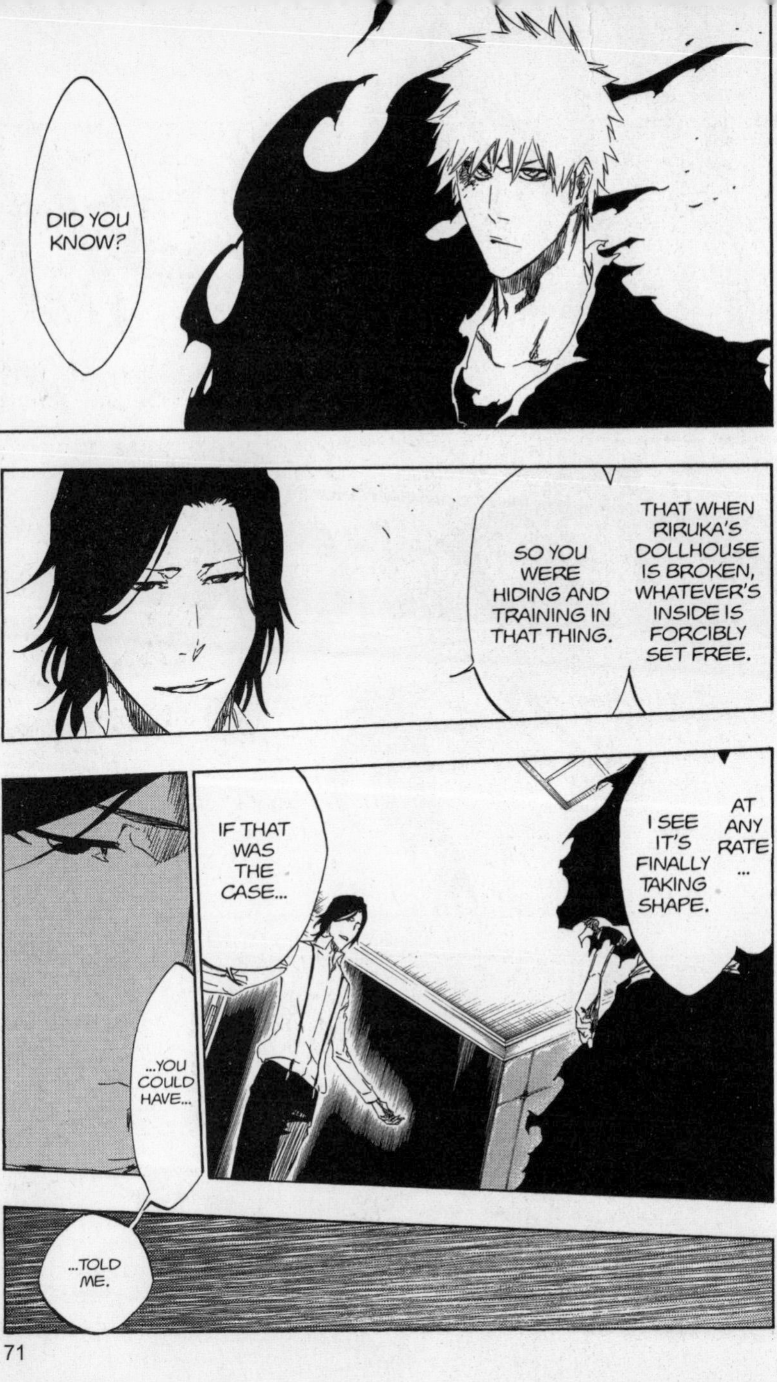
DID YOU KNOW?
THAT WHEN RIRUKA'S DOLLHOUSE IS BROKEN, WHATEVER'S INSIDE IS FORCIBLY SET FREE.
SO YOU WERE HIDING AND TRAINING IN THAT THING.
AT ANY RATE...
I SEE IT'S FINALLY TAKING SHAPE.
IF THAT WAS THE CASE...
...YOU COULD HAVE...
...TOLD ME.

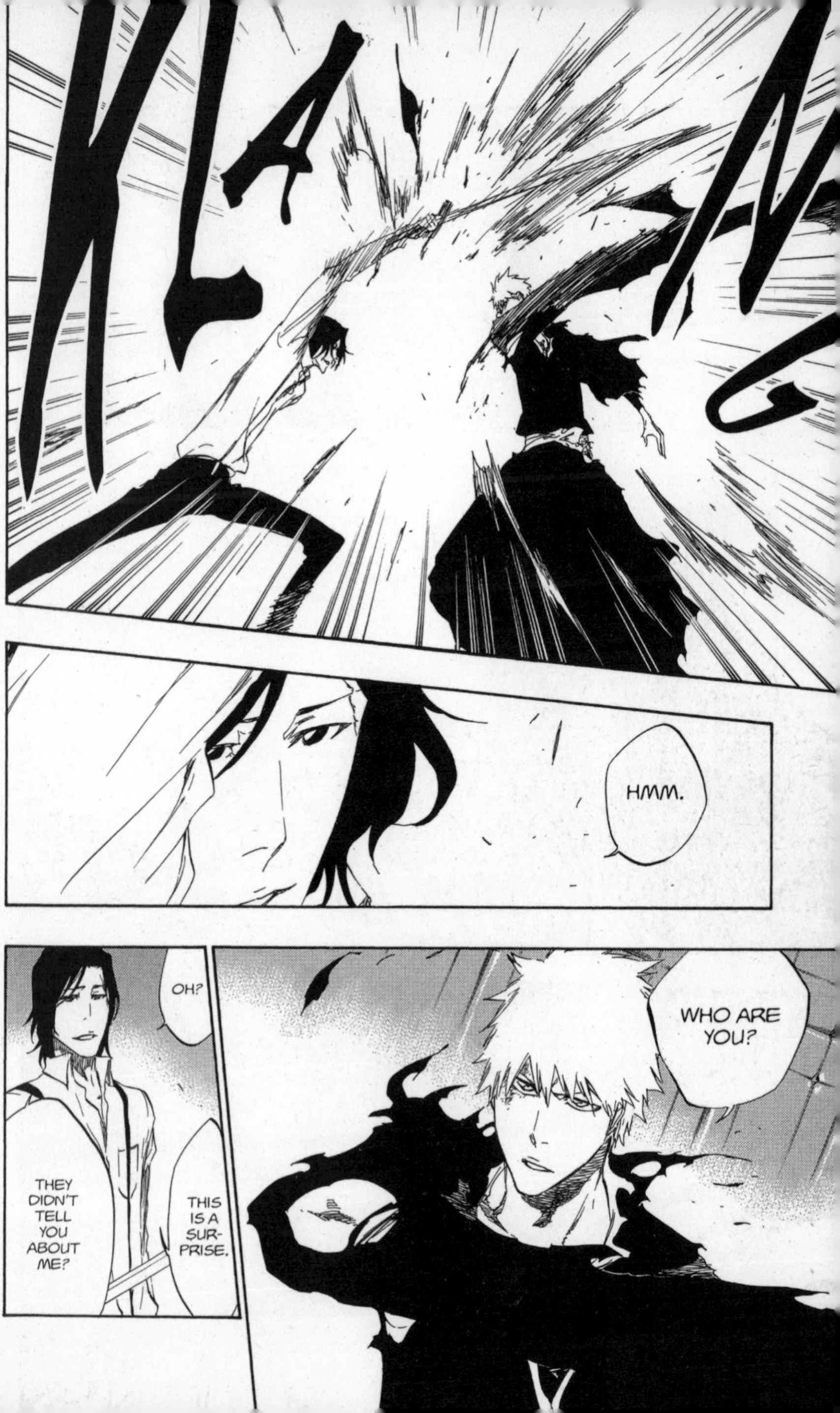
KLANG
HMM.
WHO ARE YOU?
OH?
THIS IS A SUR-PRISE.
THEY DIDN'T TELL YOU ABOUT ME?

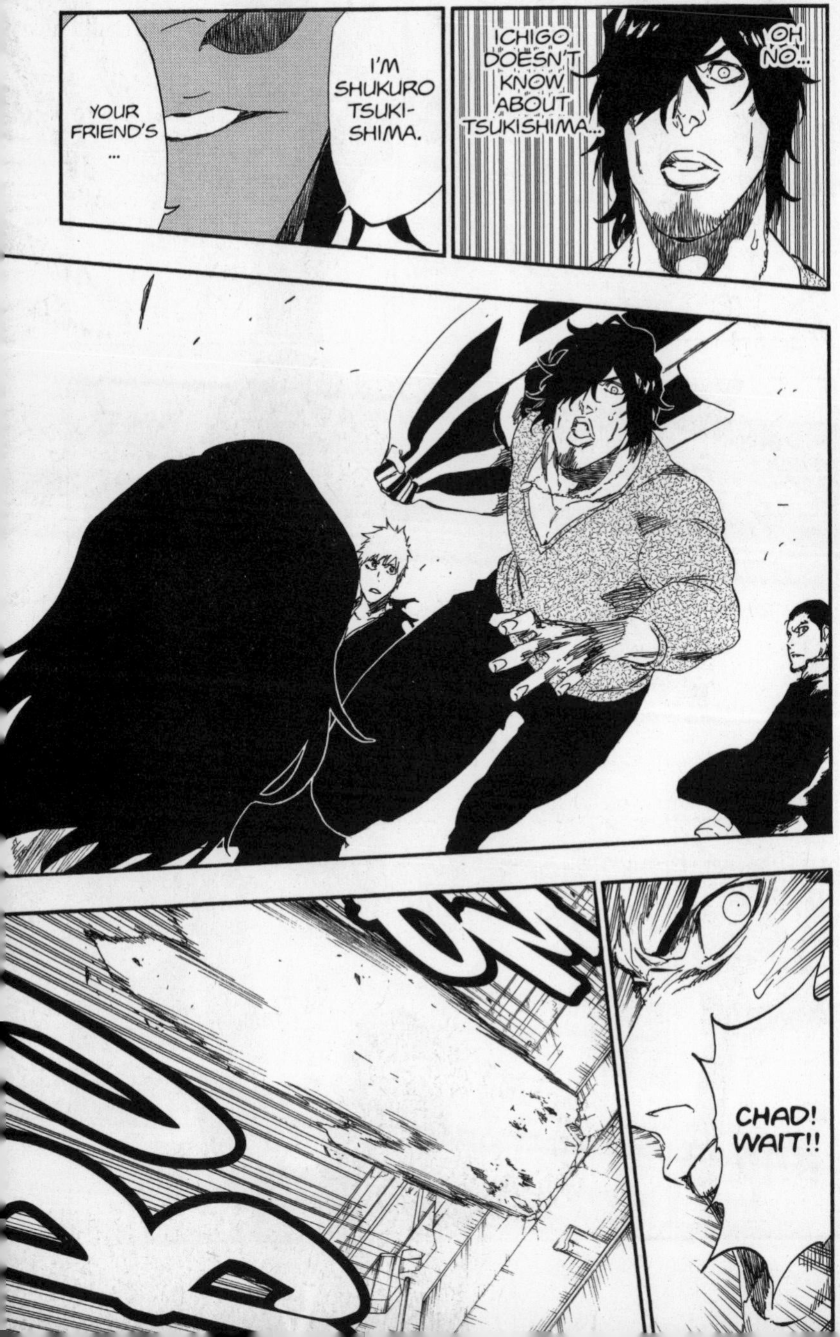
OH NO...
ICHIGO DOESN'T KNOW ABOUT TSUKISHIMA...
I'M SHUKURO TSUKI-SHIMA.
YOUR FRIEND'S ...
CHAD! WAIT!!

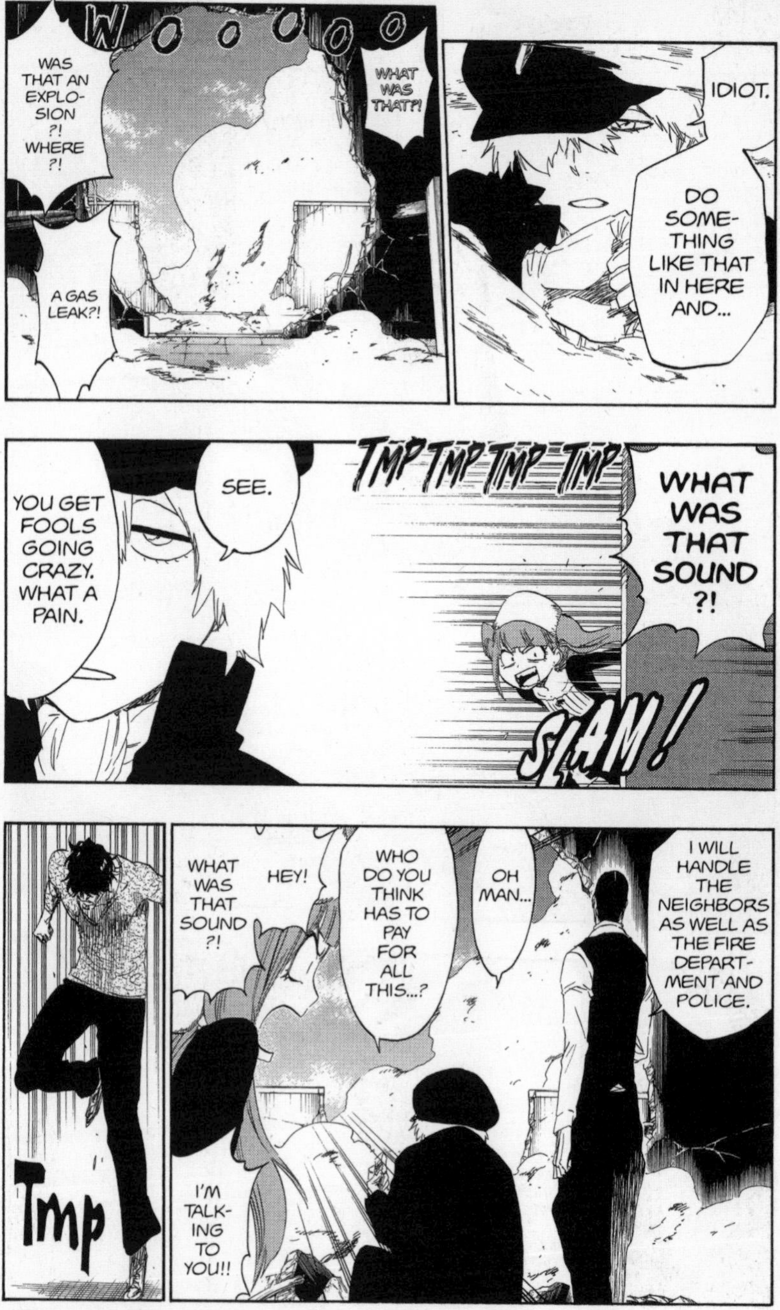
IDIOT.
DO SOMETHING LIKE THAT IN HERE AND...
WOOOOO
WHAT WAS THAT?!
WAS THAT AN EXPLOSION?! WHERE?!
A GAS LEAK?!
WHAT WAS THAT SOUND?!
TMP TMP TMP TMP
SLAM!
SEE.
YOU GET FOOLS GOING CRAZY. WHAT A PAIN.
I WILL HANDLE THE NEIGHBORS AS WELL AS THE FIRE DEPARTMENT AND POLICE.
OH MAN...
WHO DO YOU THINK HAS TO PAY FOR ALL THIS...?
HEY!
WHAT WAS THAT SOUND?!
I'M TALKING TO YOU!!
Tmp

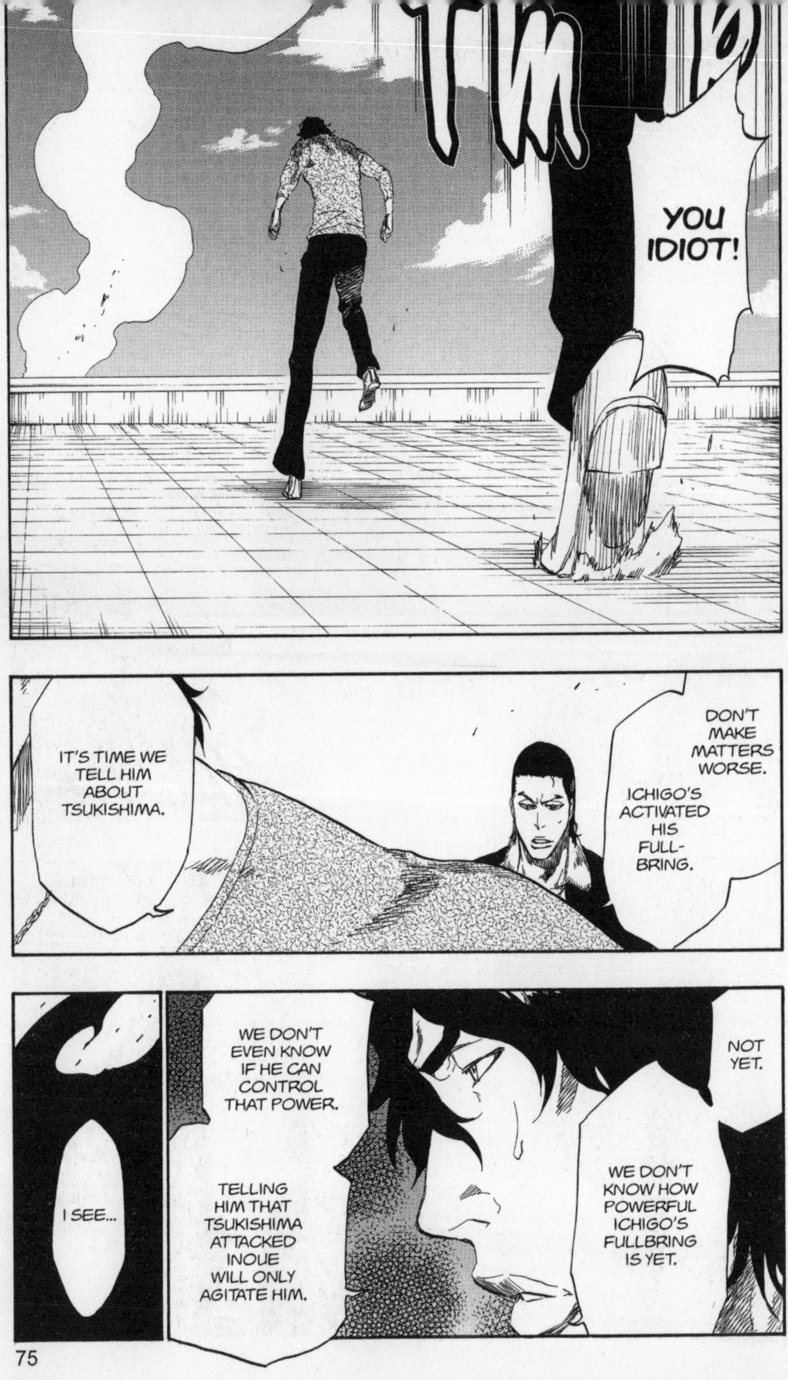
YOU IDIOT!
DON'T MAKE MATTERS WORSE.
ICHIGO'S ACTIVATED HIS FULL-BRING.
IT'S TIME WE TELL HIM ABOUT TSUKISHIMA.
NOT YET.
WE DON'T KNOW HOW POWERFUL ICHIGO'S FULLBRING IS YET.
WE DON'T EVEN KNOW IF HE CAN CONTROL THAT POWER.
TELLING HIM THAT TSUKISHIMA ATTACKED INOUE WILL ONLY AGITATE HIM.
I SEE...

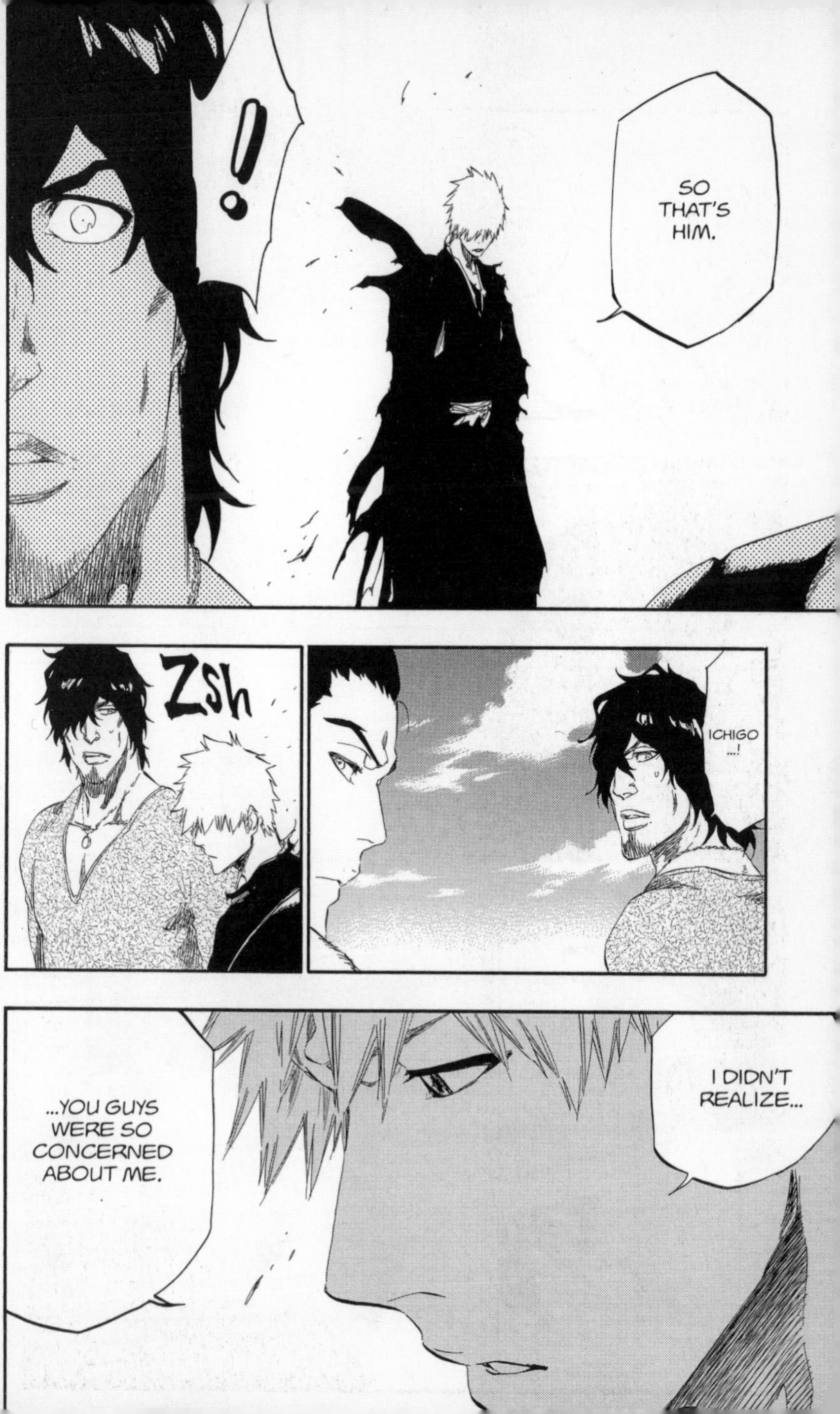
SO THAT'S HIM.
!
Zsh
ICHIGO ...!
I DIDN'T REALIZE...
...YOU GUYS WERE SO CONCERNED ABOUT ME.

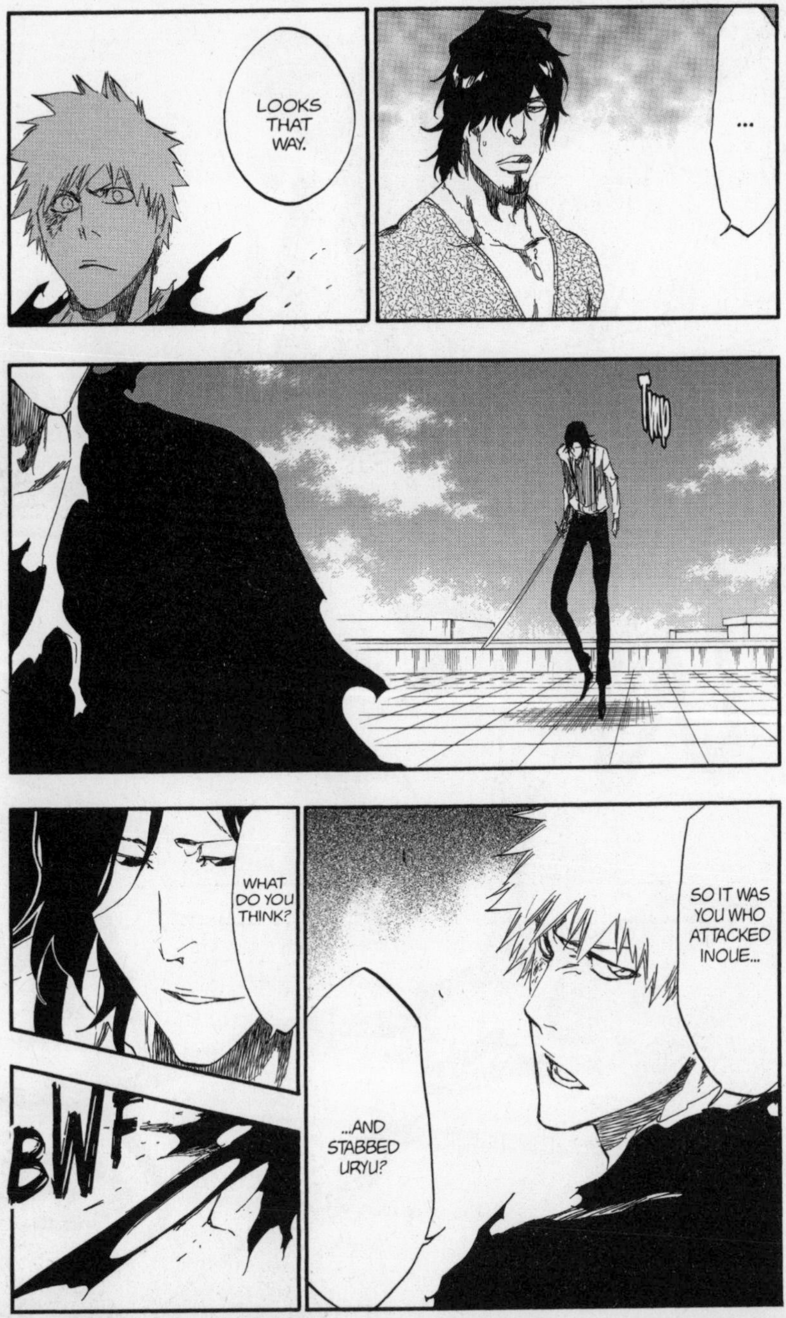
...
LOOKS THAT WAY.
Tmp
SO IT WAS YOU WHO ATTACKED INOUE...
...AND STABBED URYU?
WHAT DO YOU THINK?
BWF

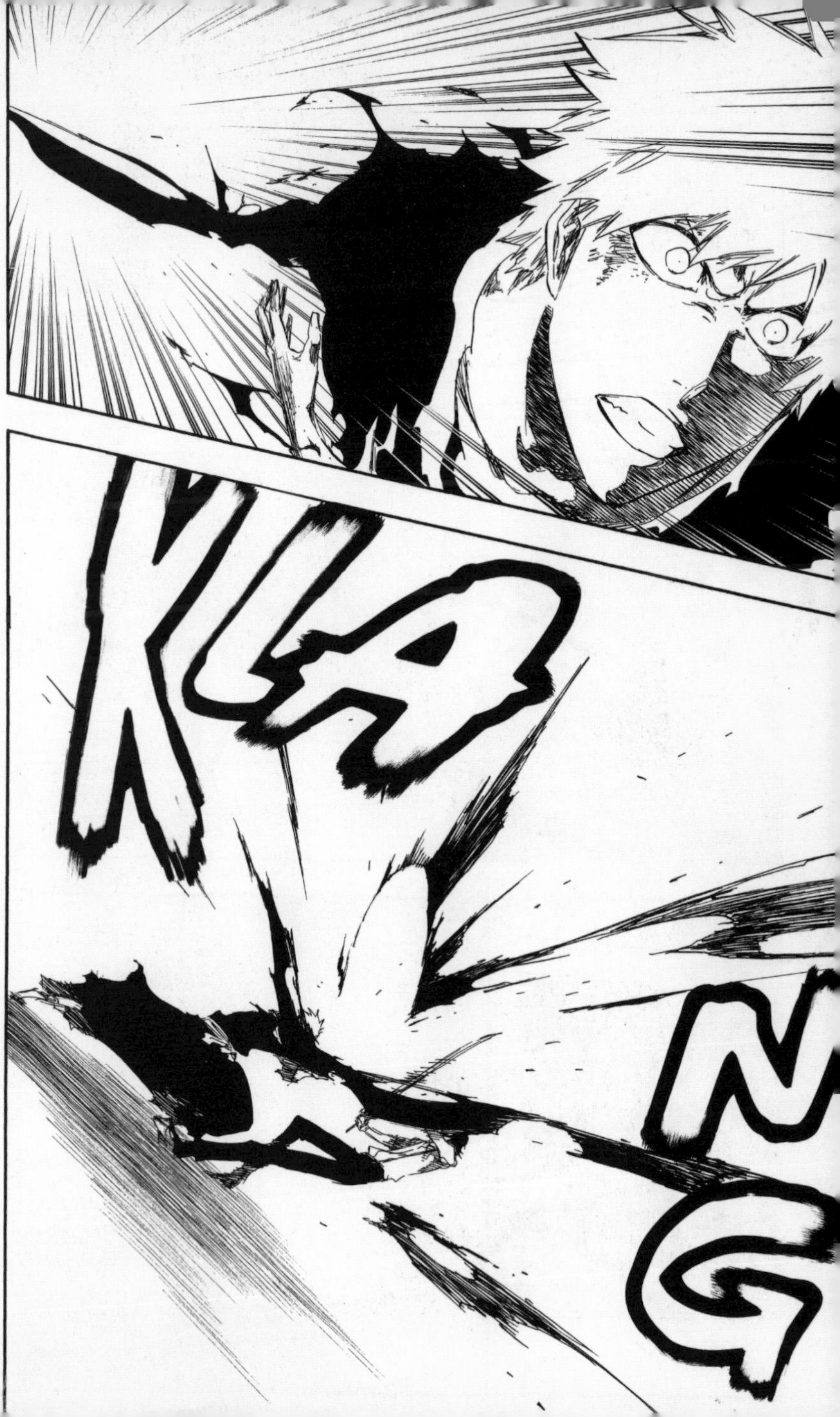
KLANG

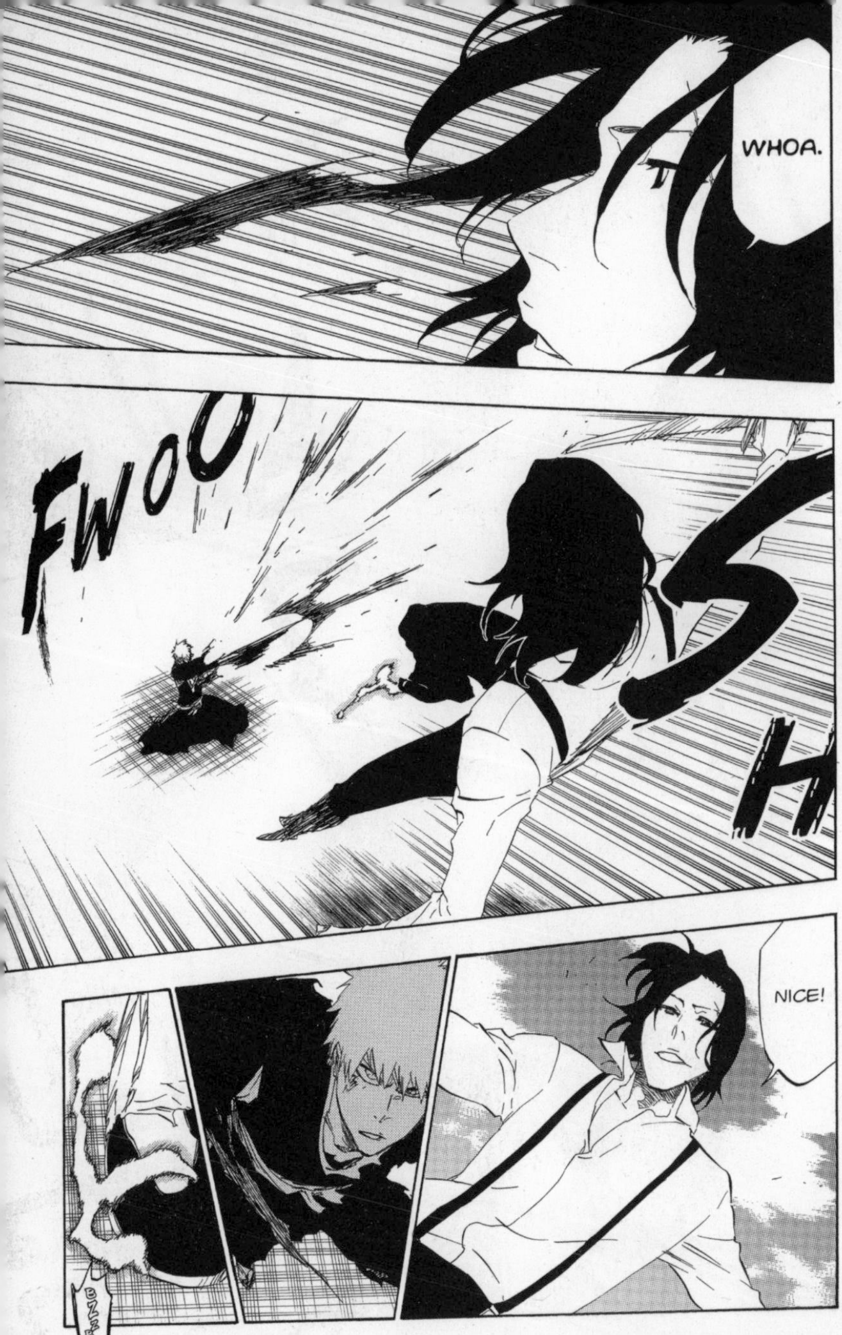
WHOA.
FWOOSH
NICE!
BZZBZZ

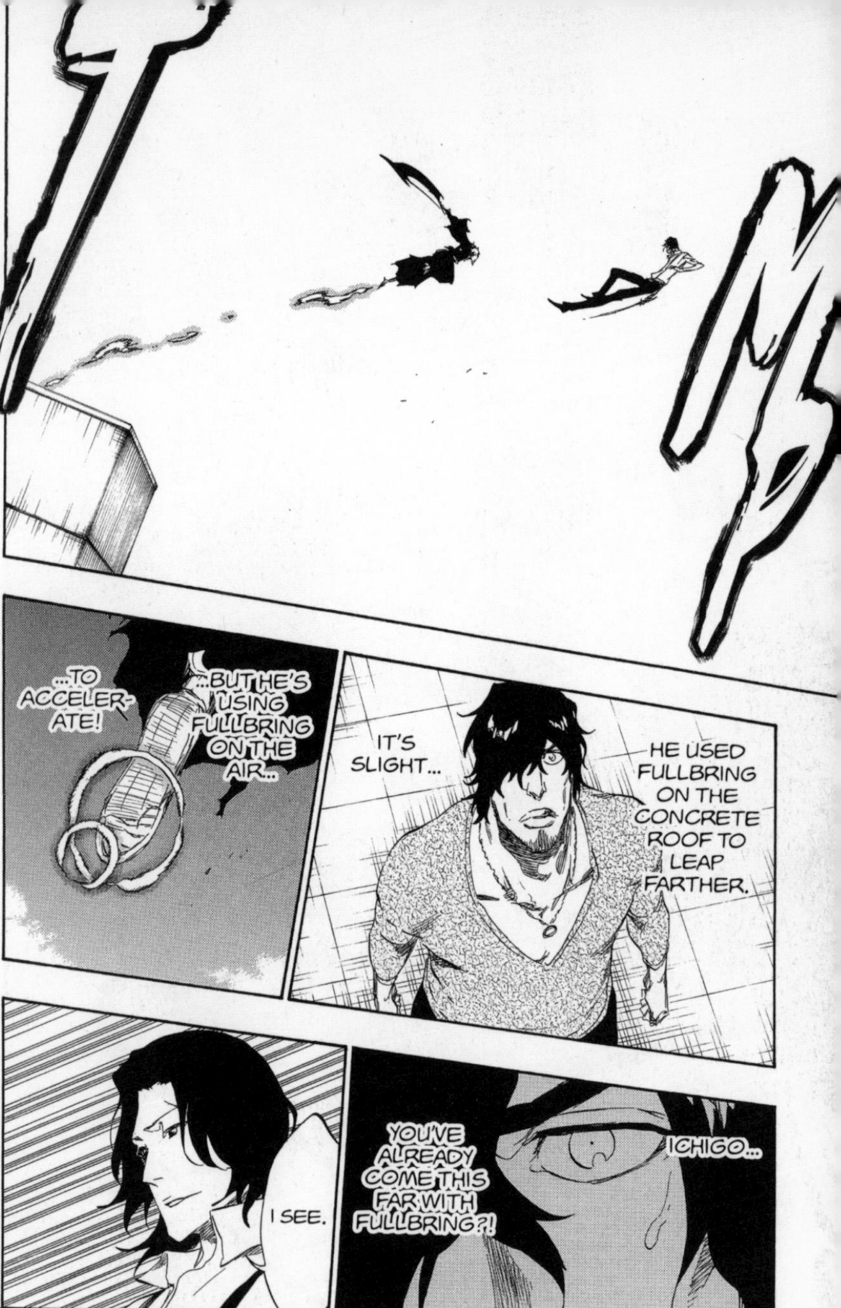
HE USED FULLBRING ON THE CONCRETE ROOF TO LEAP FARTHER.
IT'S SLIGHT...
...BUT HE'S USING FULLBRING ON THE AIR...
...TO ACCELER-ATE!
ICHIGO...
YOU'VE ALREADY COME THIS FAR WITH FULLBRING?!
I SEE.

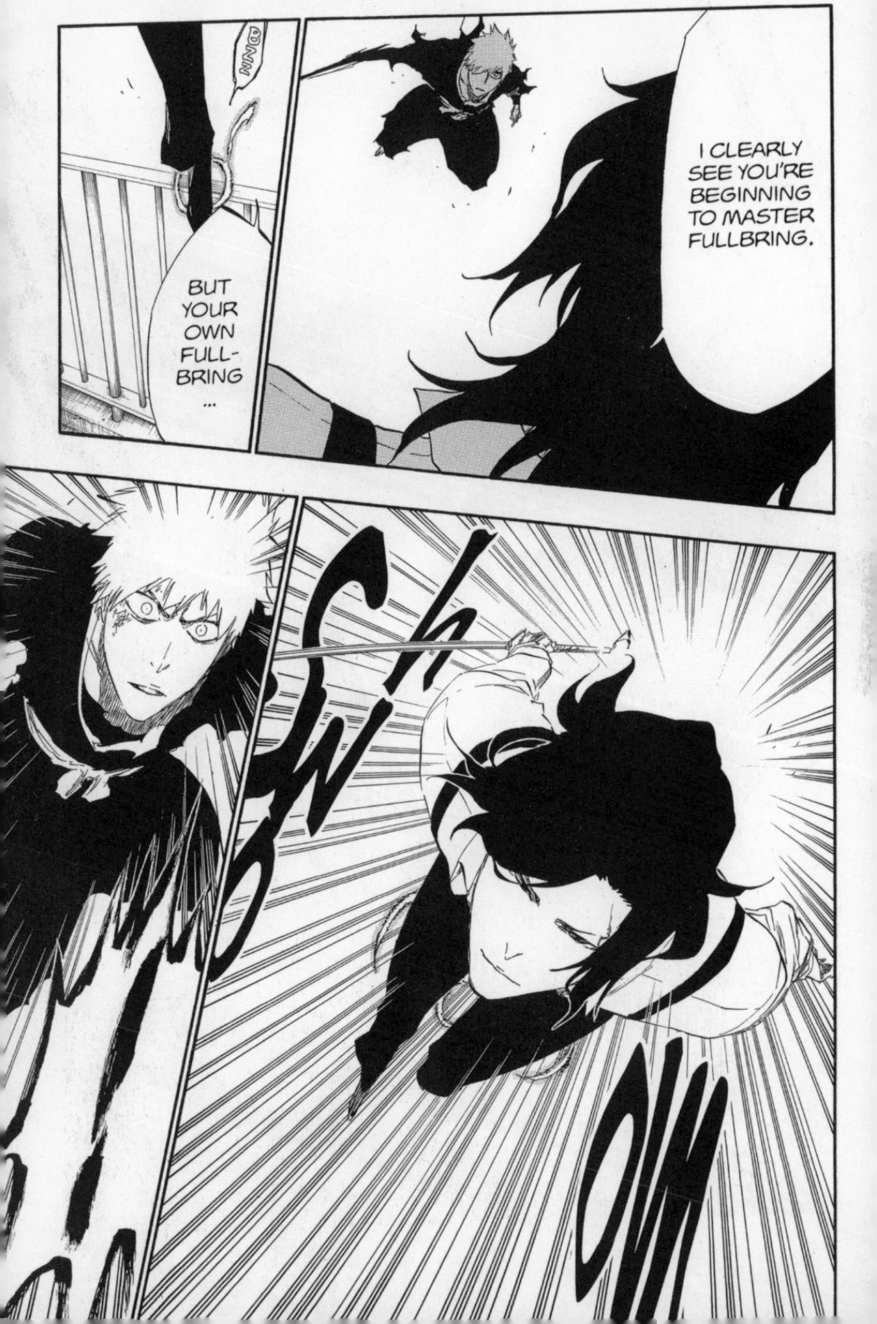
I CLEARLY SEE YOU'RE BEGINNING TO MASTER FULLBRING.
GNN
BUT YOUR OWN FULL-BRING ...

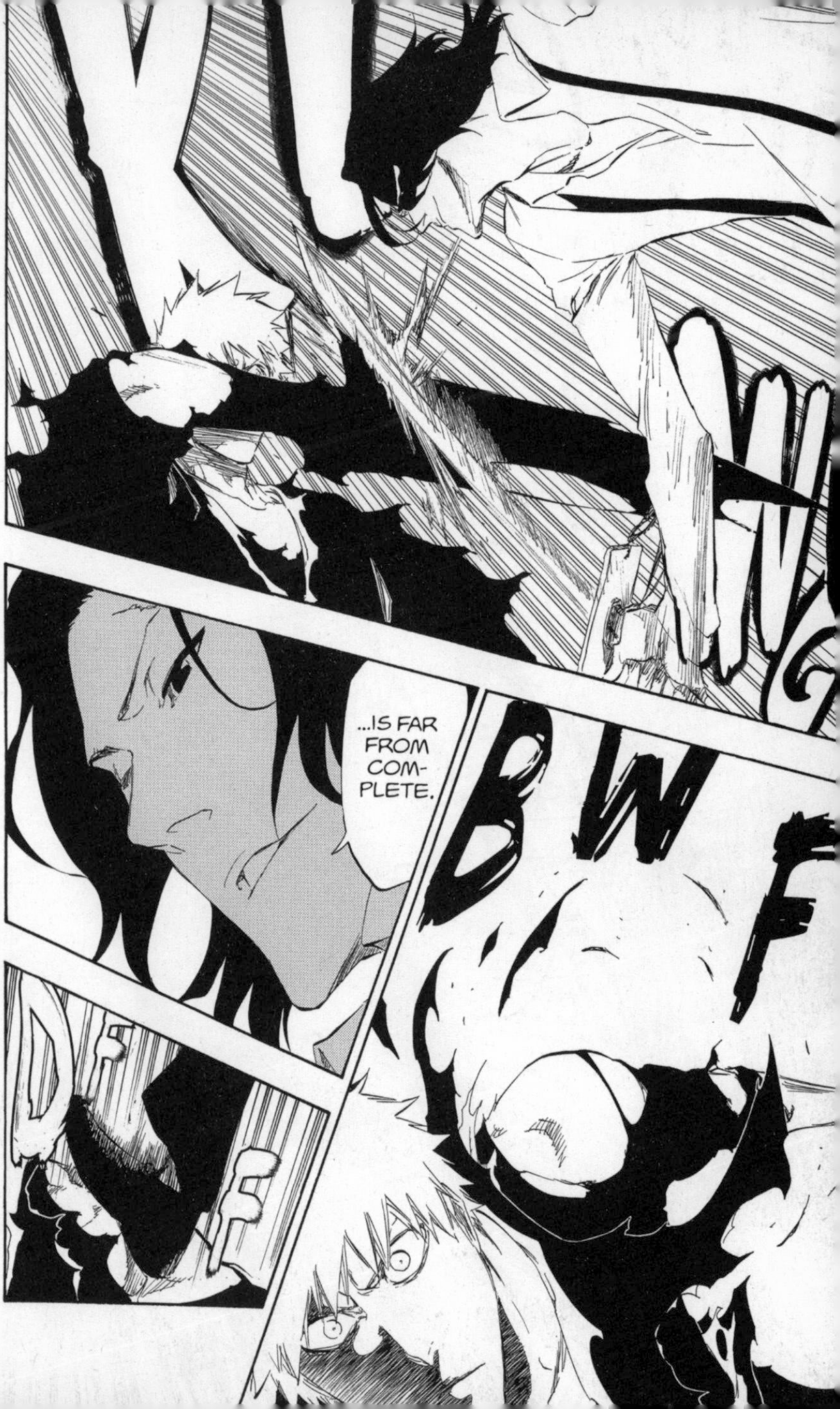
...IS FAR FROM COM-PLETE.
BWF

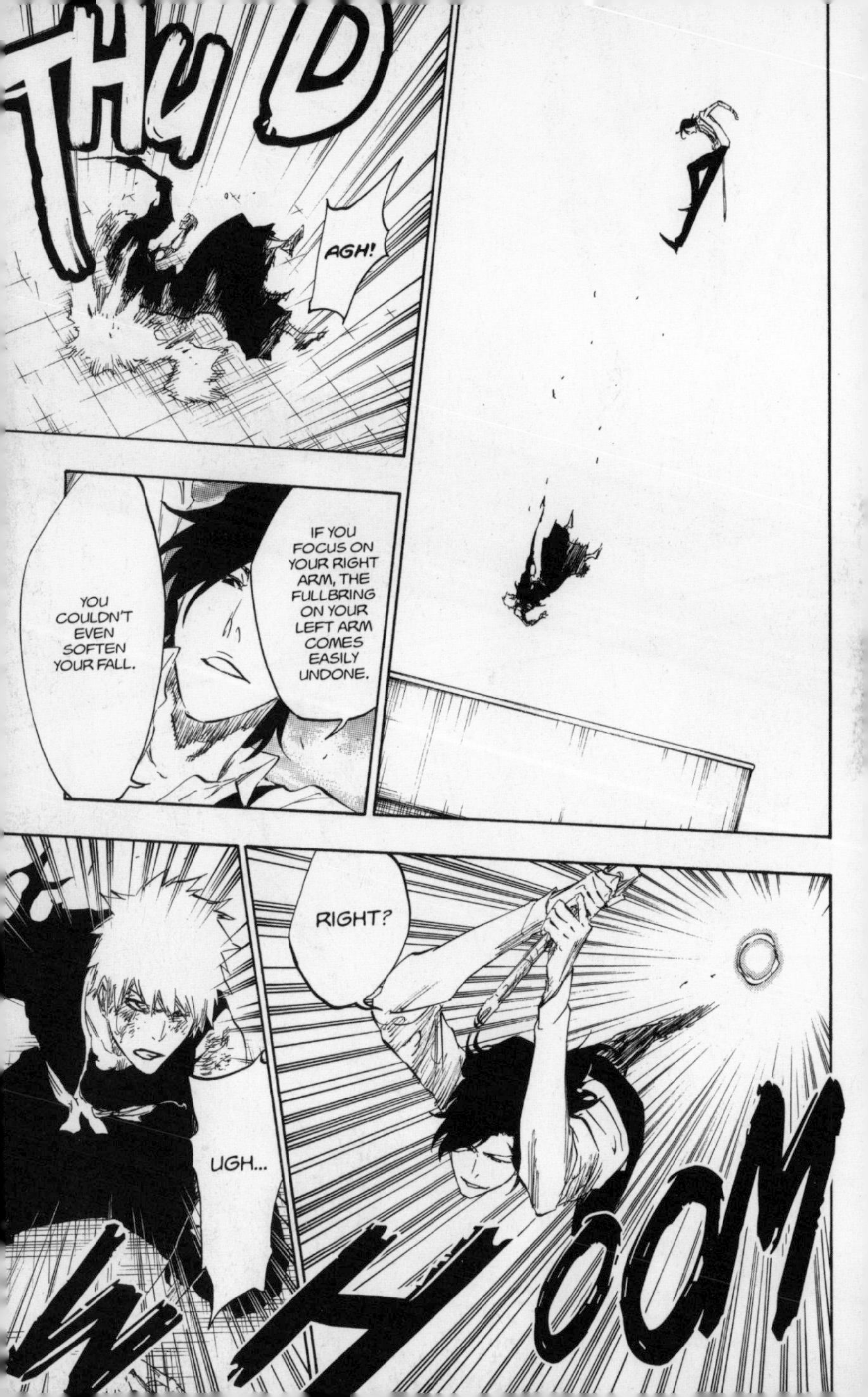
THUD
AGH!
IF YOU FOCUS ON YOUR RIGHT ARM, THE FULLBRING ON YOUR LEFT ARM COMES EASILY UNDONE.
YOU COULDN'T EVEN SOFTEN YOUR FALL.
RIGHT?
WHOOM
UGH...

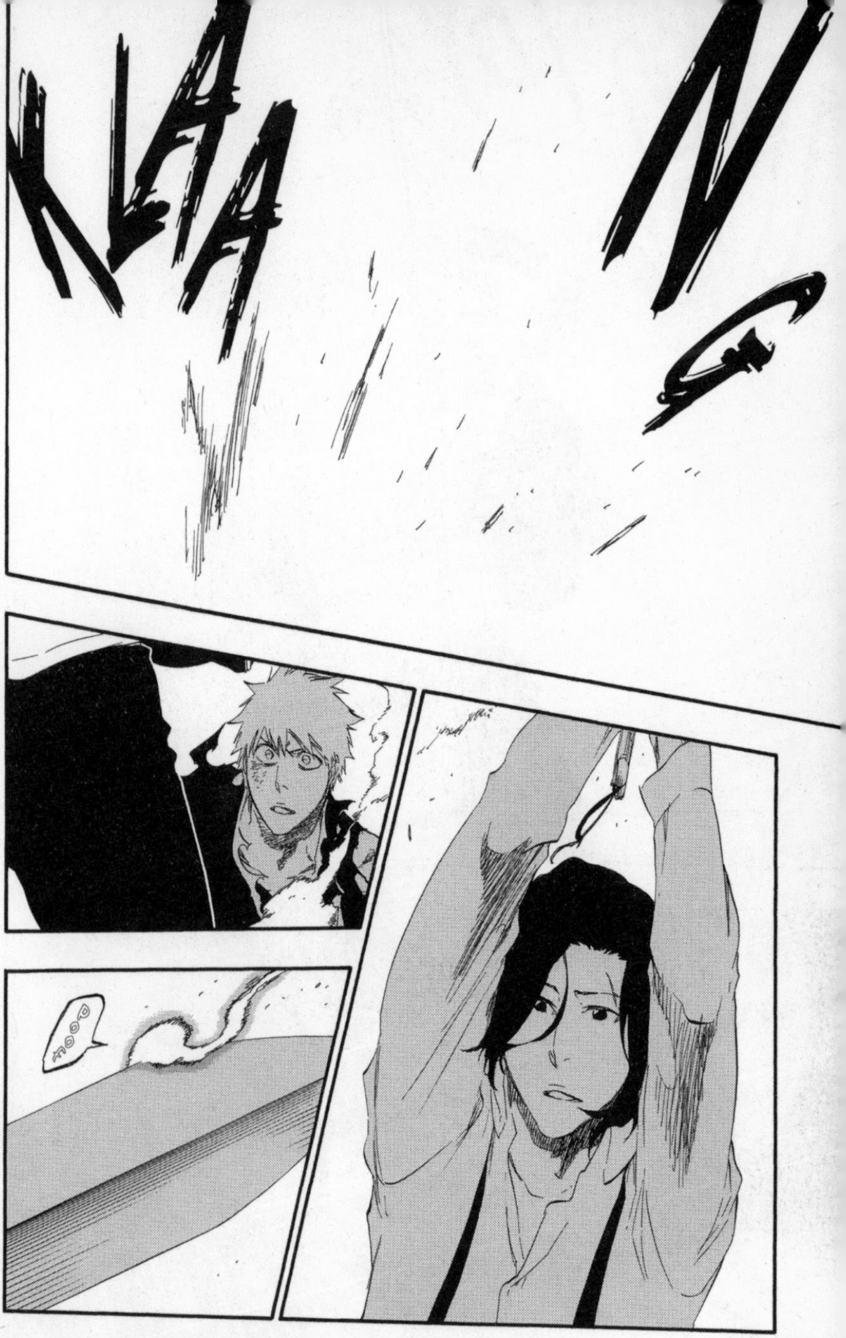
KLAANG
POOF

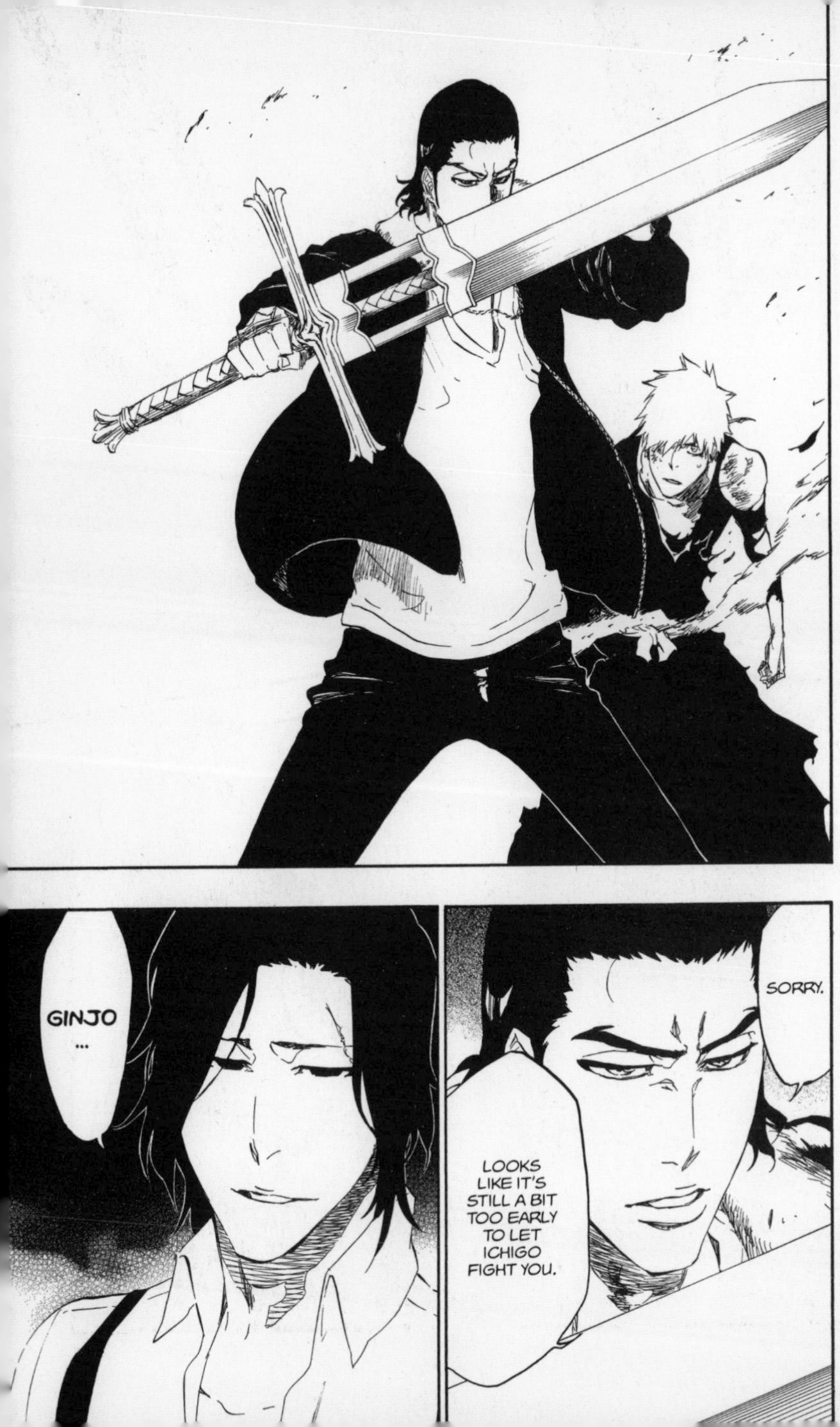
SORRY.
LOOKS LIKE IT'S STILL A BIT TOO EARLY TO LET ICHIGO FIGHT YOU.
GINJO ...

THE STORY
KEEPS
GOING ON
WHILE I'M
LYING
HERE...

446. THE DARK BEAT 2

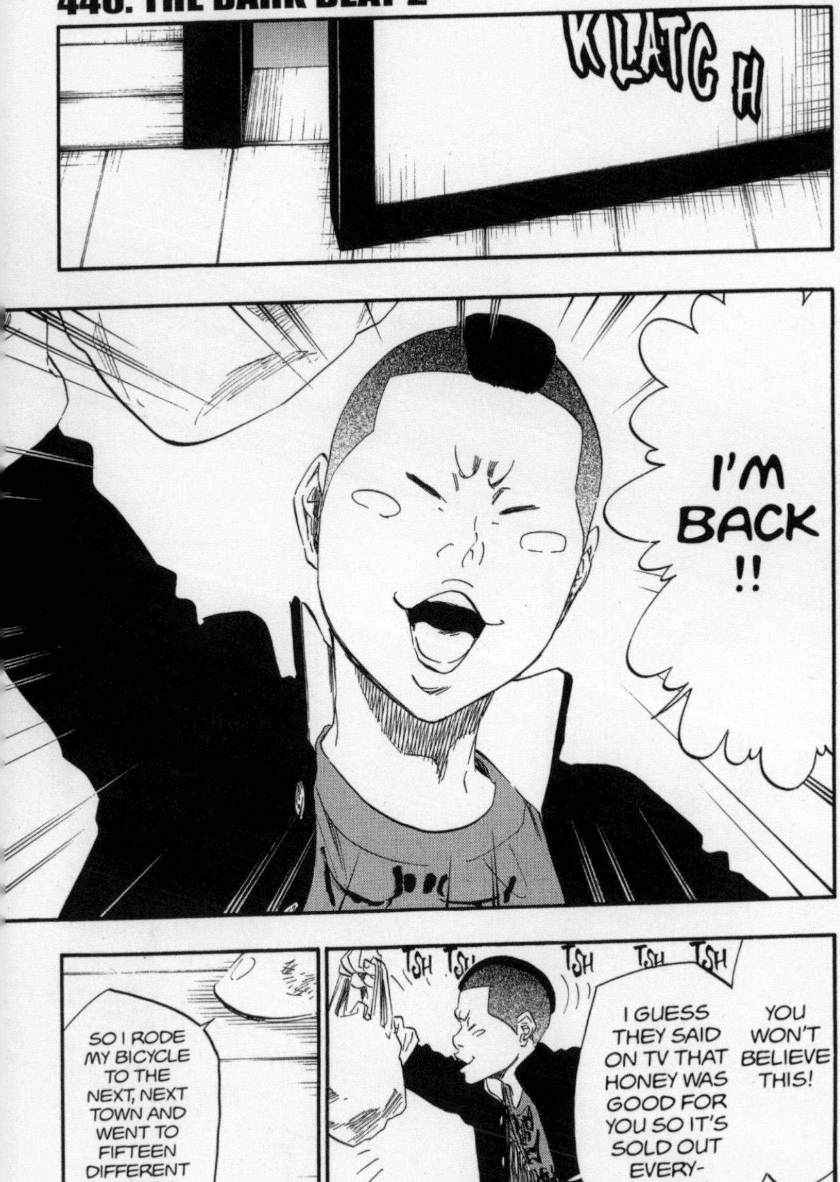
KLATCH
I'M BACK!!
TSH TSH TSH TSH TSH
YOU WON'T BELIEVE THIS!
I GUESS THEY SAID ON TV THAT HONEY WAS GOOD FOR YOU SO IT'S SOLD OUT EVERY-WHERE!
SO I RODE MY BICYCLE TO THE NEXT, NEXT TOWN AND WENT TO FIFTEEN DIFFERENT STORES AND...

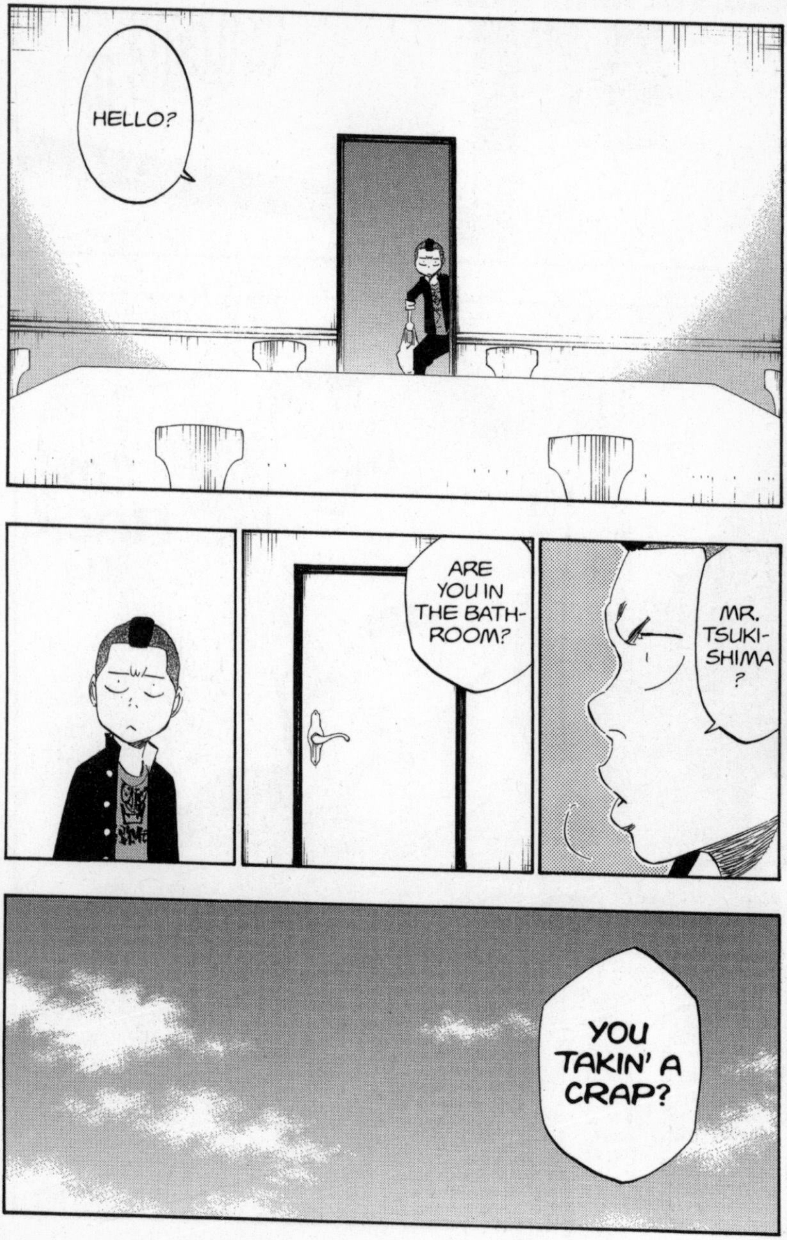
HELLO?
MR. TSUKI-SHIMA?
ARE YOU IN THE BATH-ROOM?
YOU TAKIN' A CRAP?

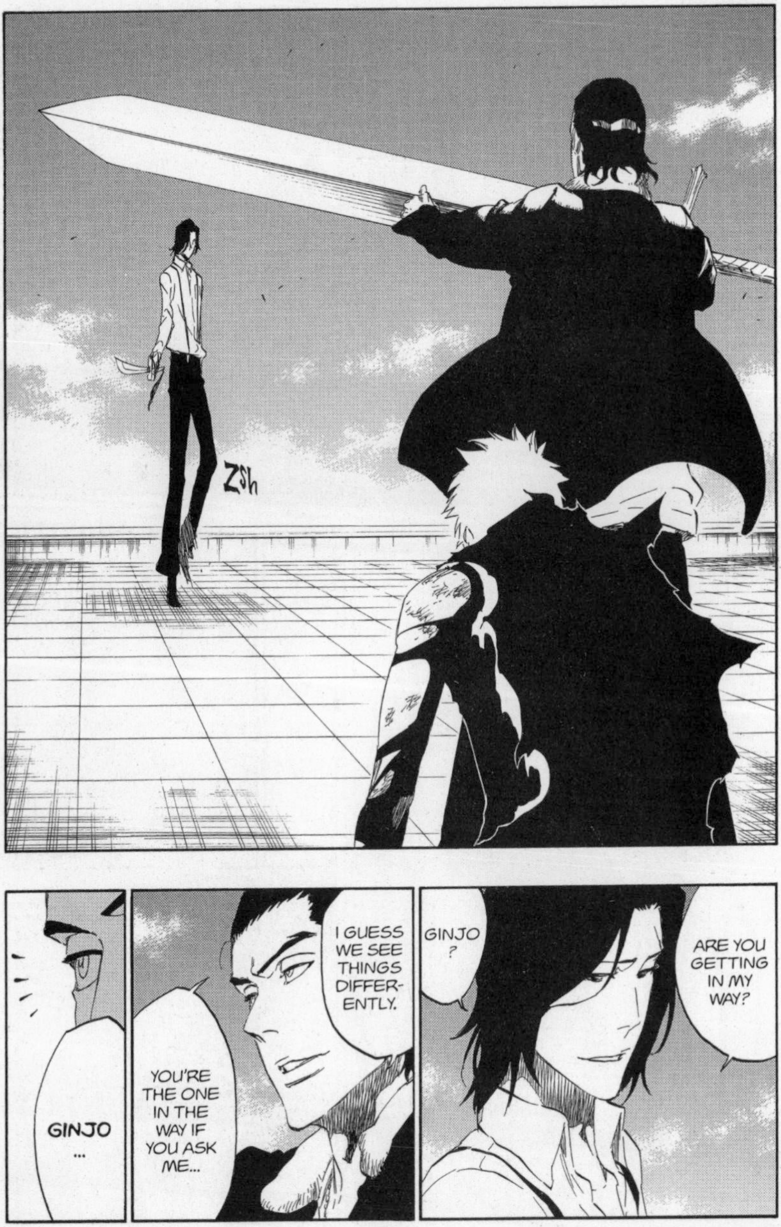
ZSh
ARE YOU GETTING IN MY WAY?
GINJO?
I GUESS WE SEE THINGS DIFFER-ENTLY.
YOU'RE THE ONE IN THE WAY IF YOU ASK ME...
GINJO...

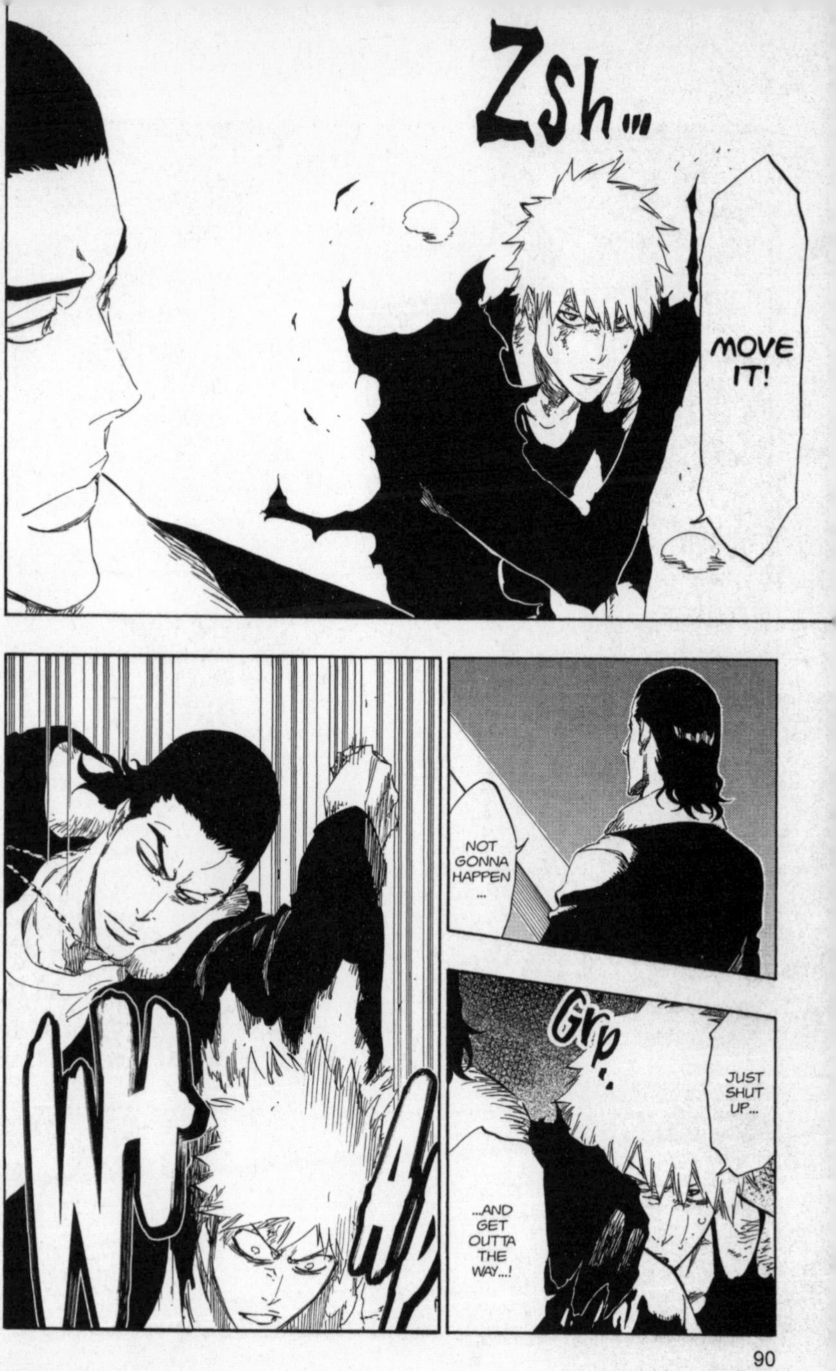
Zsh...
MOVE IT!
NOT GONNA HAPPEN...
Grp..
JUST SHUT UP...
...AND GET OUTTA THE WAY...!

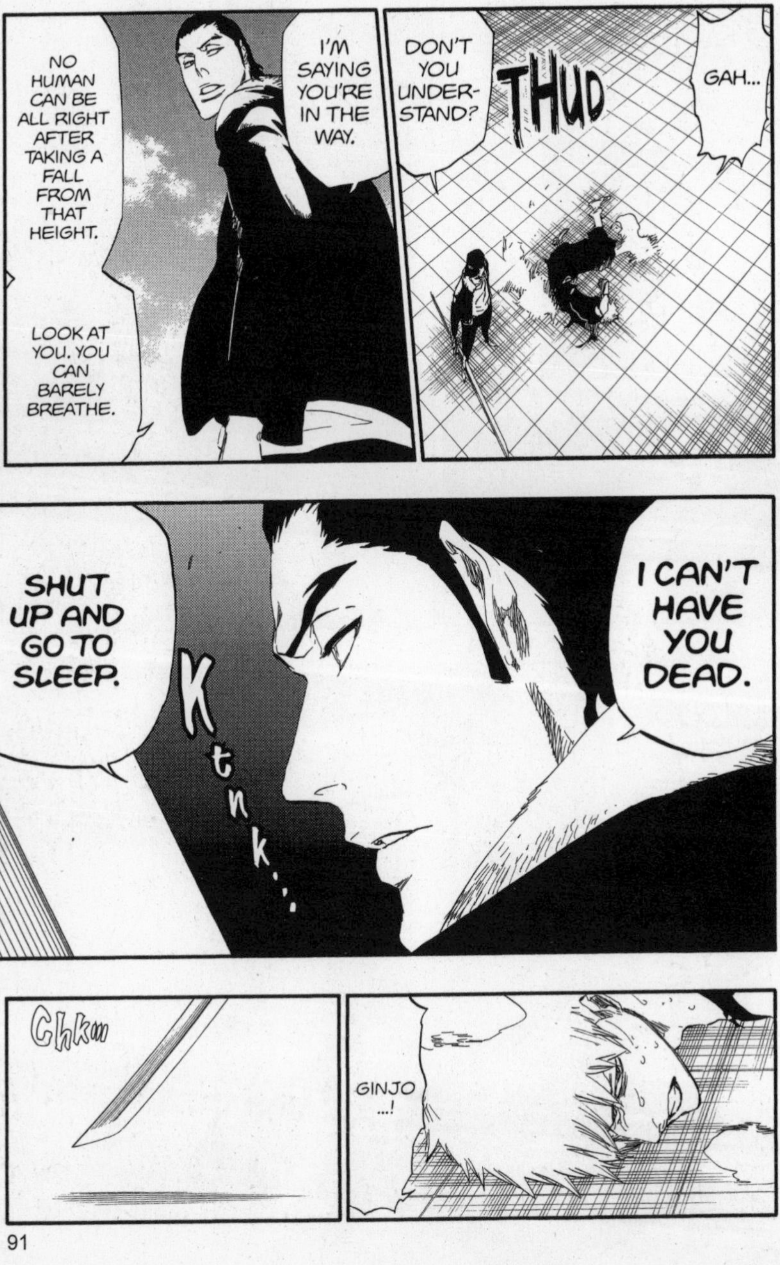
GAH...
THUD
DON'T YOU UNDER-STAND?
I'M SAYING YOU'RE IN THE WAY.
NO HUMAN CAN BE ALL RIGHT AFTER TAKING A FALL FROM THAT HEIGHT.
LOOK AT YOU. YOU CAN BARELY BREATHE.
I CAN'T HAVE YOU DEAD.
Ktnk...
SHUT UP AND GO TO SLEEP.
GINJO ...!
Chk

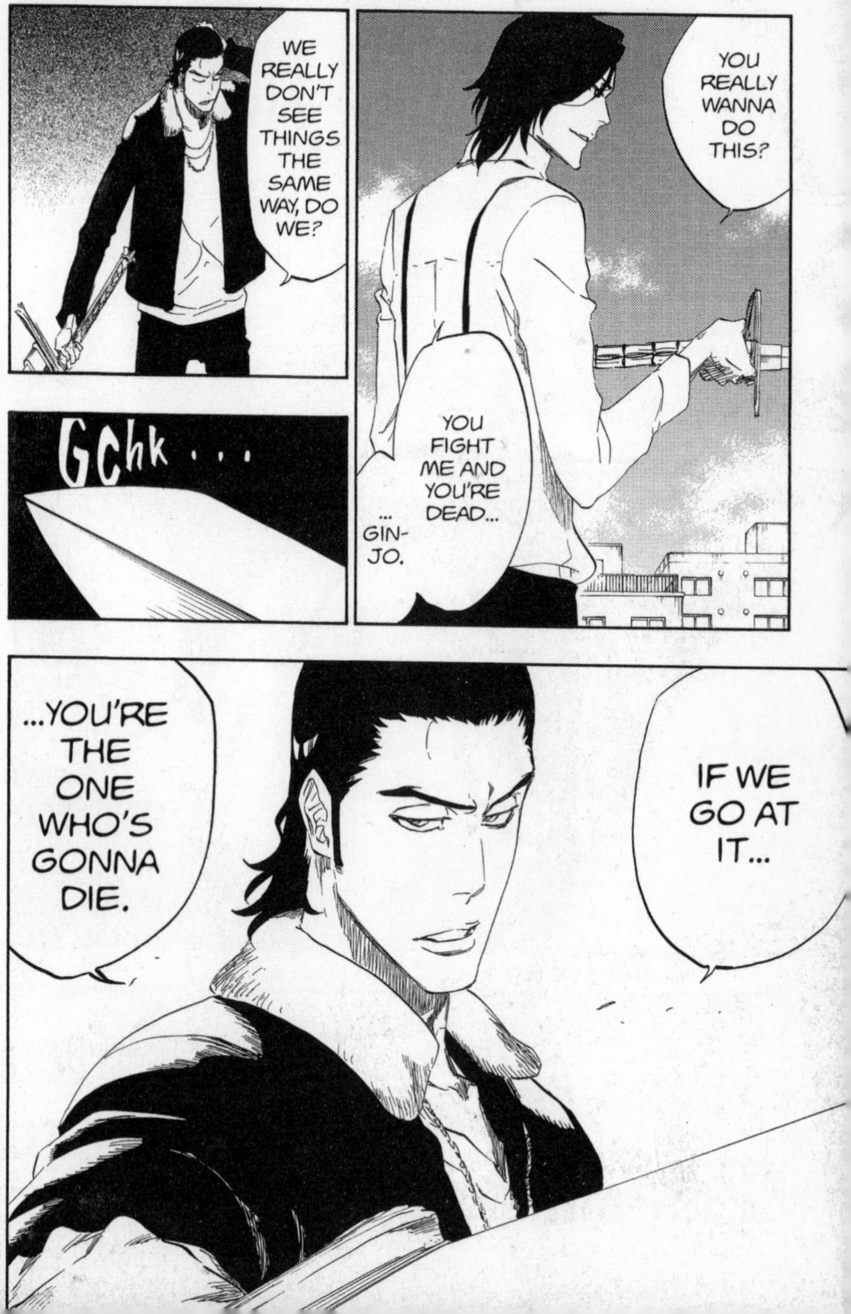
YOU REALLY WANNA DO THIS?
YOU FIGHT ME AND YOU'RE DEAD...
...GIN-JO.
WE REALLY DON'T SEE THINGS THE SAME WAY, DO WE?
GCHK...
IF WE GO AT IT...
...YOU'RE THE ONE WHO'S GONNA DIE.

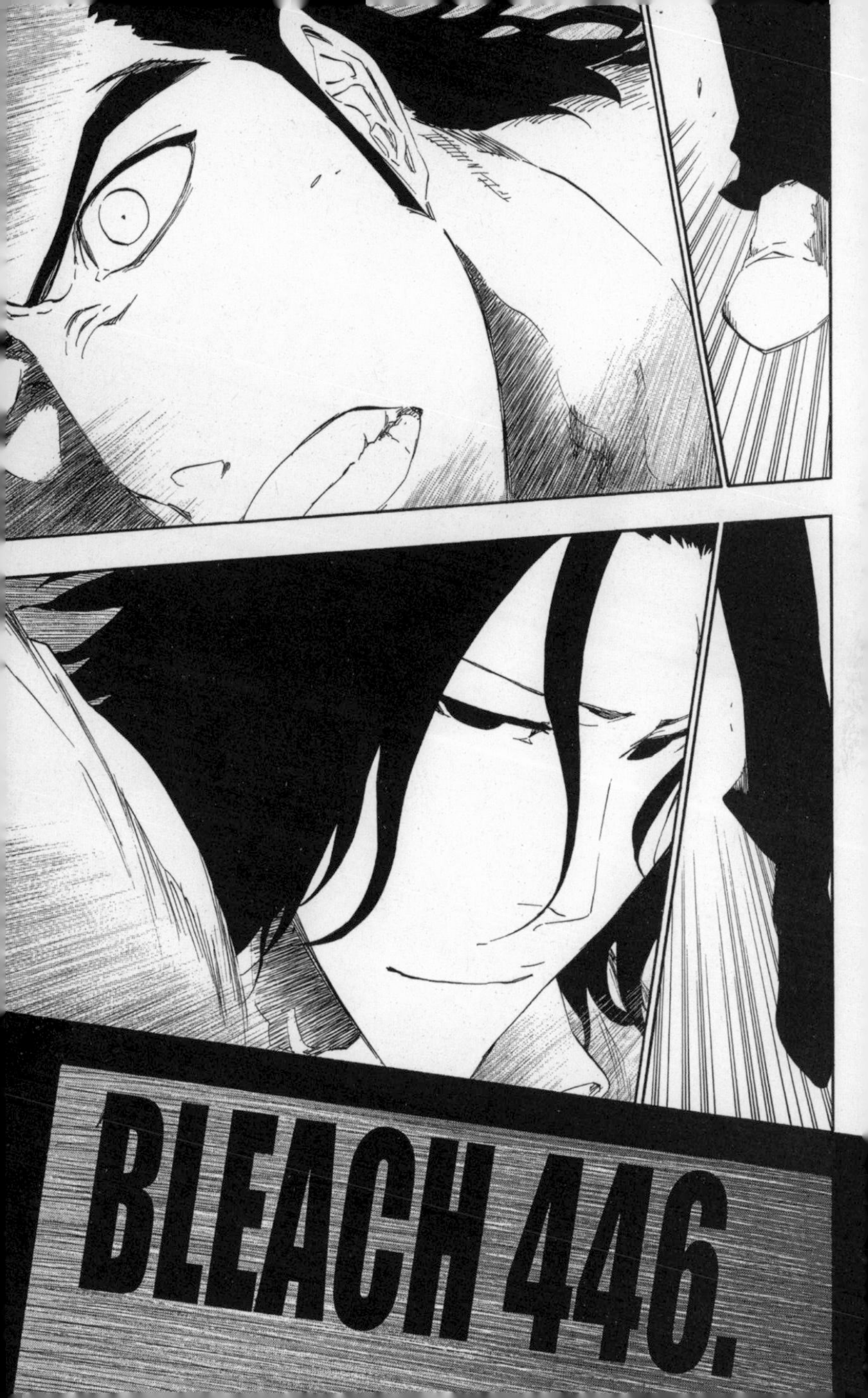
BLEACH 446.

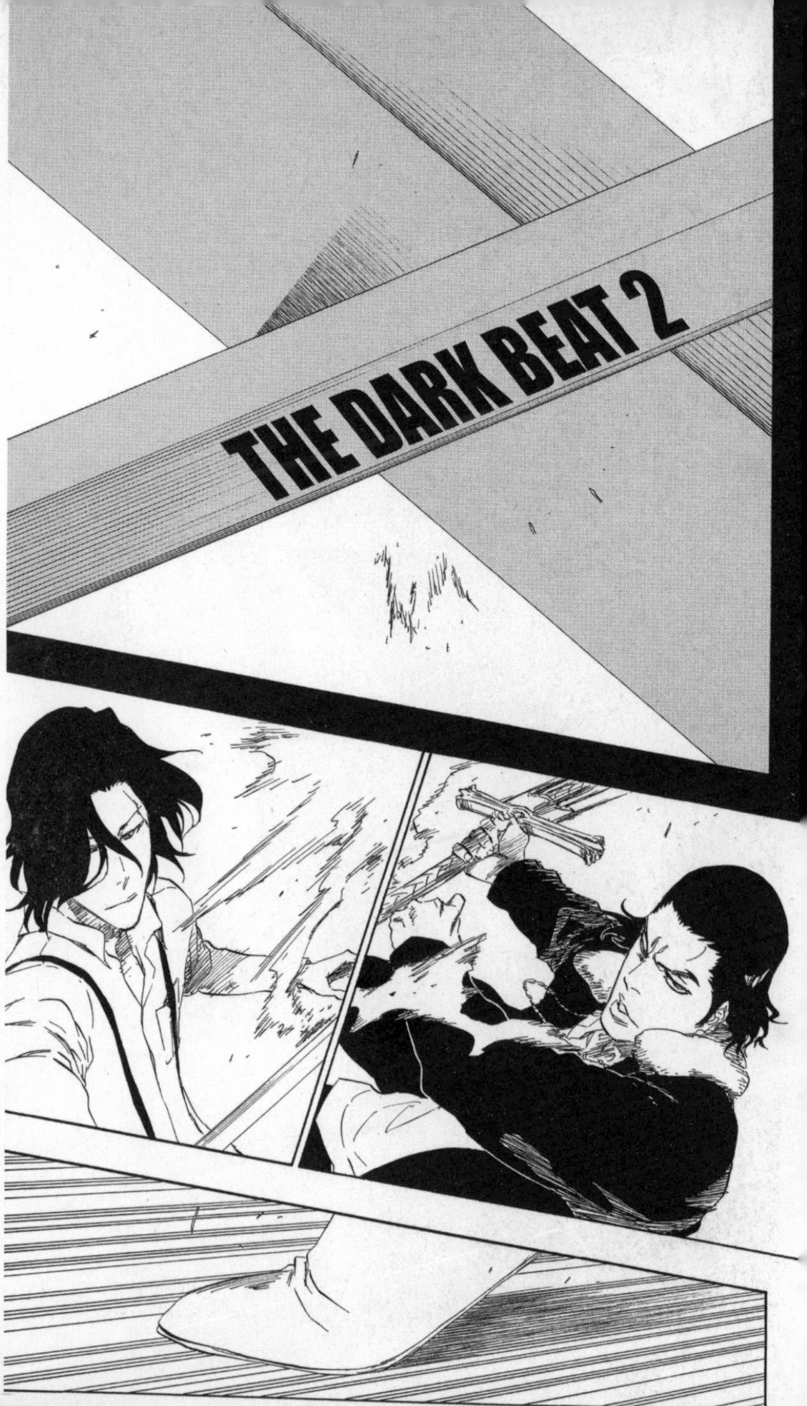
THE DARK BEAT 2

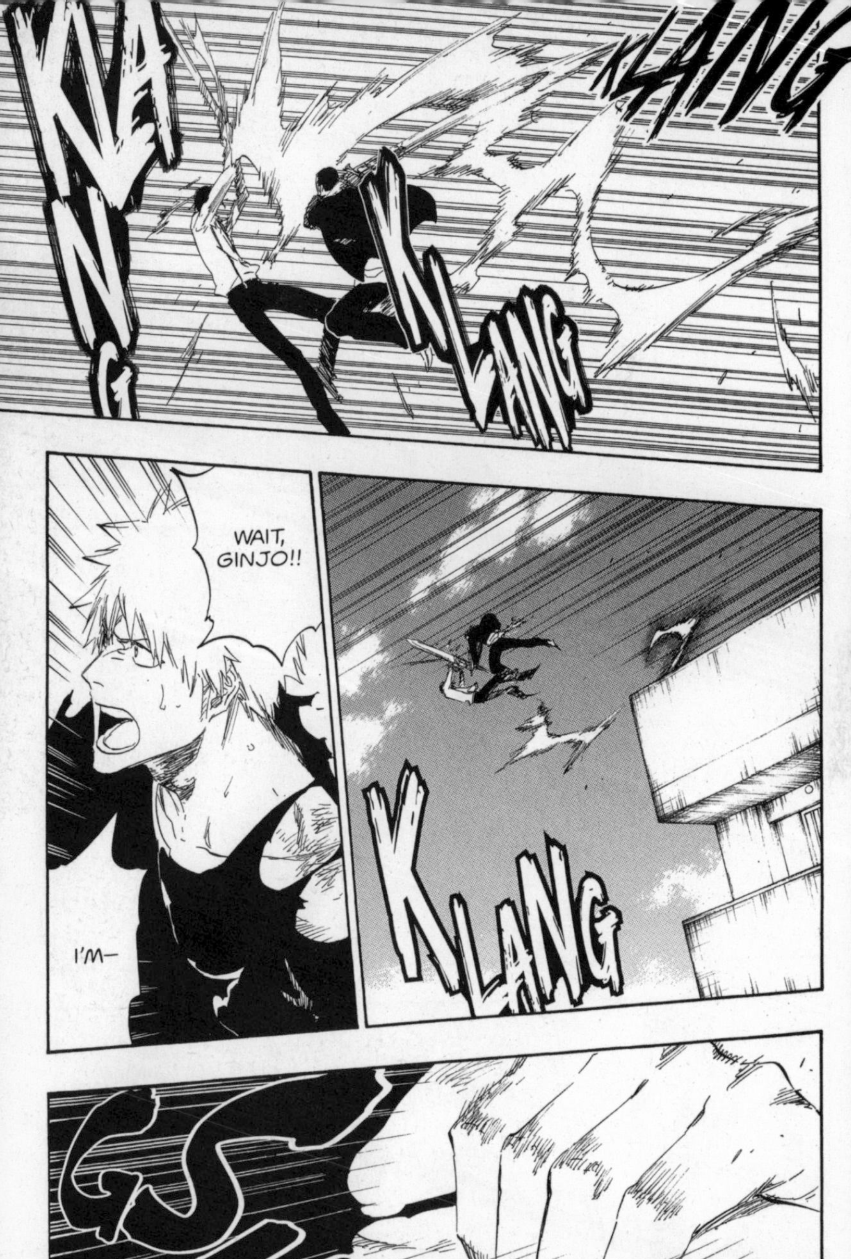
KLANG
KLANG
KLANG
KLANG
WAIT, GINJO!!
I'M—

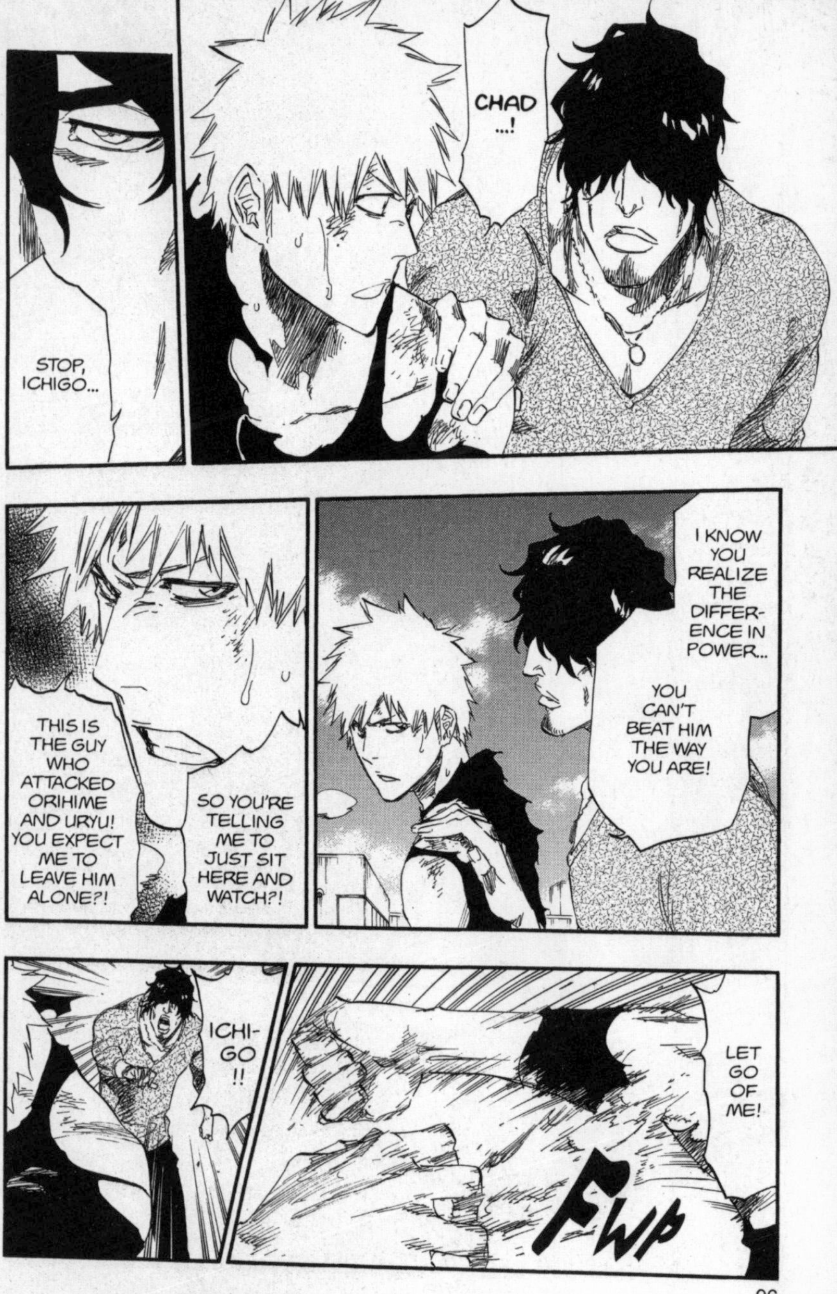
CHAD ...!
STOP, ICHIGO...
I KNOW YOU REALIZE THE DIFFER-ENCE IN POWER...
YOU CAN'T BEAT HIM THE WAY YOU ARE!
SO YOU'RE TELLING ME TO JUST SIT HERE AND WATCH?!
THIS IS THE GUY WHO ATTACKED ORIHIME AND URYU! YOU EXPECT ME TO LEAVE HIM ALONE?!
LET GO OF ME!
FWP
ICHI-GO !!

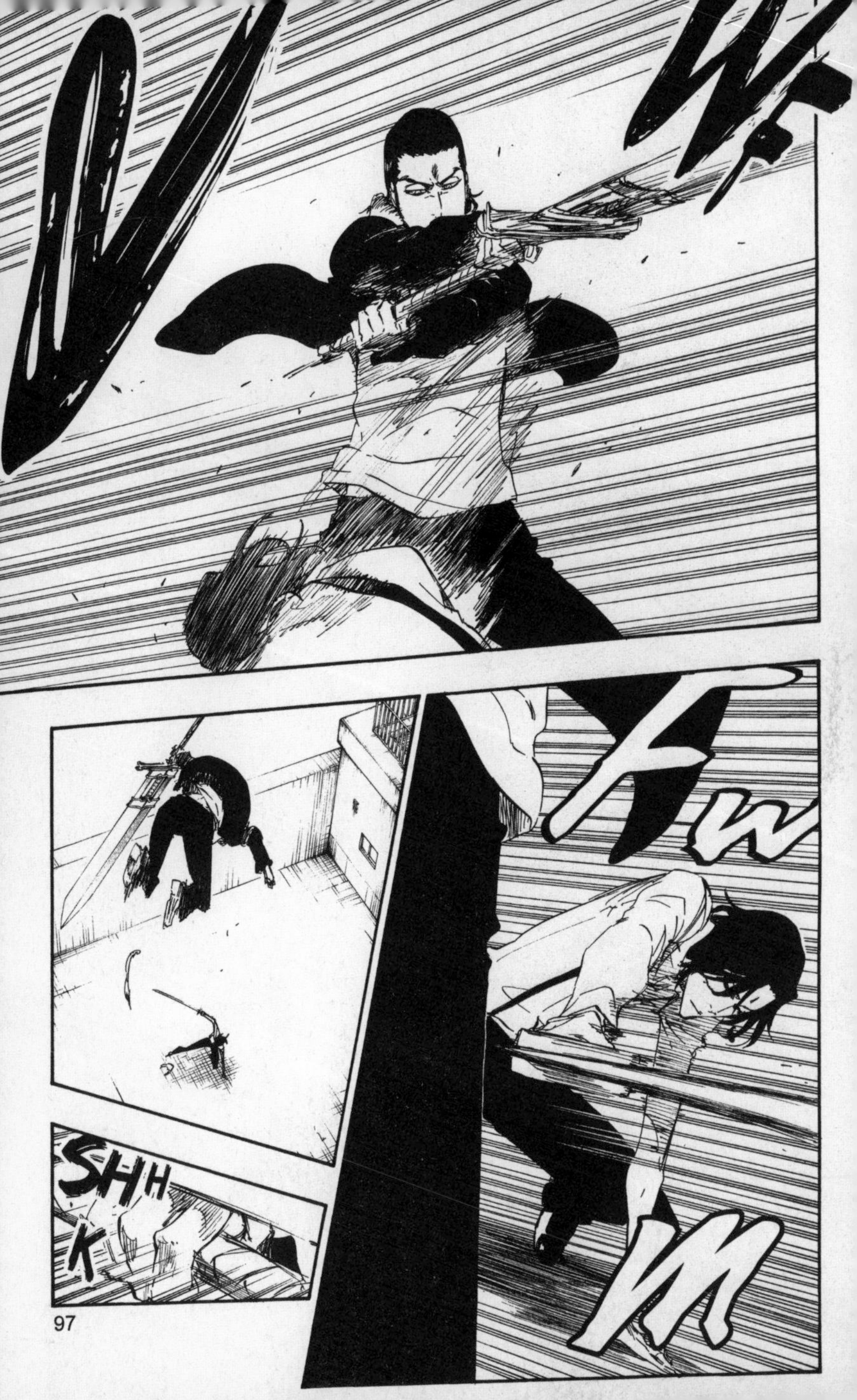
SHHK

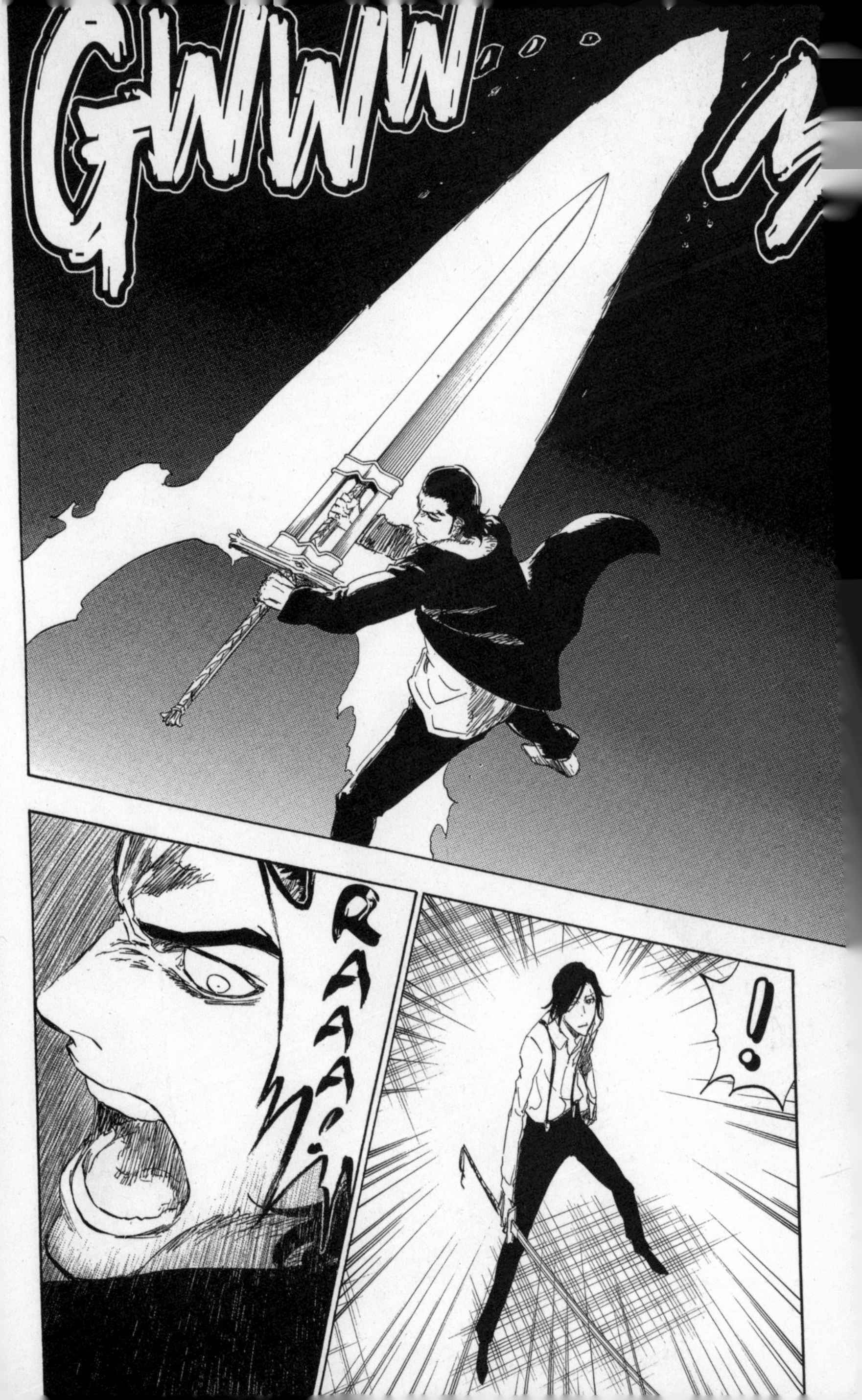
GWWWM
!
RAAAAHH

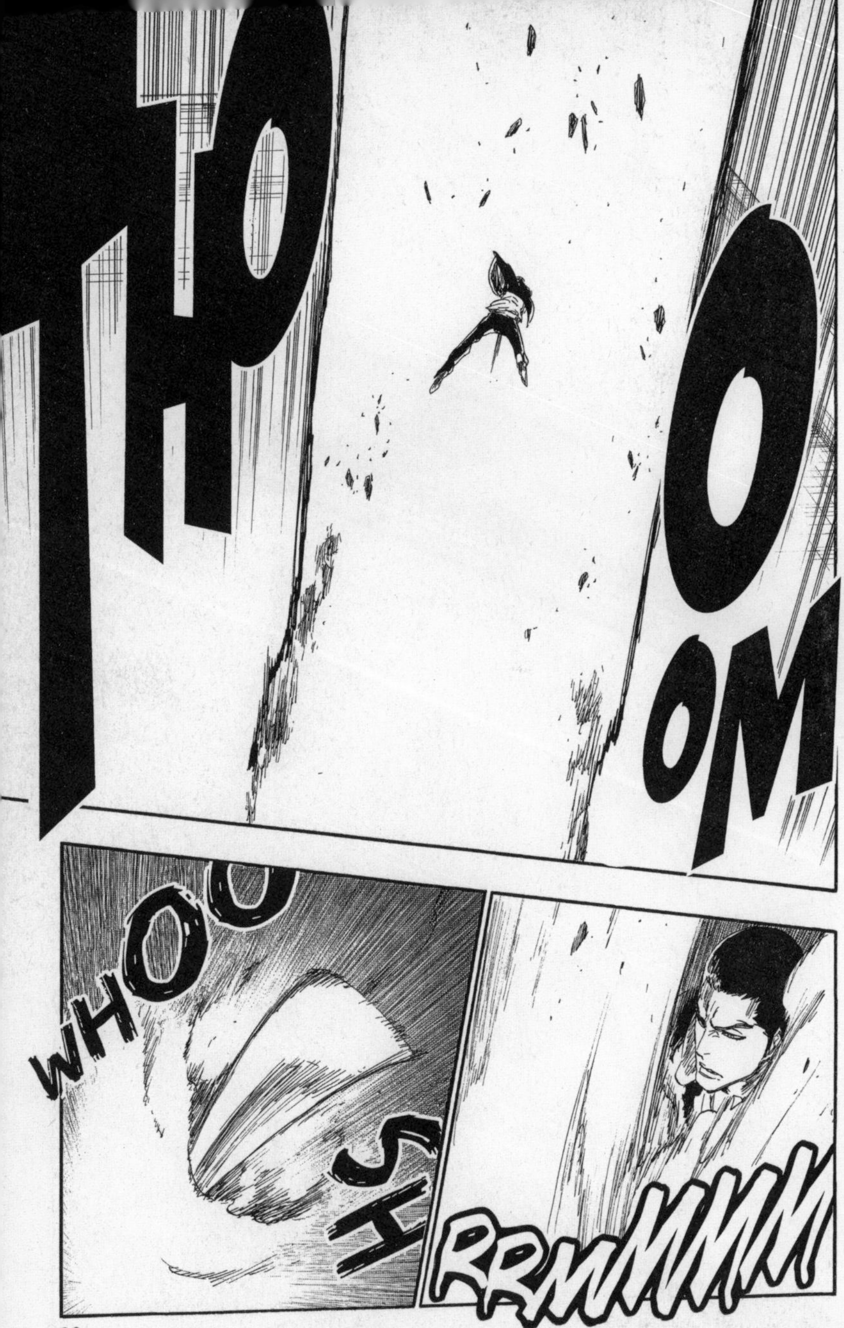
THOOOM
RRMMMMM
WHOOOSH

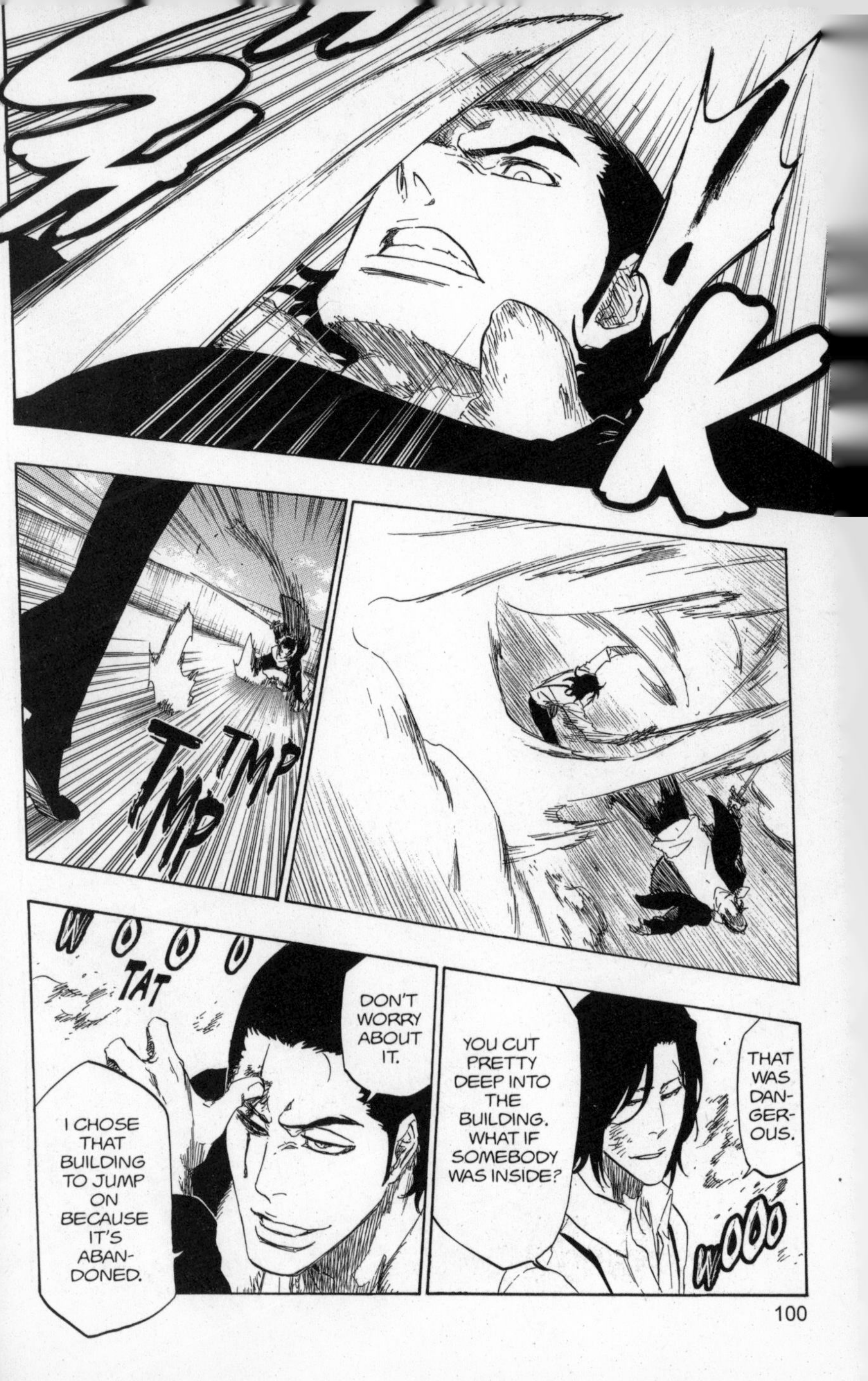
TMP
TMP
THAT WAS DAN-GER-OUS.
YOU CUT PRETTY DEEP INTO THE BUILDING. WHAT IF SOMEBODY WAS INSIDE?
WOOO
WOOOO
TAT
DON'T WORRY ABOUT IT.
I CHOSE THAT BUILDING TO JUMP ON BECAUSE IT'S ABAN-DONED.

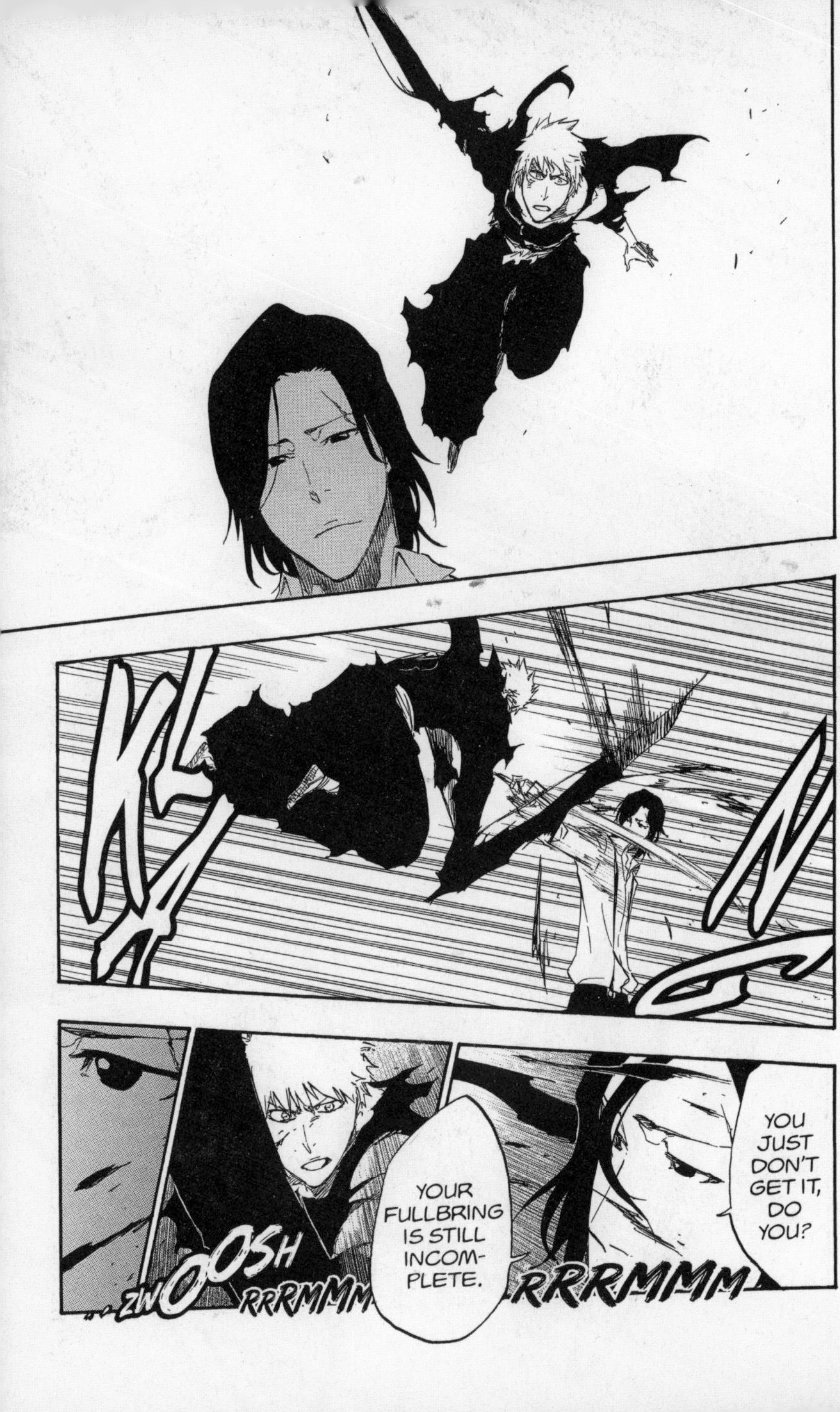
YOU JUST DON'T GET IT, DO YOU?
RRRMMMM
YOUR FULLBRING IS STILL INCOMPLETE.
RRRMMMM
ZWOOOSH

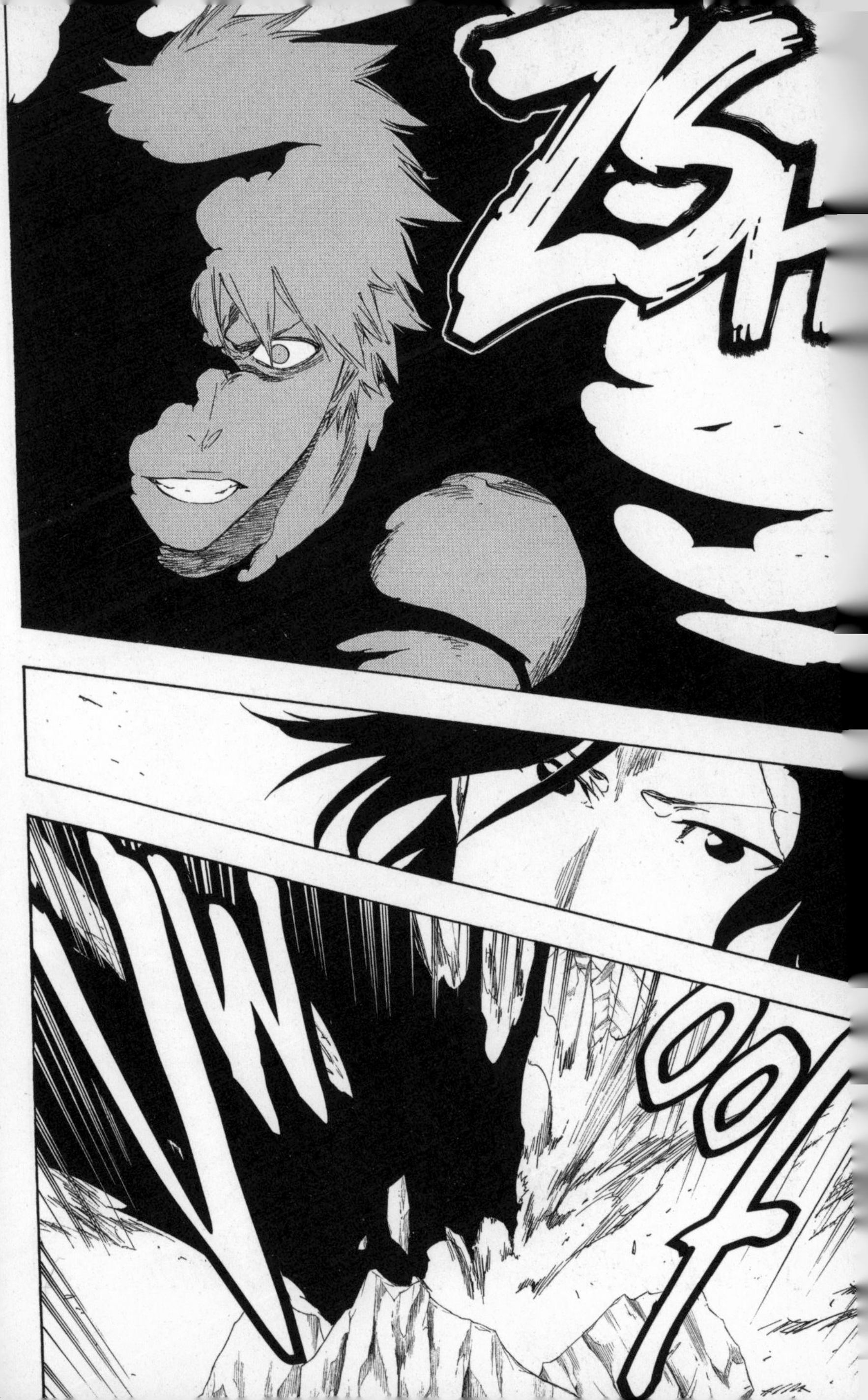

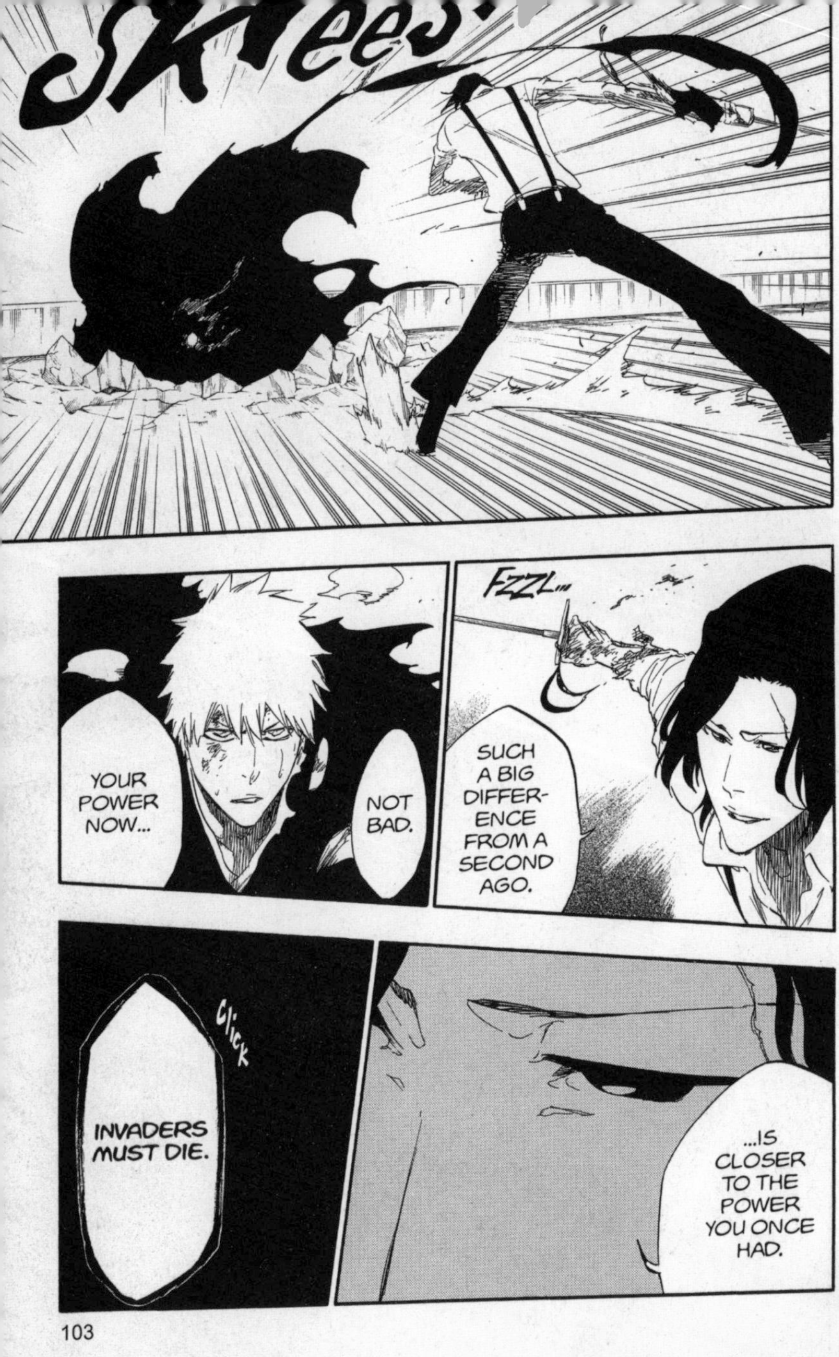
SKEES
FZZL...
SUCH A BIG DIFFERENCE FROM A SECOND AGO.
NOT BAD.
YOUR POWER NOW...
...IS CLOSER TO THE POWER YOU ONCE HAD.
Click
INVADERS MUST DIE.

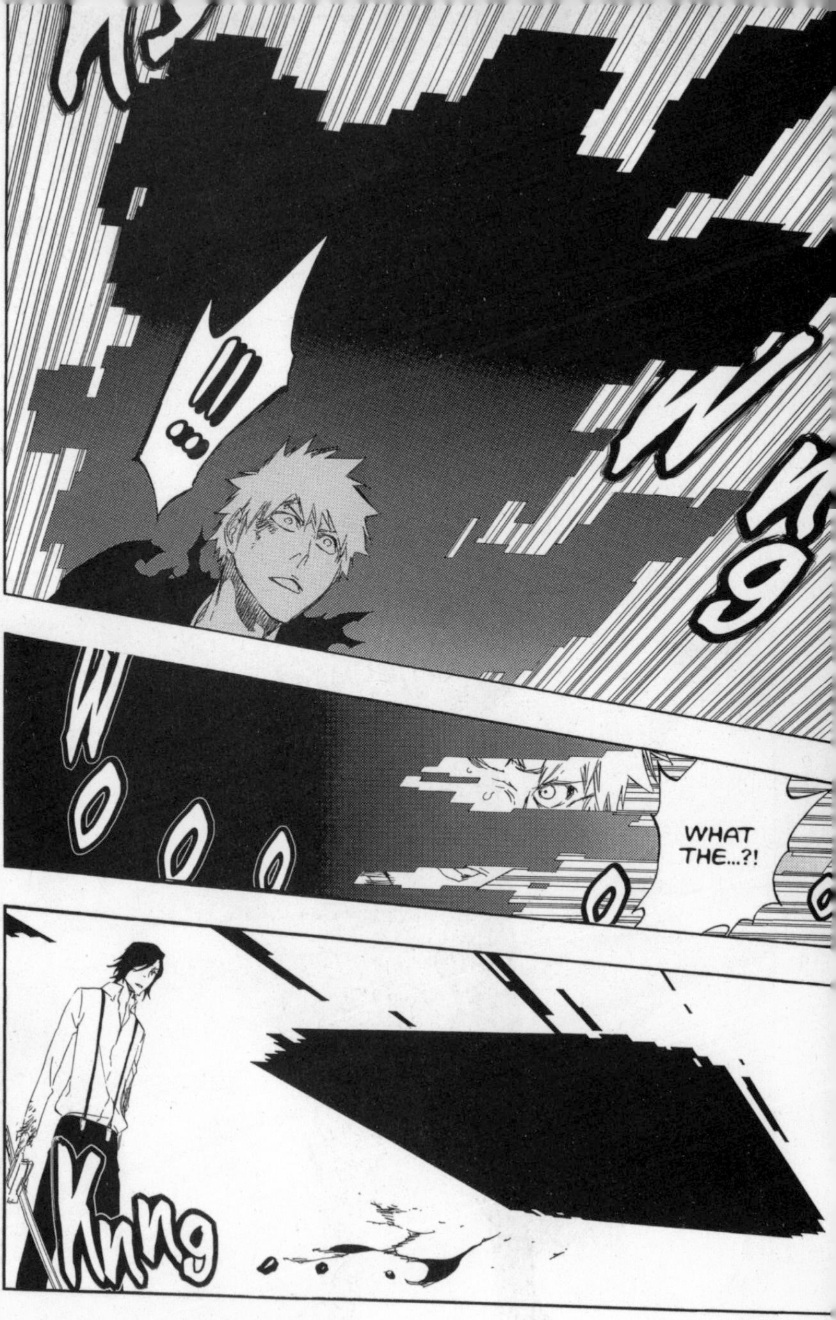
Wnng
WHAT THE...?!
Knng

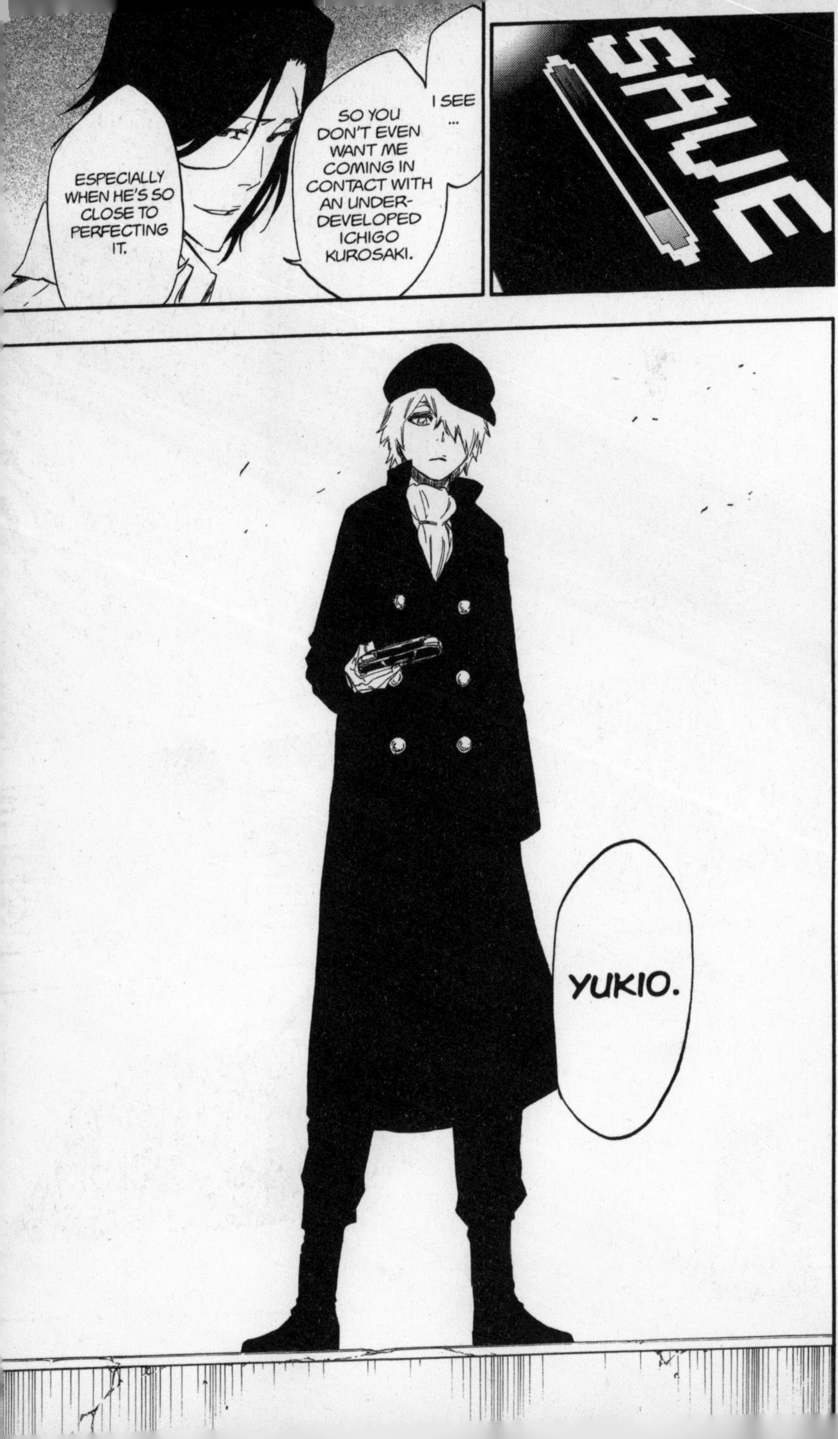
SAVE
I SEE ...
SO YOU DON'T EVEN WANT ME COMING IN CONTACT WITH AN UNDER-DEVELOPED ICHIGO KUROSAKI.
ESPECIALLY WHEN HE'S SO CLOSE TO PERFECTING IT.
YUKIO.

Mr. Tsukishima takes a long crap...

447. Load

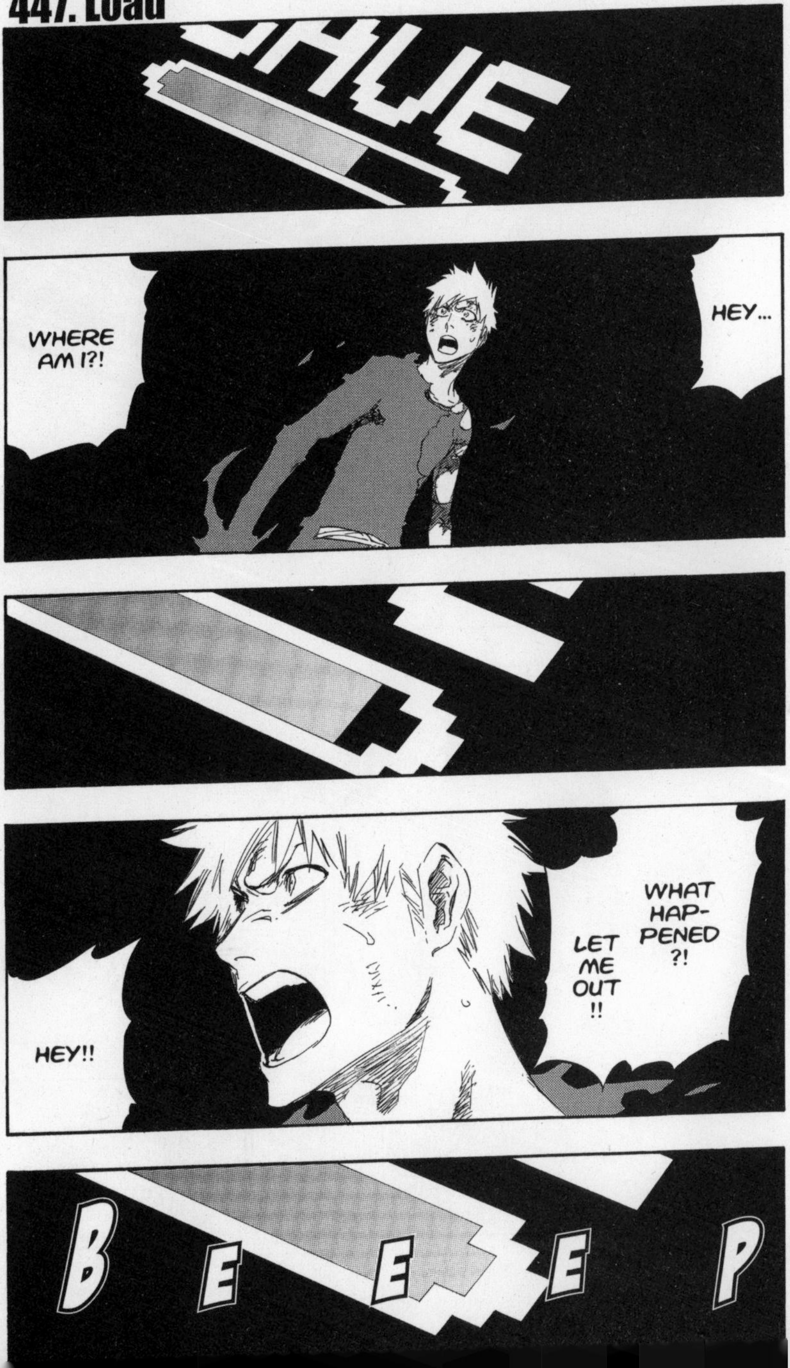
HEY...
WHERE AM I?!
WHAT HAP-PENED?!
LET ME OUT!!
HEY!!
BEEEP

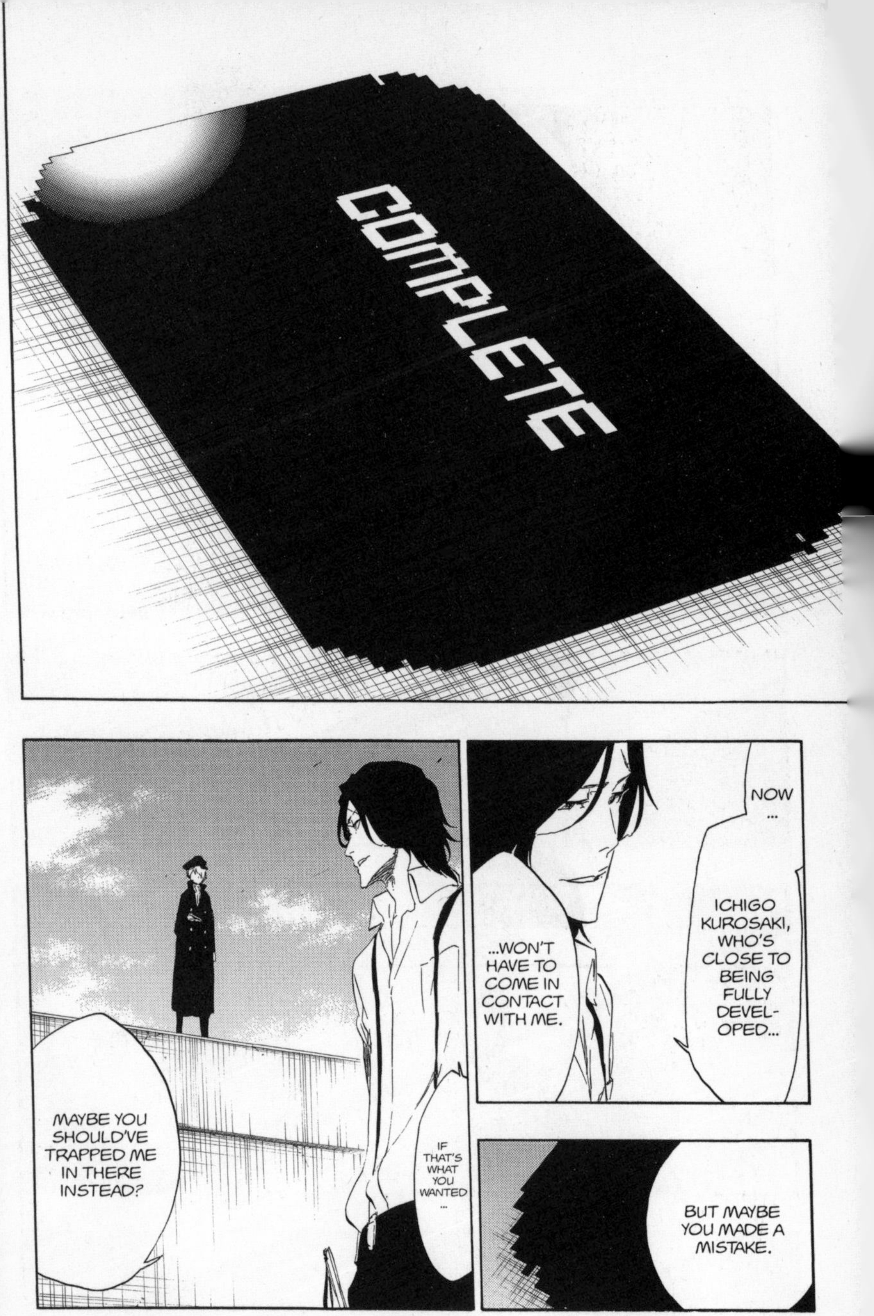
COMPLETE
NOW ...
ICHIGO KUROSAKI, WHO'S CLOSE TO BEING FULLY DEVEL-OPED...
...WON'T HAVE TO COME IN CONTACT WITH ME.
BUT MAYBE YOU MADE A MISTAKE.
IF THAT'S WHAT YOU WANTED ...
MAYBE YOU SHOULD'VE TRAPPED ME IN THERE INSTEAD?

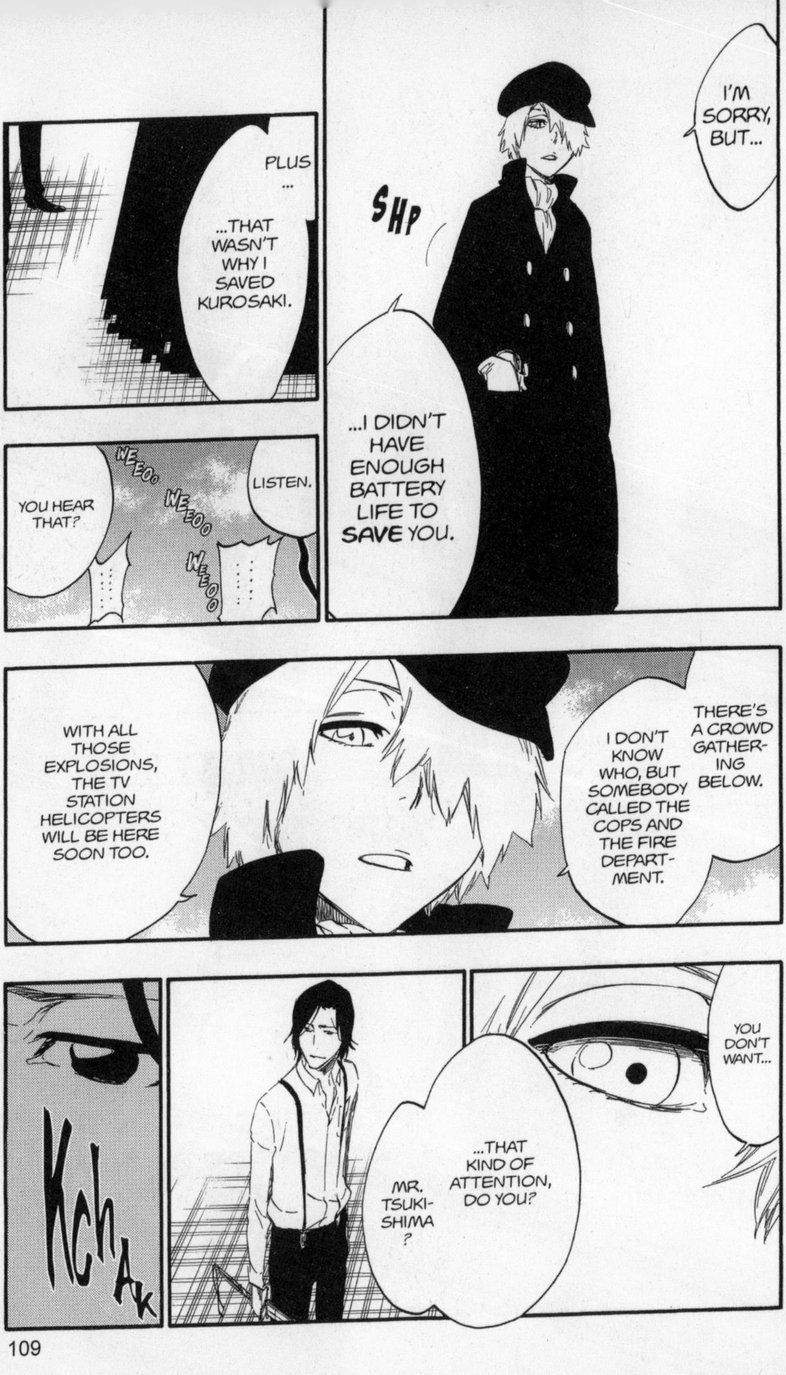
I'M SORRY, BUT...
SHP
...I DIDN'T HAVE ENOUGH BATTERY LIFE TO SAVE YOU.
PLUS... ...THAT WASN'T WHY I SAVED KUROSAKI.
LISTEN.
WEEOO WEEOO WEEOO
YOU HEAR THAT?
THERE'S A CROWD GATHERING BELOW.
I DON'T KNOW WHO, BUT SOMEBODY CALLED THE COPS AND THE FIRE DEPARTMENT.
WITH ALL THOSE EXPLOSIONS, THE TV STATION HELICOPTERS WILL BE HERE SOON TOO.
YOU DON'T WANT...
...THAT KIND OF ATTENTION, DO YOU?
MR. TSUKISHIMA?
KCHAK

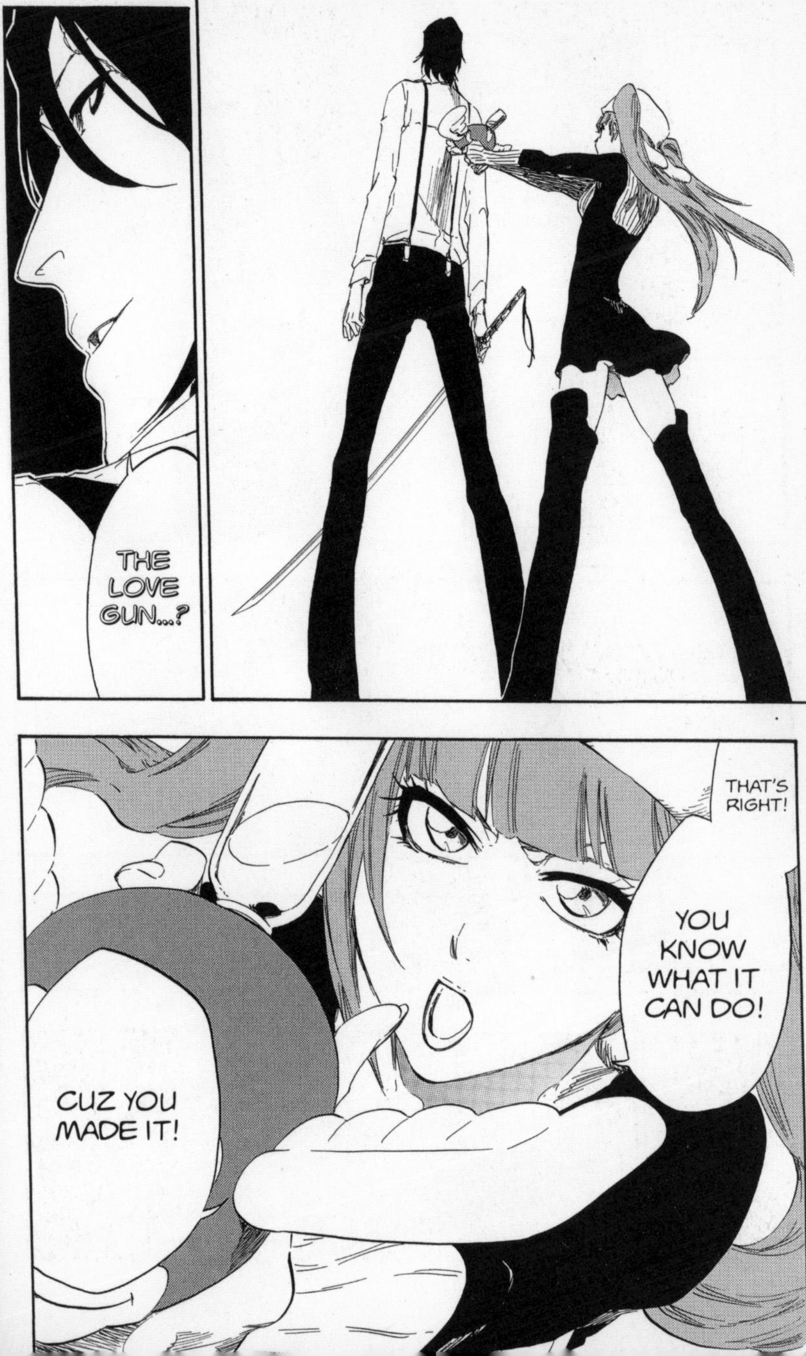
THE LOVE GUN...?
THAT'S RIGHT!
YOU KNOW WHAT IT CAN DO!
CUZ YOU MADE IT!

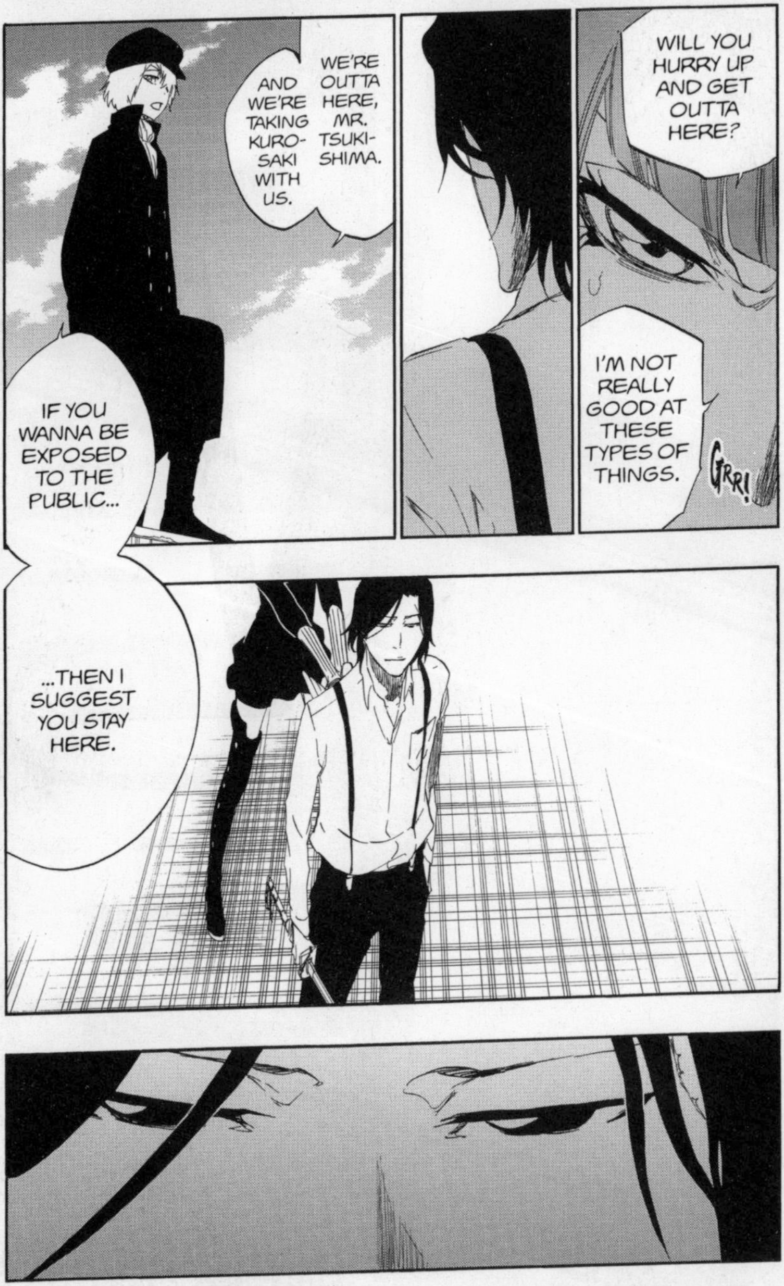
WILL YOU HURRY UP AND GET OUTTA HERE?
I'M NOT REALLY GOOD AT THESE TYPES OF THINGS.
GRR!
WE'RE OUTTA HERE, MR. TSUKISHIMA.
AND WE'RE TAKING KUROSAKI WITH US.
IF YOU WANNA BE EXPOSED TO THE PUBLIC...
...THEN I SUGGEST YOU STAY HERE.

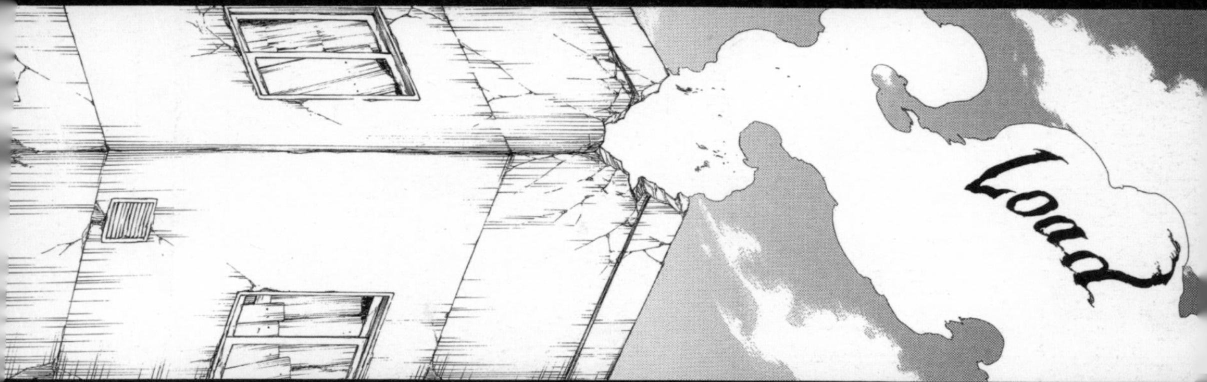
Load

BLEACH 447.

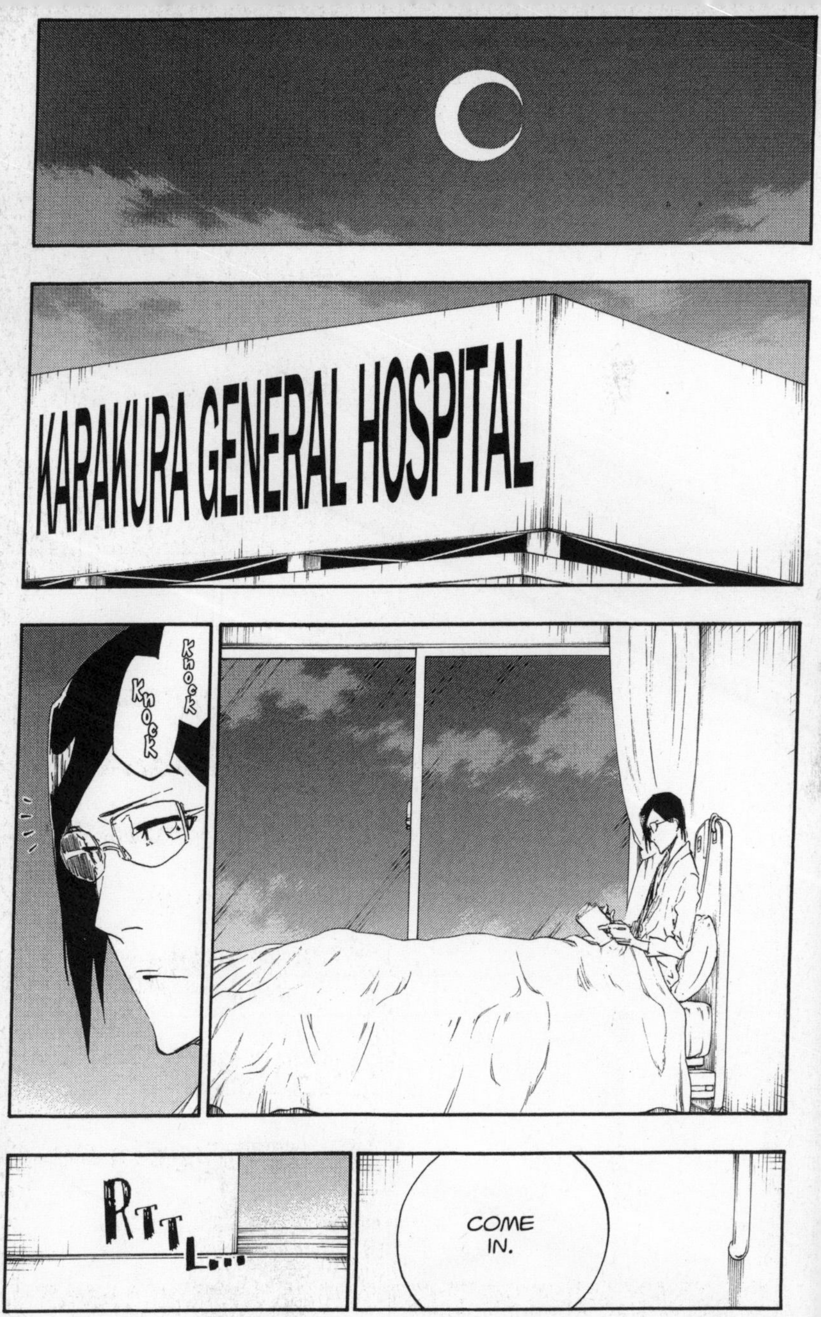
KARAKURA GENERAL HOSPITAL
Knock Knock
COME IN.
RTTL...

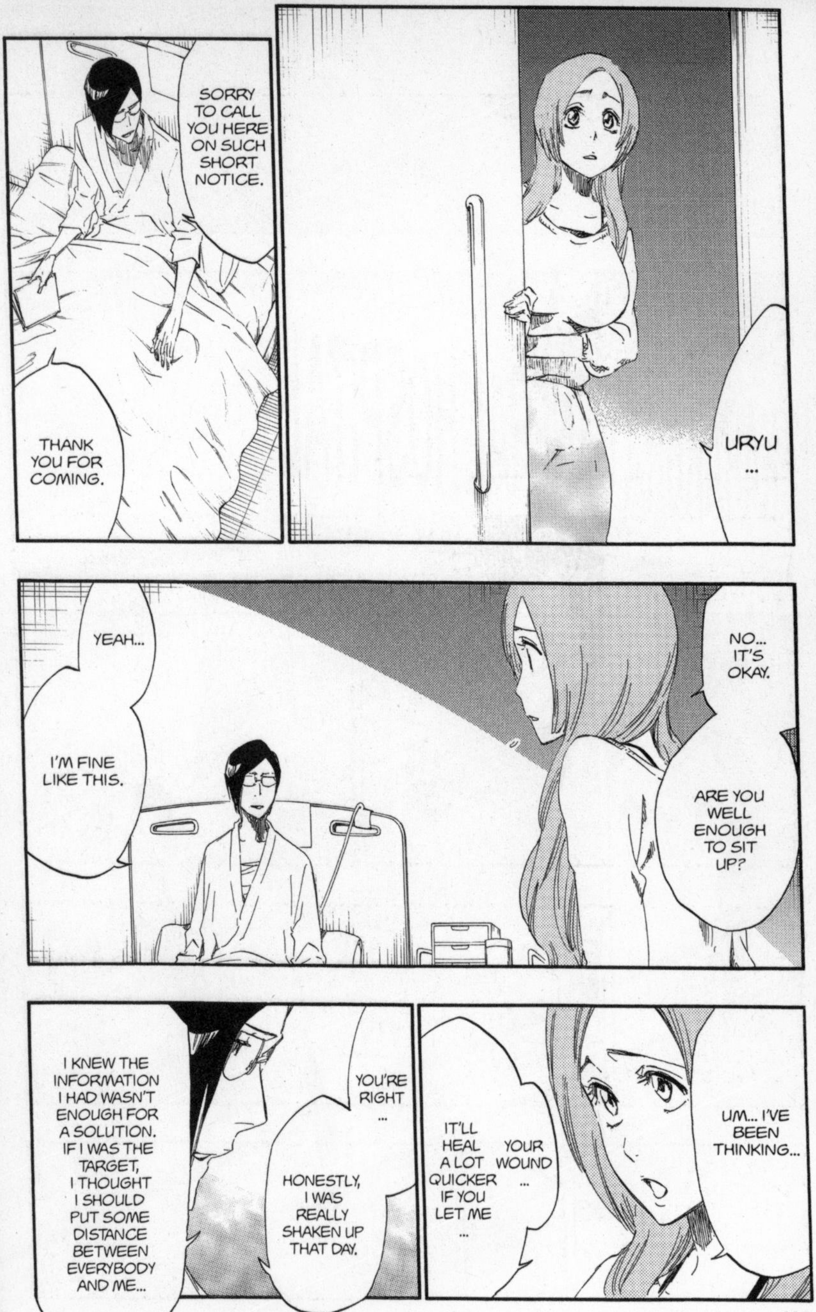
URYU ...
SORRY TO CALL YOU HERE ON SUCH SHORT NOTICE.
THANK YOU FOR COMING.
NO... IT'S OKAY.
ARE YOU WELL ENOUGH TO SIT UP?
YEAH...
I'M FINE LIKE THIS.
UM... I'VE BEEN THINKING...
YOUR WOUND ...
IT'LL HEAL A LOT QUICKER IF YOU LET ME ...
YOU'RE RIGHT ...
HONESTLY, I WAS REALLY SHAKEN UP THAT DAY.
I KNEW THE INFORMATION I HAD WASN'T ENOUGH FOR A SOLUTION. IF I WAS THE TARGET, I THOUGHT I SHOULD PUT SOME DISTANCE BETWEEN EVERYBODY AND ME...

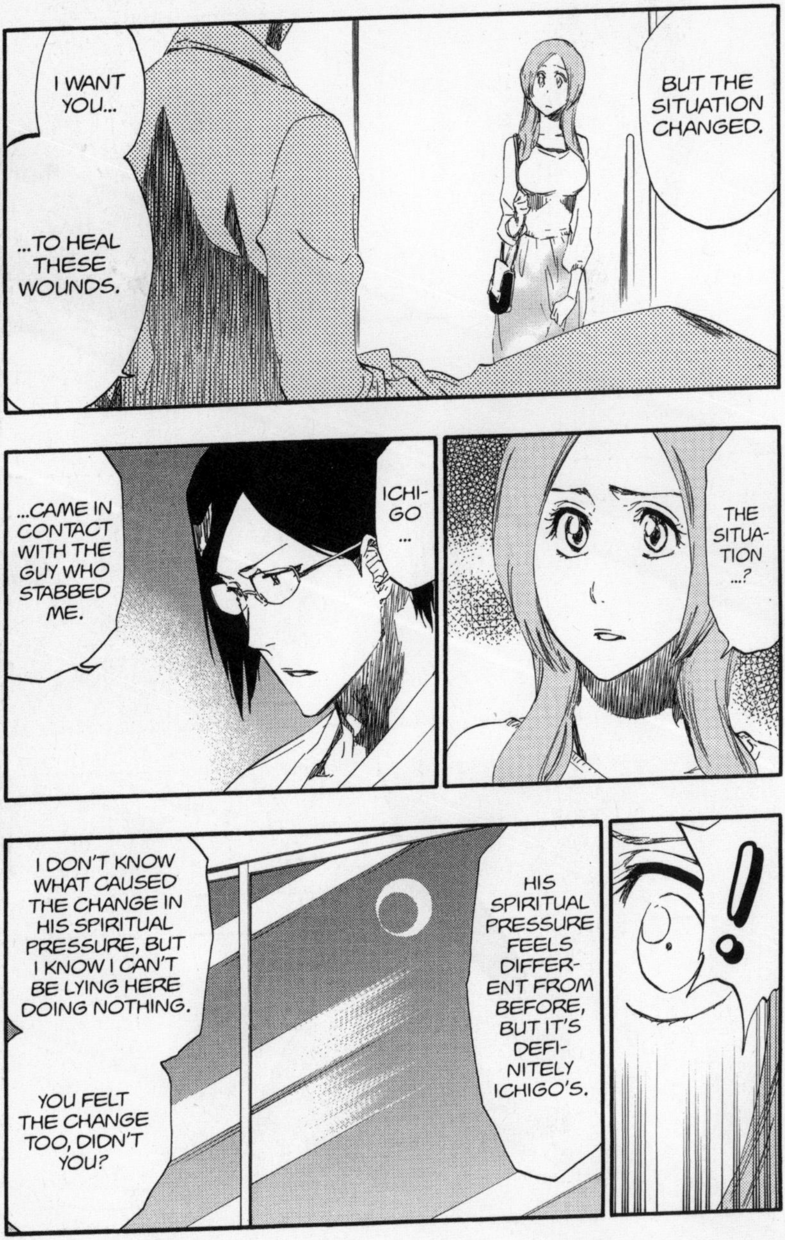
BUT THE SITUATION CHANGED.
I WANT YOU...
...TO HEAL THESE WOUNDS.
THE SITUA-TION ...?
ICHI-GO ...
...CAME IN CONTACT WITH THE GUY WHO STABBED ME.
!!
HIS SPIRITUAL PRESSURE FEELS DIFFER-ENT FROM BEFORE, BUT IT'S DEFI-NITELY ICHIGO'S.
I DON'T KNOW WHAT CAUSED THE CHANGE IN HIS SPIRITUAL PRESSURE, BUT I KNOW I CAN'T BE LYING HERE DOING NOTHING.
YOU FELT THE CHANGE TOO, DIDN'T YOU?

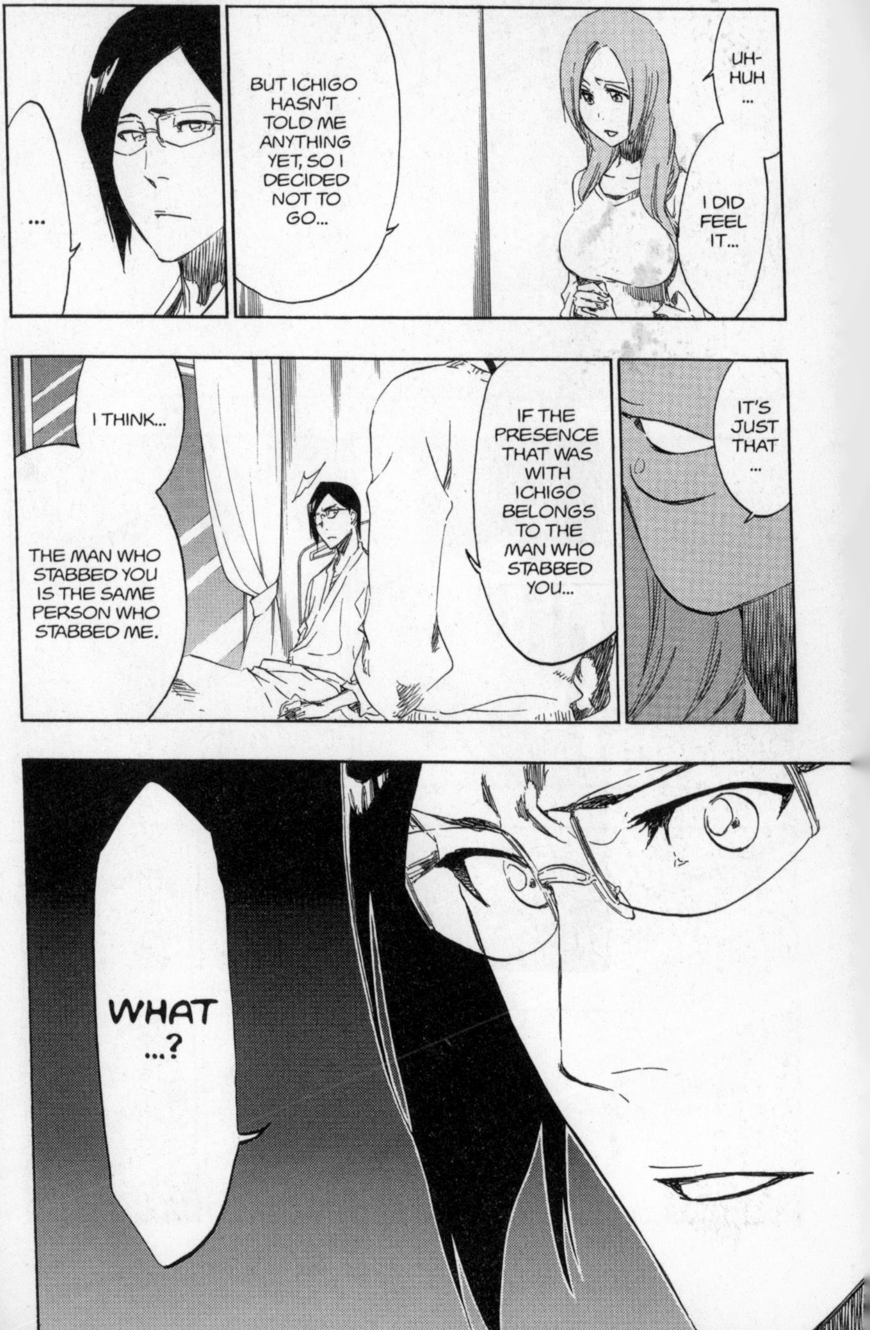
UH-HUH ...
I DID FEEL IT...
BUT ICHIGO HASN'T TOLD ME ANYTHING YET, SO I DECIDED NOT TO GO...
...
IT'S JUST THAT ...
IF THE PRESENCE THAT WAS WITH ICHIGO BELONGS TO THE MAN WHO STABBED YOU...
I THINK...
THE MAN WHO STABBED YOU IS THE SAME PERSON WHO STABBED ME.
WHAT ...?

NOW LOADING···

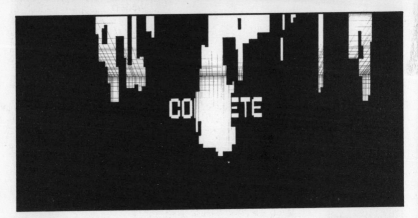

CO   ETE

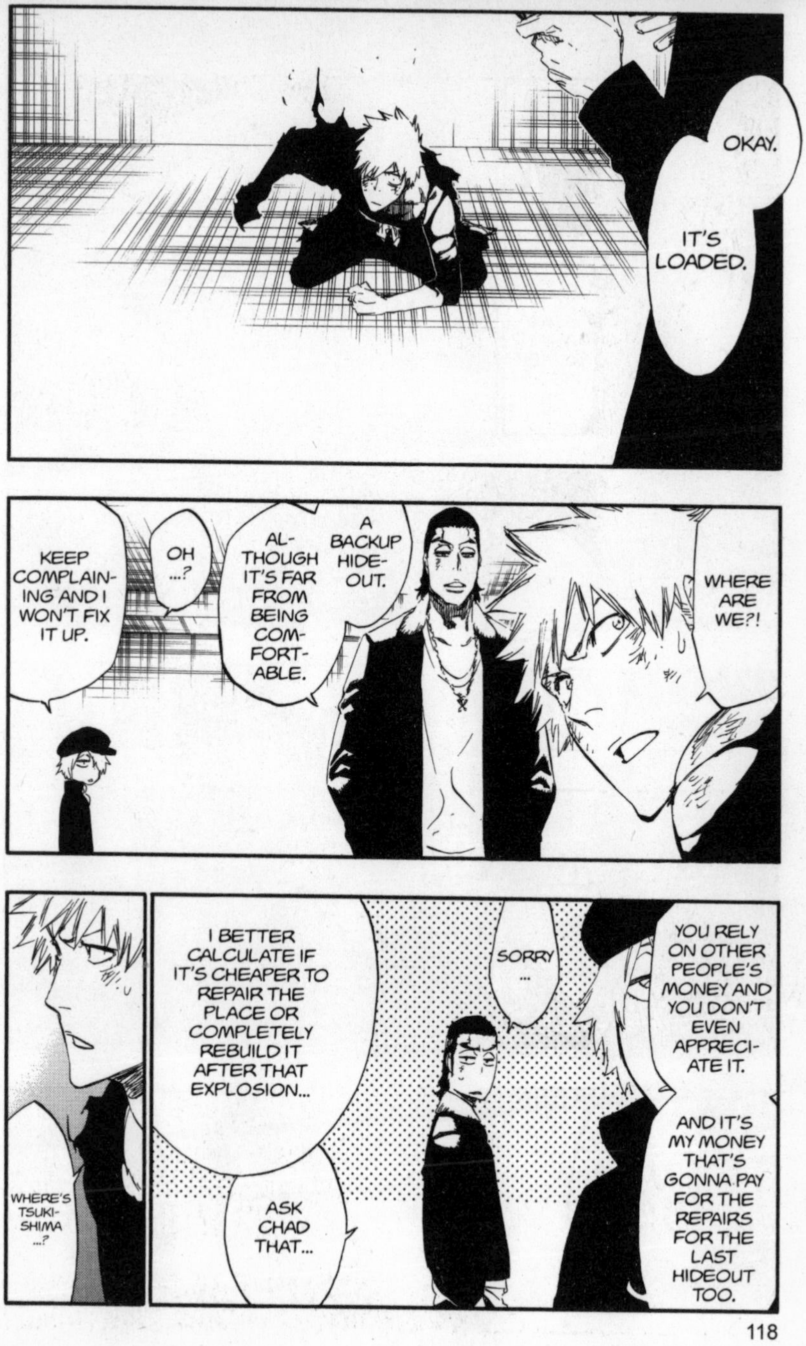
OKAY.
IT'S LOADED.
WHERE ARE WE?!
A BACKUP HIDE-OUT.
AL-THOUGH IT'S FAR FROM BEING COM-FORT-ABLE.
OH ...?
KEEP COMPLAIN-ING AND I WON'T FIX IT UP.
YOU RELY ON OTHER PEOPLE'S MONEY AND YOU DON'T EVEN APPRECI-ATE IT.
AND IT'S MY MONEY THAT'S GONNA PAY FOR THE REPAIRS FOR THE LAST HIDEOUT TOO.
SORRY ...
I BETTER CALCULATE IF IT'S CHEAPER TO REPAIR THE PLACE OR COMPLETELY REBUILD IT AFTER THAT EXPLOSION...
ASK CHAD THAT...
WHERE'S TSUKI-SHIMA ...?

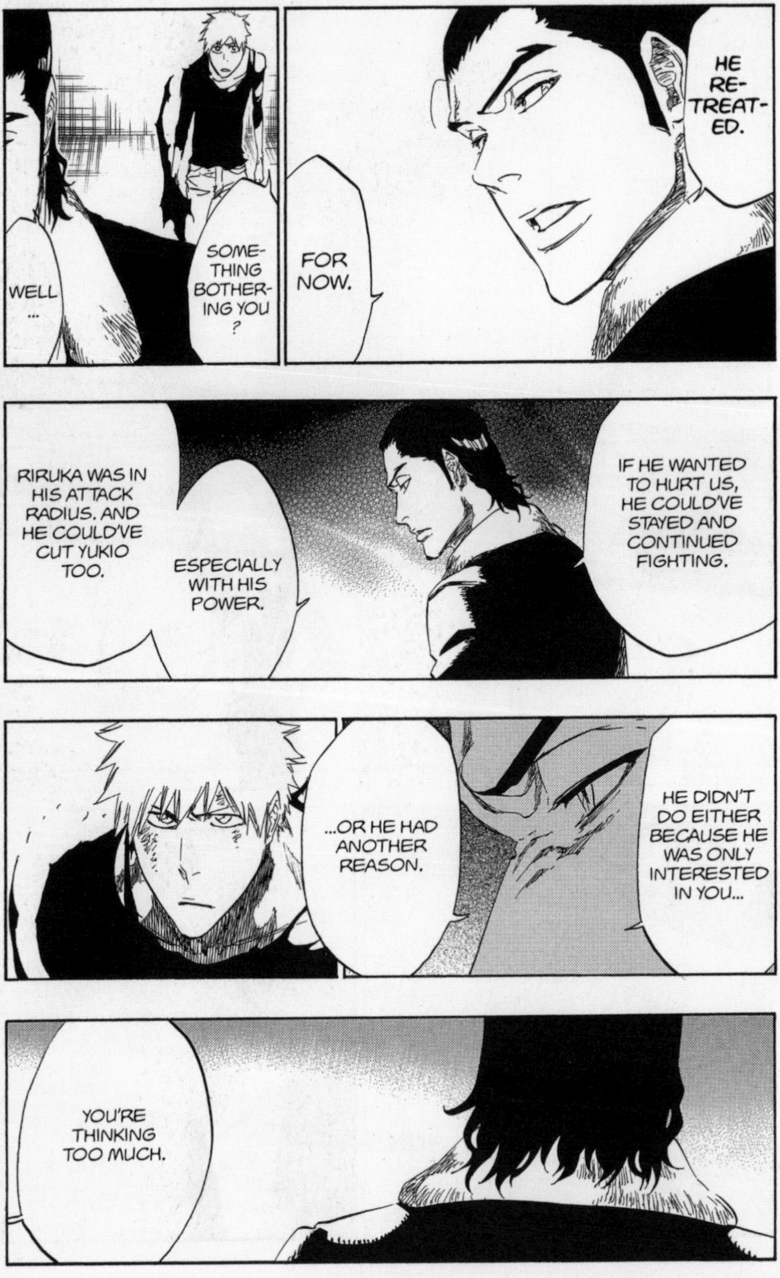
HE RE-TREAT-ED.
FOR NOW.
SOME-THING BOTHER-ING YOU ?
WELL ...
IF HE WANTED TO HURT US, HE COULD'VE STAYED AND CONTINUED FIGHTING.
ESPECIALLY WITH HIS POWER.
RIRUKA WAS IN HIS ATTACK RADIUS. AND HE COULD'VE CUT YUKIO TOO.
HE DIDN'T DO EITHER BECAUSE HE WAS ONLY INTERESTED IN YOU...
...OR HE HAD ANOTHER REASON.
YOU'RE THINKING TOO MUCH.

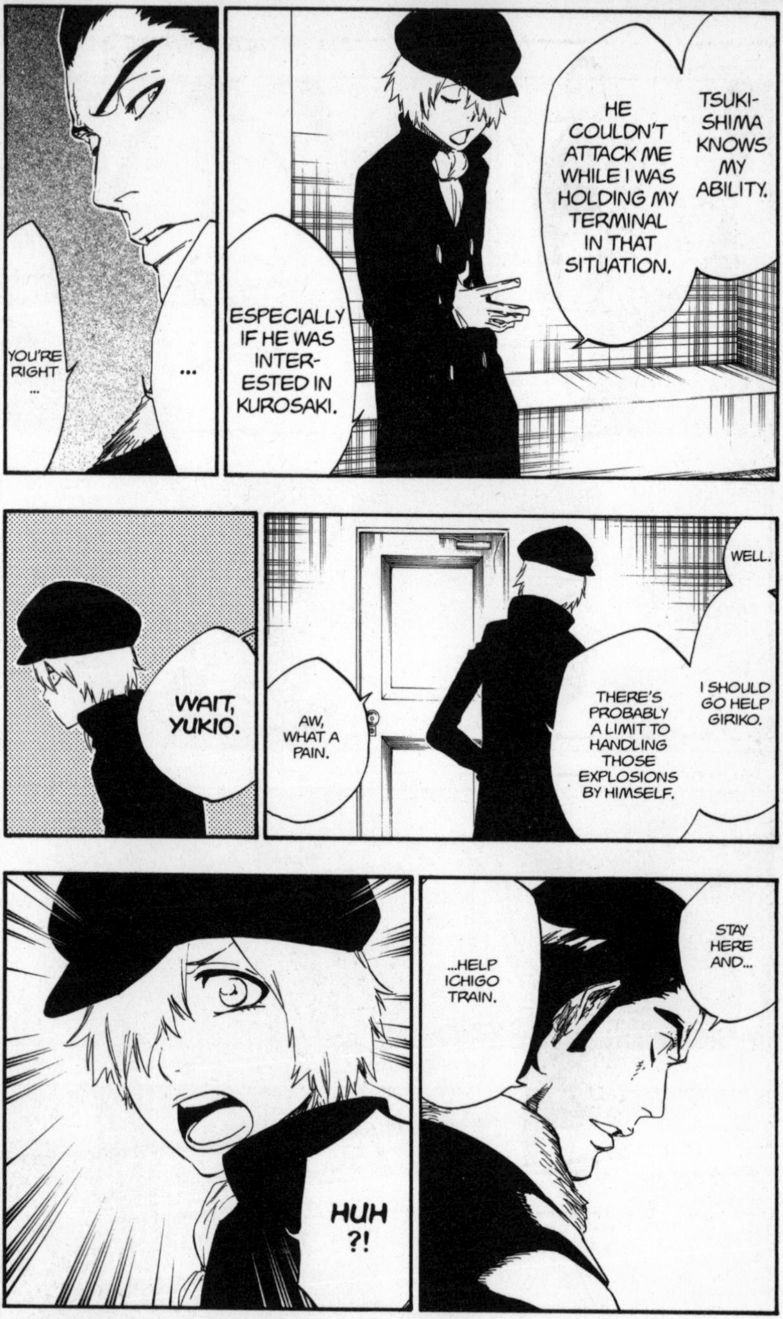
TSUKISHIMA KNOWS MY ABILITY.
HE COULDN'T ATTACK ME WHILE I WAS HOLDING MY TERMINAL IN THAT SITUATION.
ESPECIALLY IF HE WAS INTERESTED IN KUROSAKI.
...
YOU'RE RIGHT ...
WELL.
I SHOULD GO HELP GIRIKO.
THERE'S PROBABLY A LIMIT TO HANDLING THOSE EXPLOSIONS BY HIMSELF.
AW, WHAT A PAIN.
WAIT, YUKIO.
STAY HERE AND...
...HELP ICHIGO TRAIN.
HUH?!

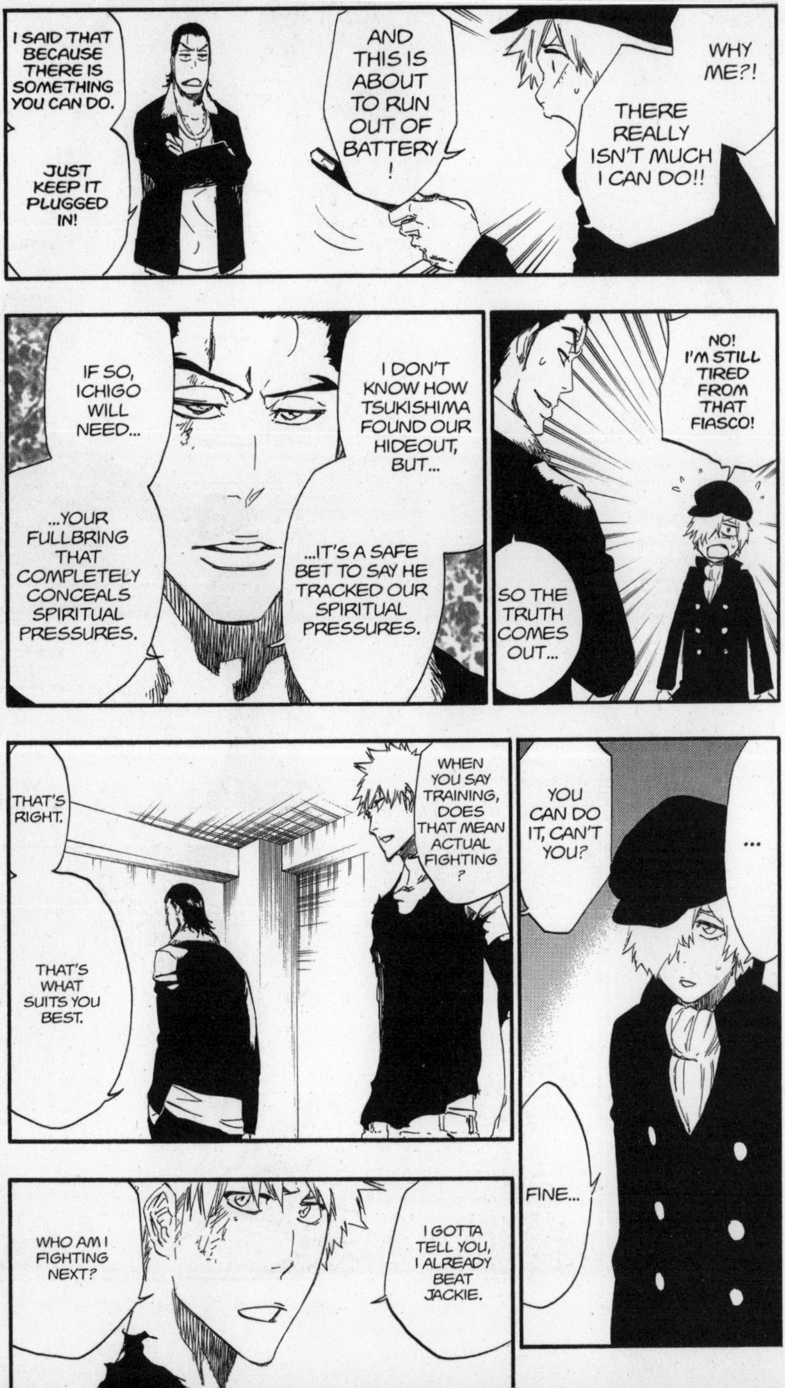
WHY ME?!
THERE REALLY ISN'T MUCH I CAN DO!!
AND THIS IS ABOUT TO RUN OUT OF BATTERY!
I SAID THAT BECAUSE THERE IS SOMETHING YOU CAN DO.
JUST KEEP IT PLUGGED IN!
NO! I'M STILL TIRED FROM THAT FIASCO!
SO THE TRUTH COMES OUT...
I DON'T KNOW HOW TSUKISHIMA FOUND OUR HIDEOUT, BUT...
...IT'S A SAFE BET TO SAY HE TRACKED OUR SPIRITUAL PRESSURES.
IF SO, ICHIGO WILL NEED...
...YOUR FULLBRING THAT COMPLETELY CONCEALS SPIRITUAL PRESSURES.
YOU CAN DO IT, CAN'T YOU?
...
FINE...
WHEN YOU SAY TRAINING, DOES THAT MEAN ACTUAL FIGHTING?
THAT'S RIGHT.
THAT'S WHAT SUITS YOU BEST.
I GOTTA TELL YOU, I ALREADY BEAT JACKIE.
WHO AM I FIGHTING NEXT?

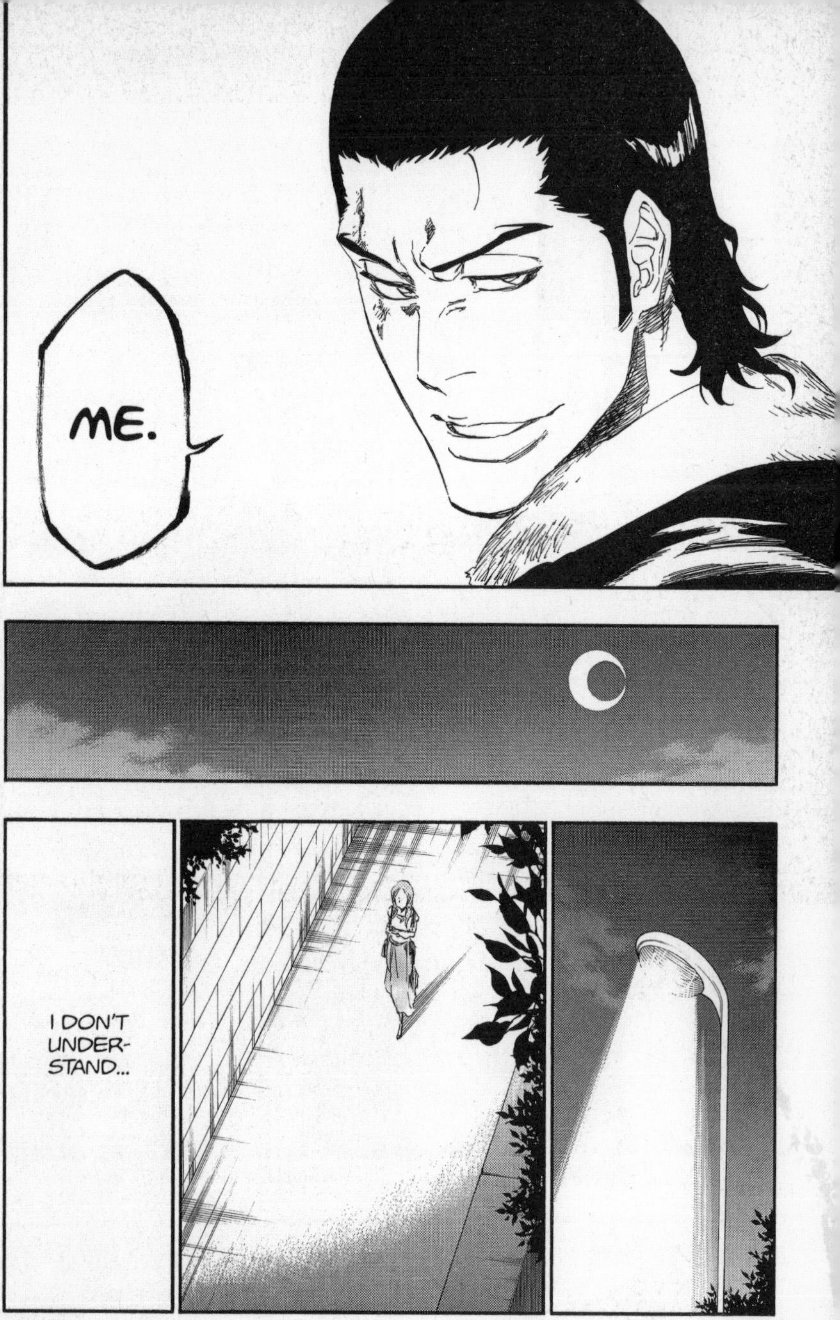
ME.
I DON'T UNDER-STAND...

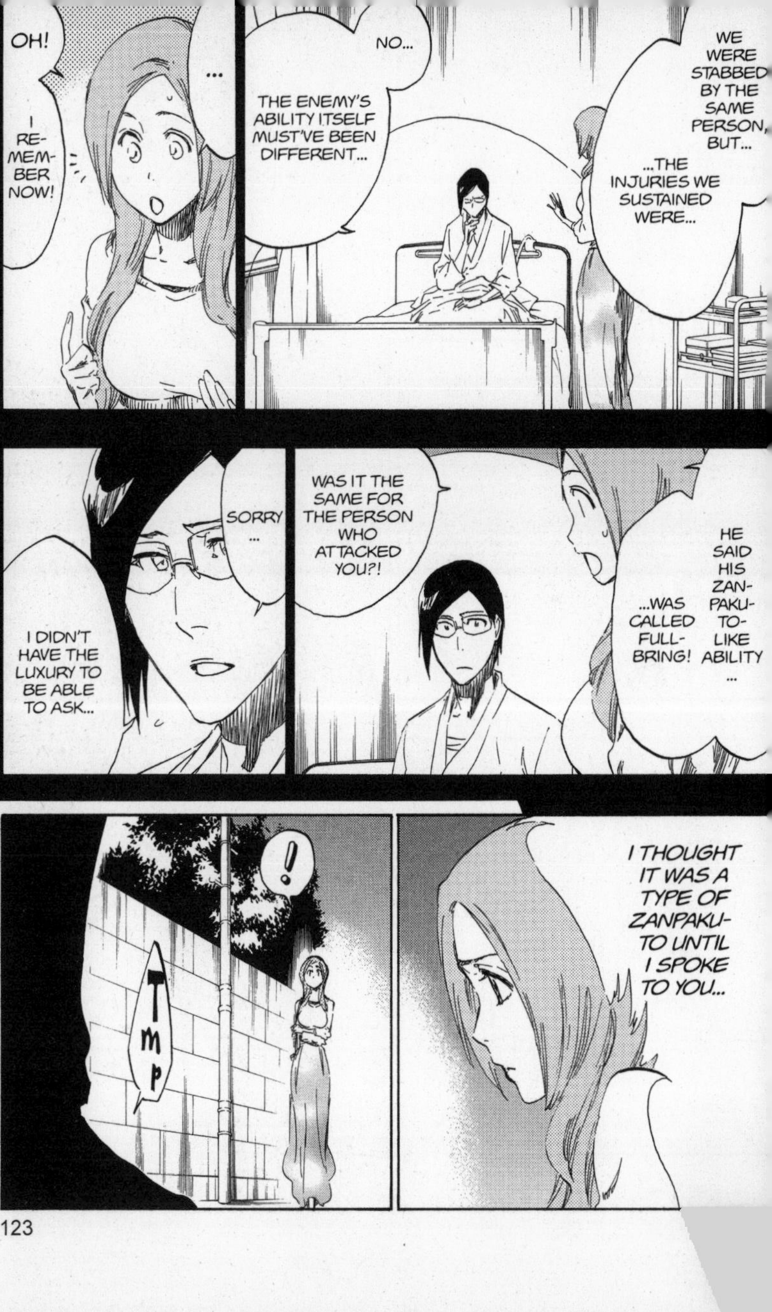
WE WERE STABBED BY THE SAME PERSON, BUT...
...THE INJURIES WE SUSTAINED WERE...
NO...
THE ENEMY'S ABILITY ITSELF MUST'VE BEEN DIFFERENT...
...
OH!
I RE-MEM-BER NOW!
HE SAID HIS ZAN-PAKU-TO-LIKE ABILITY...
...WAS CALLED FULL-BRING!
WAS IT THE SAME FOR THE PERSON WHO ATTACKED YOU?!
SORRY...
I DIDN'T HAVE THE LUXURY TO BE ABLE TO ASK...
I THOUGHT IT WAS A TYPE OF ZANPAKU-TO UNTIL I SPOKE TO YOU...
!
Tmp

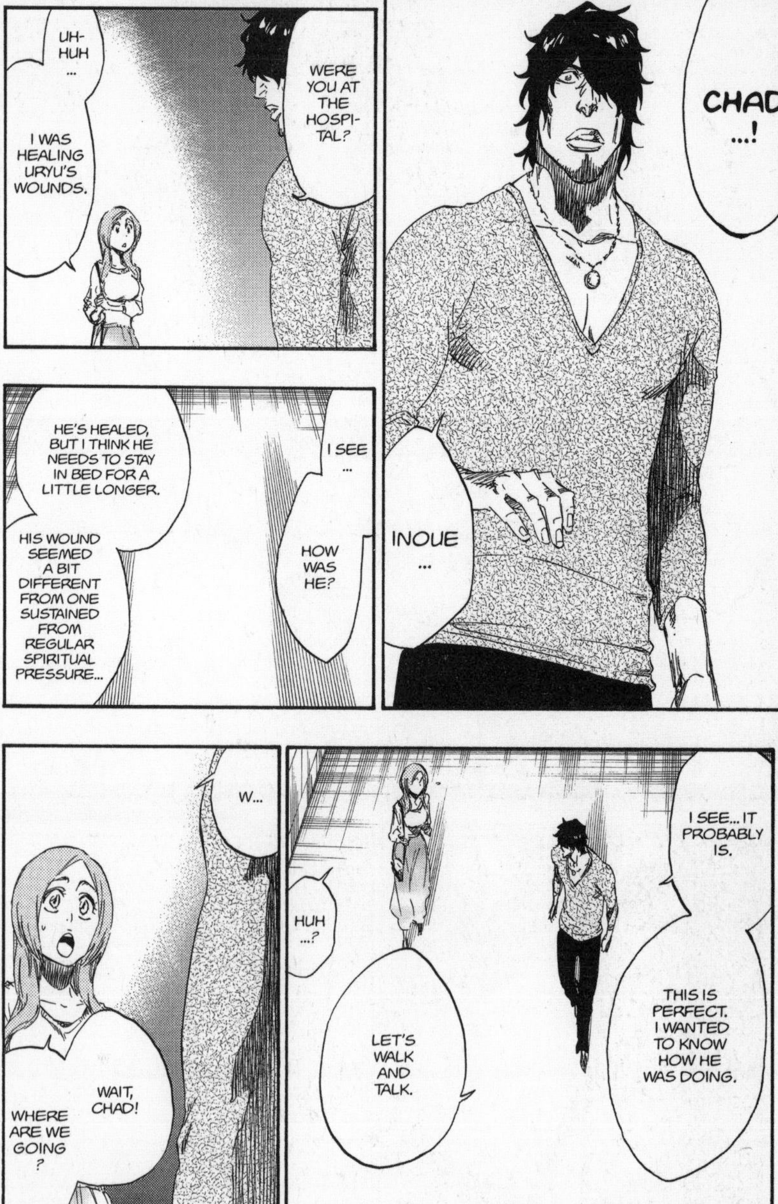
CHAD ...!
INOUE ...
WERE YOU AT THE HOSPITAL?
UH-HUH ...
I WAS HEALING URYU'S WOUNDS.
I SEE ...
HOW WAS HE?
HE'S HEALED, BUT I THINK HE NEEDS TO STAY IN BED FOR A LITTLE LONGER.
HIS WOUND SEEMED A BIT DIFFERENT FROM ONE SUSTAINED FROM REGULAR SPIRITUAL PRESSURE...
I SEE... IT PROBABLY IS.
THIS IS PERFECT. I WANTED TO KNOW HOW HE WAS DOING.
LET'S WALK AND TALK.
HUH ...?
W...
WAIT, CHAD!
WHERE ARE WE GOING ?

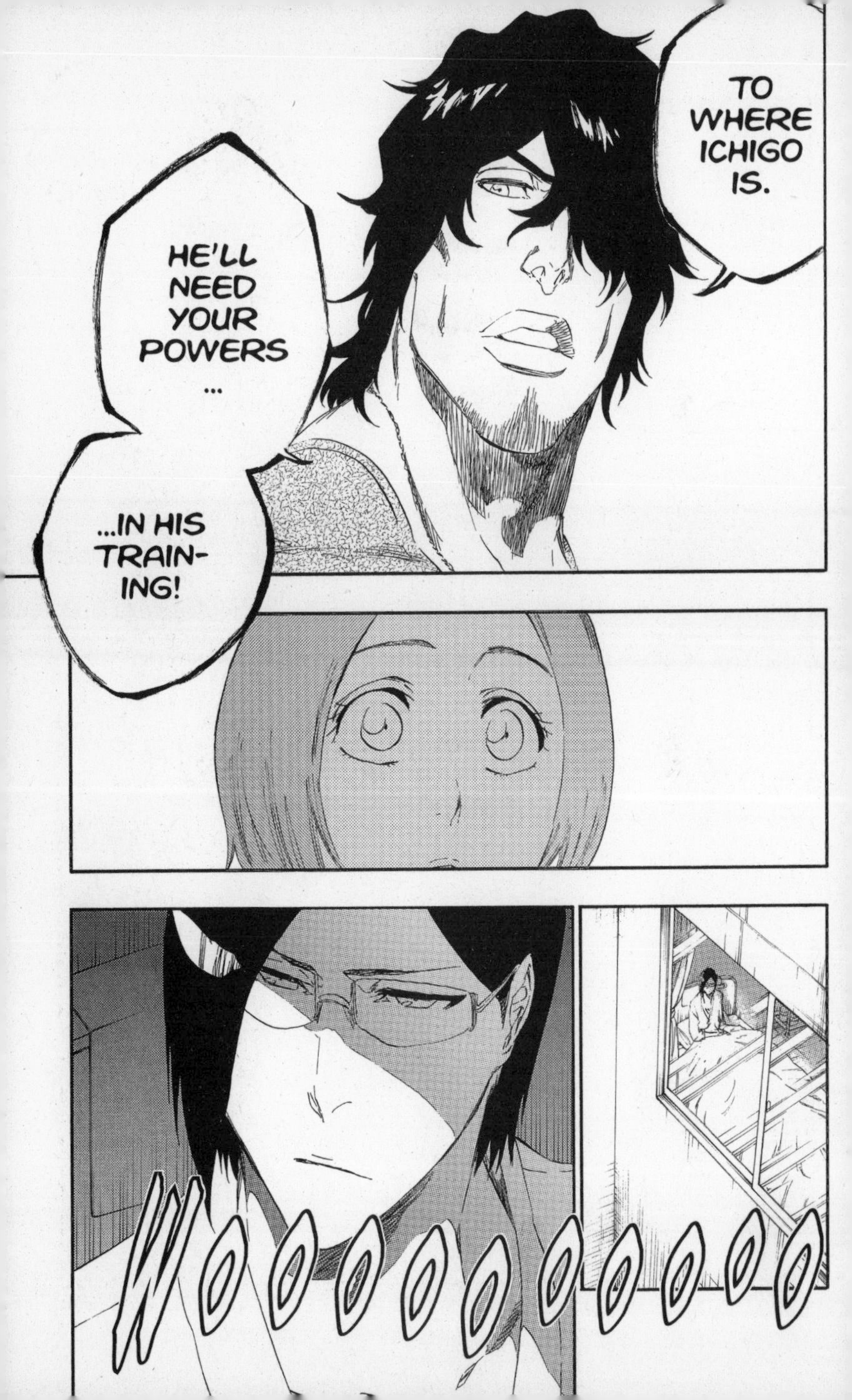
TO WHERE ICHIGO IS.
HE'LL NEED YOUR POWERS...
...IN HIS TRAIN-ING!
WOOOOOOOOOOOO

448. LOADING TO LIE

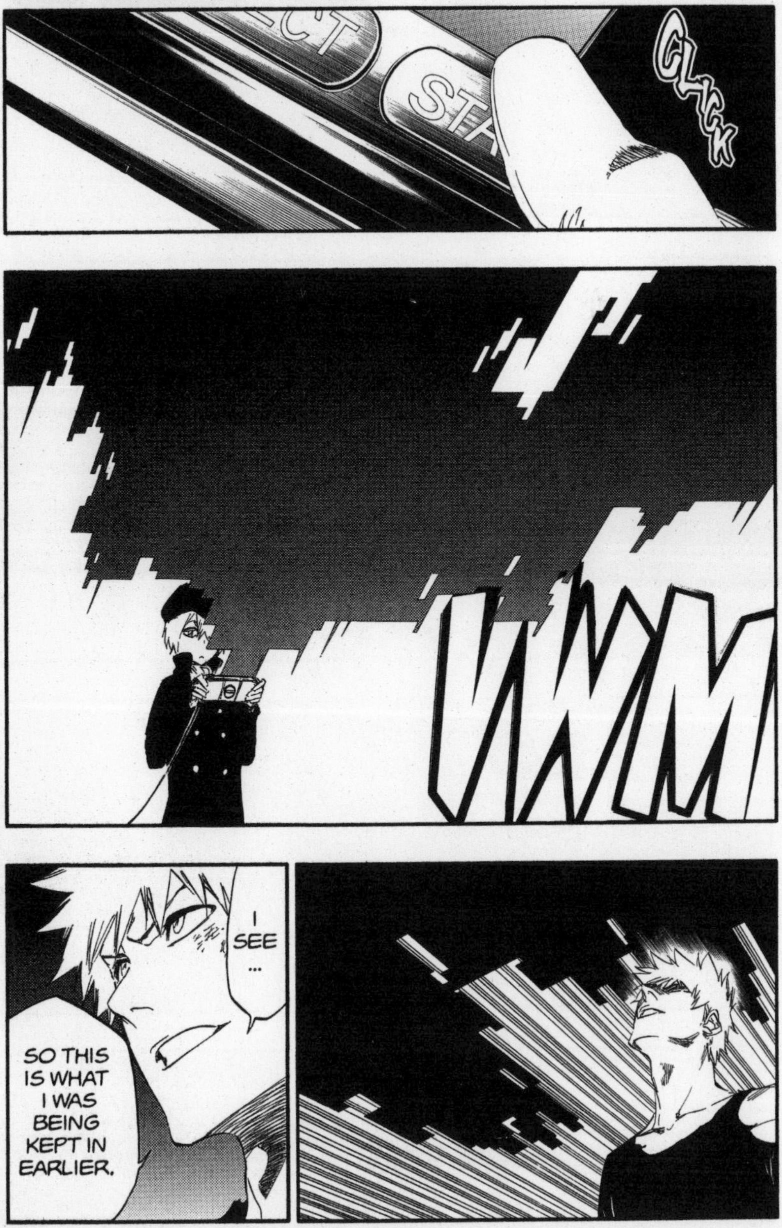
CLICK
VWM
I SEE ...
SO THIS IS WHAT I WAS BEING KEPT IN EARLIER.

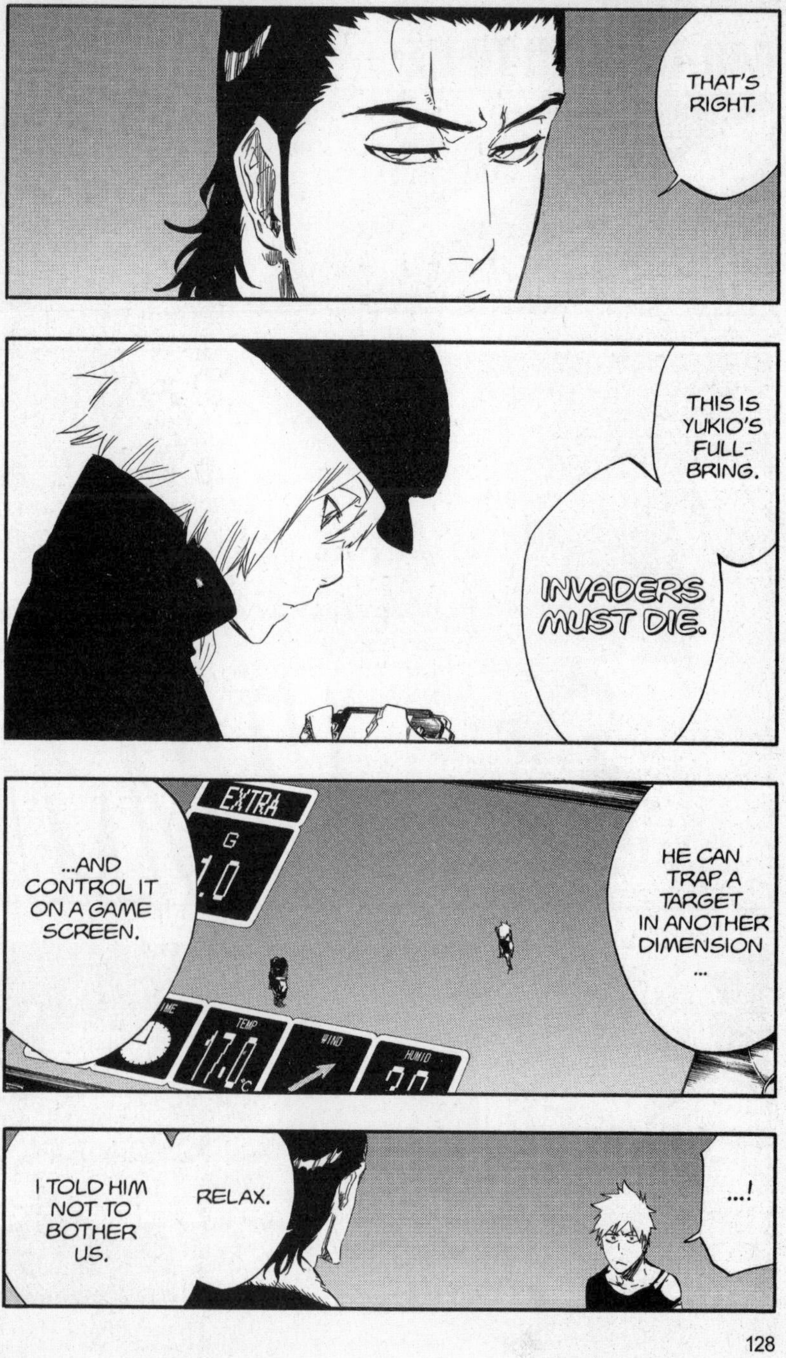
THAT'S RIGHT.
THIS IS YUKIO'S FULL-BRING.
INVADERS MUST DIE.
HE CAN TRAP A TARGET IN ANOTHER DIMENSION ...
...AND CONTROL IT ON A GAME SCREEN.
EXTRA
G
TEMP
17.0 °C
WIND
...!
RELAX.
I TOLD HIM NOT TO BOTHER US.

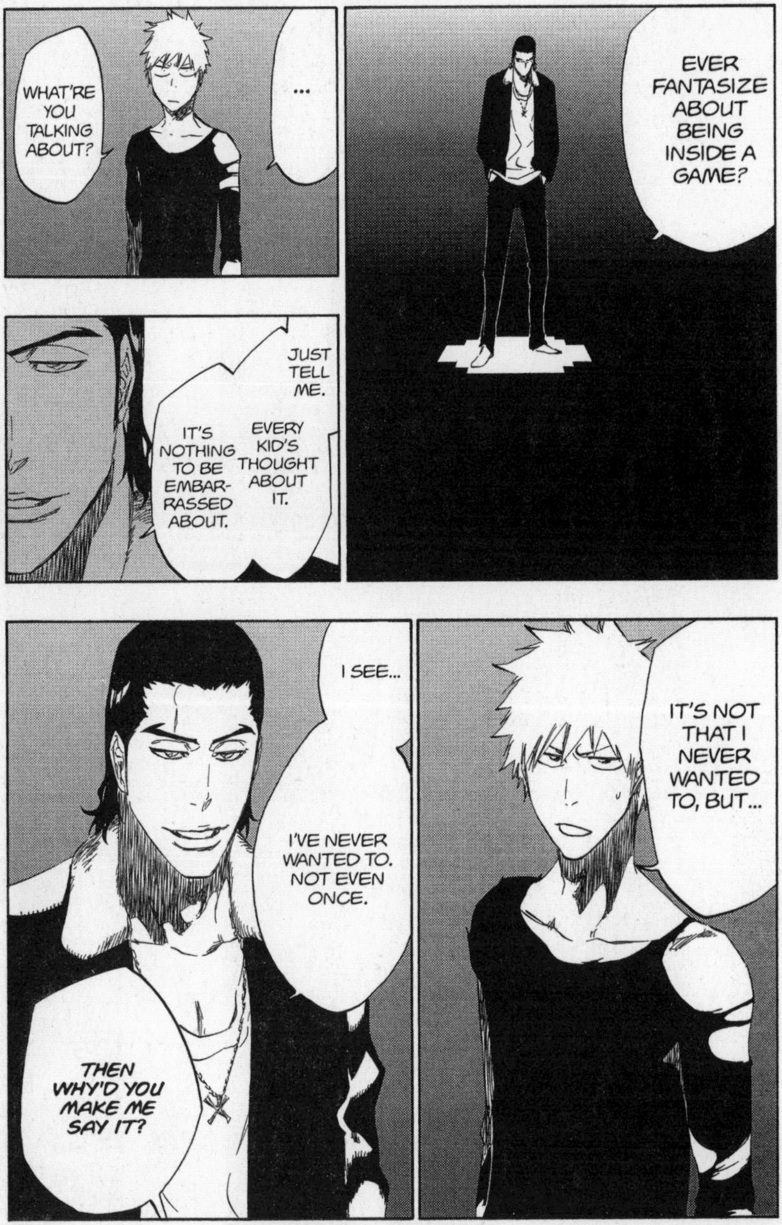
EVER FANTASIZE ABOUT BEING INSIDE A GAME?
...
WHAT'RE YOU TALKING ABOUT?
JUST TELL ME.
EVERY KID'S THOUGHT ABOUT IT.
IT'S NOTHING TO BE EMBARRASSED ABOUT.
IT'S NOT THAT I NEVER WANTED TO, BUT...
I SEE...
I'VE NEVER WANTED TO. NOT EVEN ONCE.
THEN WHY'D YOU MAKE ME SAY IT?

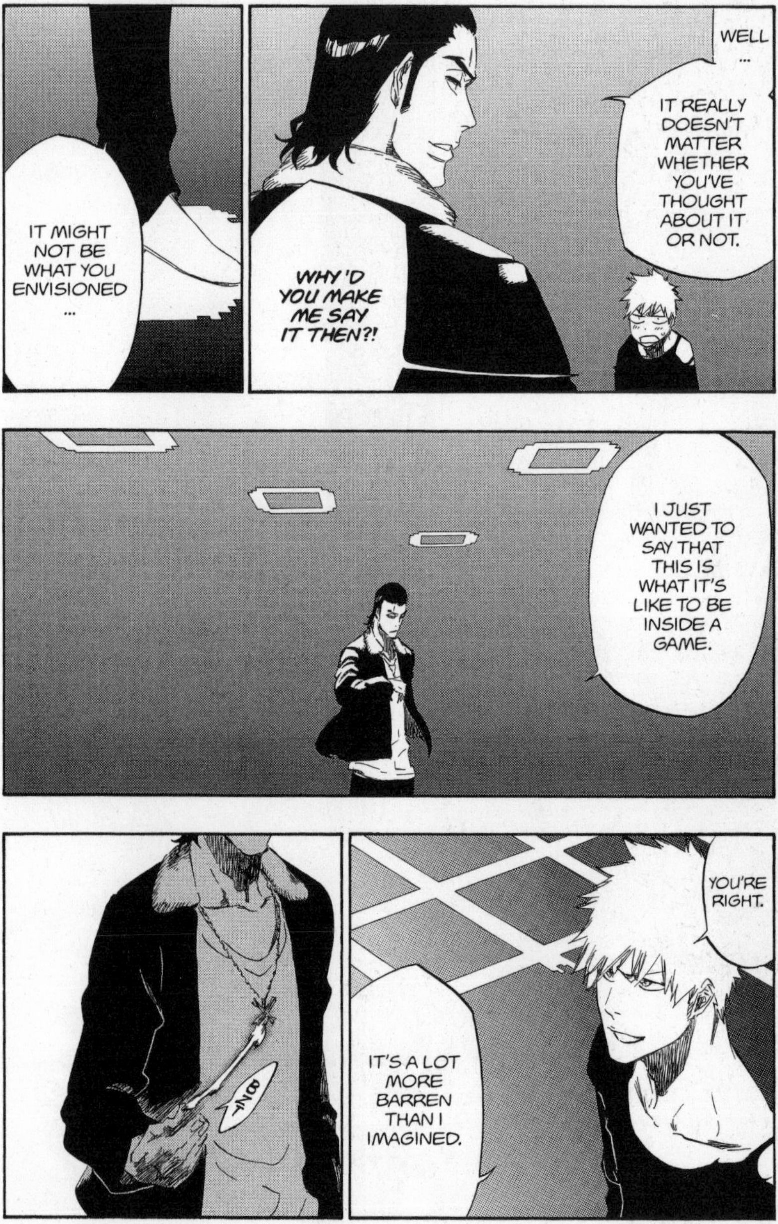
WELL ...
IT REALLY DOESN'T MATTER WHETHER YOU'VE THOUGHT ABOUT IT OR NOT.
WHY'D YOU MAKE ME SAY IT THEN?!
IT MIGHT NOT BE WHAT YOU ENVISIONED ...
I JUST WANTED TO SAY THAT THIS IS WHAT IT'S LIKE TO BE INSIDE A GAME.
YOU'RE RIGHT.
IT'S A LOT MORE BARREN THAN I IMAGINED.
BONK

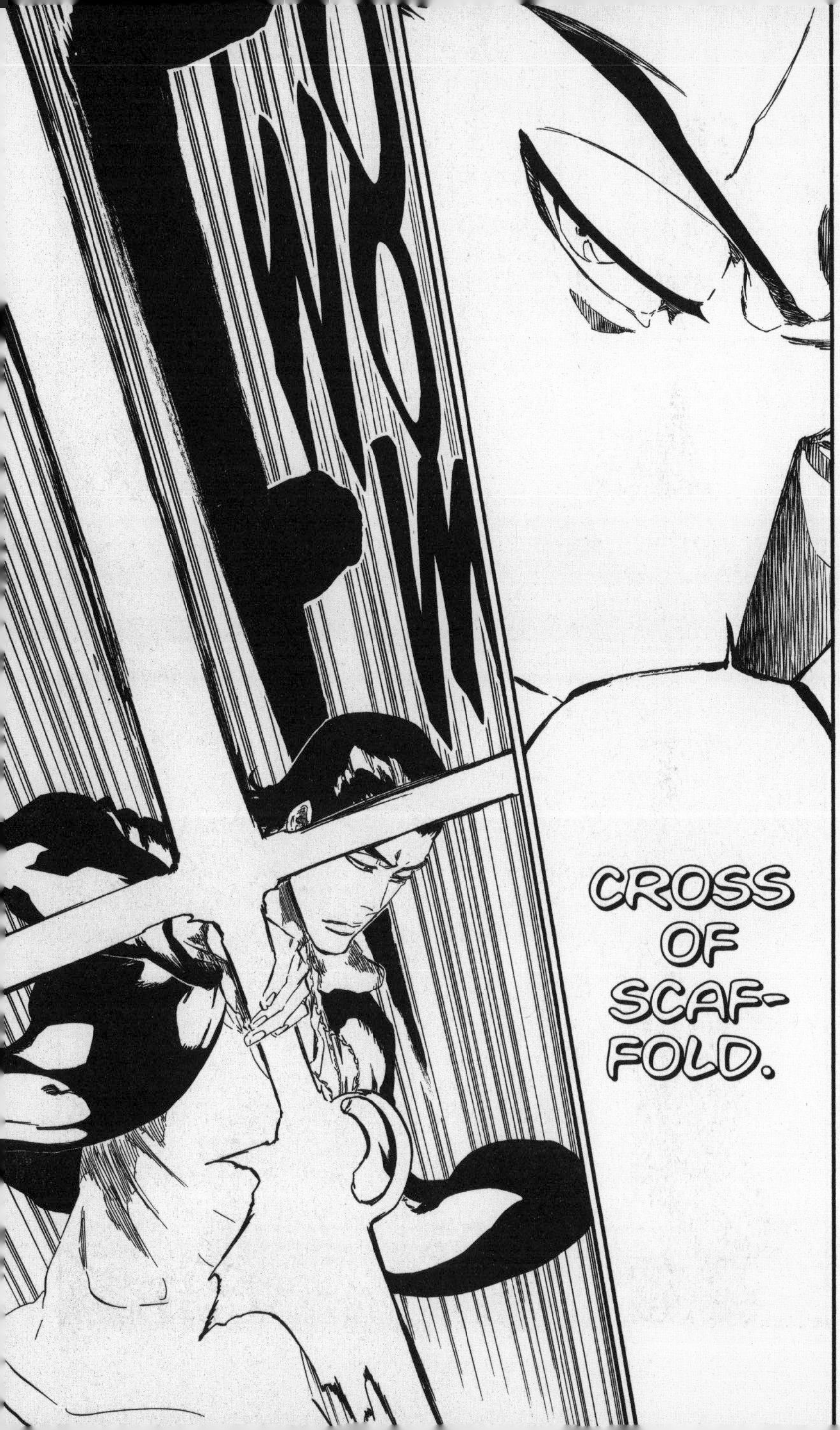
CROSS OF SCAF-FOLD.

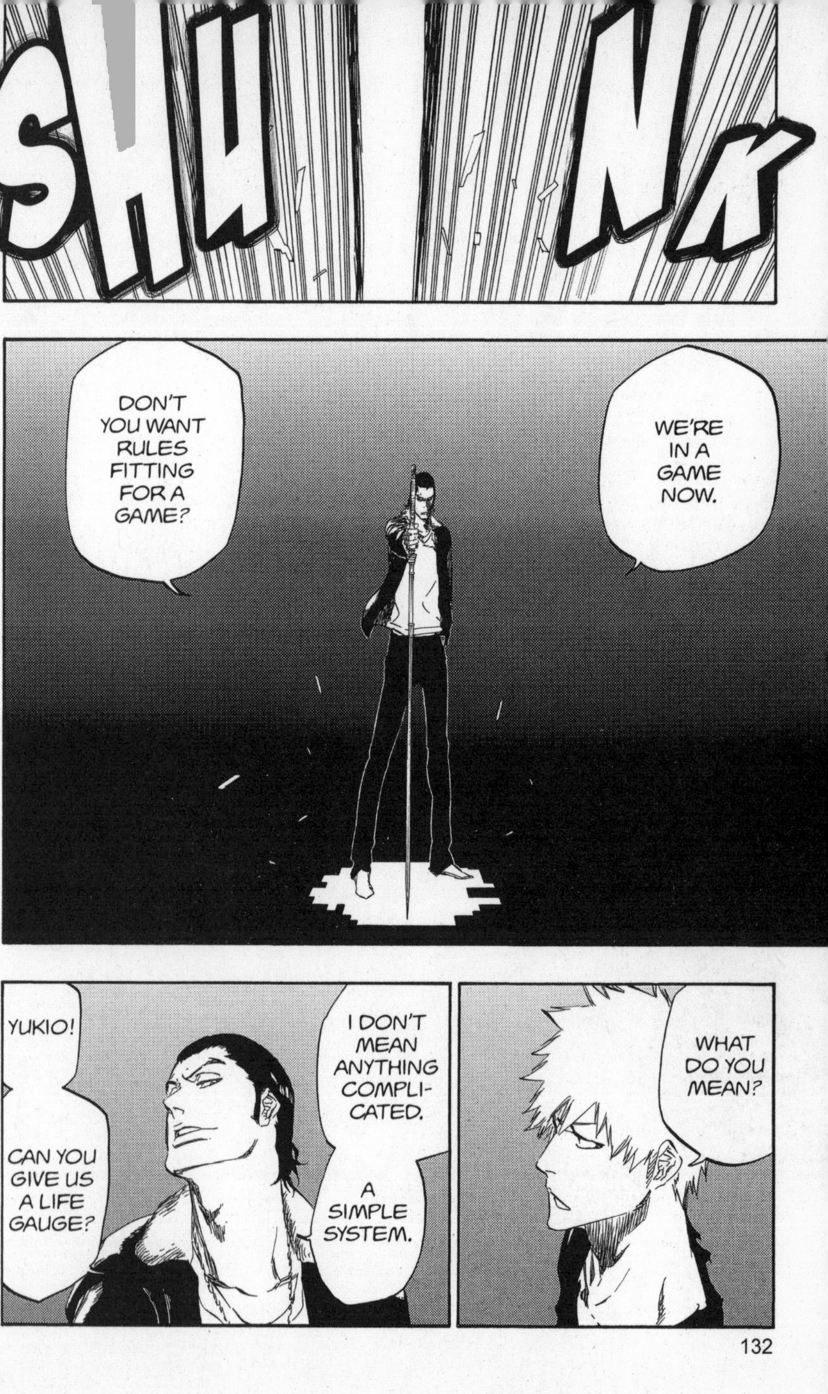
SHH NK
WE'RE IN A GAME NOW.
DON'T YOU WANT RULES FITTING FOR A GAME?
WHAT DO YOU MEAN?
I DON'T MEAN ANYTHING COMPLICATED.
A SIMPLE SYSTEM.
YUKIO!
CAN YOU GIVE US A LIFE GAUGE?

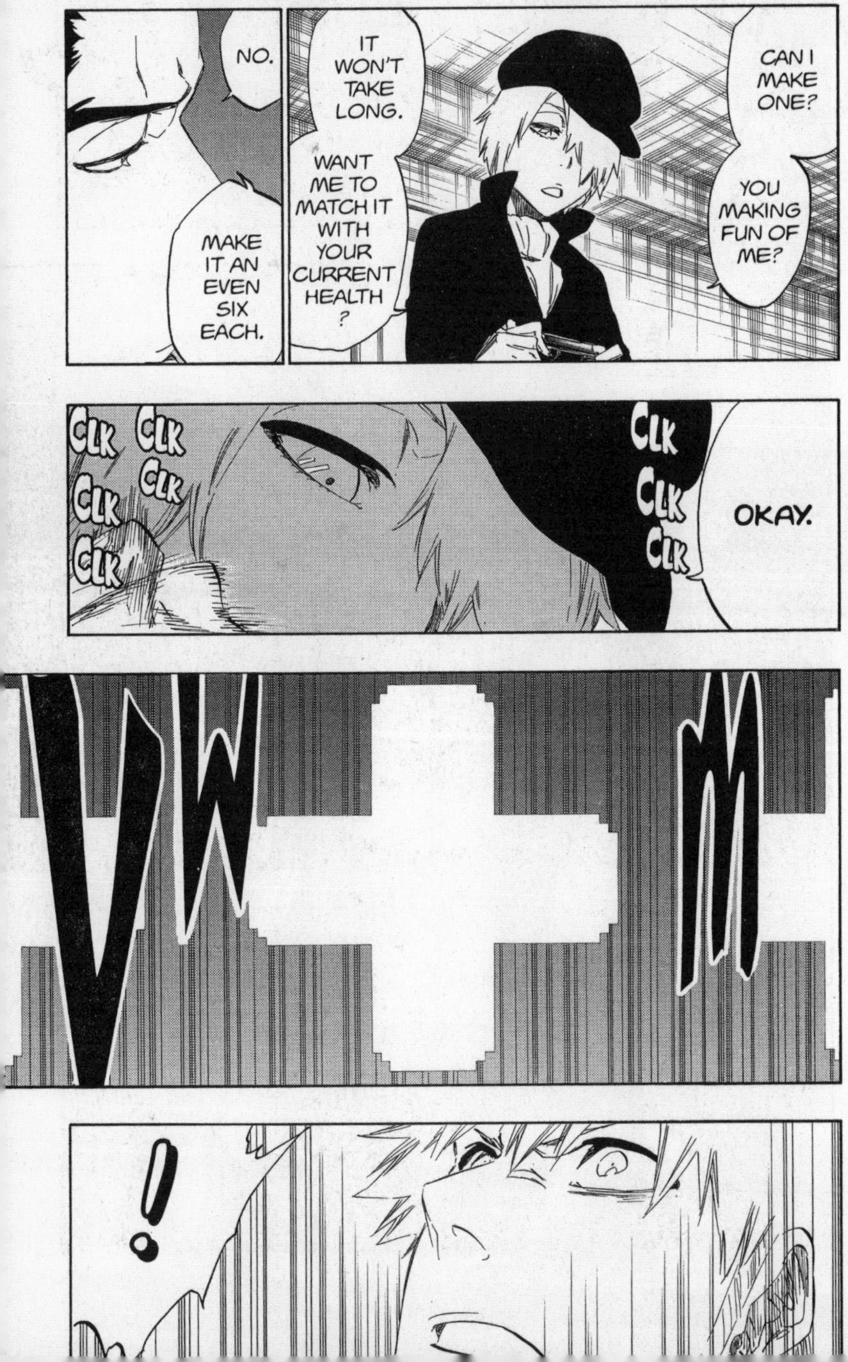

CAN I MAKE ONE?
YOU MAKING FUN OF ME?
IT WON'T TAKE LONG.
WANT ME TO MATCH IT WITH YOUR CURRENT HEALTH?
NO.
MAKE IT AN EVEN SIX EACH.
CLK CLK CLK
OKAY.
CLK CLK CLK CLK CLK
VWM
!

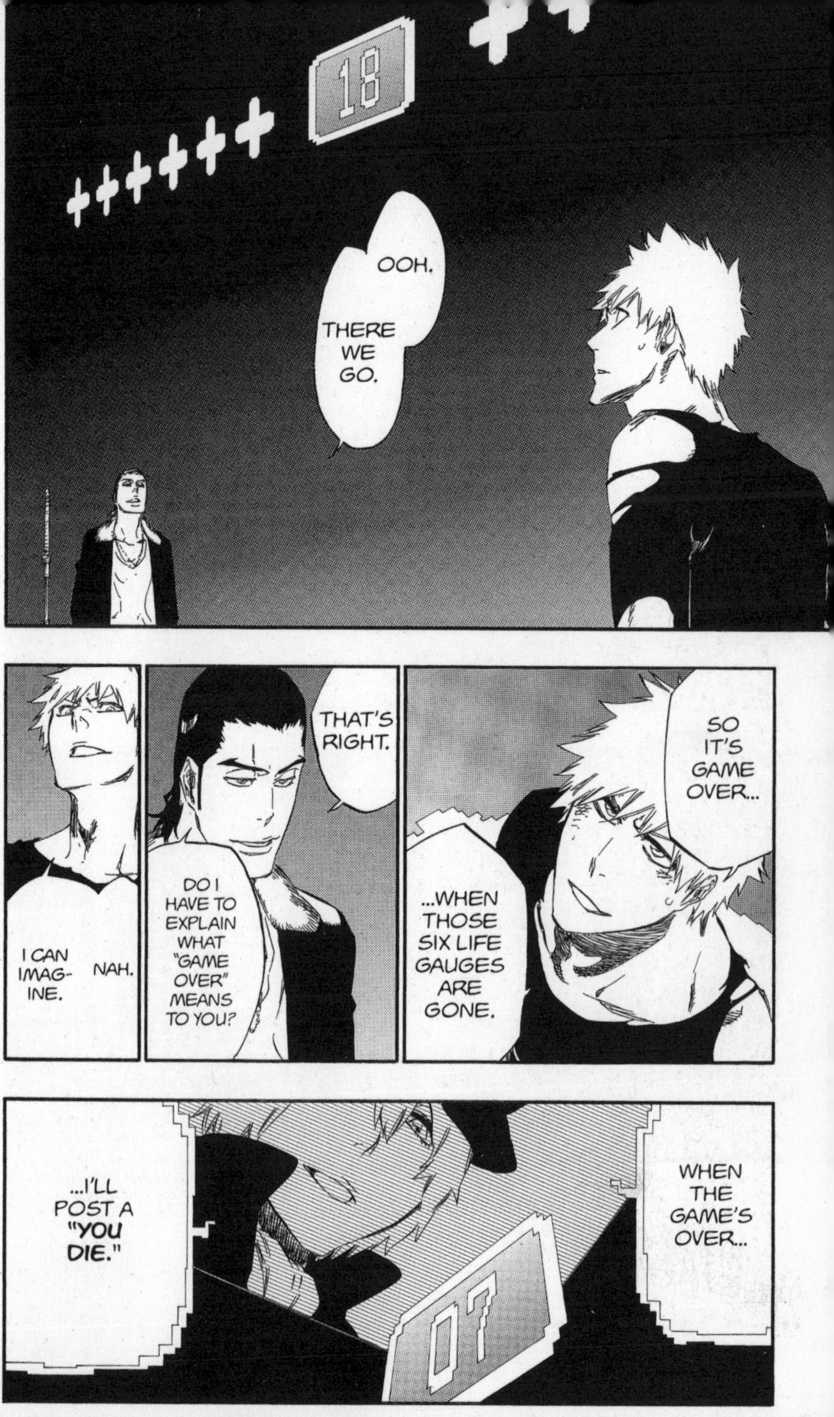
18
OOH.
THERE WE GO.
SO IT'S GAME OVER...
...WHEN THOSE SIX LIFE GAUGES ARE GONE.
THAT'S RIGHT.
DO I HAVE TO EXPLAIN WHAT "GAME OVER" MEANS TO YOU?
NAH.
I CAN IMAGINE.
WHEN THE GAME'S OVER...
...I'LL POST A **"YOU DIE."**
07

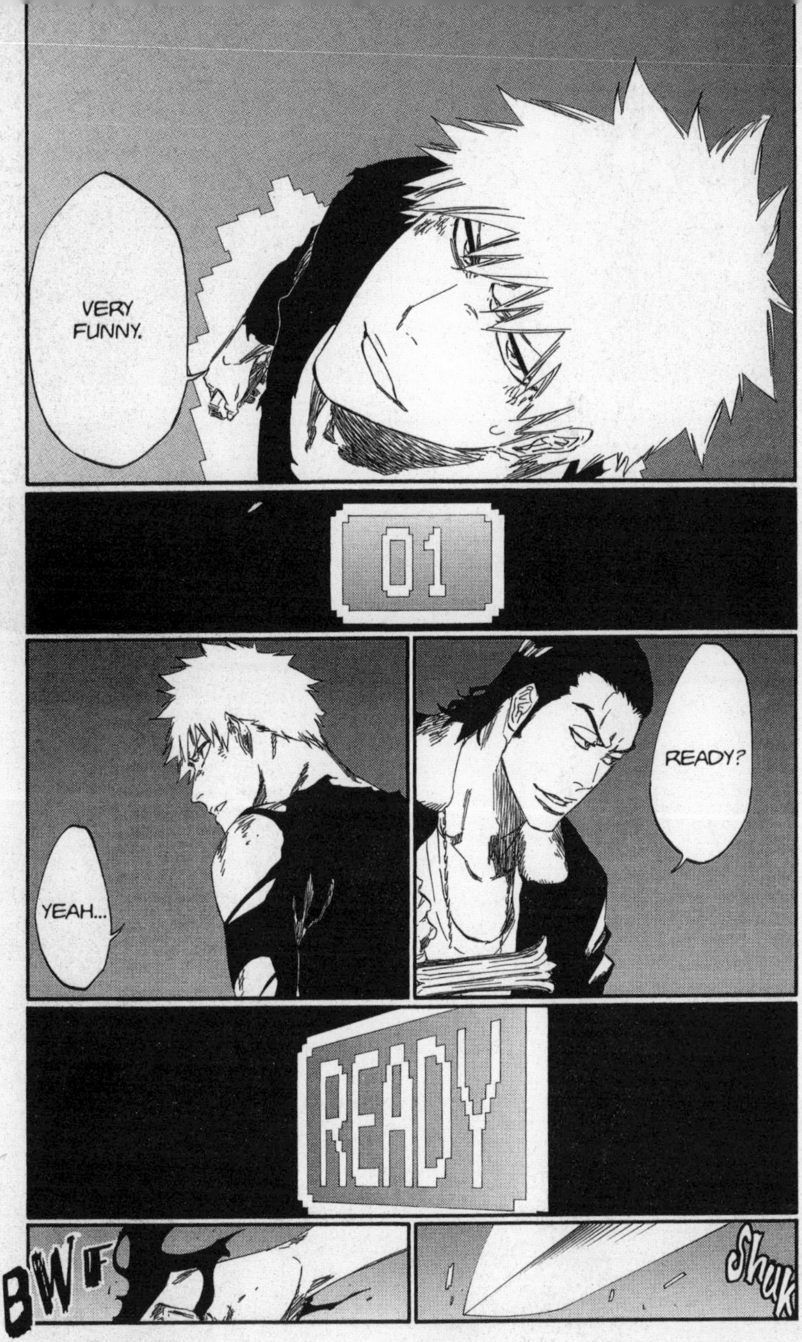
VERY FUNNY.
01
READY?
YEAH...
READY
Shuk
BWF

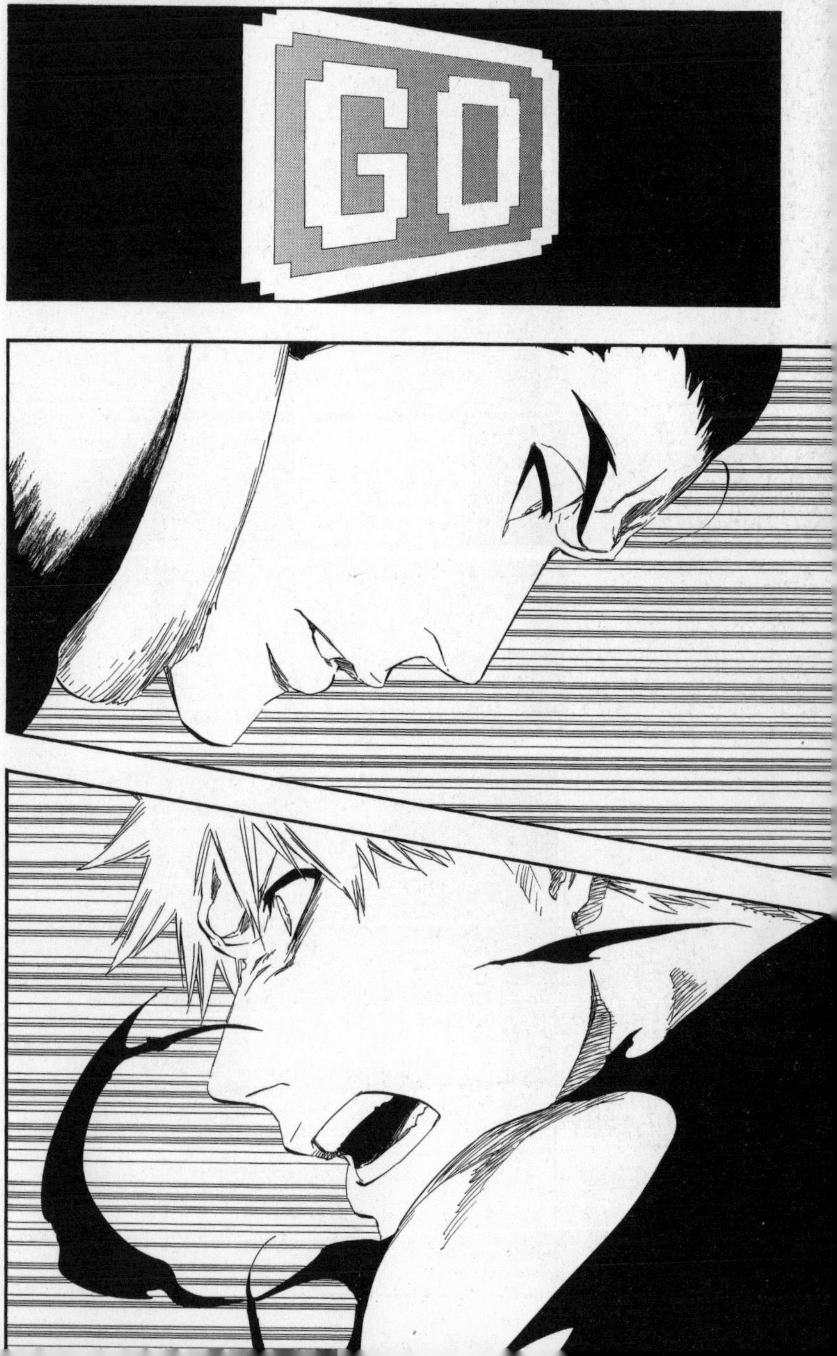
GO

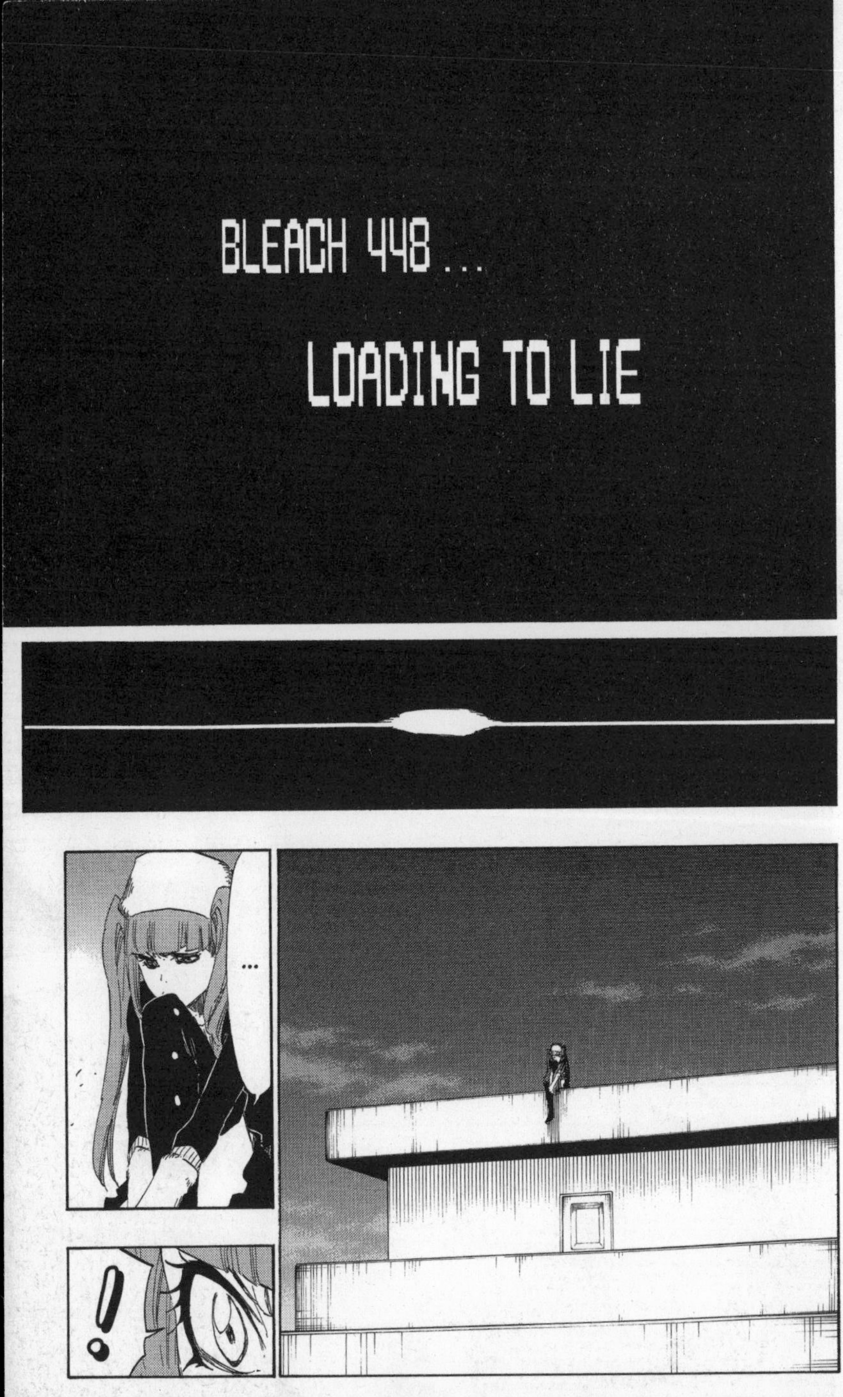
BLEACH 448...
LOADING TO LIE
...
!

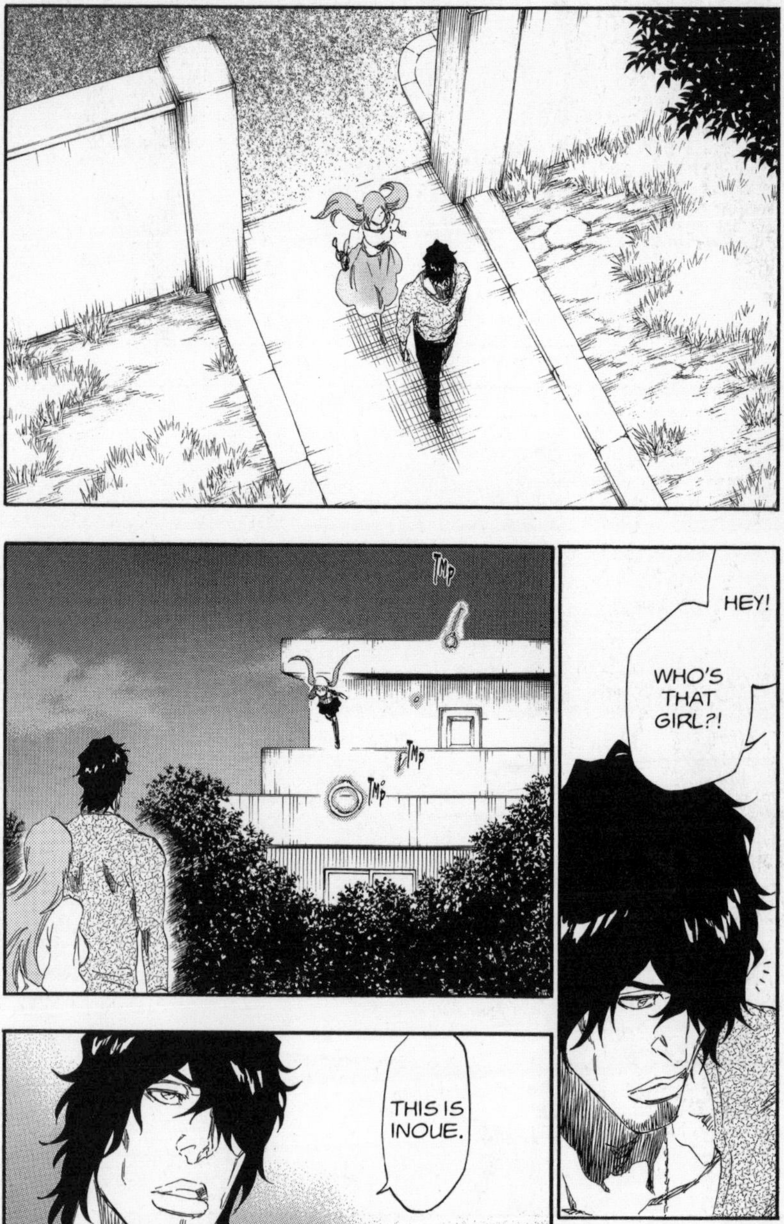
HEY!
WHO'S THAT GIRL?!
TMP
TMP
TMP
THIS IS INOUE.

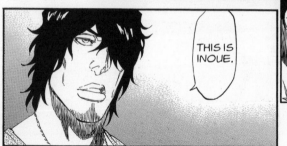

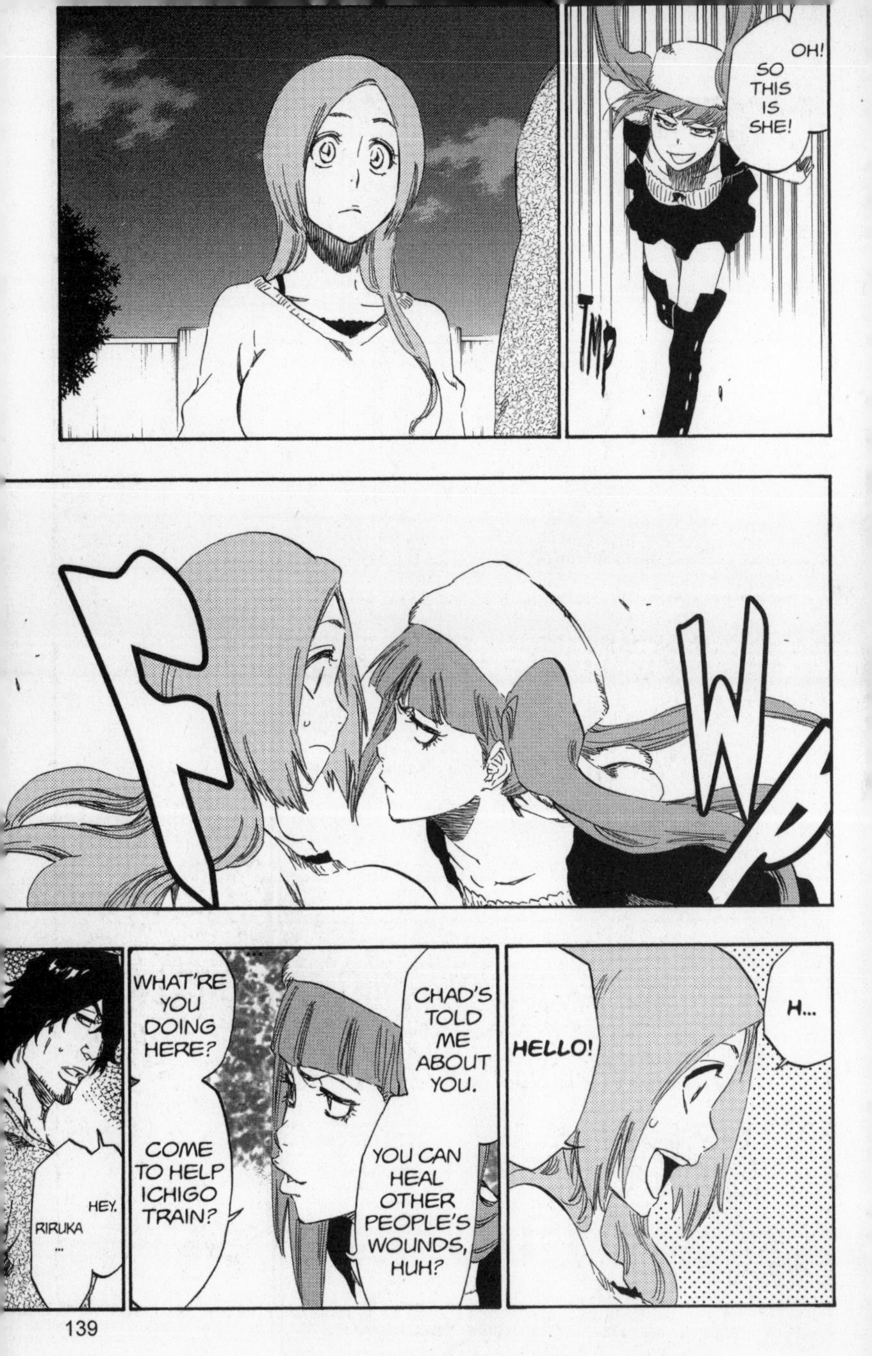
OH! SO THIS IS SHE!
TMP
FWP
H...
HELLO!
CHAD'S TOLD ME ABOUT YOU.
YOU CAN HEAL OTHER PEOPLE'S WOUNDS, HUH?
WHAT'RE YOU DOING HERE?
COME TO HELP ICHIGO TRAIN?
HEY.
RIRUKA ...

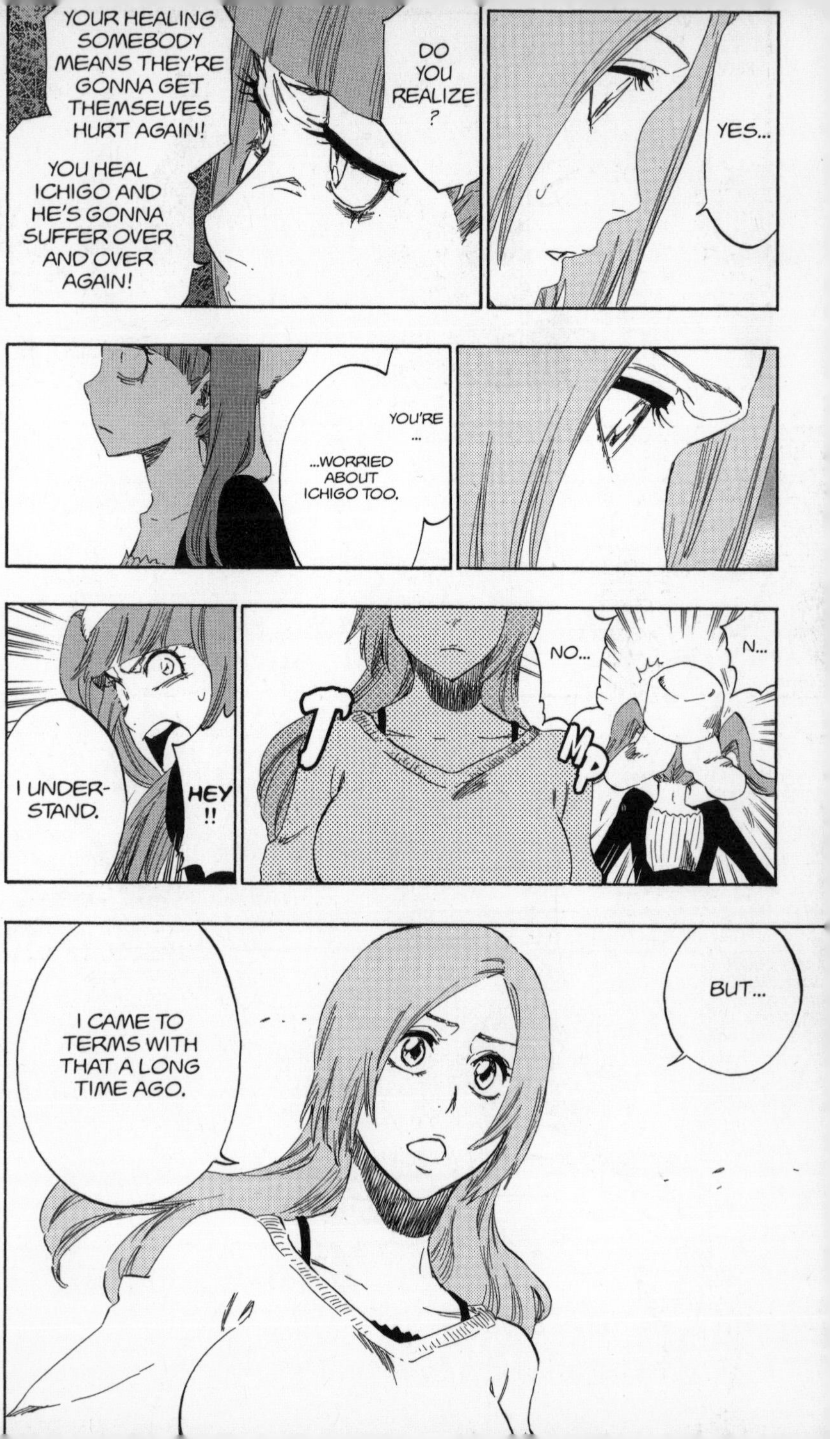
YES...
DO YOU REALIZE?
YOUR HEALING SOMEBODY MEANS THEY'RE GONNA GET THEMSELVES HURT AGAIN!
YOU HEAL ICHIGO AND HE'S GONNA SUFFER OVER AND OVER AGAIN!
YOU'RE ...
...WORRIED ABOUT ICHIGO TOO.
NO...
N...
TMP
HEY!!
I UNDER-STAND.
BUT...
I CAME TO TERMS WITH THAT A LONG TIME AGO.

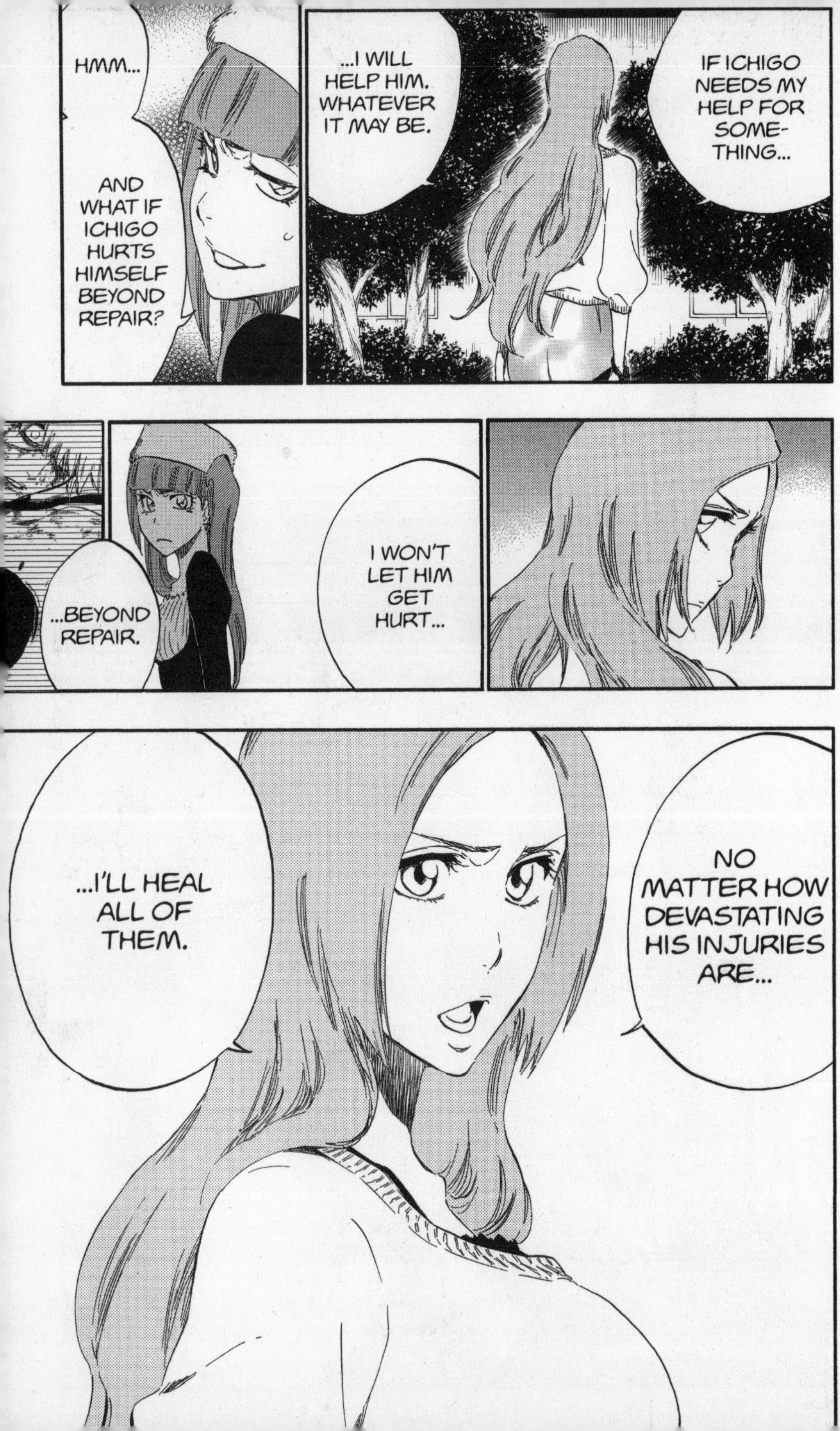
IF ICHIGO NEEDS MY HELP FOR SOME-THING...
...I WILL HELP HIM. WHATEVER IT MAY BE.
HMM...
AND WHAT IF ICHIGO HURTS HIMSELF BEYOND REPAIR?
I WON'T LET HIM GET HURT...
...BEYOND REPAIR.
NO MATTER HOW DEVASTATING HIS INJURIES ARE...
...I'LL HEAL ALL OF THEM.

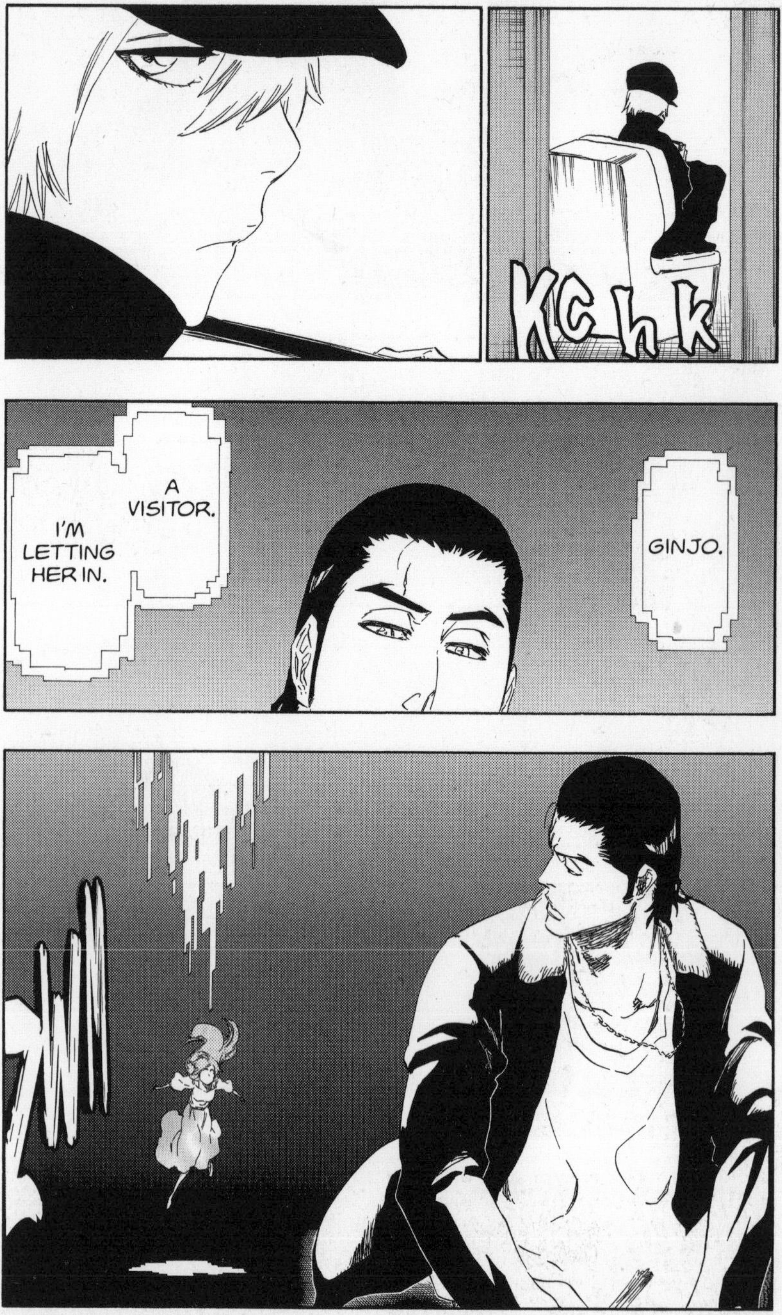
KChk
GINJO.
A VISITOR.
I'M LETTING HER IN.

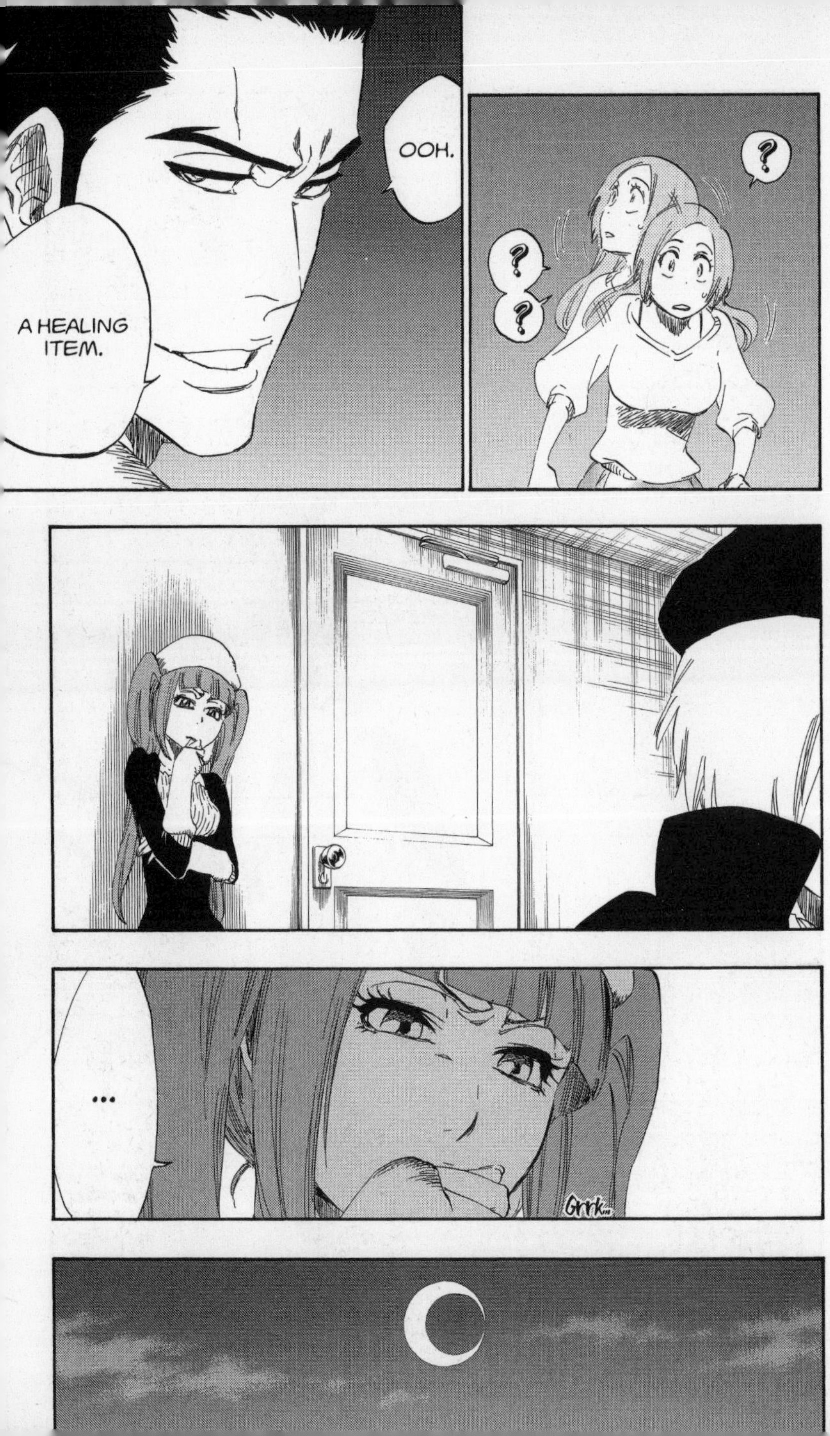

?
?
?
OOH.
A HEALING ITEM.
...
Grrk...

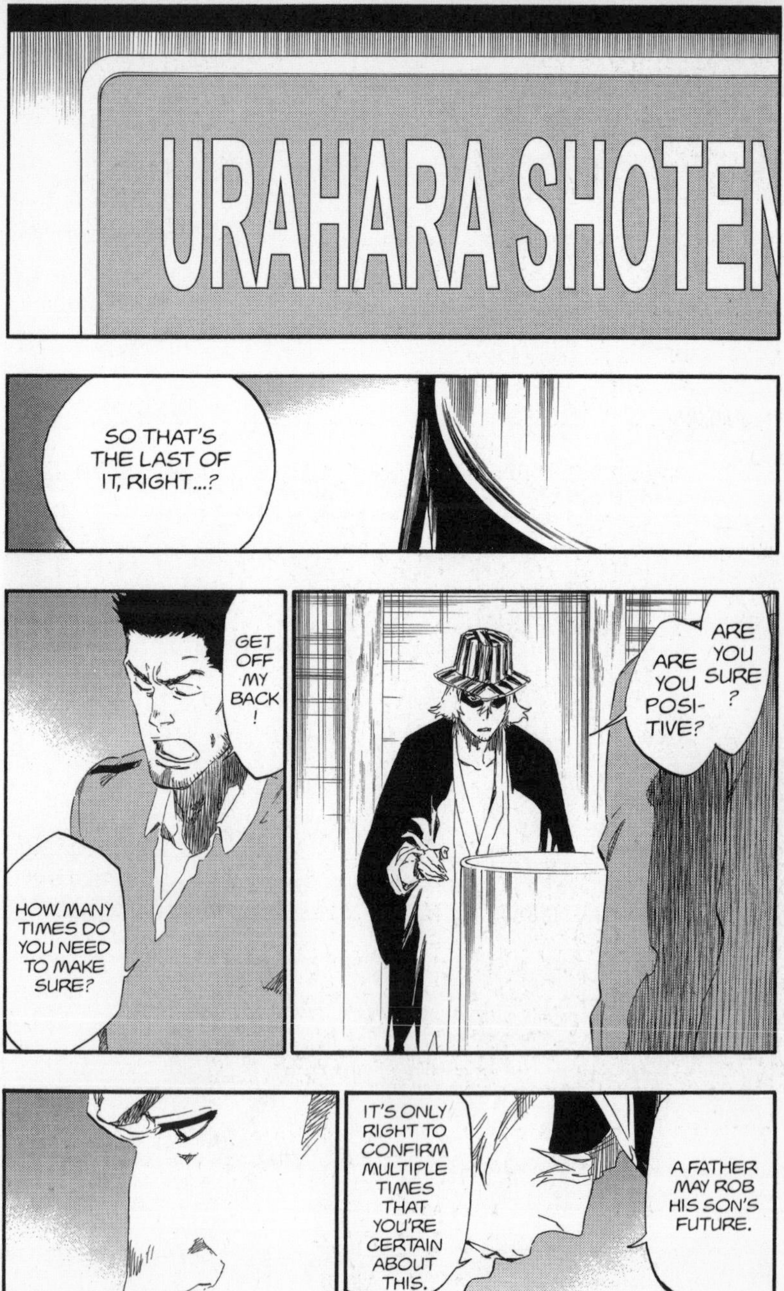
URAHARA SHOTEN
SO THAT'S THE LAST OF IT, RIGHT...?
ARE YOU SURE?
ARE YOU POSITIVE?
GET OFF MY BACK!
HOW MANY TIMES DO YOU NEED TO MAKE SURE?
IT'S ONLY RIGHT TO CONFIRM MULTIPLE TIMES THAT YOU'RE CERTAIN ABOUT THIS.
A FATHER MAY ROB HIS SON'S FUTURE.

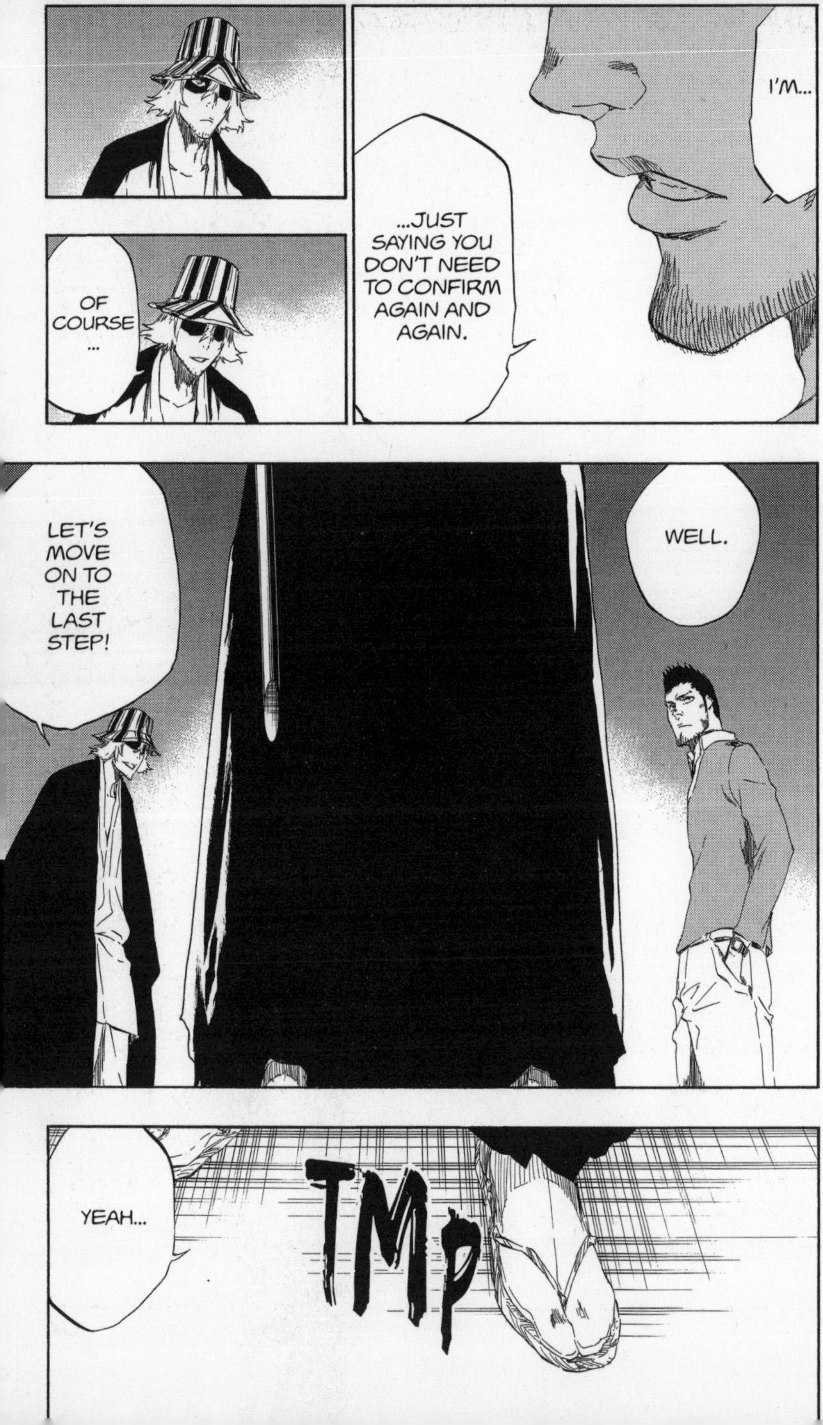
I'M...
...JUST SAYING YOU DON'T NEED TO CONFIRM AGAIN AND AGAIN.
OF COURSE ...
WELL.
LET'S MOVE ON TO THE LAST STEP!
TMP
YEAH...

PHEW...

WELL THAT WAS STRESSFUL.

449. Not be a Drug

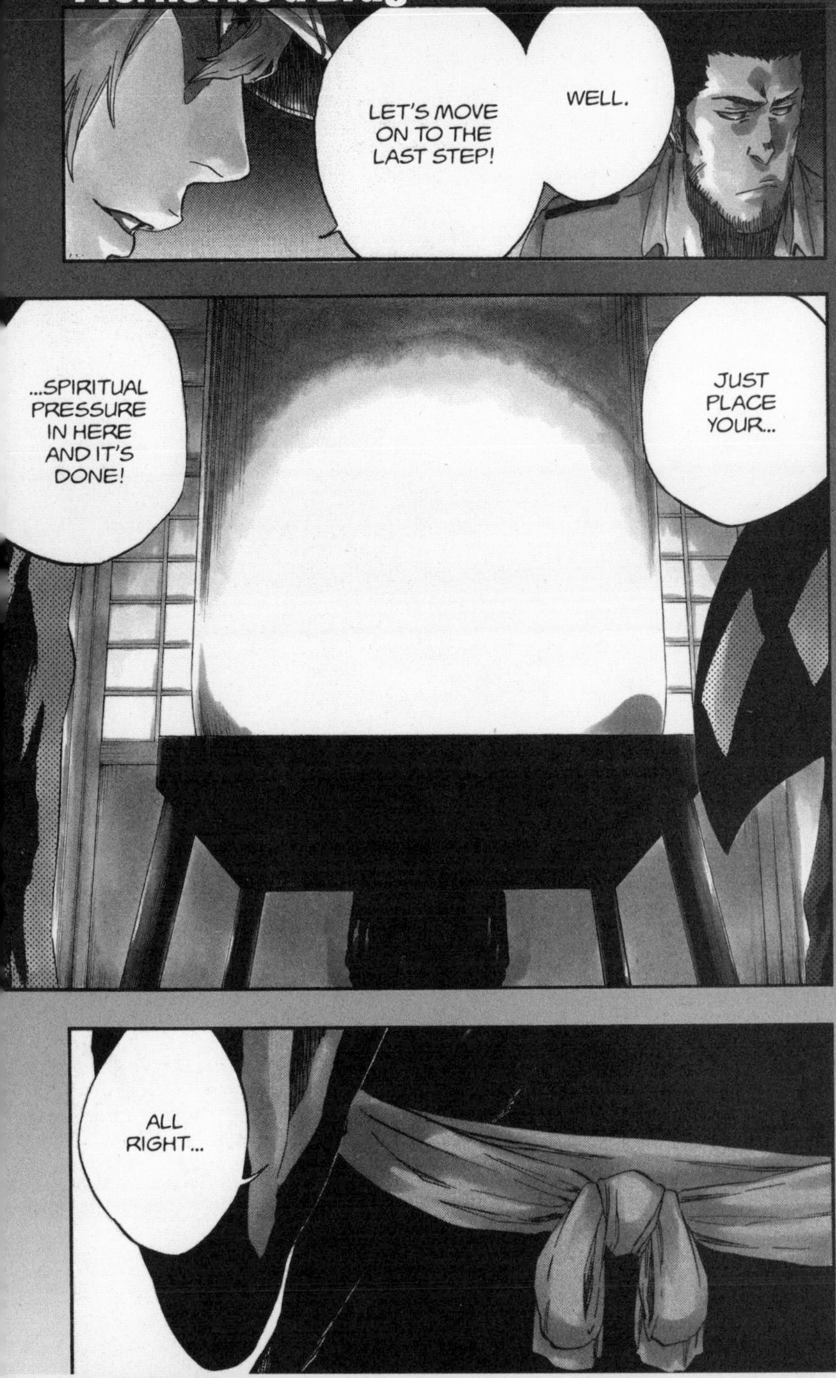
WELL.
LET'S MOVE ON TO THE LAST STEP!
JUST PLACE YOUR...
...SPIRITUAL PRESSURE IN HERE AND IT'S DONE!
ALL RIGHT...

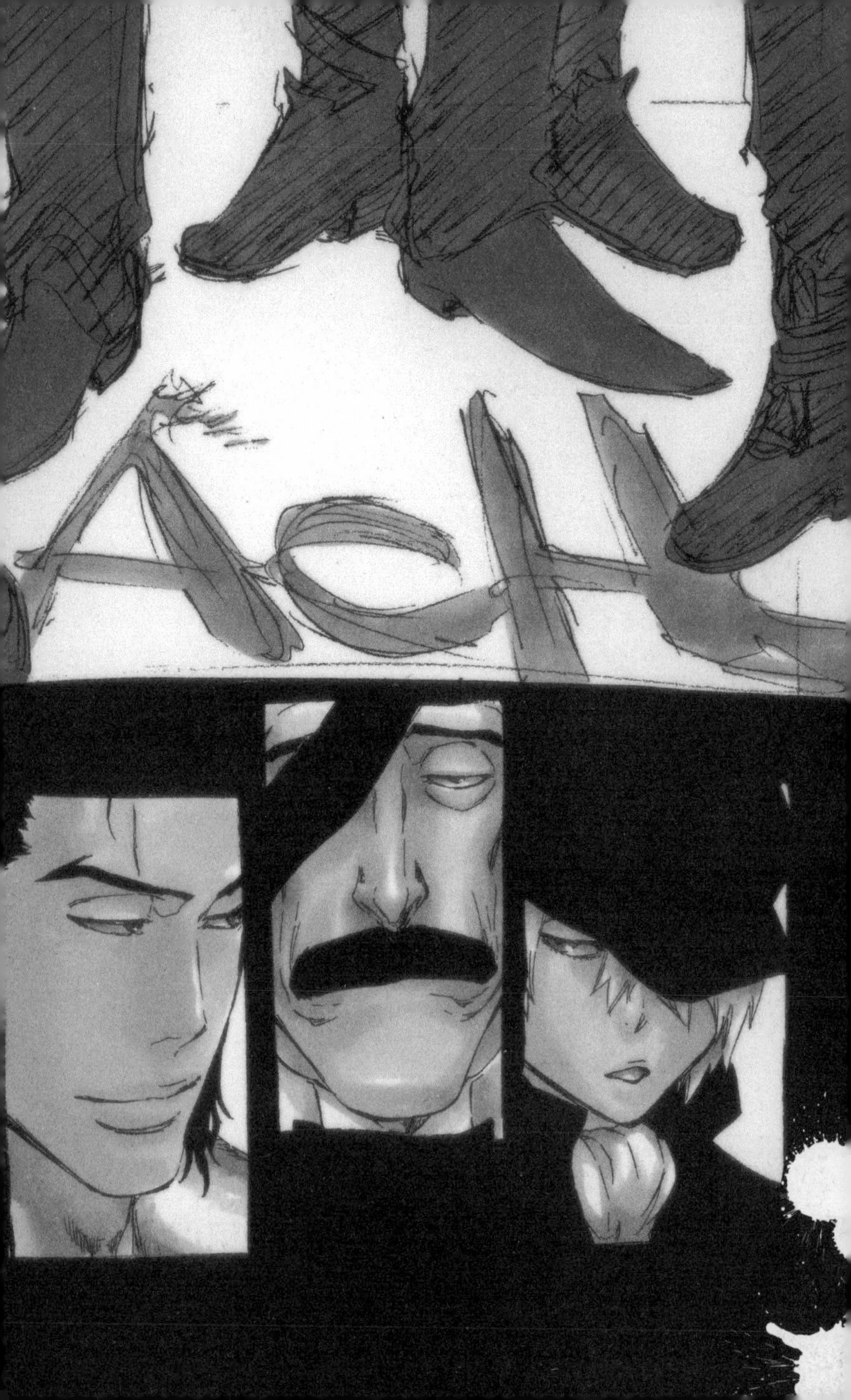

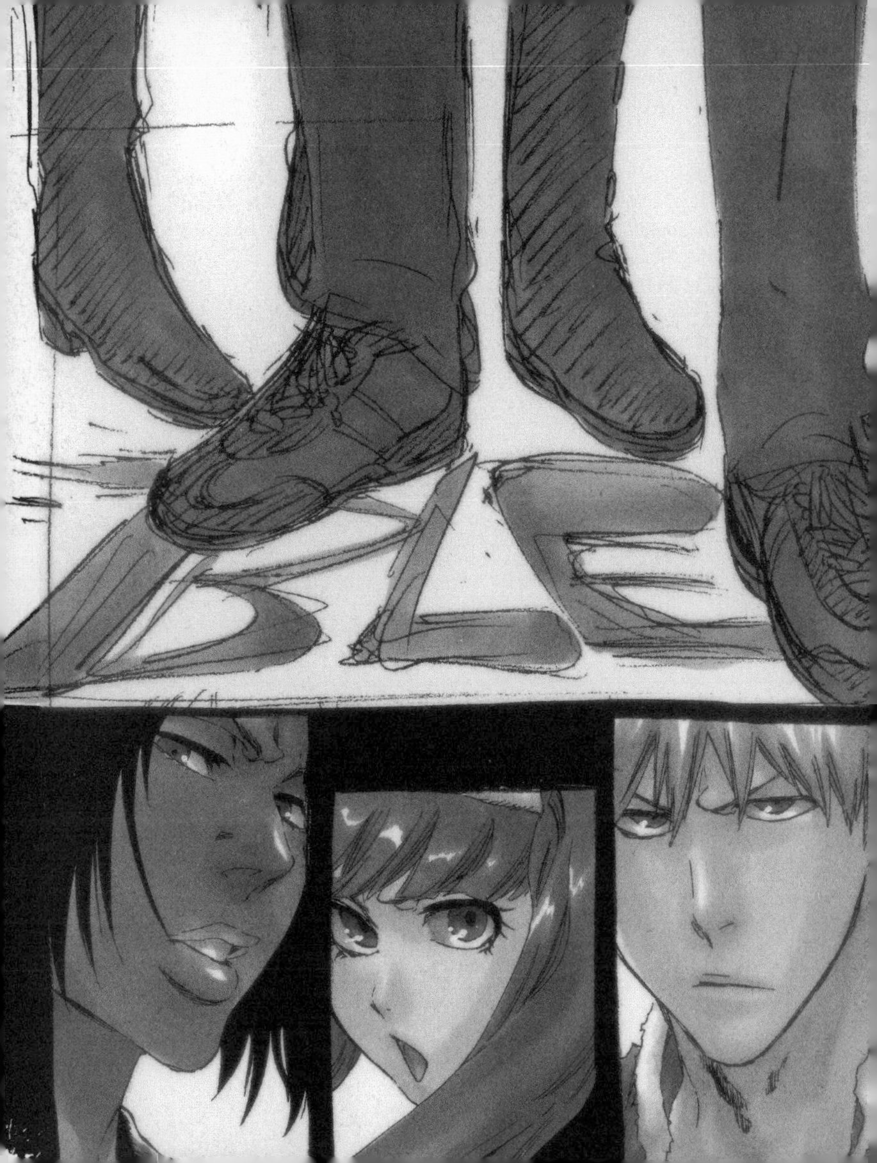
BLE

BLEACH
ブリーチ

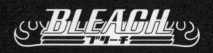

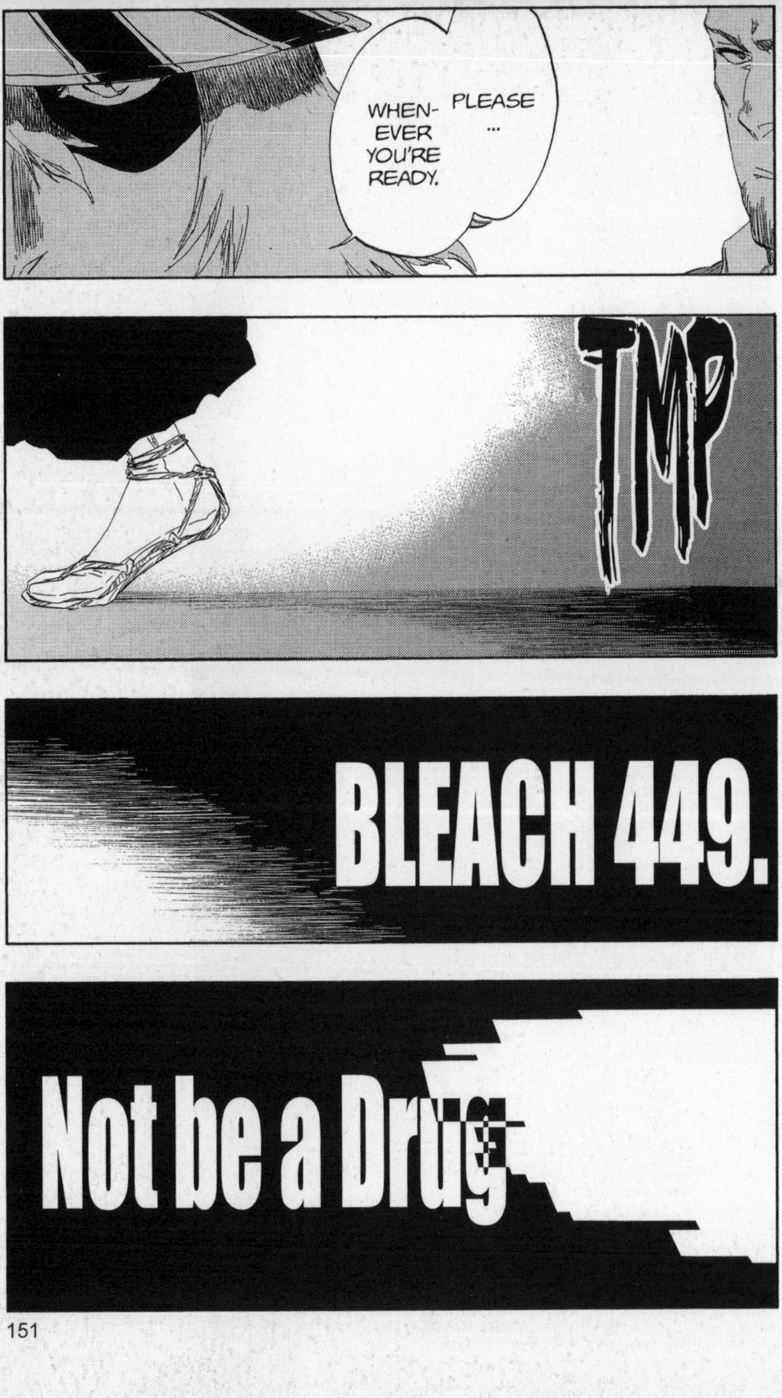
PLEASE...
WHEN-EVER YOU'RE READY.
TMP
BLEACH 449.
Not be a Drug

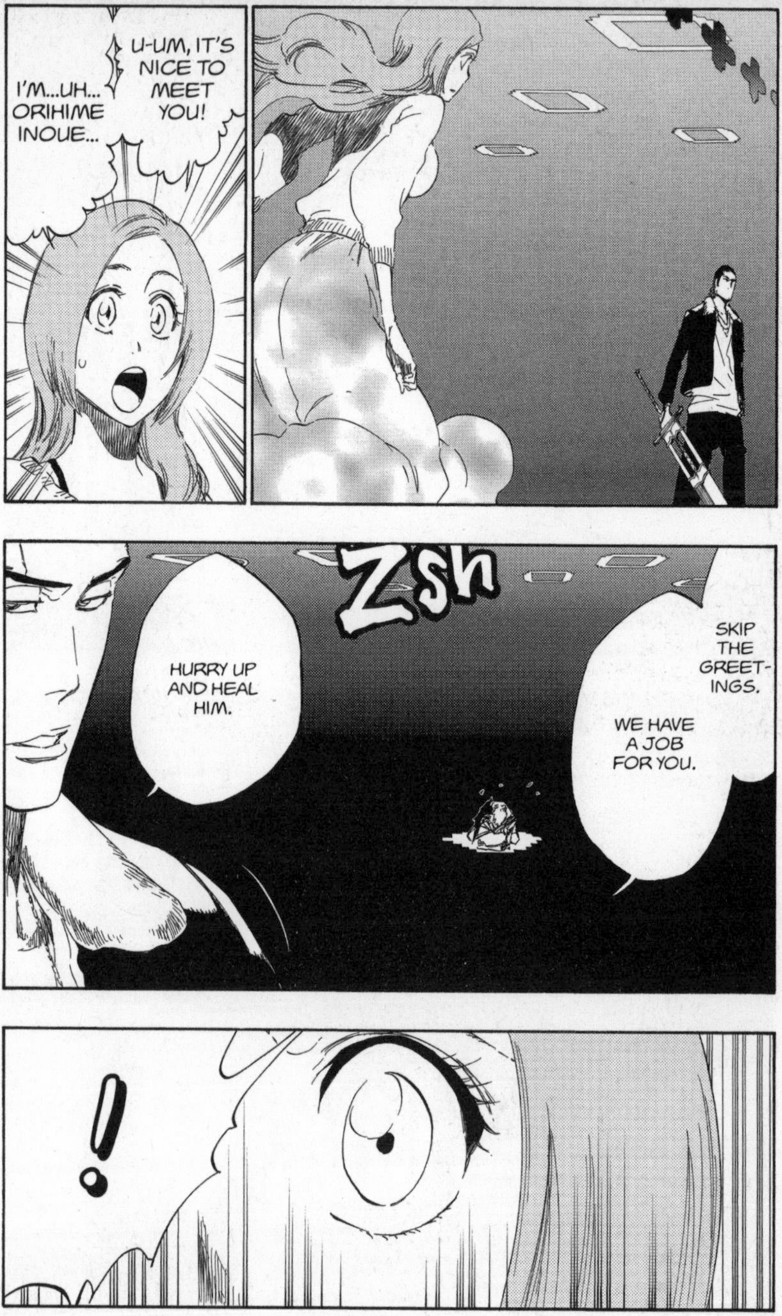
I'M...UH... ORIHIME INOUE...
U-UM, IT'S NICE TO MEET YOU!
ZSH
SKIP THE GREET-INGS.
WE HAVE A JOB FOR YOU.
HURRY UP AND HEAL HIM.
!

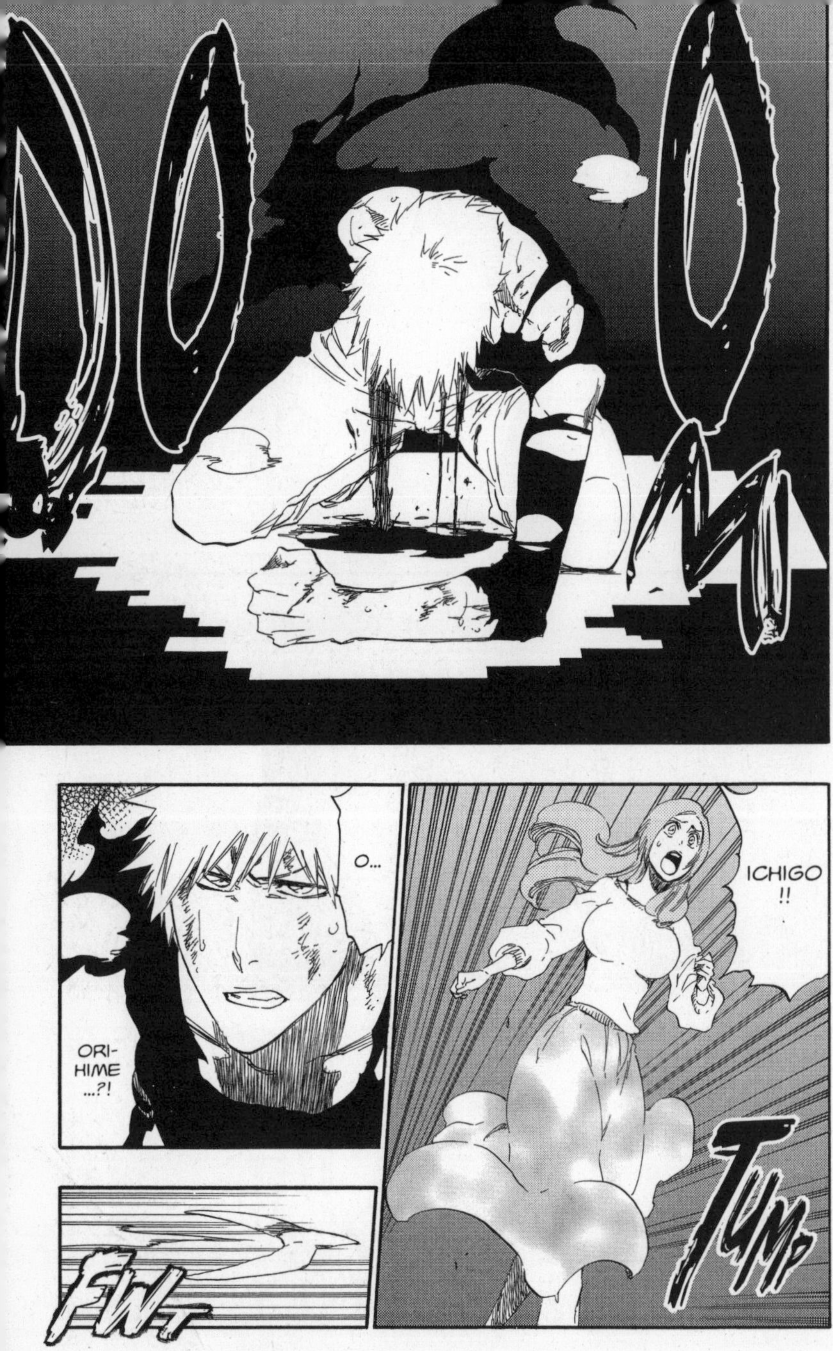
DOOM
ICHIGO !!
TUMP
O...
ORI-HIME ...?!
FWT

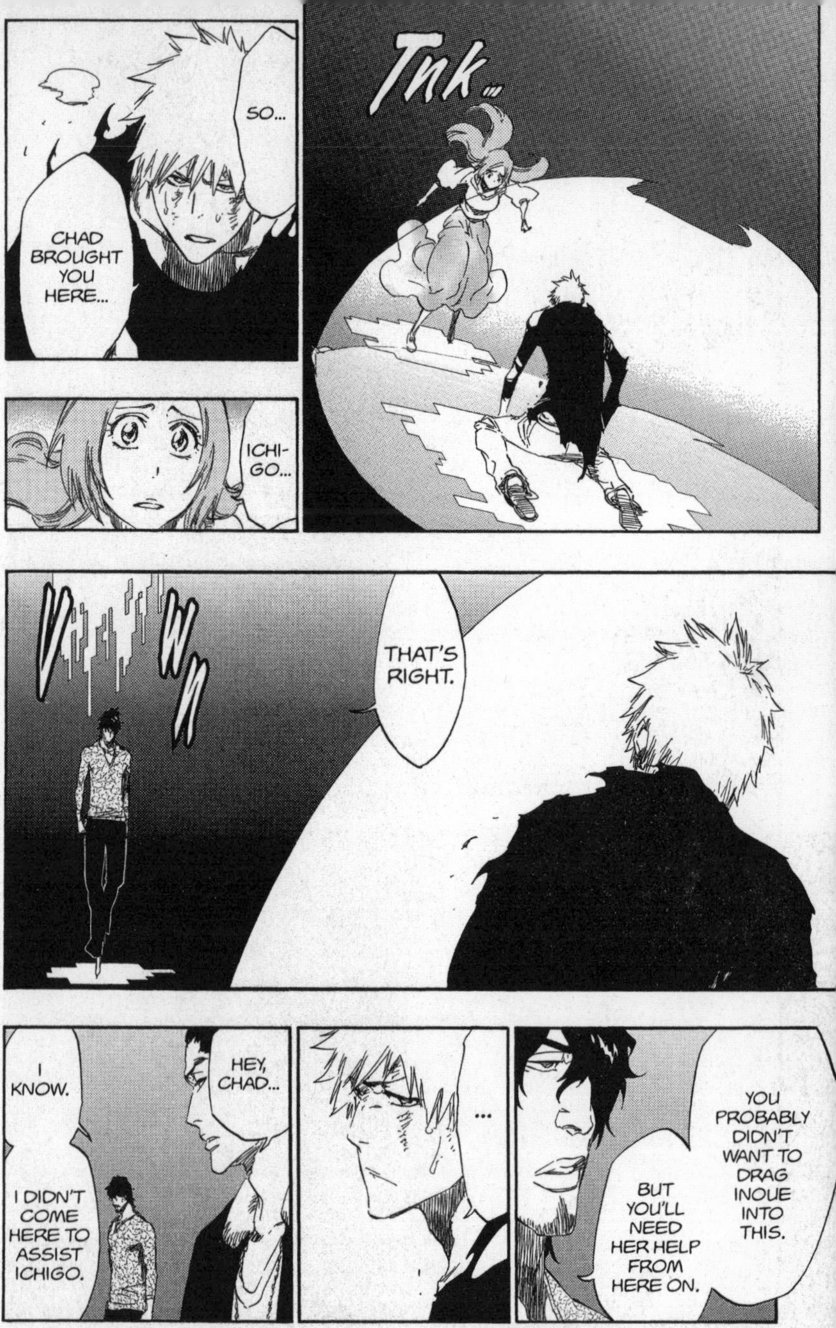
Tnk...
SO...
CHAD BROUGHT YOU HERE...
ICHI-GO...
VWWN
THAT'S RIGHT.
YOU PROBABLY DIDN'T WANT TO DRAG INOUE INTO THIS.
BUT YOU'LL NEED HER HELP FROM HERE ON.
...
HEY, CHAD...
I KNOW.
I DIDN'T COME HERE TO ASSIST ICHIGO.

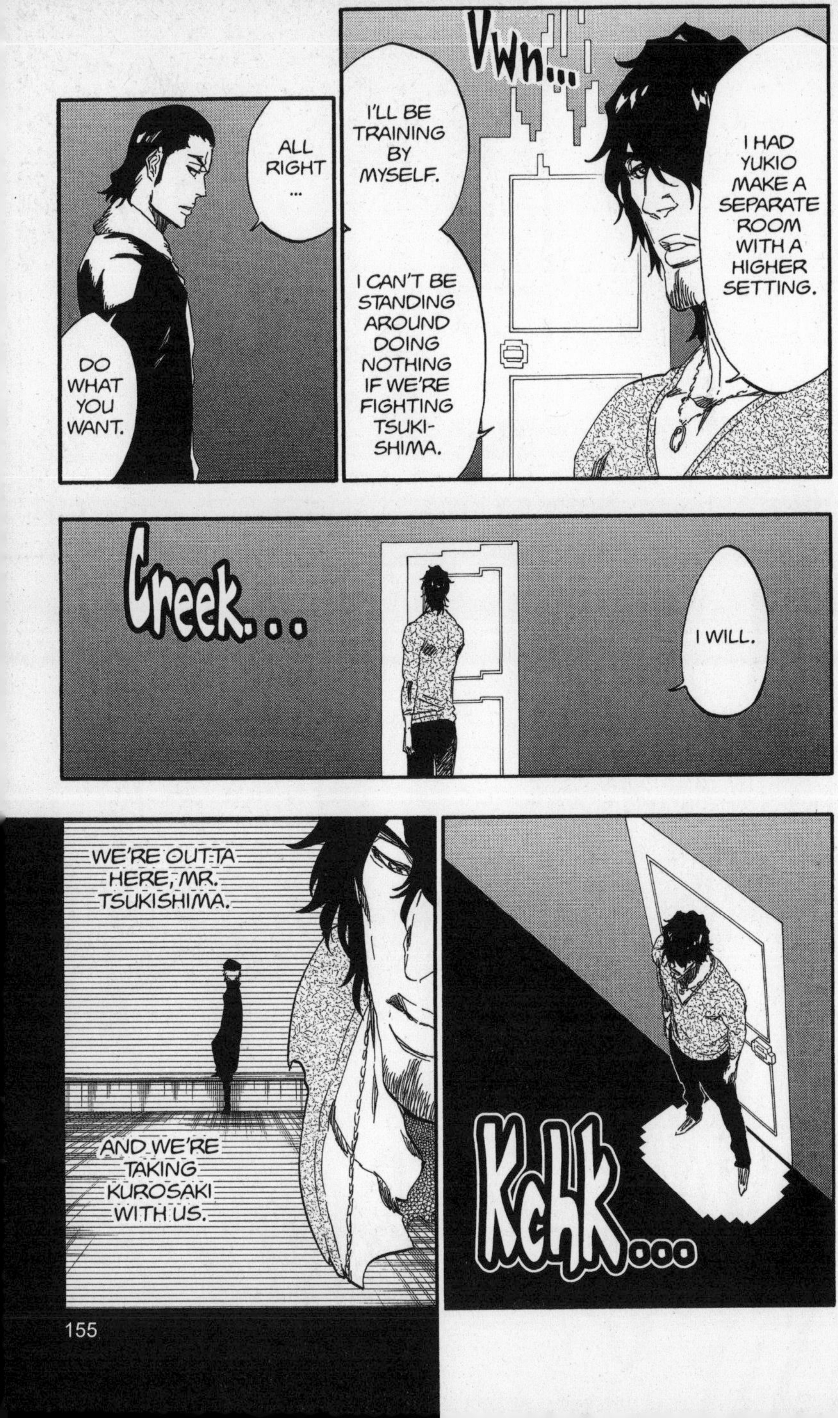
Vwn...
I HAD YUKIO MAKE A SEPARATE ROOM WITH A HIGHER SETTING.
I'LL BE TRAINING BY MYSELF.
I CAN'T BE STANDING AROUND DOING NOTHING IF WE'RE FIGHTING TSUKI-SHIMA.
ALL RIGHT ...
DO WHAT YOU WANT.
I WILL.
Creek...
Kchk...
WE'RE OUTTA HERE, MR. TSUKISHIMA.
AND WE'RE TAKING KUROSAKI WITH US.

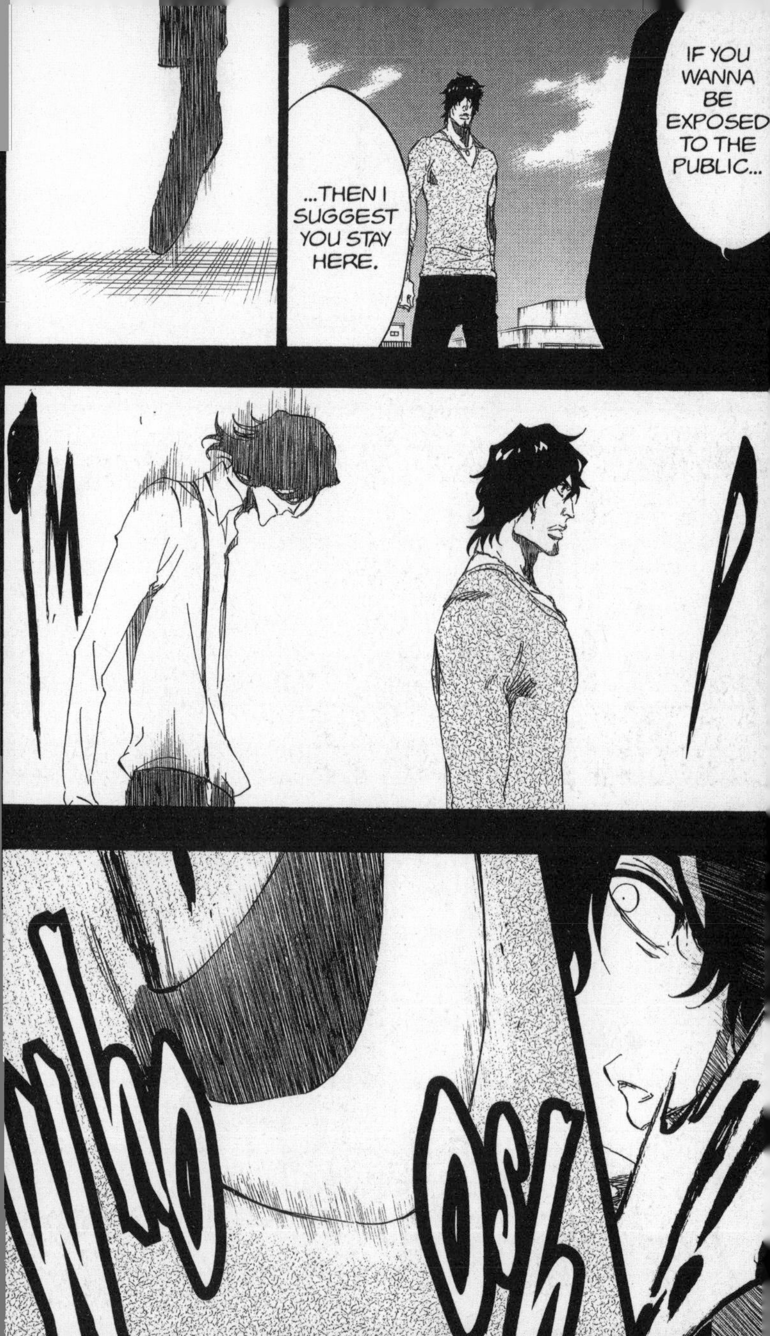
IF YOU WANNA BE EXPOSED TO THE PUBLIC...
...THEN I SUGGEST YOU STAY HERE.
WHOOSH

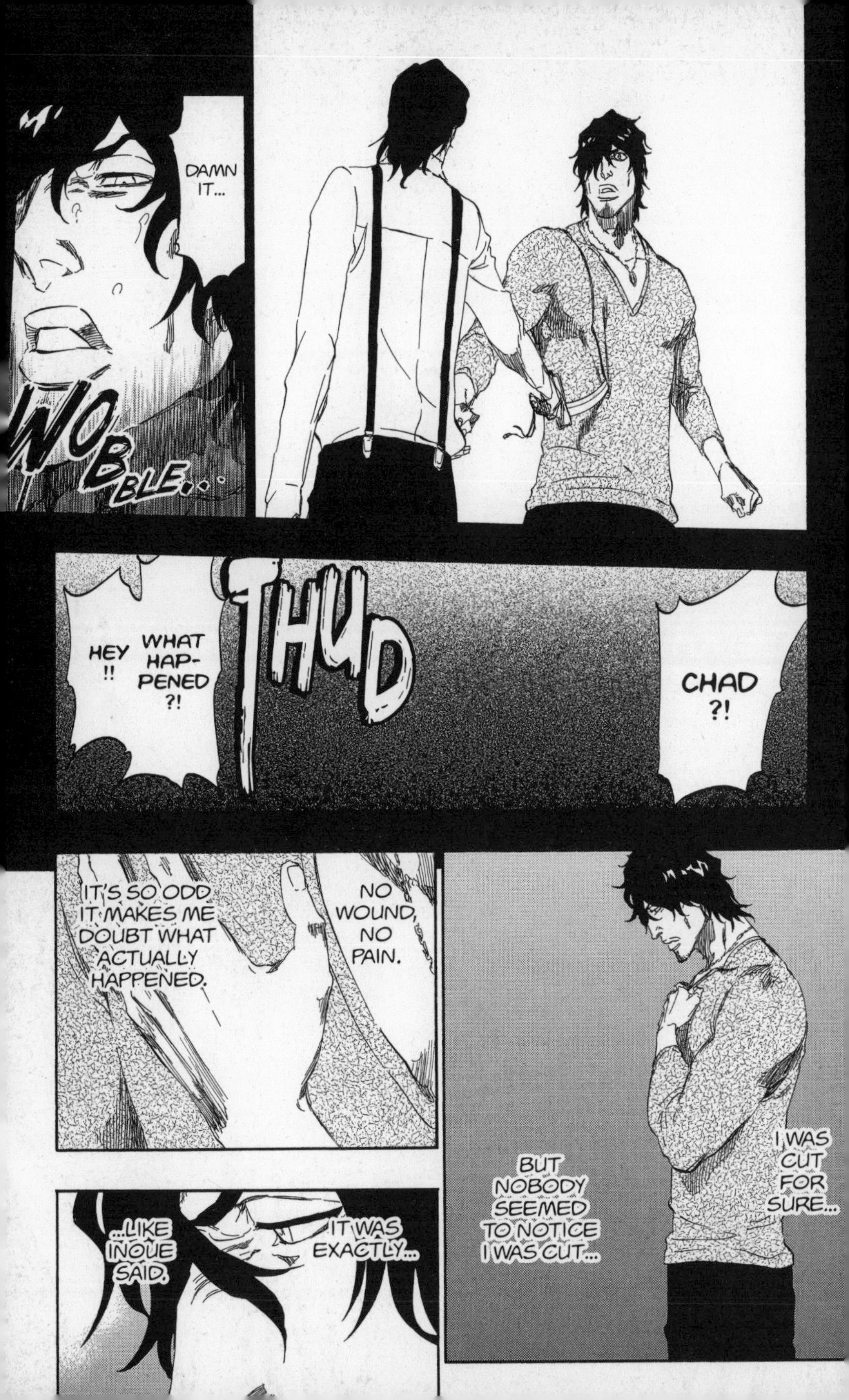
DAMN IT...
WOBBLE...
CHAD ?!
THUD
HEY !! WHAT HAPPENED ?!
I WAS CUT FOR SURE...
BUT NOBODY SEEMED TO NOTICE I WAS CUT...
NO WOUND, NO PAIN.
IT'S SO ODD IT MAKES ME DOUBT WHAT ACTUALLY HAPPENED.
IT WAS EXACTLY...
...LIKE INOUE SAID.

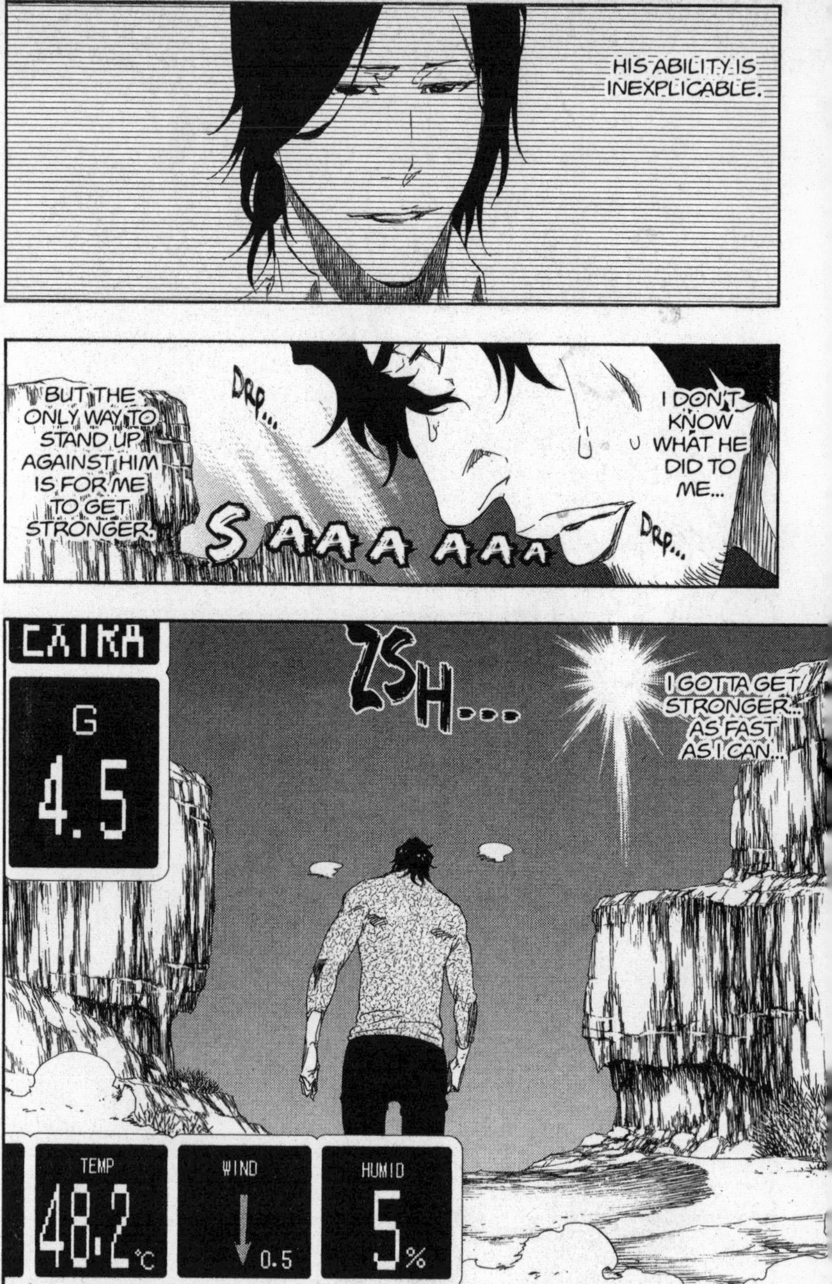
HIS ABILITY IS INEXPLICABLE.
I DON'T KNOW WHAT HE DID TO ME...
DRP...
DRP...
SAAAAAA
BUT THE ONLY WAY TO STAND UP AGAINST HIM IS FOR ME TO GET STRONGER.
I GOTTA GET STRONGER... AS FAST AS I CAN...
ZSH...
EXTRA
G
4.5
TEMP
48.2°C
WIND
0.5
HUMID
5%

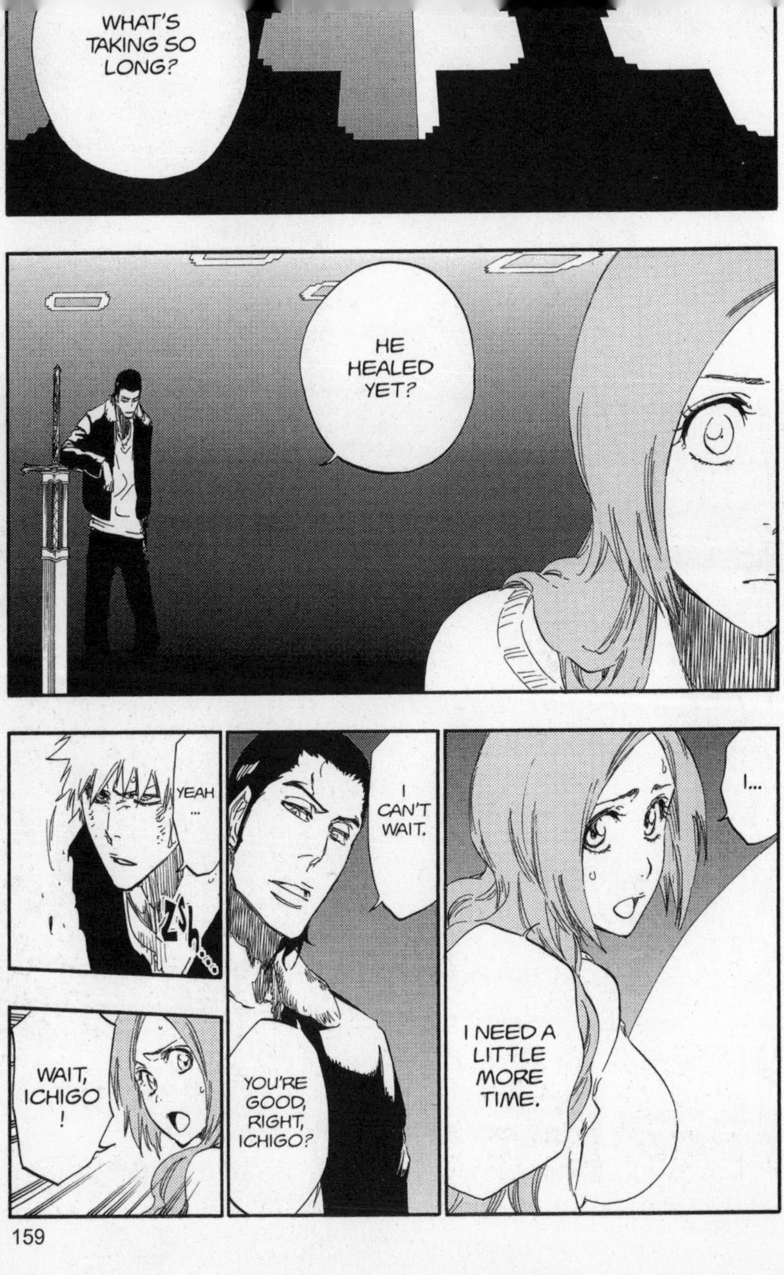
WHAT'S TAKING SO LONG?
HE HEALED YET?
I...
I NEED A LITTLE MORE TIME.
I CAN'T WAIT.
YOU'RE GOOD, RIGHT, ICHIGO?
YEAH ...
ZSH
WAIT, ICHIGO!

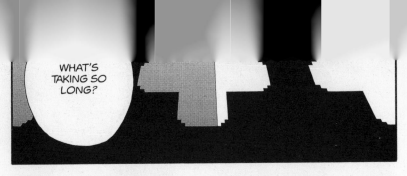

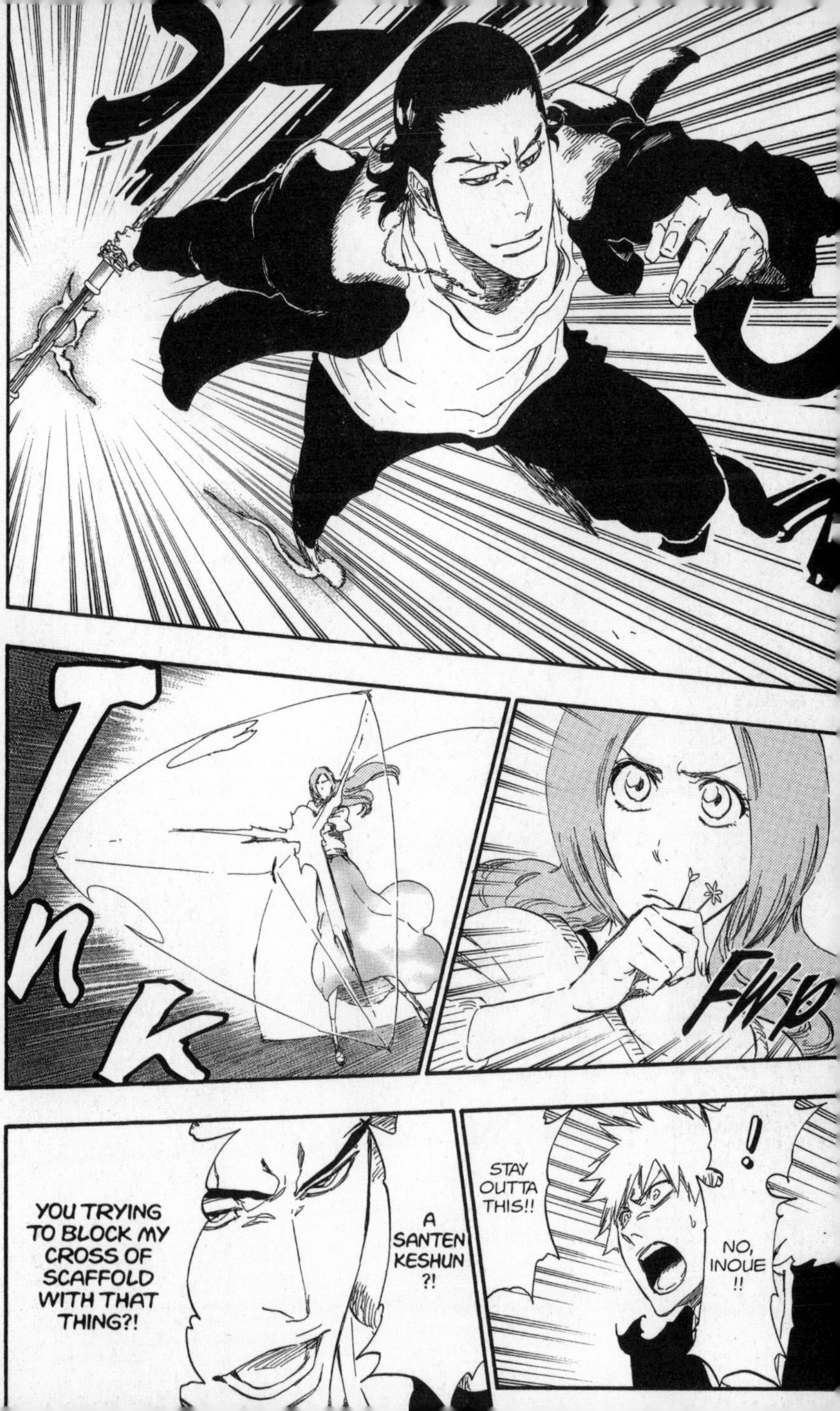
!
NO, INOUE!!
STAY OUTTA THIS!!
A SANTEN KESHUN?!
YOU TRYING TO BLOCK MY CROSS OF SCAFFOLD WITH THAT THING?!

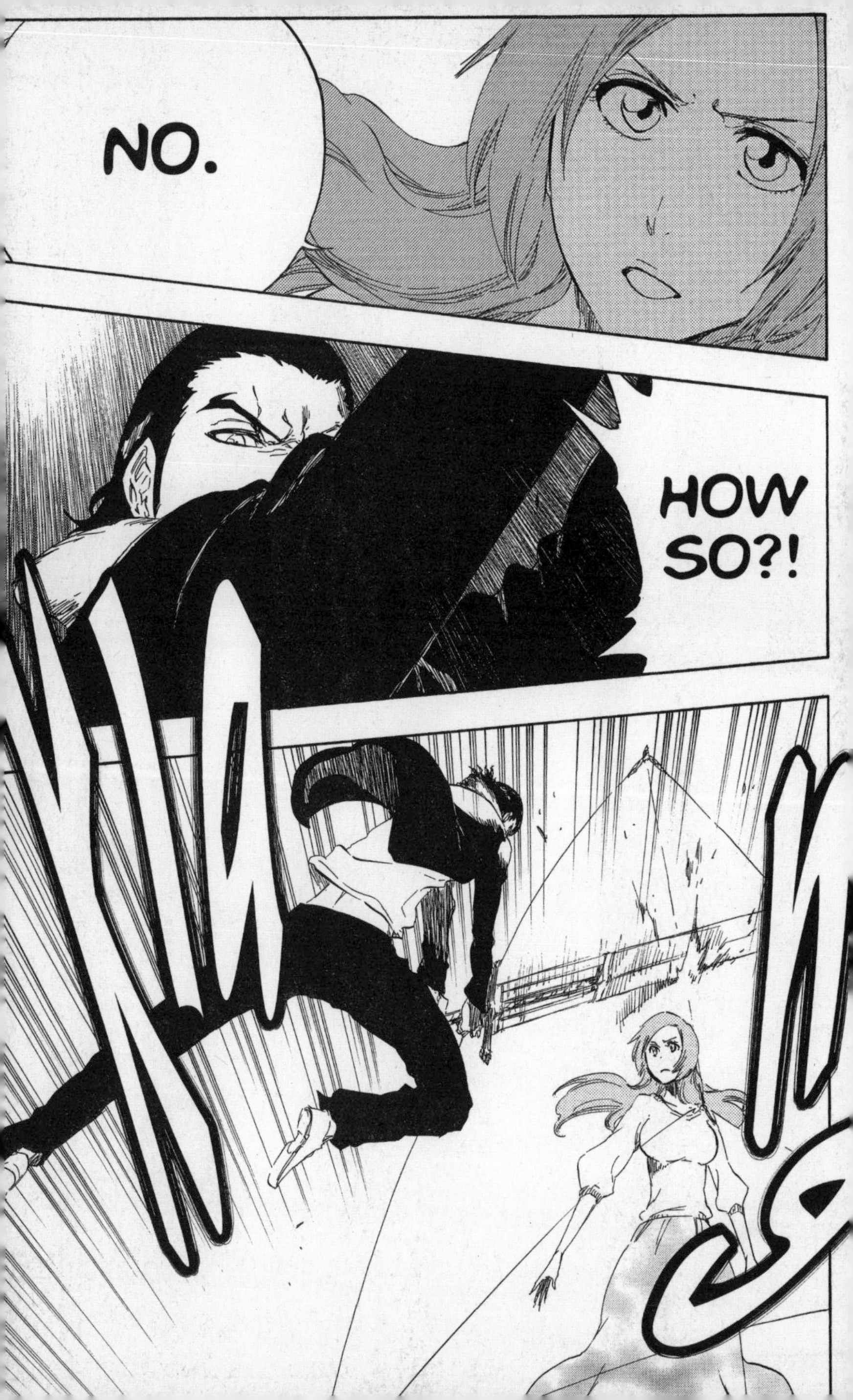
NO.
HOW SO?!

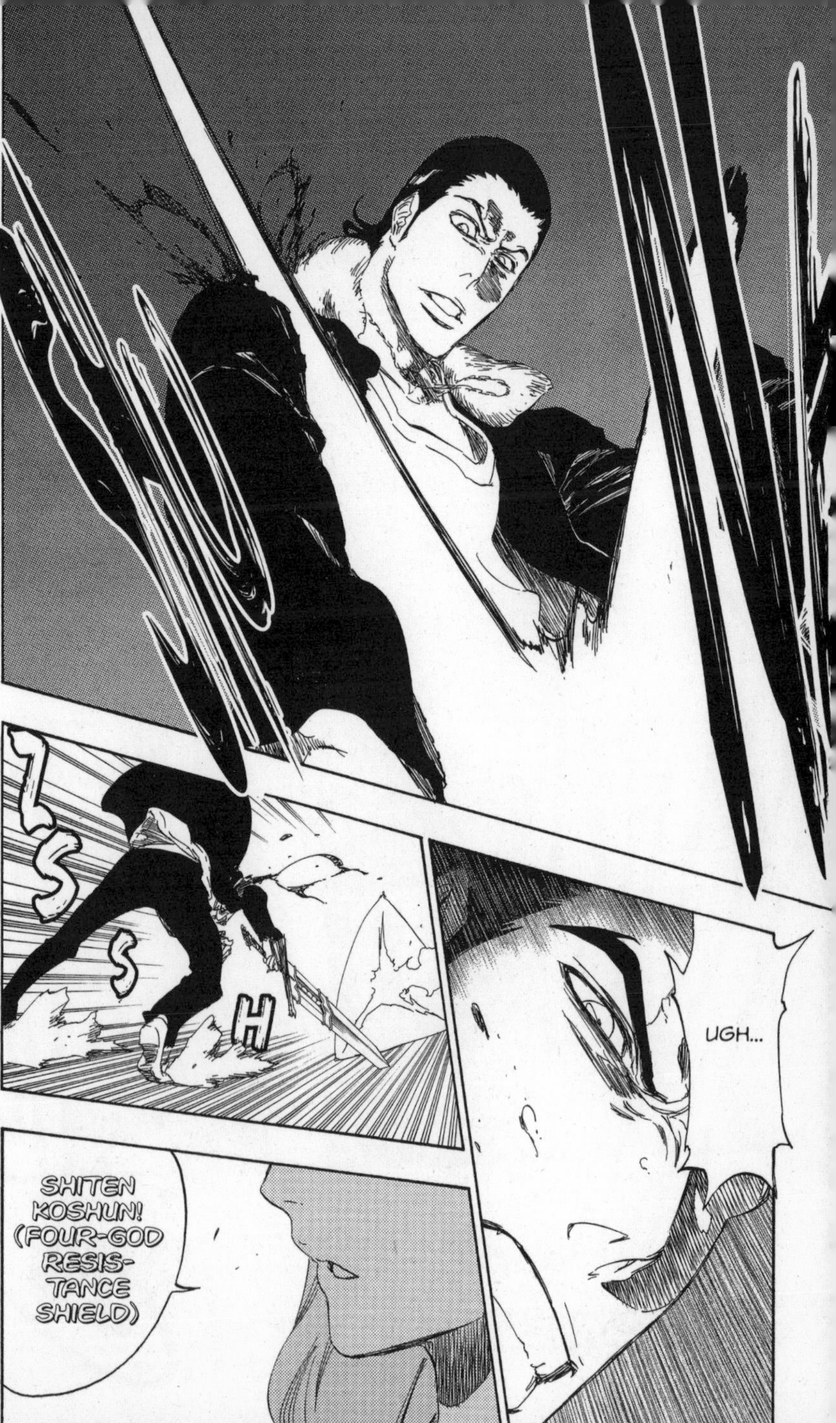
UGH...
SSH
SHITEN KOSHUN! (FOUR-GOD RESIS-TANCE SHIELD)

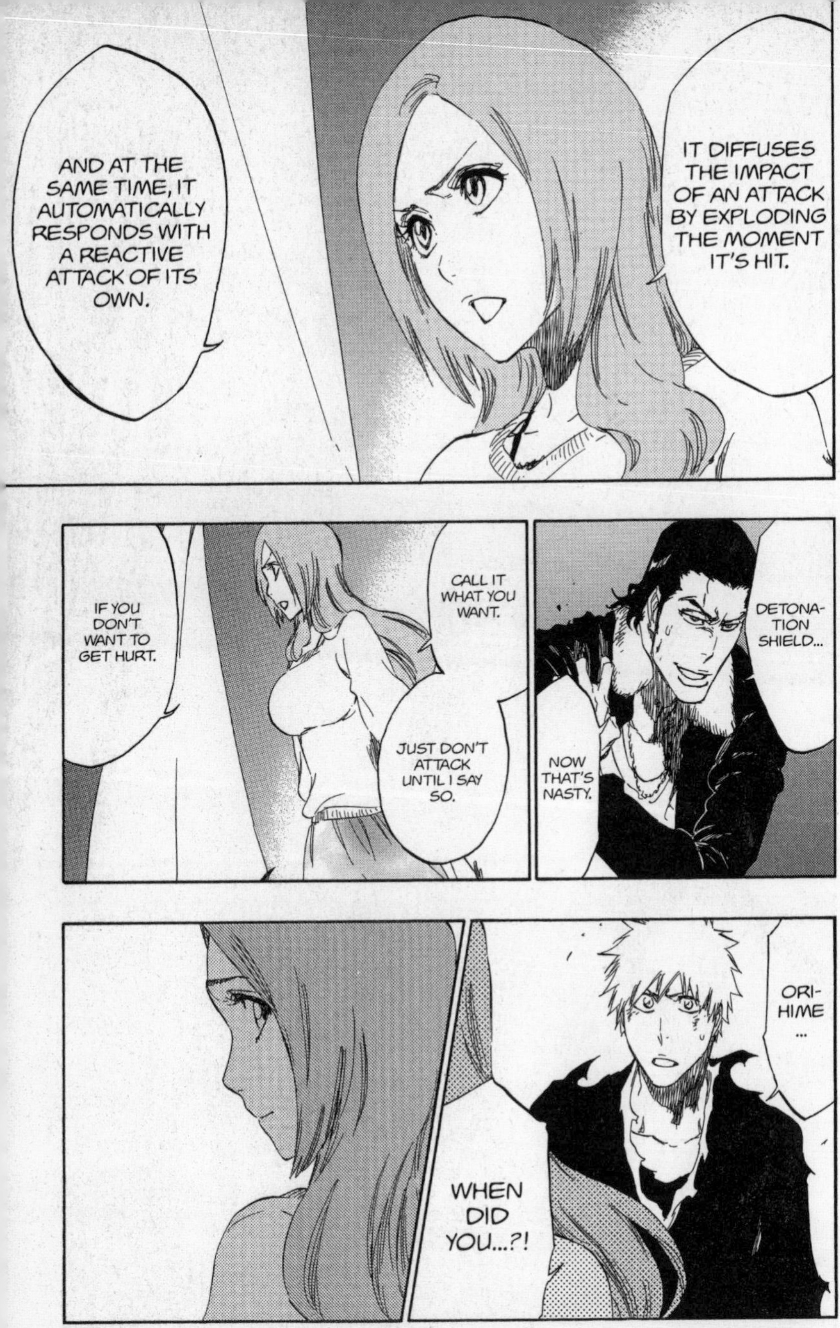
IT DIFFUSES THE IMPACT OF AN ATTACK BY EXPLODING THE MOMENT IT'S HIT.
AND AT THE SAME TIME, IT AUTOMATICALLY RESPONDS WITH A REACTIVE ATTACK OF ITS OWN.
DETONA-TION SHIELD...
NOW THAT'S NASTY.
CALL IT WHAT YOU WANT.
JUST DON'T ATTACK UNTIL I SAY SO.
IF YOU DON'T WANT TO GET HURT.
ORI-HIME ...
WHEN DID YOU...?!

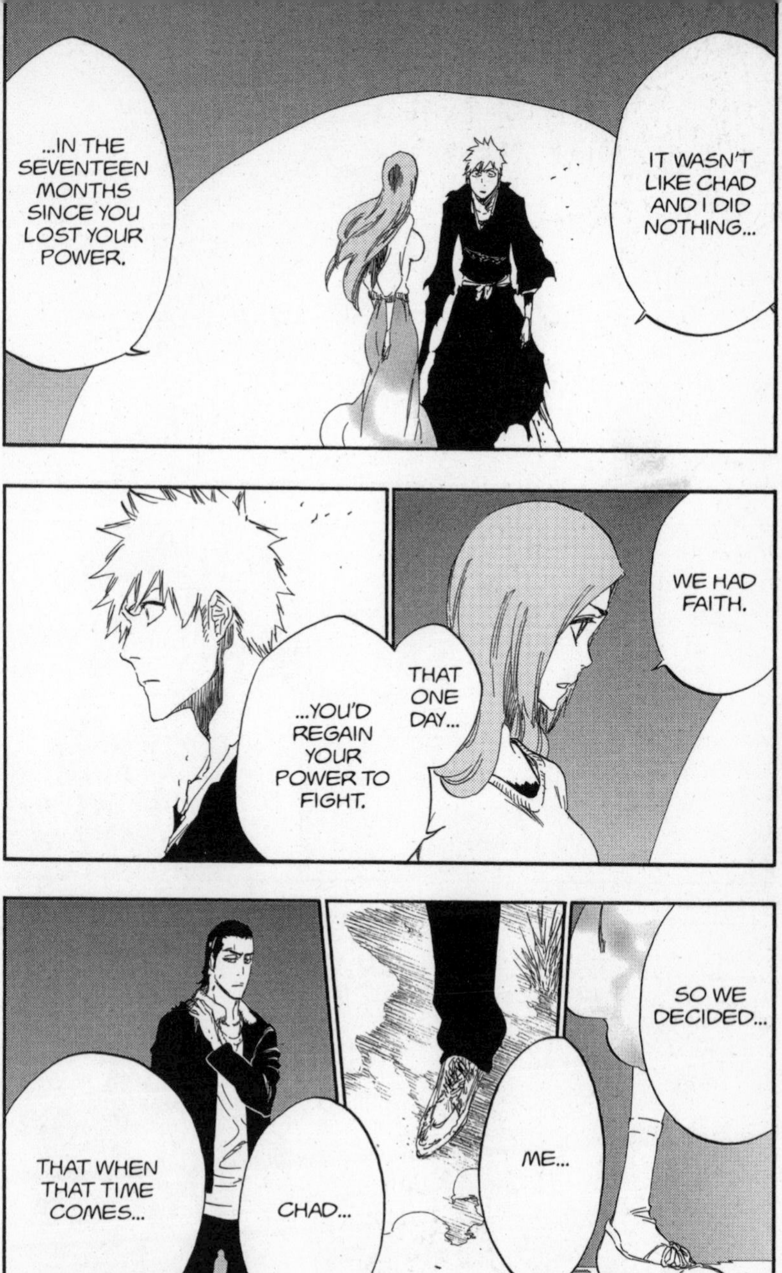
IT WASN'T LIKE CHAD AND I DID NOTHING...
...IN THE SEVENTEEN MONTHS SINCE YOU LOST YOUR POWER.
WE HAD FAITH.
THAT ONE DAY...
...YOU'D REGAIN YOUR POWER TO FIGHT.
SO WE DECIDED...
ME...
CHAD...
THAT WHEN THAT TIME COMES...

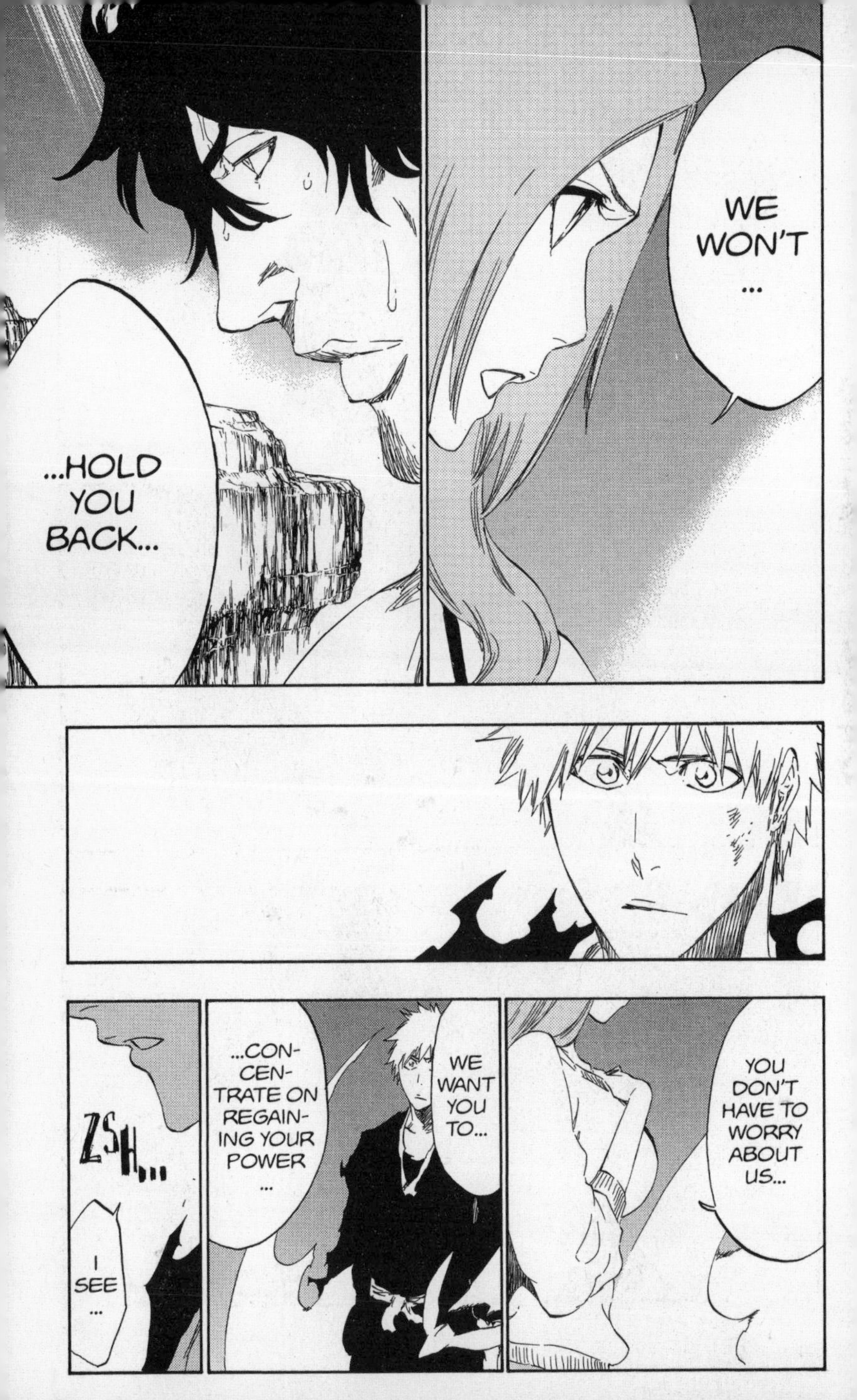
WE WON'T ...
...HOLD YOU BACK...
YOU DON'T HAVE TO WORRY ABOUT US...
WE WANT YOU TO...
...CON-CEN-TRATE ON REGAIN-ING YOUR POWER ...
ZSH...
I SEE ...

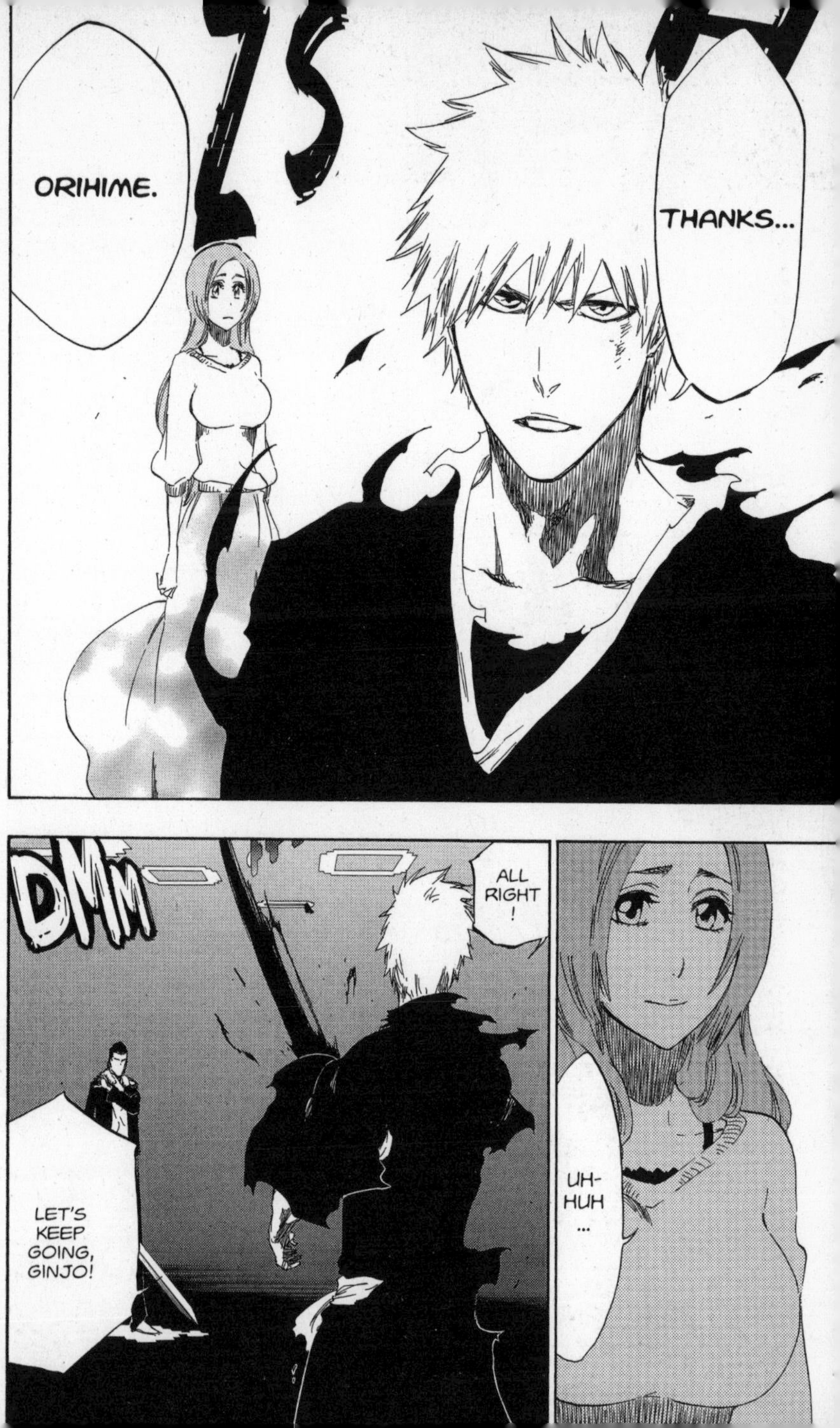
THANKS...
ORIHIME.
UH-HUH ...
ALL RIGHT!
DMM
LET'S KEEP GOING, GINJO!

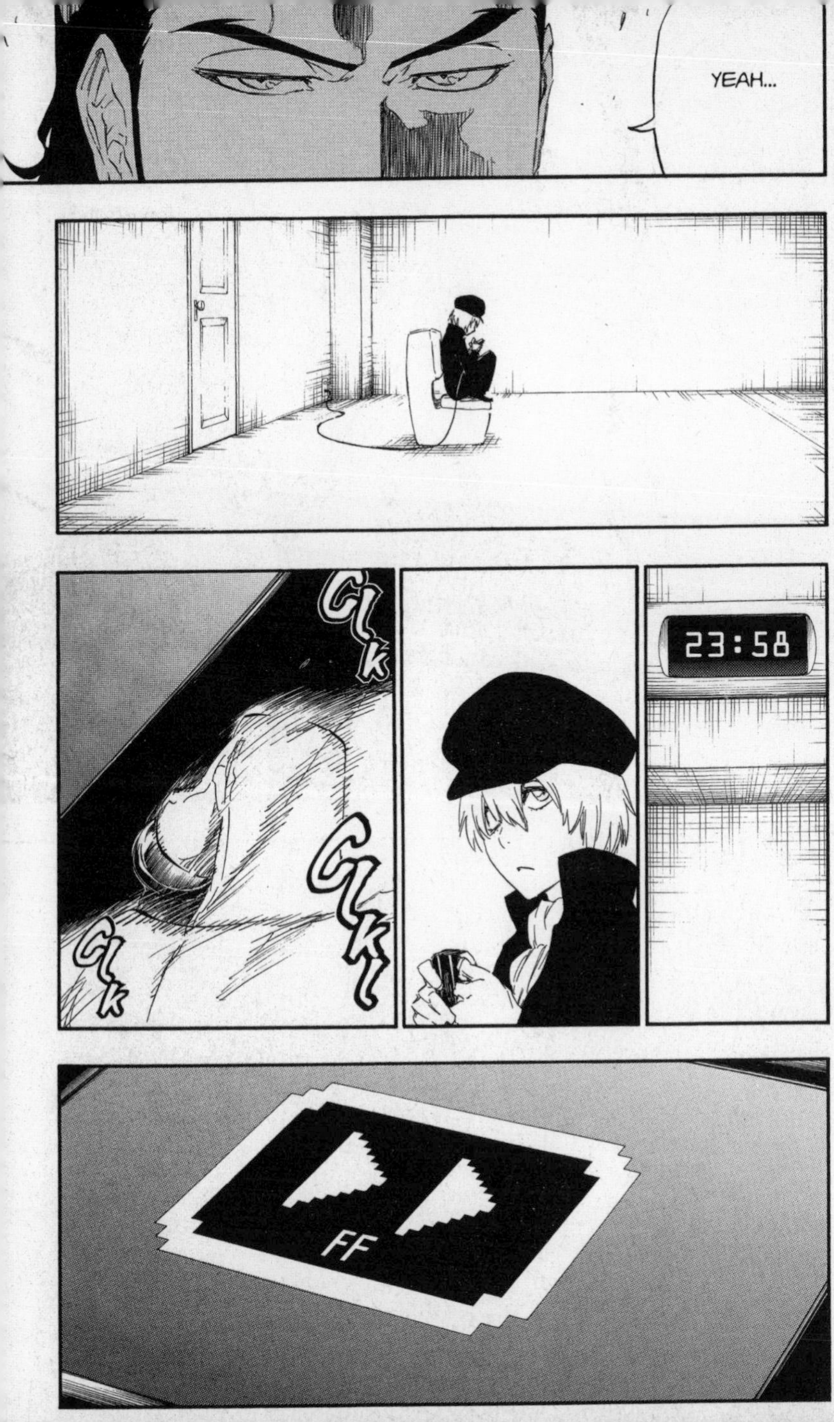
YEAH...
23:58
Clk
Clk
Clk
FF

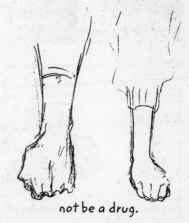

not be a drug.

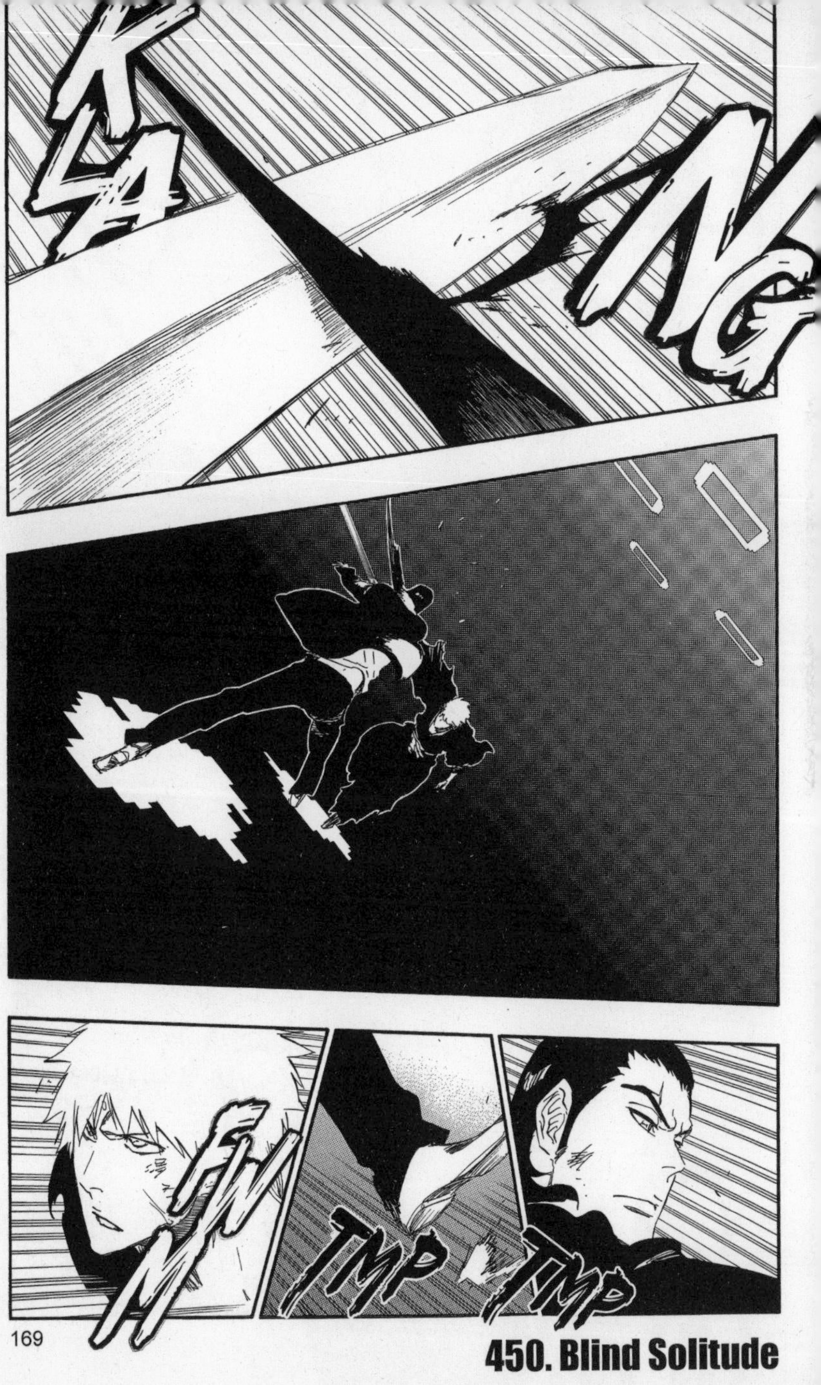
KLANG
TMP
TMP

450. Blind Solitude

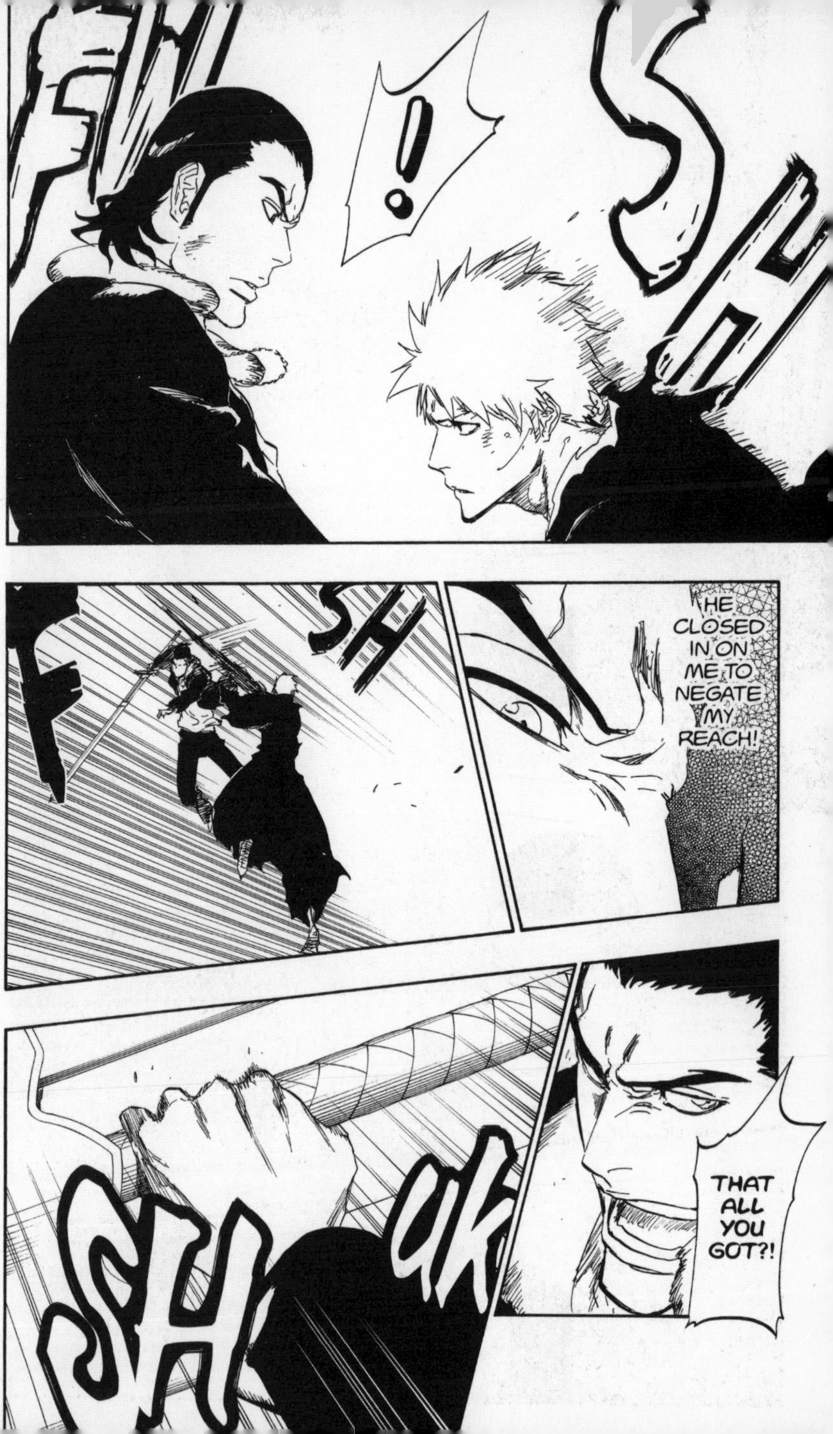
!
HE CLOSED IN ON ME TO NEGATE MY REACH!
THAT ALL YOU GOT?!

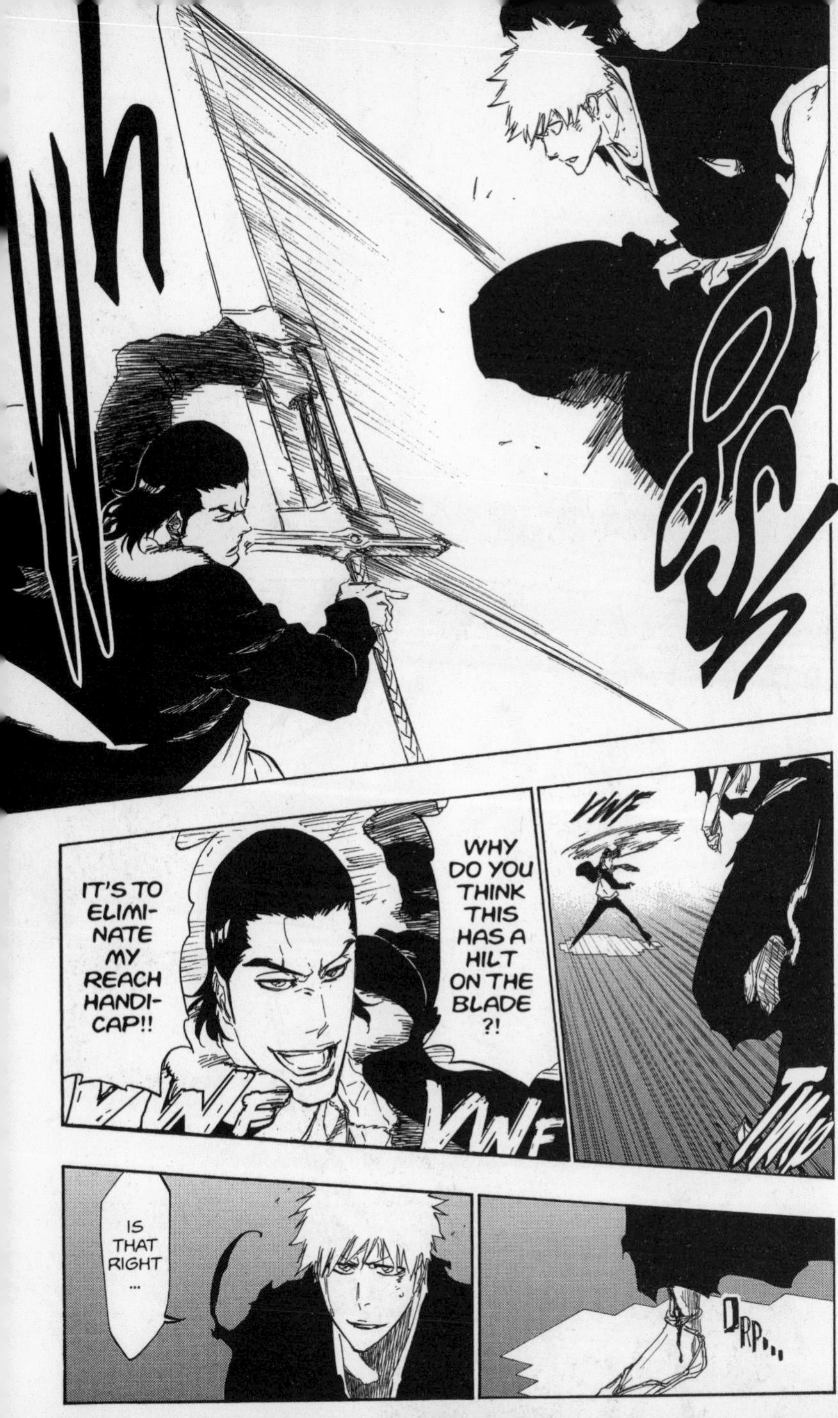
VWF
WHY DO YOU THINK THIS HAS A HILT ON THE BLADE ?!
IT'S TO ELIMI-NATE MY REACH HANDI-CAP!!
VWF
VWF
DRP...
IS THAT RIGHT ...

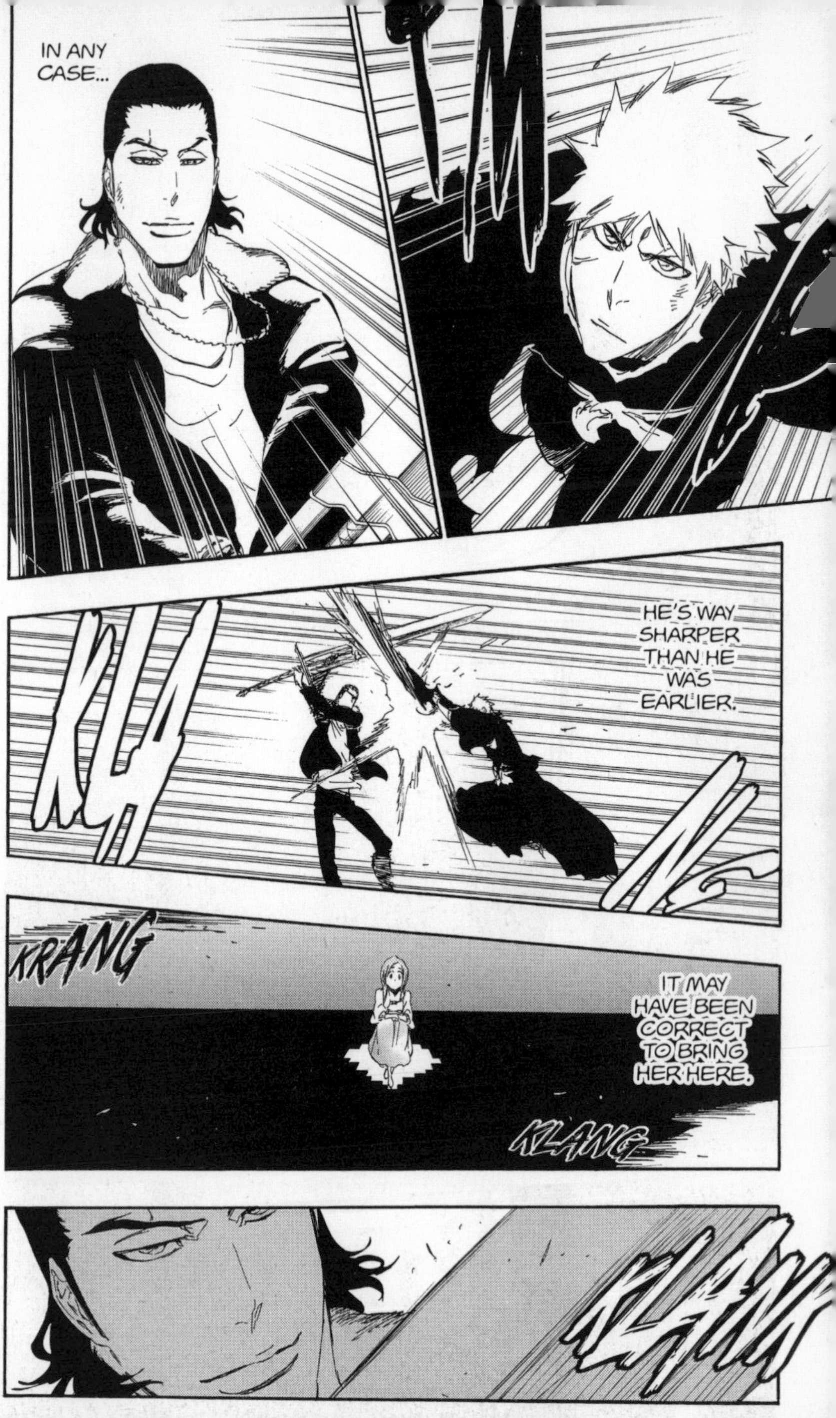
IN ANY CASE...
HE'S WAY SHARPER THAN HE WAS EARLIER.
IT MAY HAVE BEEN CORRECT TO BRING HER HERE.
KRANG
KLANG

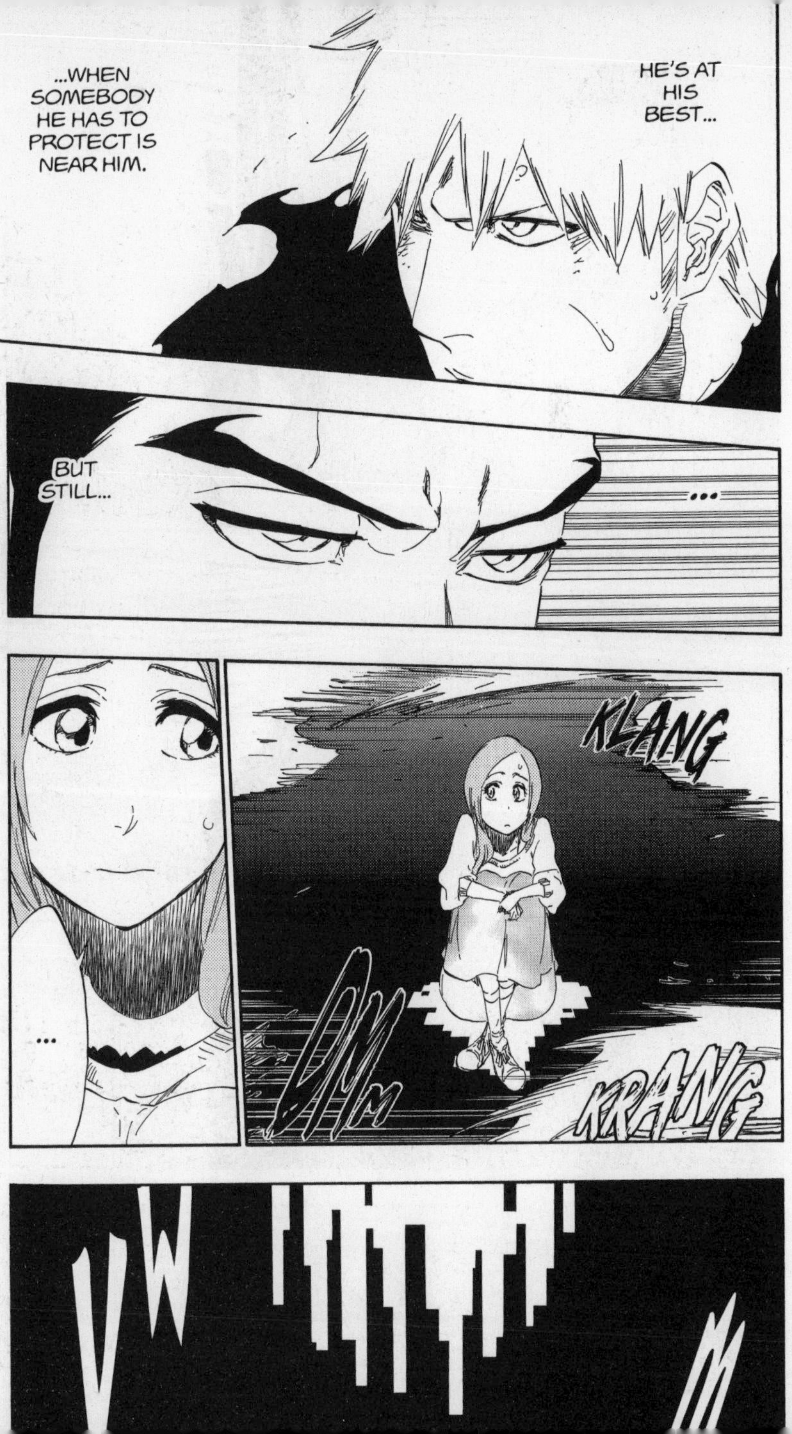
HE'S AT HIS BEST...
...WHEN SOMEBODY HE HAS TO PROTECT IS NEAR HIM.
BUT STILL...
...
KLANG
KRANG
...

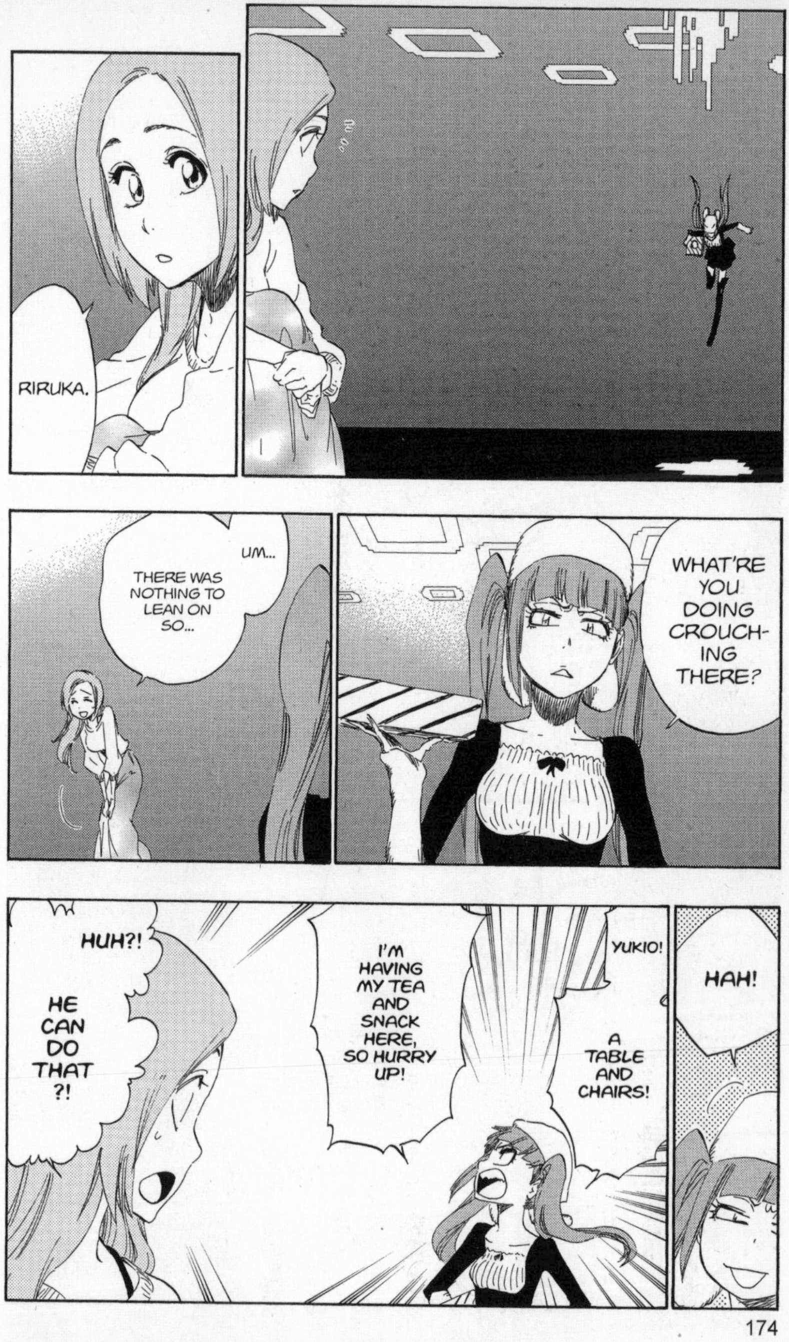
RIRUKA.
WHAT'RE YOU DOING CROUCHING THERE?
UM... THERE WAS NOTHING TO LEAN ON SO...
HAH!
YUKIO!
A TABLE AND CHAIRS!
I'M HAVING MY TEA AND SNACK HERE, SO HURRY UP!
HUH?!
HE CAN DO THAT?!

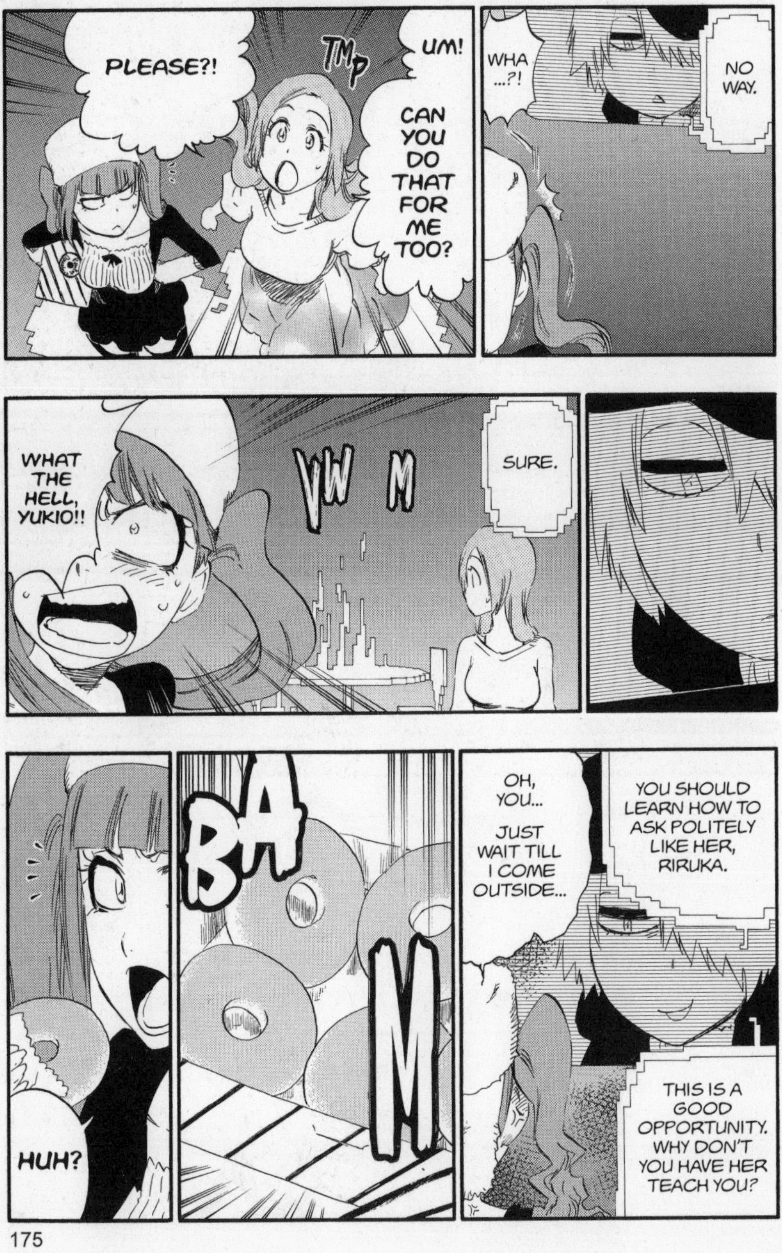
NO WAY.
WHA ...?!
UM!
CAN YOU DO THAT FOR ME TOO?
TMP
PLEASE?!
SURE.
VWM
WHAT THE HELL, YUKIO!!
YOU SHOULD LEARN HOW TO ASK POLITELY LIKE HER, RIRUKA.
OH, YOU...
JUST WAIT TILL I COME OUTSIDE...
THIS IS A GOOD OPPORTUNITY. WHY DON'T YOU HAVE HER TEACH YOU?
BAM
HUH?

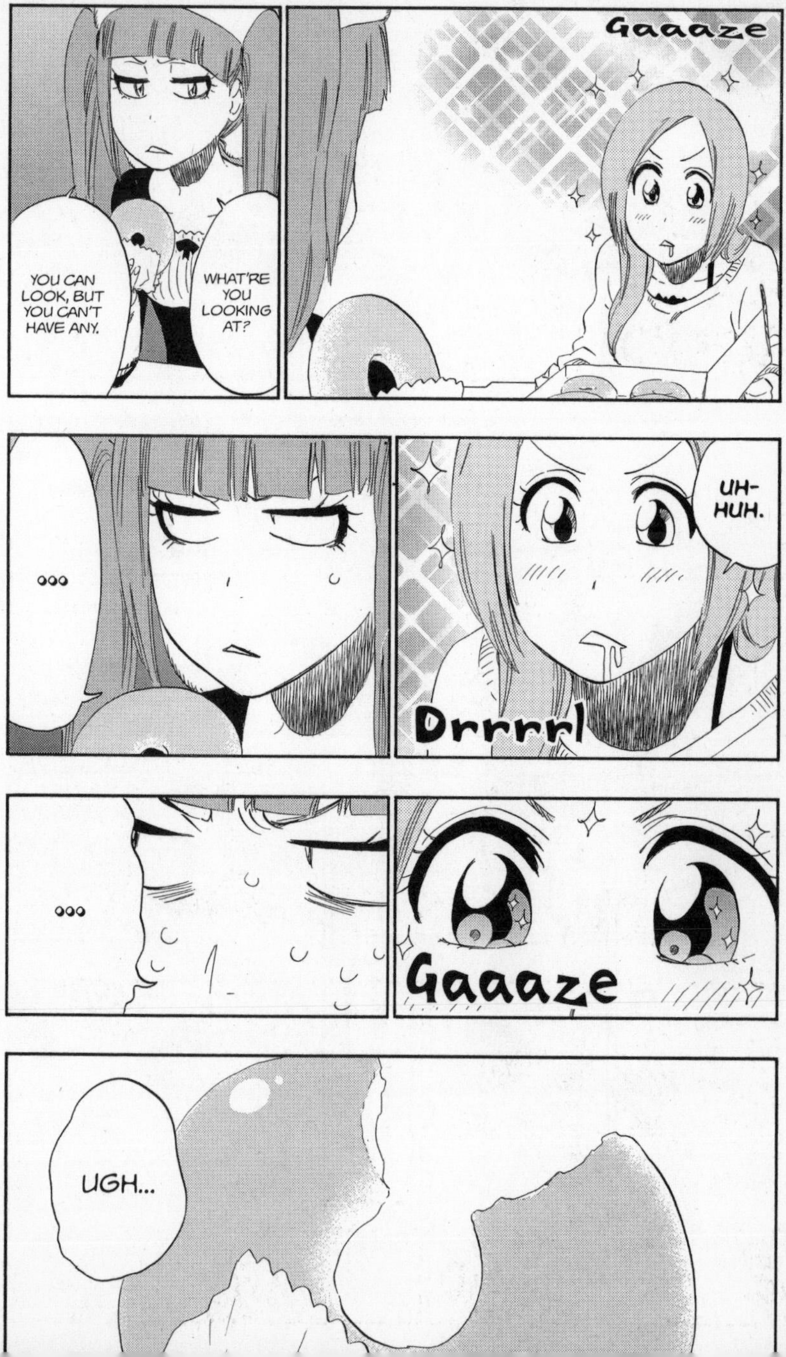
Gaaaze
WHAT'RE YOU LOOKING AT?
YOU CAN LOOK, BUT YOU CAN'T HAVE ANY.
UH-HUH.
Drrrrl
...
Gaaaze
...
UGH...

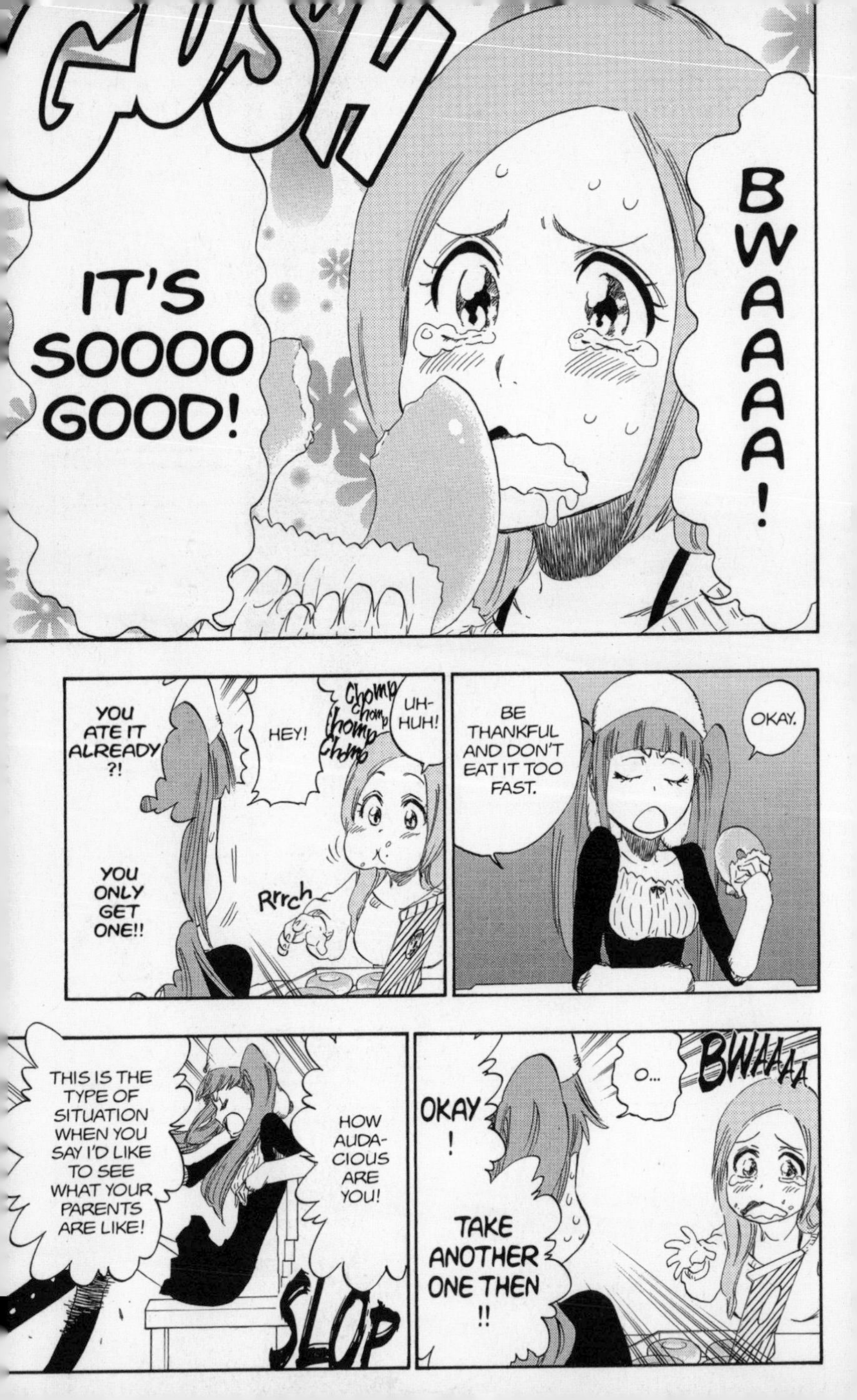
GUSH
BWAAAAA!
IT'S SOOOO GOOD!
OKAY.
BE THANKFUL AND DON'T EAT IT TOO FAST.
UH-HUH!
Chomp chomp chomp Chomp
HEY!
YOU ATE IT ALREADY?!
Rrrch
YOU ONLY GET ONE!!
BWAAAA
O...
OKAY!
TAKE ANOTHER ONE THEN!!
HOW AUDACIOUS ARE YOU!
THIS IS THE TYPE OF SITUATION WHEN YOU SAY I'D LIKE TO SEE WHAT YOUR PARENTS ARE LIKE!
SLOP

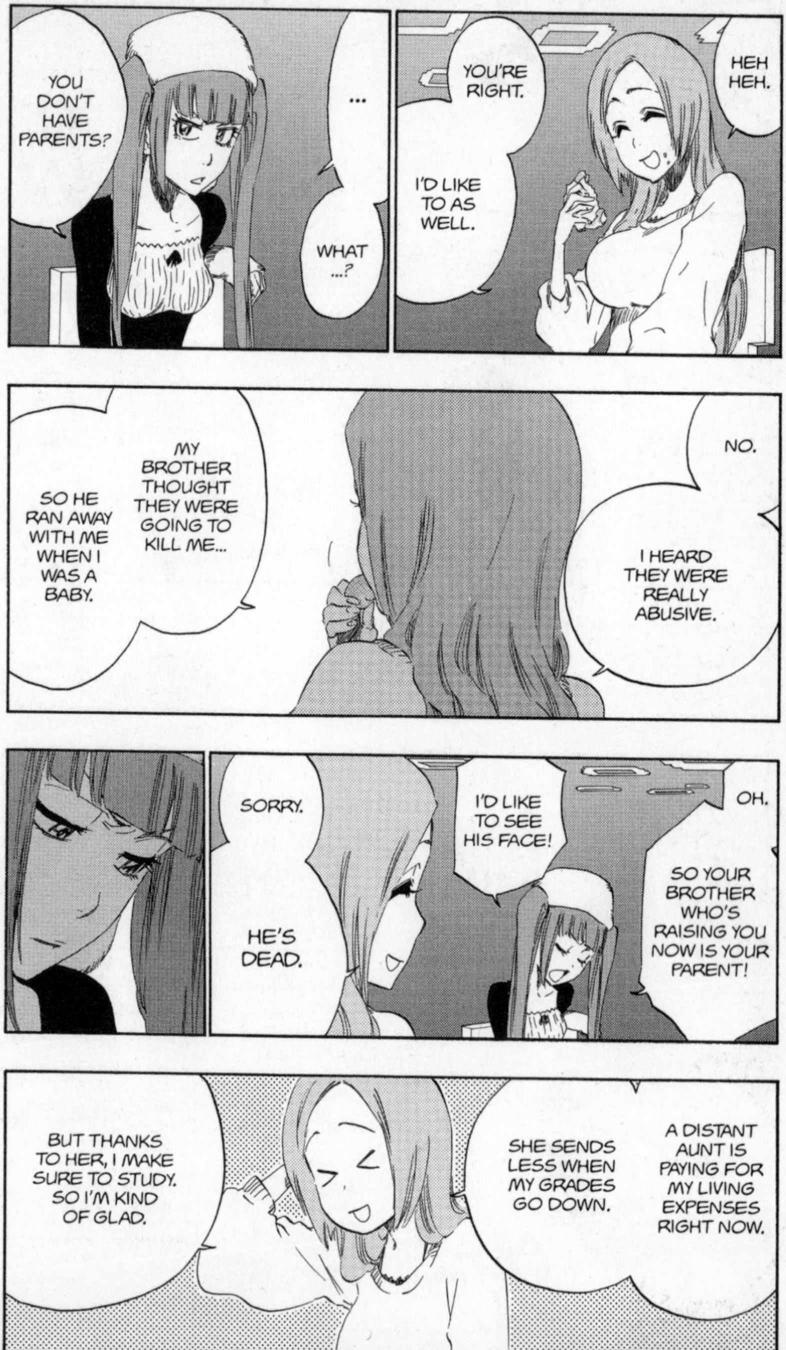
HEH HEH.
YOU'RE RIGHT.
I'D LIKE TO AS WELL.
...
WHAT ...?
YOU DON'T HAVE PARENTS?
NO.
I HEARD THEY WERE REALLY ABUSIVE.
MY BROTHER THOUGHT THEY WERE GOING TO KILL ME...
SO HE RAN AWAY WITH ME WHEN I WAS A BABY.
OH.
SO YOUR BROTHER WHO'S RAISING YOU NOW IS YOUR PARENT!
I'D LIKE TO SEE HIS FACE!
SORRY.
HE'S DEAD.
A DISTANT AUNT IS PAYING FOR MY LIVING EXPENSES RIGHT NOW.
SHE SENDS LESS WHEN MY GRADES GO DOWN.
BUT THANKS TO HER, I MAKE SURE TO STUDY. SO I'M KIND OF GLAD.

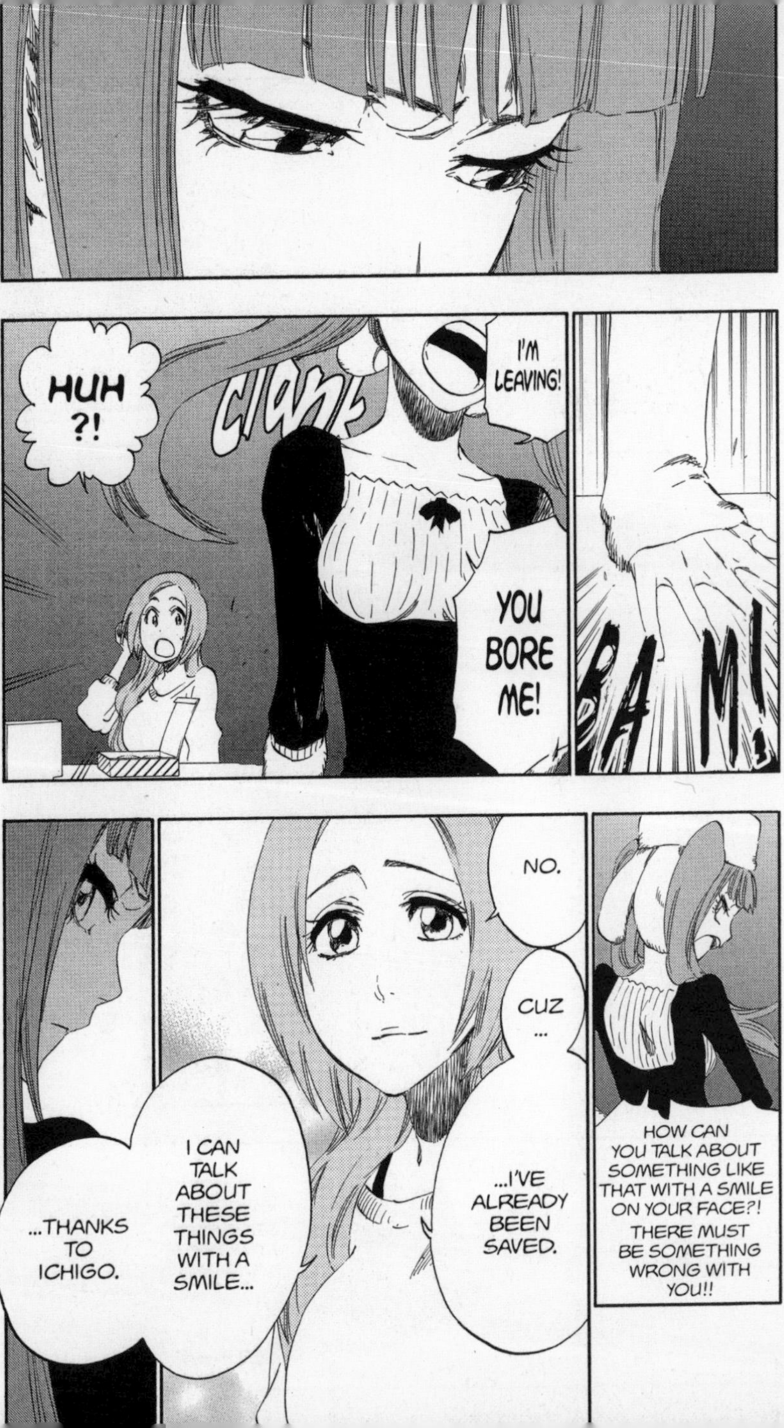
BAM!
I'M LEAVING!
YOU BORE ME!
clank
HUH?!
HOW CAN YOU TALK ABOUT SOMETHING LIKE THAT WITH A SMILE ON YOUR FACE?!
THERE MUST BE SOMETHING WRONG WITH YOU!!
NO.
CUZ...
...I'VE ALREADY BEEN SAVED.
I CAN TALK ABOUT THESE THINGS WITH A SMILE...
...THANKS TO ICHIGO.

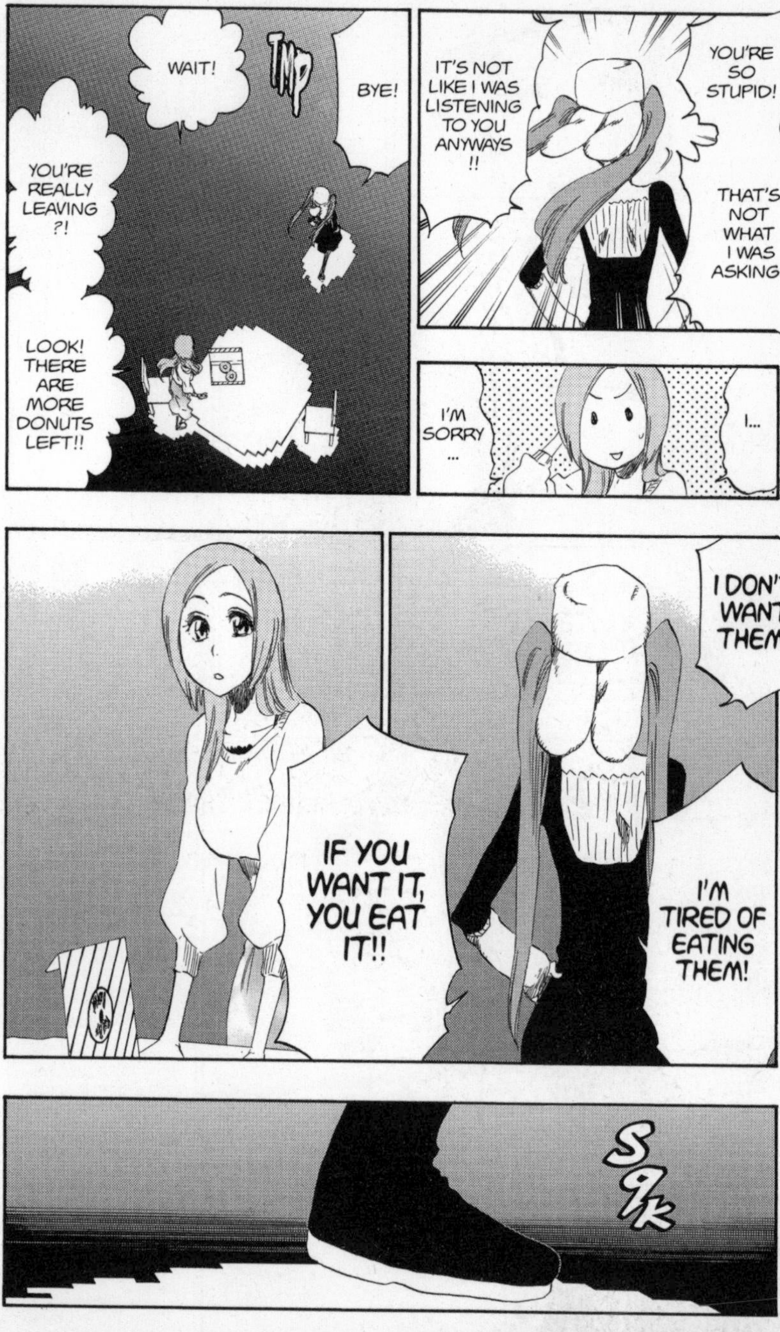
YOU'RE SO STUPID!
IT'S NOT LIKE I WAS LISTENING TO YOU ANYWAYS!!
THAT'S NOT WHAT I WAS ASKING!
I...
I'M SORRY...
BYE!
TMP
WAIT!
YOU'RE REALLY LEAVING?!
LOOK! THERE ARE MORE DONUTS LEFT!!
I DON'T WANT THEM!
I'M TIRED OF EATING THEM!
IF YOU WANT IT, YOU EAT IT!!
SQK

I KNEW YOU WERE A NICE PERSON!

...RI-RUKA!

THANK YOU...

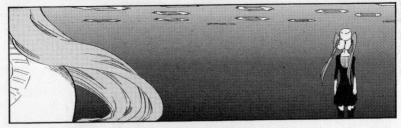

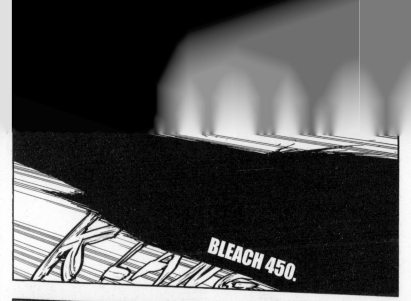

BLEACH 450.

Blind
Solitude

I DON'T
FEEL...

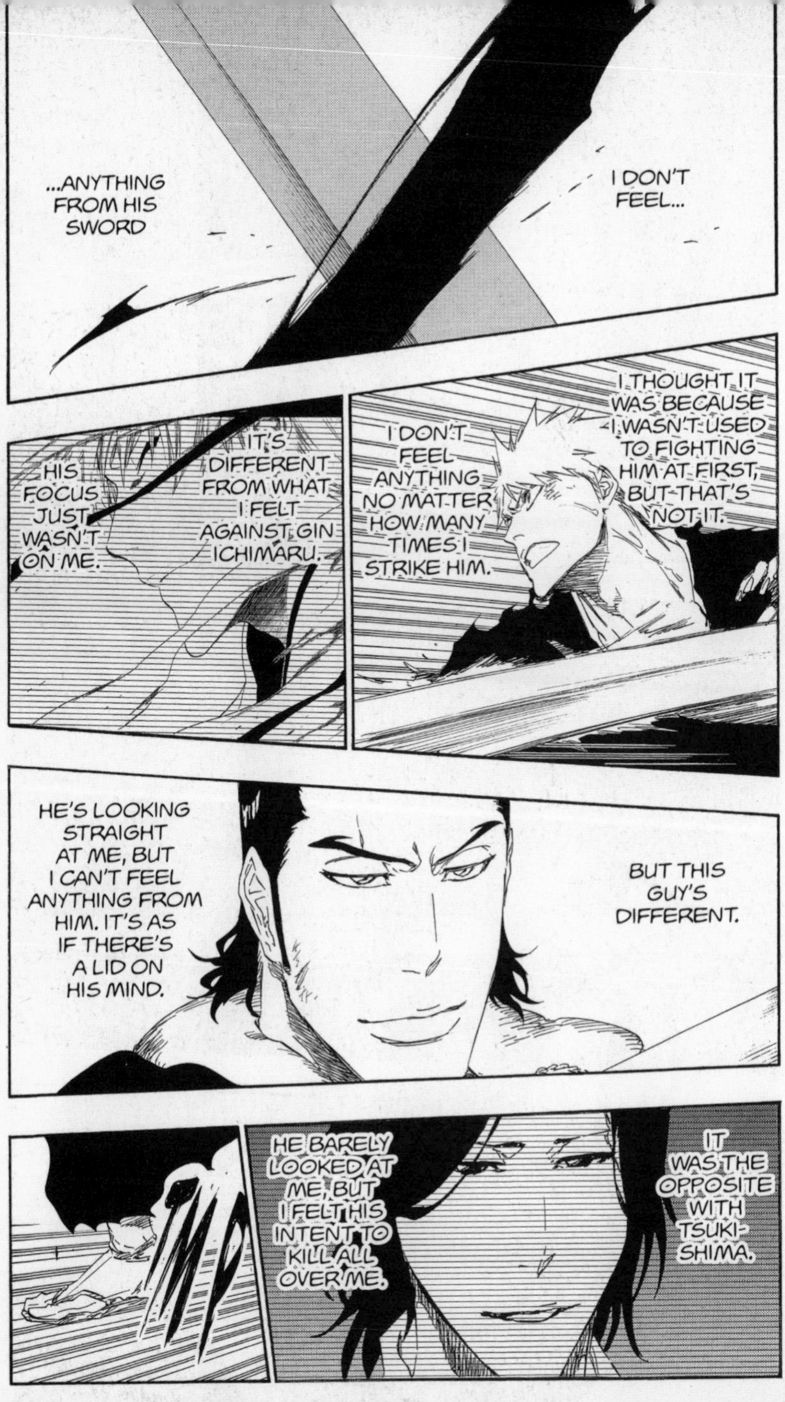
I DON'T FEEL...
...ANYTHING FROM HIS SWORD
I THOUGHT IT WAS BECAUSE I WASN'T USED TO FIGHTING HIM AT FIRST, BUT THAT'S NOT IT.
I DON'T FEEL ANYTHING NO MATTER HOW MANY TIMES I STRIKE HIM.
IT'S DIFFERENT FROM WHAT I FELT AGAINST GIN ICHIMARU.
HIS FOCUS JUST WASN'T ON ME.
BUT THIS GUY'S DIFFERENT.
HE'S LOOKING STRAIGHT AT ME, BUT I CAN'T FEEL ANYTHING FROM HIM. IT'S AS IF THERE'S A LID ON HIS MIND.
IT WAS THE OPPOSITE WITH TSUKI-SHIMA.
HE BARELY LOOKED AT ME, BUT I FELT HIS INTENT TO KILL ALL OVER ME.

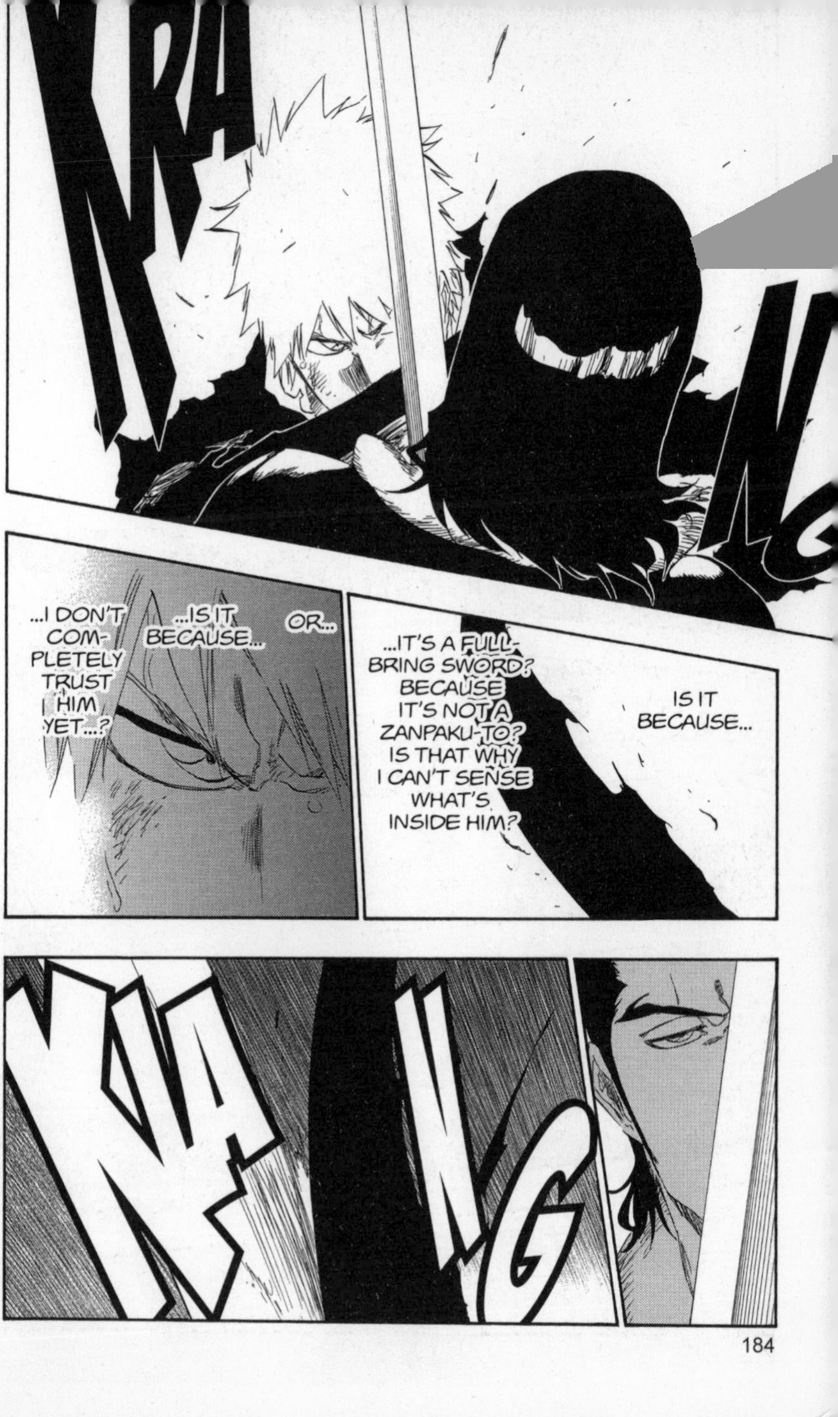
KRANG
IS IT BECAUSE...
...IT'S A FULL-BRING SWORD? BECAUSE IT'S NOT A ZANPAKU-TO? IS THAT WHY I CAN'T SENSE WHAT'S INSIDE HIM?
OR...
...IS IT BECAUSE...
...I DON'T COMPLETELY TRUST HIM YET...?
KRANG

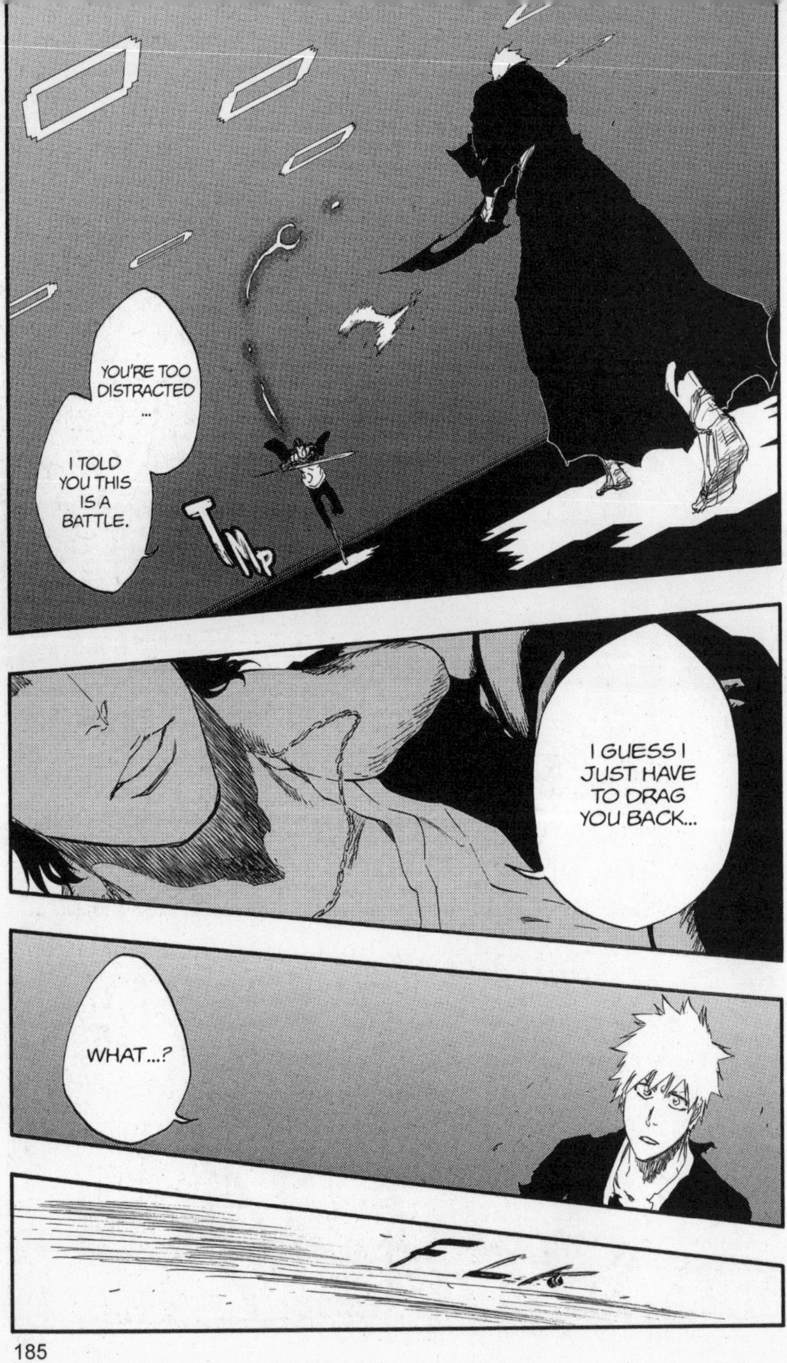
YOU'RE TOO DISTRACTED ... I TOLD YOU THIS IS A BATTLE.
TMP
I GUESS I JUST HAVE TO DRAG YOU BACK...
WHAT...?
FLK

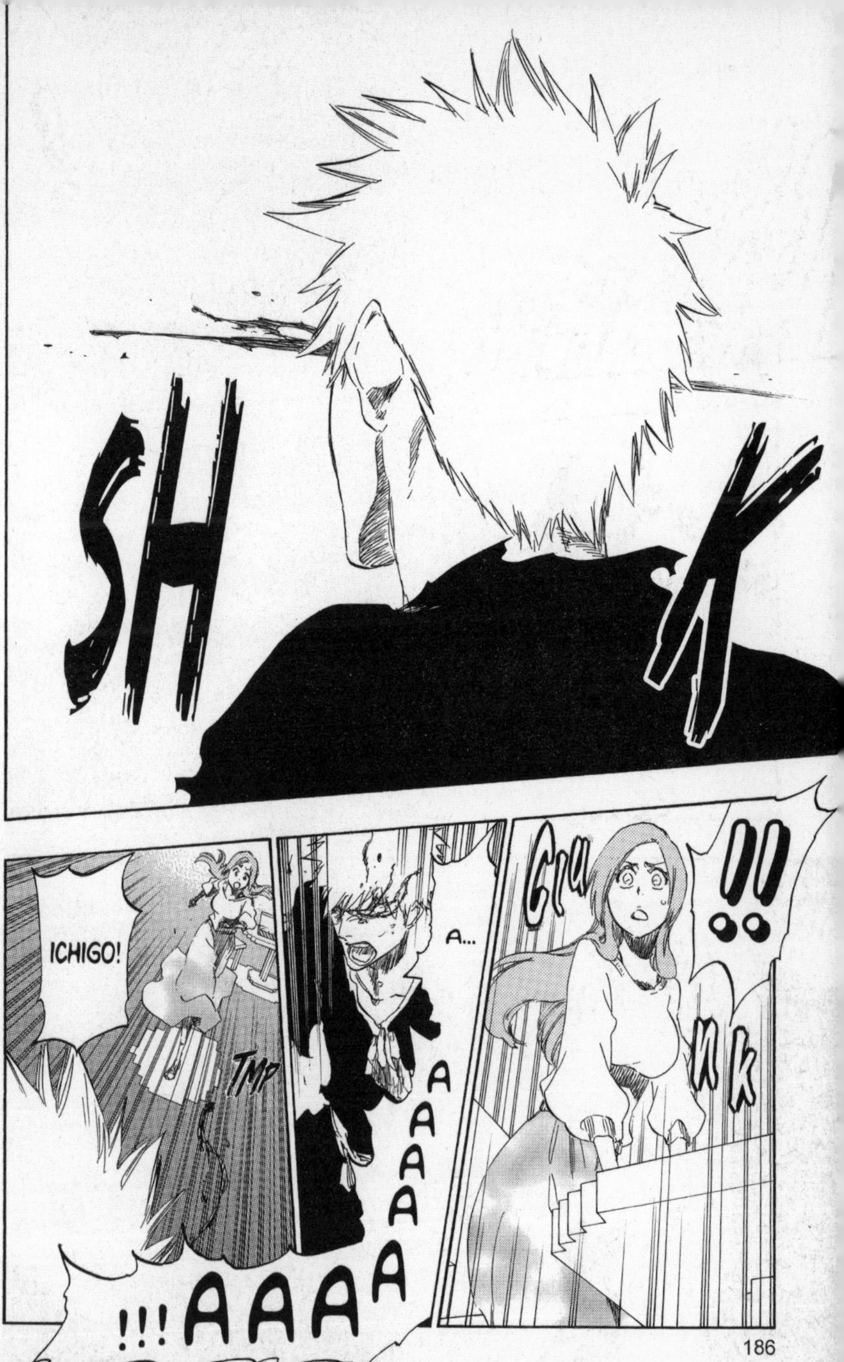
SHK
Gru
nk
!!
A...
AAAAAAAAA!!!
ICHIGO!
TMP

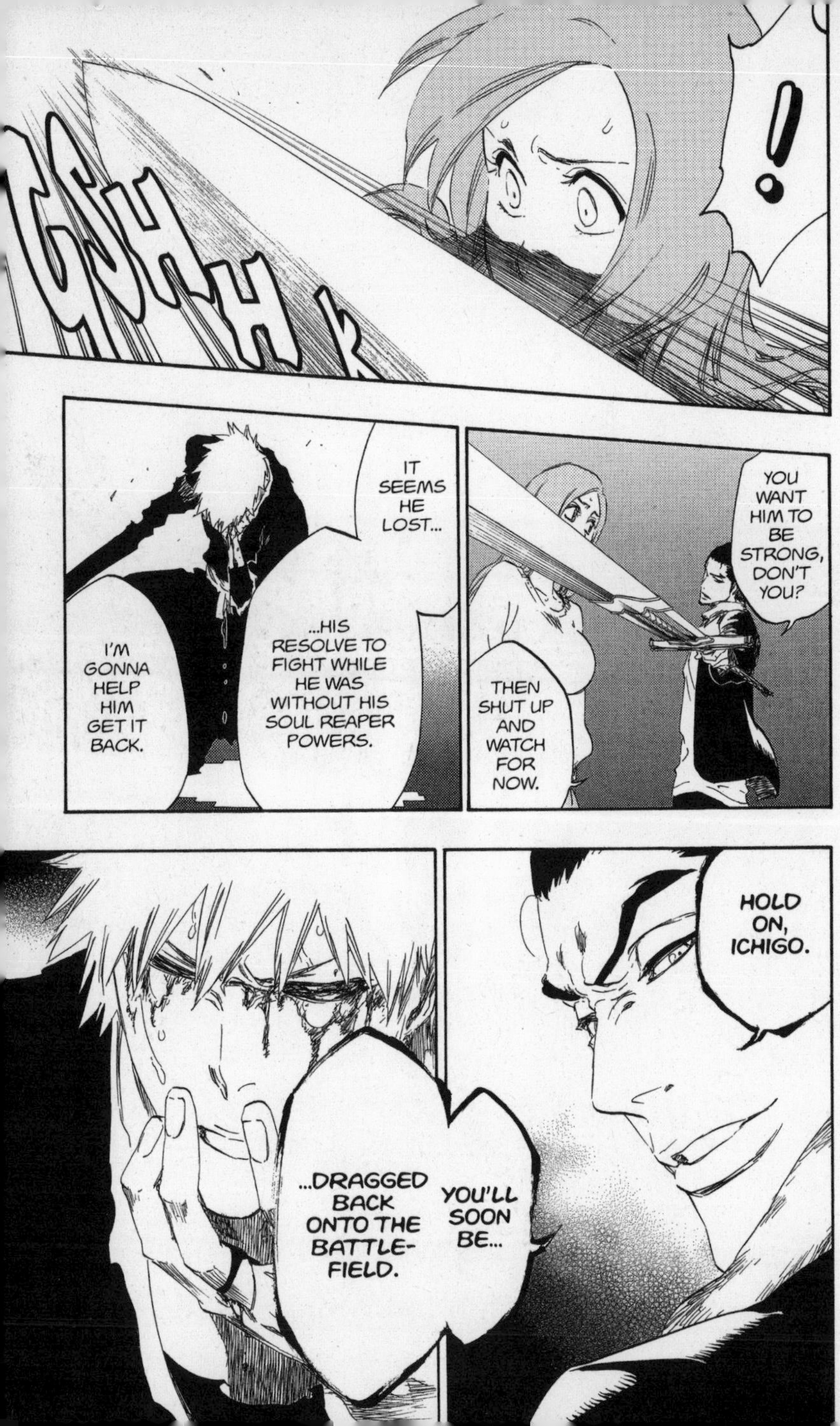
!
GSHHK
YOU WANT HIM TO BE STRONG, DON'T YOU?
THEN SHUT UP AND WATCH FOR NOW.
IT SEEMS HE LOST...
...HIS RESOLVE TO FIGHT WHILE HE WAS WITHOUT HIS SOUL REAPER POWERS.
I'M GONNA HELP HIM GET IT BACK.
HOLD ON, ICHIGO.
YOU'LL SOON BE...
...DRAGGED BACK ONTO THE BATTLE-FIELD.

CONTI
NUED
IN
BLEACH
52

Bleach
[The Lost Agent] Volume
Personal files
1

ICHIGO KUROSAKI

Height/181cm
Weight/66kg

Unagiya Employee

Karakura 1st High and

Part-Time Worker

New Member of Xcution

Membership No. 007

KUGO GINJO

Height/187cm
Weight/90kg

D.O.B. 11/15

Blood Type/AB

Xcution Leader

Membership No. 001

URYU ISHIDA

Height/177cm
Weight/57kg

Karkura 1st High School

25th Student Council

President

ASHUKURO TSUKISHIMA

Height/198cm
Weight/73kg

D.O.B. 2/4

Blood Type/BB

Xcution Ex-Leader

Next Volume Preview

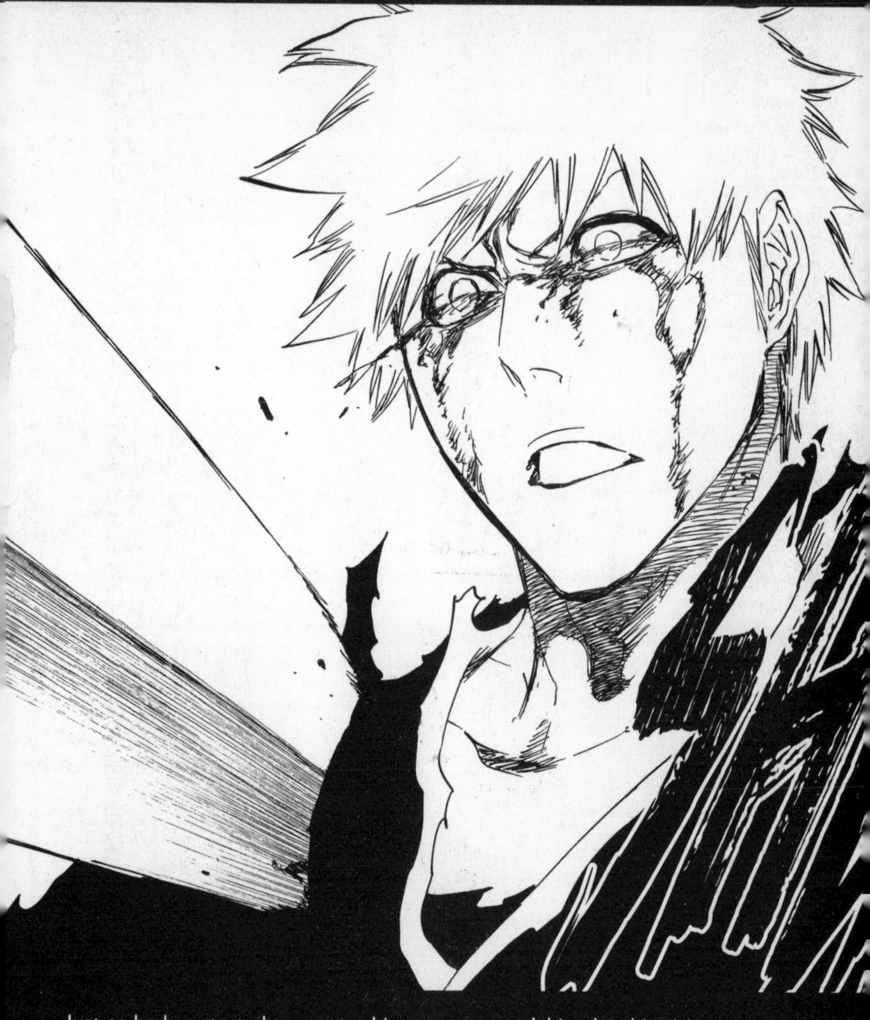

Just as he has started to master his new powers, Ichigo has his vision taken from him by Ginjo. But what is the meaning behind Ginjo's actions? And can Ichigo finally regain his lost powers?!

Coming December 2012!!